CRIMINOLOGICAL
THEORY

CRIMINOLOGICAL THEORY

A Brief Introduction

J. MITCHELL MILLER
University of South Carolina

CHRISTOPHER J. SCHRECK
Rochester Institute of Technology

RICHARD TEWKSBURY
University of Louisville

Boston   New York   San Francisco
Mexico City   Montreal   Toronto   London   Madrid   Munich   Paris
Hong Kong   Singapore   Tokyo   Cape Town   Sydney

Series Editor: *Jennifer Jacobson*
Editorial Assistant: *Elizabeth DiMenno*
Senior Marketing Manager: *Kelly May*
Production Editor: *Beth Houston*
Editorial-Production Service: *WordCraft, LLC*
Compositor: *Publishers' Design and Production Services, Inc.*
Composition and Prepress Buyer: *Linda Cox*
Manufacturing Buyer: *Megan Cochran*
Cover Administrator: *Rebecca Krzyzaniak*

For related titles and support materials, visit our online catalog at
www.ablongman.com

Between the time website information is gathered and then published it is not
unusual for some sites to have closed. Also, the transcription of URLs can result in
typographic errors. The publisher would appreciate notification of where these
errors occur so they may be corrected in subsequent editions.

Library of Congress Cataloging-in-Publication Data
Miller, J. Mitchell.
   Criminological theory : a brief introduction / J. Mitchell Miller,
Christopher J. Schreck, Richard Tewksbury.
      p. cm.
   Includes bibliographical references and index.
   ISBN 0-205-38903-1
   1. Criminology. 2. Crime. I. Schreck, Christopher J. II. Tewksbury,
Richard A. III. Title.
   HV6018.M545 2006
   364'.01—dc22

                            2005048756

Printed in the United States of America

10 9 8 7 6 5 4 3 2   09 08 07 06

CONTENTS

CHAPTER THREE

Biological Theories of Crime   29

CHAPTER FOUR

Psychological Theories of Crime   53

CHAPTER FIVE

CHAPTER SIX

CHAPTER SEVEN

Strain Theories of Crime   113

CHAPTER EIGHT

Control Theories of Crime   131

CHAPTER NINE

Theories of Social Conflict   149

CHAPTER TEN

Evaluating and Integrating Theory   169

Index   183

PREFACE

The purpose of this text is straightforward: to provide readable basic coverage of the major perspectives that constitute theoretical criminology. We offer an introductory overview of the basic assumptions and the leading principles of the various explanations. In so doing, we have arranged chapters in a general chronological order so that students may appreciate the development of criminological theory and understand ideological positions of different perspectives in some historical context. We have also attempted to illustrate major concepts and featured elements of specific theories through illustrations and examples from everyday life. Similarly, we have identified the practice and policy implications of theories, which in turn demonstrate the real-world significance of theory construction and testing.

The original plan for this text involved the late Richard Wright as a coauthor. While his involvement was not to be, many of the insights and examples throughout the manuscript reflect his participation during the planning phase. Richard, no doubt, would have been pleased that his friends and colleagues saw the project to completion.

A number of colleagues provided assistance through reading and editing chapter manuscripts. We are especially thankful for the contributions of Holly Ventura, John MacDonald, John Shutt, and Ed Wells. We appreciate the suggestions made by the reviewers during the development of the manuscript. They are: Eugene E. Bouley, Jr., Georgia College and State University; Frank Butler, Temple University; Mark E. Correia, California State University–Los Angeles; Katherine A. Culotta, Indiana State University; Jay Gilliam, Indiana University of Pennsylvania; Hua-Lun Huang, University of Louisiana; Valerie Jenness, University of California–Irvine; and Anthony W. Zumpetta, West Chester University. We are grateful to Pete Davis of Allyn and Bacon for encouraging us to pursue the project in its early stages and, especially, to Jennifer Jacobson for staying the course with us through the unforeseen setbacks along the way.

CRIMINOLOGICAL THEORY

■ ■ ■ ■ ■

CHAPTER 1

THEORETICAL CRIMINOLOGY: AN INTRODUCTORY OVERVIEW

The threat and fear of crime are constant concerns that seriously impact modern life. Television programs and newspapers remind us daily of violent acts and threats to our personal property. We are entertained, if not mesmerized, by crime, both through the glamorization of criminal genius and the bravery of law enforcement. We watch intricate plots accentuated by high drama unfold in the movies, on reality television policing shows, and during live court coverage of highly publicized trials. Crime also heavily impacts our daily lives by affecting our routine choices in ways that are so customary they seem altogether normal. Our daily patterns reflect the concern about crime in terms of where we park, how and with whom we interact, which school to attend, and the constant need to secure property. These and similar quality-of-life matters are directly attributed to both the perception and reality of crime. The safety of neighborhoods and schools, as indicated by crime rates and fear of crime, are major considerations in choosing where to live. In short, crime is a major force in contemporary society and a leading social problem that demands a considerable portion of our public resources.

The problem of crime is addressed on many levels by the criminal justice system, ranging from prevention and awareness efforts to rehabilitation of offenders. While it is essential that law enforcement, the courts, and the correctional system work to maintain a safe and orderly society, the criminal justice system is logically more effective when informed by a scientific knowledge base on the causes, patterns, and nature of crime and delinquency.

Whereas criminal justice is concerned with the actual practices of law enforcement, legal process, and corrections, **criminology** is focused on the processes of making and breaking laws (Cressey, 1978, p.3). Criminologists seek to understand how the creation of criminal law defines misbehavior according to different and sometimes competing interests and how the criminalization of behavior interrelates with culture and class status differently throughout society. More important, criminologists are concerned with the various causes for crime. It is vital to understand the underlying reasons for crime in order to best inform criminal justice practices and policies. Criminal justice science and criminology are different in that the former seeks to identify "solutions" to the crime problem while the latter is more focused on discovering the basic nature of crime and its many complex forms. The knowledge generated by criminology is an important component in society's understanding and response to crime and deviance. Anticrime strategies, for example, are ideally designed in sync with the extant knowledge base on criminal behavior and the distribution of crime throughout society.

Numerous facts are known about the causes and nature of crime, and criminologists often disagree about the reasons for crime and its relationship to other social problems. Some contend that the focus should be on individuals and their behavior—particularly the factors involved in the decision-making process leading to crime. Others look, instead, to social factors largely external to the individual, such as poverty; the quality of obtainable education; and the age, gender, racial, and ethnic composition of the population. Regardless of the particular perspective, criminologists attempt to discover, arrange, and make sense of facts about crime in a systematic manner. This process requires the creation of theory, wherein facts about crime are examined in relation to other facts—the major focus of this text.

In the following chapters, the major theories about the complex causes of criminal behavior are presented and discussed, with attention given to each theory's implications for responding to specific types of offenses or offenders. The specific theories examined across these chapters are all unique in that they identify or situate the cause or responsibility for crime in a distinct source. Accordingly, each chapter has something additional to offer in terms of furthering our understanding of crime. The various theories that will be examined address different types of offenses (such as violence, property crime, and morality infractions), the role of various internal (such as biological and psychological) and external (such as social disorganization and culture) factors, and the effects of formal (such as the production of law and enforcement initiatives) and informal (such as shaming and peer effects) social control mechanisms. An effort has been made to illustrate these theories in terms of their relevancy and applicability to everyday life.

Before examining the diversity of theories presented in this book, it is useful to establish a frame of reference or common background against which the individual theories can be considered and compared. In the context of social science theorizing, this framework consists of the following elements: (1) the origins and evolution of criminological thought leading up to the point of formal theory construction, (2) the nature of theory, (3) the criteria for assessing the quality of theory, and (4) the role of theory for criminal justice practices and policies.

THE ORIGINS AND EVOLUTION OF CRIMINOLOGY

Attention to crime can be traced back to ancient Babylonia and the Code of Hammurabi, as well as the Judeo-Christian perspective presented in the Bible. Beyond these edicts of infraction and punishment, contemporary criminologists typically recognize the origins of criminality in the Enlightenment period of the late eighteenth century, particularly the social and intellectual reforms in Western Europe. Philosophers from this period such as Voltaire, Rousseau, and Locke observed the superiority of reason based on direct experience and observation over the blind faith and superstition that characterized social life during the previous feudal era. Before this emphasis on reasoning, crime was first dealt with informally within and between families, with great emphasis placed on the realization of revenge (Larson, 1984).

The family-revenge model of justice—for example, multigenerational feuds between Scottish clans—presented social-order maintenance and governing problems for feudal lords, whose solutions were trial by battle and then trial by ordeal. Under trial by battle, either the victim or a member of the victim's family would fight the offender or a member of his or her family; under trial by ordeal, the accused was subjected to some "test" that would determine guilt or innocence, such as running through a gauntlet or being repeatedly dunked in water while bound by rope. Both approaches were vested in the spiritual notion of divine intervention. In battle, God would grant victory to the innocent side and likewise protect the falsely accused during trial by ordeal, as in the biblical report of protection afforded the prophet Daniel in the lions' den.

Clearly, these methods failed to effect justice relative to a person's guilt or innocence, instead yielding outcomes specific to a person's fighting ability, the capability to withstand various kinds of torture, or simply luck. Although the Enlightenment period introduced a new way of thinking that provided an alternative to the logic of spiritual explanations, spirituality continued to effect interpretations of both crime causation and systems of justice for several centuries. The idea of being controlled by an evil spirit or that one's criminal behavior is attributable to the influence of the devil or some other "dark" force has long been a default logic to account for the unexplainable. Primary examples from early U.S. history include the Salem witch trials, in which crime problems that could not be solved were attributed to witchcraft and demonic possession, and the origins of "correctional" institutions in Philadelphia by Quakers who believed that isolation, labor, and Bible reading would result in repentance—essentially a spiritually based form of rehabilitation. The very term *penitentiary*, which referenced institutions where society's crime problems were addressed through religious conversion, illustrates continuation of the belief in spirituality as the source of and solution to crime. Today there is renewed endorsement of the spirituality argument, evident in the current Bush administration's development and implementation of "faith-based" initiatives, many of which are crime-related or crime-specific (Allen, 2003).

While the Enlightenment period did not completely end the belief that spirituality affects crime, the momentum of experience-based reasoning led to a general view of social order that served as a forerunner to criminology. One of the primary concepts from this era that was important for the development of criminology is the idea of the **social contract**. First introduced by Thomas Hobbes (1588–1679), the social contract involves the sacrifice of some personal freedom by endorsement of governmental law enforcement in exchange for protection and the benefit of all. For example, it is likely that there is someone on campus each day from whom, either alone or with the aid of a friend, you could forcibly take personal property such as a wallet, purse, or textbook. Similarly, there is likely an individual or group that could forcibly take your property. Despite these obvious probabilities, everyone comes and goes in relative peace and safety. By sacrificing your ability to take what you might from others, you are protected from such a loss—this trade-off of loss of potential gain in exchange for law and order is an oversimplified example of the social contract.

As a result of the Enlightenment period, then, superstition- and spirituality-based orientations to crime were exchanged for innovative ways of thinking that emphasized relationships between criminal behavior and punishment. This newer approach, exemplified in the writings of the Italian Cesare Beccaria (1738–1794) and the Englishman Jeremy Bentham (1748–1832), is known as the **classical school of criminology**, a major point of origin from which criminological theorizing would develop (see Chapter Two). Conceptually grounded in the concept of deterrence and emphasizing free will and the dimensions of punishment (certainty, severity, and celerity), the classical school is significant for the development of criminological thought in at least two respects: (1) Crime was no longer believed to be a function of religion, superstition, or myth that placed the problem beyond the control of humankind, and (2) crime was seen as the result of free will. Viewing crime as a function of free will, essentially decision making, meant that it could now be explained as an outcome of rational choice. The notion of rational thought (a determination of gains versus risks) suggests that the crime rate is logically related to the elements impacting the decision to offend, such as the amount and relative value of criminal proceeds and the likelihood of getting caught in the act. The principles of the classical school, revised by legal reformers and now referred to as *neoclassicism,* continue to influence the nature of formal social control (the criminal justice system continues in the attempt to achieve deterrence as one of its primary objectives) as well as the study of criminal behavior.

Another perspective on social life began to emerge in Europe during the nineteenth century that first emphasized the application of the scientific method. This perspective, known as **positivism**, stressed the identification of patterns and consistencies in observable facts (Bryant, 1985). By examining known patterns, it was believed that causes of behavior could be determined that would enable predictions about outcomes when certain conditions exist. For example, we can ascertain a pattern of comparatively high criminality among the lower socioeconomic class. Given the absence of other intervening factors, we can predict a rise in lower-class criminality if a sharp increase in unemployment affects unskilled laborers. Regardless of whether this relationship is true, this line of thinking differs from the classical school's attention to free-will decision making, positing crime instead as a manifestation of **determinism**.

Determinism takes the position that human behavior is caused by factors specific to the individual, such as biological and psychological issues as discussed in Chapters Three and Four, respectively, or the environment as discussed in Chapter Five. Perhaps the most famous figure associated with determinism in the context of criminality is Cesare Lombroso (1835–1909), whose "criminal type" illustrated in his influential work *Criminal Man* (1863) suggests that some people are born criminals. Lombroso's work, along with that of Edwin Sutherland (1883–1950), was essential to viewing crime in a newer, more scientific light.

In the evolution of American criminology, positivism began replacing the classical approach to crime during the 1920s, largely due to the rise of the **Chicago school**, a movement resulting from a series of seminal studies conducted by the University of Chicago Sociology Department. From the 1920s through the 1940s, the Chicago school demonstrated that crime is a product of social ecology, particularly the disorganization that characterizes urban life.

The social ecological approach to crime is less concerned with the ways in which criminals and noncriminals differ in terms of intelligence, physical characteristics, and personality and more attentive to economic disadvantage, community cohesion, and social stability. The Chicago school crime studies of Shaw and McKay (1924), Merton (1938), and Sutherland (1939) grounded U.S. criminology in sociology and established a dominant *paradigm*, or model of inquiry oriented toward environmental causes of crime. These works (discussed in Chapter Five) represent some of the first American criminological theories and, more important, established a context in which the majority of future theories (presented throughout this text) would be developed. At this point, we need to examine more closely the nature and role of theory.

THE NATURE OF THEORY

What exactly is theory? A one-word definition of **theory** is "explanation." Too often, theory is erroneously thought of as philosophy or logic that has little relevance for real-world situations. In reality, theory is a part of everyday life, an attempt to make sense and order of events that are otherwise unexplainable. Think, for example, about the following common scenario. After dating for two years, a college couple's relationship is suddenly ended by one of the parties. Shocked and upset by news of the unwanted breakup, the rejected person will often consider, at great length and with the advice of friends, the reasons or causes leading to the outcome. Even if knowing *why* will not change the reality, we still want to know the answers, perhaps because making sense of seemingly random events reassures us that the social world is not chaotic and arbitrary. On a more pragmatic level, knowing why things happen enables us to modify our behavior or change relevant circumstances for a more preferable outcome in the future.

Developing explanations for everyday events, then, is a common practice that entails mentally sorting causes and effects, which is a form of theoretical expression. Academics, on the other hand, often refer to scientific theory. Simply put, scientific theories are a means of explaining natural occurrences through statements about the relationships between observable phenomena. Observable phenomena are specified as either a cause or an effect and then positioned in a relationship statement. The causes and effects are termed *variables* (a variable is simply something that varies and is not constant). These formal statements, which are often presented as a hypothesis, are formed in order to explain or predict how some observable factor or a combination of factors relate to the phenomena being examined. These relationships, which form specific theories of crime, are developed according to the logic of *variable analysis.* This analytic strategy specifies causal elements as *independent variables* and effects as *dependent variables.*

In criminology, not surprisingly, crime itself is the foremost dependent variable. It is vital to note here that the strategy of variable analysis is not interested in explaining crime per se; that is, the objective is not to explain what crime is in a definitional or legal sense. Rather, the variable analysis process seeks to account for *variation* in crime. Most theories conceptualize crime as a generic *dichotomy*—that is, the separation of phenomena into one of two categories. When crime is the dependent variable in a theory, further scrutiny usually reveals that theorists are actually referring to either **criminality** or **crime rate**. Criminality denotes the extent and frequency of offending by a societal group, such as the young, minorities, noncitizens, the unemployed, or people from a certain region. Crime rate, on the other hand, denotes the level of crime in a given locale. The focus on either criminality or crime rate is observable in the framing of different research questions: Why is there more homicide in Memphis than in Phoenix? Why are males more criminal than females? Again, the goal is not to explain the crime itself, but rather to account for the fluctuation in behavior across time, place, or social group.

After specifying causal and dependent variables, criminologists consider the nature of the relationships to determine inference and possible implications. The information revealed from a theoretical proposition is interpreted by the condition of **correlation**. Correlation speaks to the *covariance* of variables, the direction and strength of fluctuation in a dependent variable attributed to one or more independent variables. Directional correlation refers to either a positive or negative relationship. These terms do not carry the same connotation as when normally used in everyday language. The expressions "The running back rushed for positive yardage" and "She has a negative attitude" are value-laden and indicate desirable and undesirable conditions. In the social sciences, a positive correlation means that an independent variable and dependent variable fluctuate in the same direction, such as a group's level of drug use and criminal involvement. A negative correlation means that independent and dependent variables covary in different directions, such as educational attainment and crime (with the obvious exception of white-collar offenses).

Consideration of the relationship between school grades and the status offense of truancy provides a good example of directional correlation. Suppose a researcher gathers data on both absences and grades from a large sample of randomly selected middle and high school students. Findings supporting the logical hypothesis that increased absences cause lower grades would be a negative correlation, as would better grades covarying with a decrease in absences. In the latter scenario, the correlation, though negative, is also the desirable outcome.

The strength of correlation, on the other hand, specifies the degree of covariance between independent and dependent variables. For example, a gang awareness program delivered to middle school parents (in this case, the independent variable), may effect a minimal decrease in gang membership (the dependent variable). This relationship suggests an undesirable outcome, not because the correlation is negative but due to the finding that the independent variable generated only little change in the dependent variable— perhaps because the parents of gang members are less likely to participate in an awareness program in the first place. The strength of a correlation is ascertained through statistical analysis enabling the exact determination of covariance between variables, a calculation related in terms of statistical significance.

In order to analyze theoretical propositions, independent and dependent variables are respecified from a categorical and conceptual level to a measurable level, a process known as *operationalization.* Operational definitions, then, enable empirical examination of cause-and-effect relationships by specifying measurable indicators for variables. How a variable is defined will affect the nature of a relationship and yield different (and possibly undesirable) implications for addressing crime. The following example of measuring recidivism demonstrates how important the measurement process is and how easily measurement error can occur.

Recidivism (repeat criminal offending) is one of the most common theoretically based dependent variables used in criminological research, especially as an indicator of effectiveness for criminal justice program evaluation. Depending on whether an evaluation is being conducted in a law enforcement, court, or correctional context (all three of which conduct deterrence and rehabilitation programs whose success is largely indicated by recidivism), the act of reoffending is likely to be operationally defined differently according to the immediate context. Repeat offenses are typically measured in a law enforcement context—for example, as the rate of re-arrest. While it is seemingly natural and understandable that re-arrest be used as a measure of police activity, it conveys the false assumption that everyone who is re-arrested will be convicted and thus overestimates or exaggerates the perceived level of reoffending. Court-based operational definitions more accurately measure repeat offending as reconvictions, which is technically more consistent with legally determined official realities, but in correctional contexts reoffending is often calculated as reincarceration. Measuring reincarceration as an indicator of recidivism can also distort the true level of reoffending by not including those convicted whose sanction did not include jail or prison time.

The strength and direction of correlations, then, serve the objective of determining *causation,* that is, whether the independent variable(s) prompt change in a dependent variable and, if so, in what manner. In order to have confidence in observed causal relationships, there must also be both specificity and accuracy in the measurement process referred to by researchers as operationalization.

ASSESSING THEORY

What makes a theory scientific? And what makes a scientific theory good? As mentioned before, theorizing is a natural part of everyday life. We all need and attempt to make sense of what happens around us; it is just human nature to want to understand. If a one-word definition for theory is "explanation," we can argue that a one-word definition for untested theory is "opinion." Just as multiple opinions often exist as to why certain events occur in social and business contexts, alternative and competing theories often attempt to explain the same types of crime. How do we know which theories are accurate and which ones are mistaken?

Characterizing theory as scientific means that inferential claims about relationships (the observed correlations) can be falsified. Research entails gathering data according to the operationalization process so that the theory is framed for systematic observation of cause and effect. The analysis and conclusions concerning the existence and nature of relationships are then compared to the conceptual logic of the theory itself. When observations are inconsistent with the basic premises of a theory, it is falsified. Observations that are consistent with a theory's statements about the relationship between cause-and-effect statements are often deemed more credible, but this does not mean the theory is necessarily true, as alternative theories might explain the same relationships.

Criminologists especially seek the answers to a wide range of research questions that focus on causality: Will increasing the severity of punishment lower the amount of crime in society? Do fines levied against the parents of truant children increase levels of parental responsibility and ultimately result in less truancy? Does a substance abuse treatment program in a correctional setting impact prisoners' rate of recidivism and drug relapse? These and similar questions reflect the desire to specify causal relationships that, in turn, may yield implications for criminal justice practice. Causation, in the context of scientific theorizing, requires four main elements: (1) logical basis, (2) temporal order, (3) correlation, and (4) a lack of spuriousness.

Scientific theory, just like any type of accurate explanation, requires sound reasoning. There must be a *logical basis* for believing that a causal relationship exists between observable phenomena. Criminologists are not concerned with offenders' hair or eye color when attempting to account for their behavior, for example, because there simply is no logical connection between these physical traits and criminal behavior.

A second necessary element for scientific theory construction is *temporal order*—that is, the time sequence of cause-and-effect elements. In short, causal factors must precede outcomes, as in the relationship between religious involvement and morality crime. Faith-based initiatives are vested in the belief that religious-based programs will better social conditions, including a reduction in crime. If offenders participate in religious programs (the independent variable) and subscribe to the convictions of religious doctrine condemning behavior such as gambling, commercial sex, and recreational substance use and abuse, a reduction in their commission of these vice crimes (the dependent variable) would appear to be a causal relationship because the religious programming both preceded and logically prompted the decreased involvement in the specified behaviors. Another example involves a scenario in which parents' concern about a child's misbehavior involves discipline. Theorists would not hypothesize that discipline caused the misbehavior, because it was applied after the fact.

Correlation, described earlier in this chapter, is a third required element of a scientific theory. Correlation, again, indicates the presence of a relationship between observable phenomena and the nature of the relationship in terms of direction and strength.

The last essential element for scientific theory development involves the condition of *spuriousness*. Some theorists argue that internalization of subculturally defined values (the independent variable) causes or influences involvement in crime (the dependent variable). Many subcultures, however, are also characterized by poverty. Poverty confuses the causal relationship between subculture and crime, as it may be poverty that causes crime, and subcultures simply emerge within impoverished groups. So the relationship between subculture, poverty, and crime is spurious because cause and effect cannot be determined. Theorists, then, must frame relationship statements that reflect an absence of spuriousness.

By incorporating these elements, theorists increase the likelihood or probability that relationship statements are accurate, but this does not mean a theory is certain or necessarily true. Also, it is important to observe that these elements neatly align with the logic of variable analysis, reflecting a positivistic inquiry strategy to theory construction.

THE INFLUENCE OF GENERAL SOCIAL PERSPECTIVES ON THEORIES OF CRIME

Criminological theories identify causes of crime at different levels of social realities and interactions. *Micro-level theory* focuses on individual and small-group behavior, such as face-to-face interaction. A decision to rob one person instead of another based on perception of ability to resist or parental role modeling, regardless of whether it is positive or negative, are examples. *Macro-level theory* looks to the structural properties of society, such as social inequality, culture, and demographic characteristics of the population (such as age, gender, race, educational attainment, and citizenship).

Specific theories of crime are framed within larger conceptual frameworks or theoretical traditions. Because criminology is typically considered a specialization within the discipline of sociology, the three leading perspectives of social life significantly condition the development of crime and deviance theories (see Table 1.1). These three perspectives are functionalism, social conflict, and symbolic interactionism (Collins, 1985).

Functionalism is a theoretical perspective developed by the famous sociologists Emile Durkheim and Talcott Parsons, which contends that social order is realized because people reach a general *normative consensus;* that is, they agree on what is acceptable. Though norms can be either formal or in-

TABLE 1.1   **Criminological Theories Grouped by Social Perspective**

FUNCTIONALISM	SOCIAL CONFLICT	SYMBOLIC INTERACTIONISM
Classical criminology	Labeling theory	Differential association
Deterrence theory	Marxist radical theory	Learning theory
Rational choice theory	Feminist criminology	Routine activities theory
Subculture theory	Peacemaking criminology	Social control theory
Social ecological theory	Cultural criminology	Reintegrative shaming theory

formal, functionalist criminology categorically accepts formal norms as stated in the criminal law as a point of departure for theoretical development. Classical, neoclassical, and many positivistic theories of crime reflect the functionalist tradition of seeing crime as nonconformity.

The *social conflict* perspective does not view norms as representative of societal consensus, but rather as expressions of the interests of those in power. Crime is considered less a violation of normative behavioral standards and more a reflection of conflicting values between social groups and classes, ideas put forth by Karl Marx and Friedrich Engels. The conflict perspective is evident in a number of critical and radical criminological theories, including Marxist criminology, feminist criminology, left-realism, and cultural criminology, all of which view crime as a by-product of social alienation stemming from social inequalities.

The third sociological theoretical tradition influencing criminology is *symbolic interactionism,* an approach developed by the twentieth-century American sociologists George Mead and Herbert Blumer that focuses on shared meanings of social life determining communication and a range of human interaction, including crime. This perspective has shaped the development of several prominent theories including learning theory, reintegrative shaming theory, and routine activities theory.

THE ROLE OF THEORY

Theory is vital to criminology for several reasons. It provides a scientific orientation to the phenomenon of crime, in which observations of facts are specified and classified as causes and effects. It grounds several styles of inquiry in a logic of systematic analysis. More important, the relationships between causes and effects can be identified, thus composing a knowledge base to guide decision making and planning concerning how to best address the problems presented by crime. Some theorists examine the relationships between observable phenomena to simply find out for the sake of advancing knowledge, the goal of *basic* or *pure research.* Most criminological theorizing, however, generates practice and policy implications and, as such, is *applied research.* Even the pure theorists, who may have no particular interest in addressing a specific crime or delinquency issue, may generate the knowledge necessary for others to modify the criminal justice system's efforts.

There is, then, a connection between theory and policy. Theoretically based research may, for example, shed light on a better way of doing things, meaning that new programs should be developed and implemented or that existing programs are not working. Different theories may suggest similar or quite alternative practices and policies, often depending on what is proposed as the root cause of criminal behavior. The leading theories of crime described in this text suggest various paths of action. This is to be expected because it is only natural that the identification of a problem's source and its defining attributes will affect the solution. As you become familiar with the different perspectives in the following chapters, notice that each unique theory indicates different directions for how society should address crime.

SUMMARY

Criminological theorizing is vital to both the study of and response to crime. It is illogical to solve the problem of crime without first fully understanding its complex nature. Theory furthers this understanding by identifying factors associated with crime and examining causal relationships. Criminological theory is diverse, having identified multiple sources of crime over time that are reflected in a sequence of philosophical perspectives: spirituality and superstition, free will, determinism, and positivism. Theories reflect both macro and micro perspectives on both criminality and crime rate, as evidenced in the following chapters of this book.

KEY TERMS

Chicago school an important movement influencing the social sciences that was concentrated in the University of Chicago Sociology Department during the 1920s through the 1940s; demonstrated that crime is a product of an area's social ecology, particularly social disorganization in urban areas

classical school of criminology a movement accentuating rational thought as the major influence on human behavior; major theorists include Jeremy Bentham (1748–1832) and Cesare Beccaria (1738–1794), whose works emphasized the concepts of free will and deterrence in the context of crime and punishment

correlation the presence of a relationship between observable phenomena, usually characterized in terms of strength and direction

crime rate the level of crime attributable to a geographic locale such as a city, county, or country

criminality the extent and frequency of criminal offending by a group of people

criminology the study of the various factors and processes of making and breaking laws; a social science address of crime characterized by a theoretical-methodological symmetry

determinism a philosophy contending that human behavior is caused by biological and psychological factors specific to individuals and/or structural factors composing the environment

positivism a philosophy contending that scientific inquiry should focus on the study of relationships between observable facts

social contract the sacrifice of individual freedoms in exchange for protection and social benefit; first introduced by Thomas Hobbes (1588–1679)

theory a systematic explanation composed of statements indicating an outcome's causal and associated elements

DISCUSSION QUESTIONS

1. Theory is a systematic way of developing explanations—something we do in everyday life to solve problems and to better understand the social world around us. What are a couple of problems or issues that you've dealt with recently that have involved theoretical thinking?

2. How does criminology differ from criminal justice?

3. What are the basic assumptions and how do they differ across the three leading perspectives (classical school, determinism, and positivism) in the chronological development of criminological theorizing?

4. How are the general social perspectives of functionalism, social conflict, and symbolic interactionism important to the construction of criminological theory?

REFERENCES

Allen, M. (2003, September 23). Bush presses faith-based agenda. *Washington Post,* p. A10.

Bryant, C. G. A. (1985). *Positivism in social theory and research.* London: Macmillan.

Collins, R. (1985). *Three sociological traditions.* New York: Oxford University Press.

Cressey, D. R. (1978). *Principles of criminology* (10th ed.). Philadelphia: Lippincott.

Larson, C. J. (1984). *Crime—justice and society.* Bayside, NY: General Hall.

Lombroso, C. (1863). *Criminal Man.* Turin, Italy: Fratelli Bocca.

Merton, R. K. (1938). Social structure and anomie. *American Sociological Review, 3,* 672–682.

Shaw, C., & McKay, H. D. (1942). *Juvenile delinquency and urban areas.* Chicago: University of Chicago Press.

Sutherland, E. H. (1939). *Principles of criminology* (3rd ed.). Philadelphia: Lippincott.

CHAPTER 2

CLASSICAL THEORY
IN CRIMINOLOGY

Have you heard anyone lately, say a politician, a friend, or even yourself, complaining that the laws against crime are a joke and that criminals simply do not fear the system? Do you or someone you know often decry how long it takes simply to find someone guilty? Do you believe that the system is such that the rich can easily commit a crime and get away with it? If so, then your belief about the system and how it ought to work shares many similarities to what criminologists refer to as *classical theory,* one of the oldest and most enduring perspectives of crime. Classical theory in criminology formally began in 1764 with the publication in Italy of *Dei Delitti e Delle Pene (On Crimes and Punishments)* by Cesare Bonesana, Marchesa de Beccaria. That small document of slightly more than 100 pages was a protest piece, arguing against a system characterized by unwritten law, secret trials, hideous punishments, and methods of adjudicating guilt that, to our modern eyes, appear painfully superstitious. Beccaria desired a more enlightened, rational system for controlling crime. Initially published anonymously to avoid possible prosecution and reprisals for its criticism of the existing political and religious order (Beccaria's book was in fact banned by the Catholic church for more than a century), it was the only significant publication its author ever produced. However, the influence of this publication, which you have probably never heard about before, was such that it bears great responsibility for much of how our justice system looks today and how we think crime ought to be addressed.

Beccaria drew on the newly developing ideas of the Enlightenment movement in Europe (shaped by such figures as Rousseau, Voltaire, Locke, and Hobbes) to outline a model of criminal law, punishment, and justice that would be free of the arbitrariness, brutality, and inequality of the existing legal systems based on a supernatural or spiritual view of government, law, and human nature. Adopting a utilitarian framework that viewed the establishment of governments and legal systems as "social contracts" among free citizens (rather than divine grants imposed by God), Beccaria's theory identified social harm prevention rather than moral retribution as the legitimate function of criminal law. According to Beccaria (1764/1963, p. 93), "It is better to prevent crimes than to punish them. This is the ultimate end of every good legislation, which, to use the general terms for assessing the good and evils of life, is the art of leading men to the greatest possible happiness or to the least possible unhappiness." For Beccaria, the **deterrence** of crime (through rational, enlightened administration of legal punishments) was the central purpose of criminal justice. In *On Crimes and Punishments* Beccaria elaborated the features of a rational, enlightened justice system that would effectively deter crime while correcting the injustices of the existing system, protect the liberty and dignity of individual citizens, and achieve the greatest good for the greatest number. Such a system would embody the ideals of the Enlightenment movement, including such now familiar concepts as presumption of innocence until proven guilty, equality of all people before the law, guarantee of due process, public and impartial trials, adherence to rules of evidence and procedure to ensure fair judgments, right to a jury trial of one's peers, and equal punishment for equal crimes. According to Beccaria's model, the prevalence of crime in a society reflects irrational and ineffective law, rather than the presence of evil or abnormal human natures. Thus, legal reform implementing a more rational and fair justice system, which would effectively deter people from choosing criminal acts, was the answer to the problem of crime.

Another seminal figure whose writings heavily shaped the classical perspective was Englishman Jeremy Bentham. In opposition to the operations of eighteenth-century legal and penal systems, Bentham developed propositions for reform that were based in rationality in his famous work *An Introduction to the Principles of Morals and Legislation* (1789). Bentham is credited with developing the principle of utility, which is based on the central assumption that people inevitably pursue pleasure and avoid pain. He identified the elements by which individuals could calculate the value of pleasure or pain according to the level of intensity, duration, certainty, and extent. It is from these basic observations that later and very consequential deterrence-based models of justice and more elaborate criminological theories rooted in free will and the nature of the criminal calculus were shaped.

Classical theory constitutes one of the older and yet one of the most contemporary explanations of crime. Following only older supernatural explanations that date from the earliest attempts to account for evil acts in a demon-haunted world, classical theory is an older idea, because it derives from the ideas and writings of early Greek philosophy. That is the reason for the "classical" label—because its roots are in the classical period of Greek rationalism (the so-called golden age of Greece). Thus, while we identify classical theory as formally originating in the eighteenth century (as the fulfillment of the seventeenth- and eighteenth-century Enlightenment movement), it actually has a much older lineage (e.g., Hobbes, 1651). At the same time, the classical model is also among the "latest and greatest" theories of crime, rediscovered by modern criminologists in the 1970s and elaborated as the logical foundation for contemporary rational choice theory (Morris, 1966; Walters and Grusec 1977). In these terms, it simultaneously represents very old and very new thinking about crime.

ASSUMPTIONS ABOUT HUMAN NATURE

Theories have to begin with an idea about what people are naturally like. Are we naturally criminal, or do we naturally obey the law? Our answer to this seemingly simple question profoundly affects our outlook on crime and how we should respond to it.

Beccaria's assumptions of human nature were based on the Enlightenment image of human nature developed by Hobbes and Locke. The classical model holds simply that people deliberately do things because they expect to benefit from them in some way. In fact, everything that people do is done for its anticipated pleasures and benefits. You read this chapter or even show up for class, for instance, solely because you anticipate some advantage. Maybe you wish to gain an insight about human behavior (we professors are such optimists), so the costs of spending time doing the reading appear to be a worthwhile sacrifice. Or maybe you fear failing a test. But crime as well as conformity to the law occurs because we get something out of it and we don't sacrifice too much either. The model of human nature assumed here is that (a) people have **free will** (to choose what to do); (b) people exhibit **hedonism** (they seek pleasure and avoid pain) and *egoistic* (self-seeking) behavior; and (c) people have **rationality** (to anticipate the consequences of different actions and to calculate the most beneficial outcomes).

While the classical perspective dominated enlightened thinking about crime through the beginning of the nineteenth century, it was gradually supplanted in the nineteenth century by an alternative perspective—*positivism*—that pointedly rejected several of the key premises of the classical model, namely the assumptions of free will and rational choice. The positivist perspective, which based its analysis of behavior on empirical research and experimentation rather than logical deduction, was critical of "mere philosophy" such as the classical model (Akers, 1994). The classical theory was an idealistic philosophical doctrine that based its conclusions on universalistic assumptions about rationality and free will. It presumed that all people had free will and all behaviors were the result of rational calculation. Interpersonal differences in free will and rationality were minimized or ignored; criminals were not regarded as physically or mentally different from non-criminals—both were rational, hedonistic choice makers. In contrast, positivism embodied a scientific perspective in which events were explained in causal rather than volitional terms—as the result of cause-effect dynamics rather than free-willed choices. The natural causal framework of positivism presumed that there must be a causal reason for every event—including criminal acts. We can only really understand and explain an event when we can identify scientifically what caused it to happen. The assumption of free will was viewed by positivists as incompatible with the scientific principle of causality and the idea of general causal laws. If a behavior were explained as entirely the result of identifiable causes, then there was no room left for free will. Moreover, free will was generally identified with the *soul*, which was an inherently unobservable and unscientific concept.

The growth of positivism was spurred by dramatic scientific advances during the nineteenth century, especially in biology, botany, and the medical sciences, that illustrated that science applied to all natural phenomena—living systems as well as inanimate objects. In these terms, scientific knowledge based on careful empirical research, measurement, and experimentation has more validity than philosophical doctrines based on abstract speculation and argumentation. Thus, to be fully modern and enlightened, the study of crime must adopt a rigorously scientific perspective and abstain from explanations based on philosophical argument and intuitive appeal.

Thus, by the end of the nineteenth century the classical model came to be regarded as a "pre-scientific," philosophical construction—imaginative and enlightened—but ultimately to be replaced by more scientifically rigorous theories of behavior. Up through the middle of the twentieth century, classical theory receded from criminological view, eclipsed by positivist theories for explaining crime. While the classical model continued to provide the philosophical rationale for the American legal system, even here the positivist framework made substantial modifications to fit with scientific analysis. These changes included the widespread adoption of the rehabilitation model of corrections (based on treating the scientifically diagnosed causes of criminal behaviors rather than punishing moral/legal transgressions), the implementation of the juvenile justice system (developed at the start of the twentieth century as a rehabilitative alternative to the criminal justice system), and the expansion of the insanity defense during the twentieth century (Andenaes, 1974; Barnes & Teeters, 1951; Gibbs, 1975). The latter evolved in this period from a limited neoclassical exemption in rare cases where rationality was clearly absent to a wide-ranging defense applicable to all cases where mental illness was present in some form. Such innovations represented a fairly radical movement away from the deterrence-oriented vision of the classical theory.

And while an eclipse is not a permanent condition, but an event of limited duration in which what is hidden during the eclipse re-emerges into view, the classical theory also re-emerged. By the 1970s positivist domination of criminology and criminal justice was declining as scholars and administrators began losing faith in the social engineering model of crime control and the rehabilitative model of corrections, along with the underlying causal models of crime on which they are based. Crime rates were steadily increasing during the 1960s and 1970s as more and more positivist-based crime control policies were enacted with little apparent effect on the crime trend; recidivism rates of "corrected" prisoners remained depressingly high; and researchers were beginning to conclude that "nothing works."

This resulted in an ironic reversal of fortunes; the classical perspective was replaced by positivism in the nineteenth century because its punishment-oriented policies were seen as ineffective in controlling crime (Vold, Bernard, & Snipes, 2002). That is, as more states and nations instituted governmental and legal systems based on Beccaria's models, the crime rates in most European countries continued to rise (along with the recidivism rates of punished criminals). While this largely reflected the rapidly changing social conditions in Europe during this period, it led to a questioning of the underlying classical theory as unrealistic or misguided, and it supported a movement to replace the classical ideas with a more scientific theory of criminality. Ironically, the revival of classical theory in the United States during the 1970s represented exactly the reverse pattern. As more states implemented legal and correctional policies based on positivist theories of causality and rehabilitation, crime rates continued to climb alarmingly. Many criminologists viewed this as evidence of the failure of positivist theory and the need to reconsider other theoretical perspectives, which notably included the classical model of rational choice.

The renewal of classical theory in the 1970s was a combination of a number of different developments. As already noted, the failure of rehabilitation-based policies of punishment provided a strong motivation to change the dominant theoretical framework, but it worked along with other factors to identify classical theory as perhaps the most likely alternative. In his well-known requiem article affirming the failure of rehabilitation policy—that is, "nothing works"—Robert Martinson (1974) questioned the viability of positivist explanations for criminality and suggested that the traditional idea of deterrence should be seriously reconsidered. As crime rates continued to rise in the 1960s and 1970s, criminologists had been giving increased attention to the impact of sentencing policies on crime rates. Although most of the initial attention had been on variations in capital punishment—concluding that there was little systematic evidence of a deterrent effect of executions on capital crime rates—additional research was done on the effects of more frequent and ordinary forms of punishment, including imprisonment. This latter research found that such ordinary criminal punishments often did show deterrence-like correlations with crime rates, consistent with classical theory.

Coincident with the increasing uneasiness about the growing crime rates was a widespread "postmodern" rejection of the assumption of causal determinism as a reasonable premise for explaining human actions. This came with a renewed openness to volitional or voluntaristic models of behavior, which necessarily contained elements of free will or indeterminacy. The growing omnipresence of computers toward the end of the twentieth century brought with it a growing interest in artificial intelligence and cognitive models of information processing, which also prompted a renewed interest in decision making and an emphasis on rationality in human behavior (Becker, 1968). Thus, a variety of different factors all pointed toward a revival of interest in classical theorizing.

A final factor facilitating the re-emergence of classical theory is a recognition that it is not necessarily incompatible with scientific theory and research (Cook, 1980). The traditional argument portraying positivist and classical perspectives as antithetical were based on idealized and exaggerated premises. That is, original positivist assumptions about causal determinism were as overstated and scientifically untenable as were the original classical assumptions about universal free will and rational thinking. Contemporary theories depict people as having limited free will (in which many external and internal factors limit the options people have) and their behaviors as being shaped by a "soft" causal determinism (in which causal variables influence behavioral outcomes but do not completely determine them).

The **neoclassical theory** appearing in the 1970s presents a slightly modified version of the original perspective, changing it in some subtle but very important ways. For one thing, it synthesizes the original philosophical argument with a more scientific orientation, expressing the original philosophical concepts as measurable variables and behavioral hypotheses. For another, the neoclassical model—or *postclassical*, as Roshier (1989) calls it— moderates the original universalistic assumptions, allowing for individual differences in motivation, rationality, and free will, and allowing these to be situationally variable as well. Rather than universal free will, the new model assumes a "bounded free will" (acknowledging some environmental and biological constraints on behavioral choice) and a "bounded rationality" (presuming only that most people *usually* behave in a "mostly rational" manner). However, while the new version allows for individual differences in motivation, it regards such variations as smaller and less important than external structures of rewards and punishments.

HOW DETERRENCE WORKS

To understand how deterrence works, you must at least momentarily accept basic classical ideas about human nature. You are someone who loves pleasure and hates pain, who is egoistic, and who can anticipate the consequences of your actions. Now pretend you are at a party at someone's home, and you have the opportunity to sneak into a bedroom and steal some jewelry. The advantages are obvious—you can use the baubles yourself (wear them or share with significant others), or you might pawn them for some quick money. But what would make you stop yourself in spite of these advantages? This is the fundamental question for deterrence, and Beccaria's ideas offered insights about how to get people to not selfishly gratify their desires at the cost of the happiness of others.

The problem is that crime feels so *good*. And because criminal acts are frequently beneficial—yielding pleasure or monetary gain at less effort than noncriminal actions—there is a naturally occurring, universal motivation to engage in prohibited acts. Thus, crime has to be controlled by negative means (such as by ratcheting up the costs). It must be legally discouraged by increasing the likelihood that its outcomes will be unpleasant (for example, painful, disgusting, embarrassing, aversive), at least more unpleasant than the potential rewards of the criminal act. Once the advantages are offset by the costs, then one should have no desire to commit crime. Everything so far is pretty straightforward.

Beccaria also argued that the deterrent effectiveness of criminal punishments will depend on three characteristics of how punishments are administered: (1) **severity** (the painfulness or unpleasantness of the punishing outcome), (2) **certainty** (the probability that a misdeed will be detected and punished), and (3) **celerity** (the swiftness with which punishment follows the criminal deed). To achieve maximum deterrence, a punishment needs to be unpleasant (at least more unpleasant than the benefits the act would yield), certain, and swift. Beccaria argued that of the three characteristics, maximizing certainty and swiftness is more important for deterrence than severity. The latter, if disproportionate, may result in irrational brutality and have counterproductive effects on crime, inciting revolution, defiance, revenge, even martyrdom. This is perhaps one aspect of deterrence that most students have a hard time grasping. If the punishment for selling drugs is death, then woe to the police officer who tries to arrest the drug dealer! Woe especially if the justice system is imperfect and has a habit of arresting and condemning the innocent. Put differently, you might reason that it is better to kill others to protect yourself from the excessively severe legal consequences of your actions.

For all the recent updates in the classical revival, the account of deterrence provided by Beccaria (1963/1764) remains the theoretical cornerstone. Beccaria provided a surprisingly modern analysis that clearly identified the subjective or psychological nature of deterrence and the critical role of perceptions as determinants of behavior. People's decisions to engage in criminal behavior will be shaped by their *perceptions* of what the punishment would be, how likely they *think* they are to get caught, and how personally unpleasant they *expect* the punishment to be. The objective properties of the punishment are far less relevant to these decisions than what people think these properties are. Deterrence occurs when perceptions of likely punishments for criminal acts cause would-be offenders to refrain from committing those acts (even though they are otherwise motivated and willing to do so). The specific mechanism that inhibits would-be offenders from criminal actions is their *fear* of punitive consequences. Thus, the process of deterrence is inherently psychological, based on an aversive emotional response to what people think will occur.

Recent modern analyses of deterrence have mostly affirmed the ideas developed by Beccaria, but also have noted that things are a bit more complex than Beccaria could know. For one thing, deterrence effects are divided into two distinct types, reflecting two distinct ways in which punishments may influence people's behaviors. Beccaria implicitly recognized these but did not recognize or discuss the importance of the distinction. In *specific deterrence,* the offender is inhibited from repeating criminal behavior by the unpleasant experience of being punished for the original misdeed. It involves the direct experience of punishment by the offender (who experiences the punishment). In *general deterrence,* punishing offenders has a discouraging effect on *other* would-be offenders (that is, members of the general public, other than the person getting punished, who witness or hear about the punishment). This kind of deterrence involves the indirect or vicarious experience of punishment through seeing others receive unpleasant outcomes for their actions, which provides an example of what might happen to other would-be offenders if they were to commit the same acts. These two deterrence processes seem very similar (and Beccaria lumped them together), but they refer to different psychological events and may occur quite independently of each other. Moreover, they represent separate problems in crime prevention as revealed in different patterns of criminal behaviors. Specific deterrence involves reducing recidivism (repeated offenses committed by convicted, punished offenders), while general deterrence involves reducing general crime rates (offenses committed among the general public who have not been punished).

As a scientific theory, the validity of the deterrence notion depends on the ability to carry out empirical research on it that provides empirical tests of the key premises (hypotheses). While considerable efforts have been made in the past three decades, research to persuasively test deterrence theory has been surprisingly difficult to accomplish. A large number of studies, encompassing a broad assortment of different types of research, have been carried out on this topic, but they have yielded an ambiguous and inconclusive pattern of findings (Nagin 1998; Sherman 1990).

Part of the difficulty in many of these studies may be simply their failure to fully express deterrence as a scientific theory with clearly defined (measurable) concepts and fully specified (testable) hypotheses. But the most fundamental difficulty is that deterrence is not directly observable; it can be inferred only from observable events. Quite literally deterrence refers to *nonevents* (that is, a person does *not* commit a crime). Moreover, these occasions when "nothing happens" occur because of a psychological process not observable to an outside observer (that is, an expectation of punishment accompanied by a feeling or fear or aversion). Failure to act is meaningful information about deterrence only if we clearly expect that the action *should* have occurred but did not, as in Sherlock Holmes's famous reference to "the dog that didn't bark."

We can infer deterrence only when we know that the person would have acted criminally but refrained because he or she considered the likely consequences of the act and feared the legal punishments that might result. People may refrain from committing a crime for lots of reasons other than fear of legal sanctions. They may simply have no desire to assault another person, sexually abuse their children, steal someone else's property, set fire to a building, drive eighty miles per hour on a busy highway, or inject heroin into their veins. They may find such actions uninteresting, uncomfortable, too much work, personally unattractive, morally offensive, physically risky to personal health and safety, likely to produce strong negative reactions from their friends and family, or sure to cause their eternal damnation. If so, then deterrence is irrelevant, no matter how severe the legal punishment, since they would not have committed the crime anyway.

The obvious difficulties of trying to study something that did not happen for reasons we cannot see means that almost all research on deterrence has involved studying only the *failures of deterrence*—that is, occurrence of criminal acts, which we *can* observe (at least in theory). But even here, we do not directly observe even deterrence failure, but must still infer it. We can observe when people commit crimes, but whether this indicates a failure of deterrence depends on what they knew and thought about before committing their crimes. To infer a failure of deterrence, we must know (or assume) that they were aware of and considered the punitive consequences of their acts before deciding to act anyway; otherwise, it is not a failure of deterrence but rather a thoughtless behavior oblivious to its possible outcomes.

In the face of these difficulties, how can researchers prove the scientific validity of the deterrence theory? A large body of deterrence studies have accumulated using a variety of research procedures, yielding a diverse array of findings. These range from strongly consistent with deterrence theory to strongly contradictory, with the vast majority being in the ambiguous or inconclusive middle. These studies include four broad types of research, each with its strengths and weaknesses for informing us about deterrence effects. First are anecdotal studies that rely on qualitative interviews, observations, and impressions of serious criminal offenders for evidence that their actions did or did not embody deterrence processes. Katz's (1988) qualitative analysis of the "nonrational seductions" of crime provided insightful evidence that rational calculations may not cover the thought processes of real criminals very adequately. Tunnell's (1990) in-depth interview study of incarcerated repeat property offenders amply documented that most of the offenders studied did not really think about the likely legal consequences of their actions. They had unrealistic perceptions about the likelihood of being caught and irrational expectations about what would happen to them if they did get caught. However, while such anecdotal studies are insightful and revealing about the perceptions and feelings of criminals, they are also selective and difficult to replicate or generalize from. For this reason, even though they may tell us a lot about the phenomenology of crime and punishment, they cannot provide a very definitive test of deterrence theory.

The second type of research involves ecological studies of aggregate crime and justice statistics, such as correlation of imprisonment rates and index crime rates across states or counties in the United States. *Index crimes* refers to the eight major commonly occurring crimes reported annually in the uniform crime reports, which are compiled by the Federal Bureau of Investigation. These crimes include: homicide, aggravated assault, arson, theft, robbery, motor vehicle theft, forcible rape, and burglary. These range from the original simple bivariate correlation studies in the late 1960s to the latest elaborate multivariate, multiple-equation econometric analyses. In this approach, the deterrence prediction is that punishment and crime rates will be negatively correlated, even after controlling for other social factors that may be confounded with crime and punishment patterns. Many of these studies show results consistent with a deterrence prediction, but these correlations vary considerably in size and direction, making interpretation ambiguous. The difficulty with this approach is its indirect assessment of deterrence events. It deals only with aggregated events and does not measure individual perceptions or correlate perceptions with individual behaviors. Thus, the findings of the ecological studies are, at best, suggestive but inconclusive.

The third category of deterrence research has involved what are called natural experiments or field experiments—that is, tracking patterns of crime levels before and after a dramatic change in punishment or enforcement policy (Nagin, 1978; 1998). The change or intervention that constitutes the experimental treatment may be a political event—such as a reinstitution of the death penalty, a statutory revision of the criminal law to provide mandatory prison terms for certain crimes, a judicial moratorium on death sentences, or a police strike. The change might also be a deliberately targeted intervention—such as a scheduled police crackdown on DUI drivers, implementation of a mandatory arrest policy for domestic violence cases in some precincts—that creates a kind of natural experiment. In all such cases, the deterrence prediction is that crime levels will be higher after an interruption that lowers the risk of punishment (such as during a police strike or a judicial moratorium on death sentences). Correspondingly, crimes will be lower after an intervention that increases the risk of punishment (such as reinstituting the death penalty or instituting random roadblocks to catch drunk drivers). This kind of research design seems more rigorous than the ecological studies, which are merely correlational. However, it still provides only indirect assessment of actual deterrence events, since individual perceptions and behaviors are not measured in these studies. Although they seem more scientific, the findings from these kinds of studies have shown only mixed evidence for deterrence. Some of the studies show a definite deterrence-like effect. Some studies show an opposite pattern from the predicted deterrence effect—one in which more punishment seems to lead to more crimes (sometimes termed a brutalization or a facilitation effect).

The fourth type of research relies on sample surveys of the general public using self-reported measures of people's punishment perceptions (such as perceived likelihood of getting caught or expected harshness of punishments) and their criminal behaviors (Williams and Hawkins, 1986; Zimring and Hawkins, 1973). Here again, deterrence predicts a negative correlation between people's perceptions of the certainty and severity of punishment and their reports of actually doing the illegal behavior. Alternative versions of the surveys have asked people not about their actual perceptions and behaviors, but about their predicted reactions in hypothetical scenarios. This type of deterrence research has the obvious advantage of dealing much more directly with perceptions and with directly correlating individual perceptions and behaviors. However, two weaknesses limited the ability of this kind of research to yield conclusive tests. One is the cross-sectional nature of surveys, which make the time ordering of variables somewhat ambiguous. The other limitation is the hypothetical nature of the questionnaires, which deal with abstract predictions about what people would do in hypothetical situations rather than their actual responses and behaviors. Thus, even though they deal more directly with the psychological aspects of deterrence, perceptual surveys provide suggestions, rather than definite conclusions, about deterrence effects (Ross, 1982).

After considering all the research carried out on deterrence, most scholars agree that it is impossible to assign a simple "true" or "false" to the deterrence doctrine (Paternoster and Piquero, 1995). It is clear that the general question "Does punishment of criminals deter crime?" is too simple to be answered meaningfully. It is clear from the considerable research carried out over the past three decades that punishment of criminals can and does have deterrent effects. However, the effects are generally weaker, and far more variable and inconsistent, than classical theory predicts. Thus, while there is considerable support for classical theory, it is by no means the complete and final explanation for crime that the classical model suggests. Classical theory remains a viable and useful theory for explaining many crime patterns, as well as for developing crime control policies, but it does not replace or eliminate any of its theoretical competitors—at least on scientific grounds.

Overall, it is clear that the dominant appeal of the theory is not entirely an outcome of scientific progress. The appeal of classical rational choice theory is substantially ideological rather than utilitarian. That is, it agrees with other values and beliefs people have about human nature, law, and morality; it fits with other things they believe about human nature and moral philosophy. Classical theory "works well enough" in terms of empirical research and policy evaluations, but it does not work demonstrably better than its more positivist theoretical competitors. And it does not work as well—as invariably and universally—as the theory claims it will. We know from research and criminal justice policy analysis that legal punishments provide an effective deterrent for crime in many circumstances. However, we also know that the effects of criminal punishments are limited and variable across situations and individuals. They are not universally and invariably effective; they do not always work as our philosophy prescribes.

SUMMARY

The classical school of criminology is the first general perspective on crime that attempted to understand its complex nature in a systematic and scientific nature. The perspective has had lasting impact as a leading explanation of crime for well over a century and has been vital in influencing the very nature of criminal justice systems around the world and, especially, in the Western Hemisphere. The daily efforts of law enforcement, the sanctions delivered through our court system, and certainly the deterrence and rehabilitation programs of our correctional institution all directly reflect ongoing efforts to lower the crime rate generally, and recidivism rates especially, by manipulating the criminal calculus. Deterrence theories and similar neoclassical perspectives incorporate deterministic and environmental factors that mitigate the decision-making process, but crime is ultimately seen as an outcome of free will and ineffective deterrence.

KEY TERMS

celerity   the swiftness with which punishment follows a crime

certainty   the probability that a crime will be detected and punished

deterrence   prevention of a certain act or acts (such as crime)

free will   humans' ability to control their own actions and destiny

hedonism   humans' tendency to maximize pleasure and minimize pain

neoclassical theory   a revised version of classical theory that acknowledges individual and situational differences in motivation, rationality, and free will (that is, bounded free will)

rationality   humans' ability to anticipate the consequences of different actions and to calculate the most beneficial outcomes

severity   the painfulness or unpleasantness of a sanction

DISCUSSION QUESTIONS

1. How did the Enlightenment period influence classical theories?

2. Identify some of the classical theory's key assumptions about human

nature. Do you think that humans generally behave according to these assumptions?

3. Why did classical theory come under fire from the positivistic school of criminological thought?

4. What are some modifications of the neoclassical movement that influenced deterrence theory?

5. Discuss some of the ways criminologists test deterrence theory today. Can you envision a study that would also test modern deterrence theory?

REFERENCES

Akers, R. L. (1994). *Criminological theories: introduction and evaluation.* Los Angeles: Roxbury.

Andenaes, J. (1974). *Punishment and deterrence.* Ann Arbor: University of Michigan Press.

Barnes, H. E., & Teeters, N. K. (1951). *New horizons in criminology* (2nd ed.) Upper Saddle River, N. J.: Prentice Hall.

Beccaria, C. (1963). *On crimes and punishments* (H. Paolucci, Trans.). Indianapolis: Bobbs-Merrill. (Original work published 1764)

Becker, G. S. (1968). Crime and punishment: An economic approach. *Journal of Political Economy, 76,* 169–217.

Cook, P. (1980). Research in criminal deterrence: Laying the groundwork for the second decade. In N. Morris & M. Tonry (Eds.), *Crime and justice: An annual review of research* (Vol. 2, pp. 211–268). Chicago: University of Chicago Press.

Gibbs, J. P. (1975). *Crime, punishment, and deterrence.* New York: Elsevier.

Gibbs, J. P. (1986). Deterrence theory and research. In G. B. Melton (Ed.), *The law as a behavioral instrument* (pp. 87–130). Lincoln: University of Nebraska Press.

Hobbes, T. (1962). *Leviathan.* New York: Macmillan. (Original work published 1651)

Katz, J. (1988). *Seductions of crime: Moral and sensual attractions in doing evil.* New York: Basic Books.

Marvell, T., & Moody, C. (1994). Prison population growth and crime reduction. *Journal of Quantitative Criminology, 10,* 109–140.

Morris, N. (1966). Impediments to penal reform. *University of Chicago Law Review, 33,* 627–656.

Nagin, D. (1978). General deterrence: A review of the empirical evidence. In A. Blumstein, J. Cohen, and D. Nagin (Eds.), *Deterrence and incapacitation: Estimating the effects of criminal sanctions on crime rates* (pp. 95–139). Washington, DC: National Academy Press.

Nagin, D. (1998). Criminal deterrence research at the outset of the twenty-first century. In M. Tonry (Ed.), *Crime and justice: A review of research* (Vol. 23, pp. 1–42). Chicago: University of Chicago Press.

Paternoster, R., & Piquero, A. (1995). Reconceptualizing deterrence: An empirical test of personal and vicarious experiences. *Journal of Research in Crime and Delinquency, 32,* 251–286.

Ross, H. L. (1982). *Deterring the drinking driver: Legal policy and social control.* Lexington, MA: Heath.

Sherman, L. W. (1990). Police crackdowns: Initial and residual deterrence. In M. Tonry and N. Morris (Eds.), *Crime and justice: A review of research* (Vol. 12, pp. 1–48). Chicago: University of Chicago Press.

Sherman, L. W. (1993). Defiance, deterrence, and irrelevance: A theory of the criminal sanction. *Journal of Research in Crime and Delinquency, 30,* 445–473.

Tunnell, K. D. (1990). Choosing crime: Close your eyes and take your chances. *Justice Quarterly, 7,* 673–690.

Walters, G. C., & Grusec, J. E. (1977). *Punishment.* San Francisco: Freeman.

Williams, K. R., & Hawkins, R. (1986). Perceptual research on general deterrence: A critical overview. *Law and Society Review, 20,* 545–572.

Zimring, F. E., & Hawkins, G. J. (1973). *Deterrence: The legal threat in crime control.* Chicago: University of Chicago Press.

CHAPTER 3

BIOLOGICAL THEORIES
OF CRIME

One of the easiest ways for many of us to try to understand why some people commit crime and others do not is to look for some type of unique quality or characteristic of the individual that we can blame for crime. Among the easiest to understand, and for some of us the "safest" way to think about why some people are and some people are not criminal, is to focus on physical traits of individuals. When we can point to something specific and tangible about a person and see this as the cause of behavior, we remove all (or at least much of) the blame and grayer areas of social influences. This approach usually makes logical sense, and it is easy to think of different parts of people's brains, bodies, or chemical makeup that we could point to as explanations for why people are the way they are. Biological theories also allow us to look at crime and criminals in less judgmental ways; after all, if someone commits crime because he is "programmed" or "born" that way, it really is not right to blame him for his behavior.

However, if someone is "bad" because of some characteristic that she was born with, it might also make sense to look for a cure to what is wrong with her body or brain. This is called a medical model view of crime and behavior. In this view, criminality is not something that people choose to do, nor something over which they have any (or much) control. Instead, being a criminal is similar to having a disease or a birth defect. And the way we can, and should, respond to crime is similar to how we can and should react to people with a disease or birth defect. The appropriate response is to try to find a medical approach that can intervene or "fix" what is wrong with the body. However, just as with some diseases and birth defects, it may not be possible to cure or fix what is wrong. In these cases, then, it may be necessary to segregate, quarantine, or in extreme cases, permanently remove the sick person from society (so he or she does not infect or harm other people).

The medical model view of crime, based on biological theories for explaining why crime occurs, sees criminal behavior as a part of an individual for which he or she cannot, or at least should not, be blamed. Society has the responsibility to try to help correct the biological/physical problems that cause the behavior. Or, in cases when the biological problem cannot be fixed, it is the responsibility of society (through experts) to remove criminals so as to protect those who are not sick.

Biological theories of crime are among the oldest explanations for why people break the law. A number of theories and research evidence have emerged in the last two decades that suggest a link between biology and criminal behavior (see Fishbein, 1990). Explanations for crime that point to the size and shape of criminals' bodies and family trees (heredity and genetics), scientific "facts" that show differences in genetics and chemical compositions of individuals, and biological consequences of things such as what we eat and drink have been suggested as reasons for all types of behaviors, including crime. Some of these theories date back several centuries, and some have emerged in the last couple of years.

This approach to explaining behavior appeals to many people because it seems to make logical sense. We can all think of times when we have assumed behaviors of others based on something about their size, looks, or even eating habits. Our popular culture is also full of images and messages that reinforce these ideas. When you ask someone to describe a "criminal," it is not uncommon for him or her to suggest that such people are large, muscular, and mean-looking, with sharp piercing eyes. What type of person are we more likely to fear in a dark and deserted alley—a five-foot-tall, hundred-pound individual wearing thick glasses, or a six-foot-six muscular individual covered in tattoos? How many of us as children were warned by our parents to stay away from other children because their parents "just don't look right"? The point is, many of us already act on information that is rooted in biological theory assumptions; therefore, it is easy to see how these types of theories could have wide appeal.

Biological theories of crime and criminal behavior have been with us for a long time, but they have undergone some very significant and important changes over the past several centuries. Originally, biological theories emphasized the idea that some people had a biological/physical trait or condition that led them into crime, regardless of their social environment or other factors. More recent biological theories have expanded to recognize the importance of social environments, and today these types of theories suggest that criminals (all, or maybe just some) have some sort of biological/physical characteristic that can be "turned on" or that makes the individual more likely to commit crime. As one set of observers and commentators on biological theories suggest, the more recent biological theories are "most useful when looking at how such environmental influences as isolation, neglect, abuse, and other conditioning variables are imprinted into individuals to cause predictable, incorrigible behavioral disorders years later" (Knoblich & King, 1992, p. 2).

THE POSITIVIST SCHOOL OF THOUGHT

The foundation for biological theories of crime is a positivist way of thinking. **Positivism** is the idea that it is possible to identify specific causes of behavior using scientific approaches. The positivist school of thought has its roots in the scientific revolution of the sixteenth century. This means that when we say we can use scientific means to identify specific causes of criminal behavior, we need to think of science in a very broad way. Obviously, what we think of as science today (use of DNA, sophisticated medical procedures, and so on), is not what was meant by this idea five hundred years ago. Scientific investigation conducted by the early positivist thinkers and biological theorists compared the characteristics of known criminals with others in the population. If it could be shown that all (or at least most) criminals had a particular characteristic—such as large ears or pointy chins—and noncriminals did not have this characteristic in large numbers, it was assumed to indicate one's criminal ways.

Positivist thinking in criminology is based on three core assumptions about individuals and how their bodies relate to their behavior. First, it is assumed that all individuals are biologically unique and different from all other people. Second, these differences in our individual makeup are believed to account for our differences in behavior. Third, criminal behavior is assumed to be a result of specific differences in physical constructions and characteristics of individuals that can be identified through observation or other scientific means.

One of the most important changes in thinking about behavior to arise from the positivist way of thinking was the rejection of the idea of free will. No longer was it assumed that people chose their behavior. Rather, behavior was a part of the individual over which he or she had little (if any) control. Our behavior, including whether we committed crimes, was simply another result of our physical development, much like the color of our hair, how tall we are, or whether we are male or female.

Early positivist biological theories focused on identifying distinct characteristics of criminals' faces, sizes, shapes and bumps on their heads, and overall physical size and shape. Over time these ideas developed and were refined, remaining a part of public debate and influencing public policies and laws well into the twentieth century.

PHYSIOGNOMY AND PHRENOLOGY

The earliest biological theories of crime focused on the study of facial features and the size, shape, and contours of people's heads. The focus of these scientific investigations was to locate features that could be found among criminals but not among noncriminals, and then use these features to identify who is (or would be) criminals.

Physiognomy, made popular by Johan Caspar Lavater during the 1770s, was an early form of science that sought to identify distinct facial features of people who committed crimes. The ideas of physiognomy were well received by society, and caused people to watch out for people with a wide range of facial features believed to be associated with criminal behavior. Included among the indicators of dangerousness were men without beards (and, interestingly, women *with* beards), weak chins, and "shifty" eyes. Although these types of traits clearly are not today seen as indications that someone is dangerous or a criminal, it is most important that such "scientific" conclusions were considered important and prompted further development of the search for criminal characteristics in the faces and bodies of individuals.

A second, and similar, form of science closely followed on the heels of physiognomy, and focused on the shape and contours of the head (assumed to be indications of the shape and development of the brain) and the relation of such to behavior. **Phrenology**, as this science was called, was popular in the 1790s and early 1800s. The basic idea of phrenology was that different parts of the brain controlled different types of social activities and thinking, and when particular areas of the brain were more developed, they would be larger and therefore create bumps or protrusions on the skull. Based on beliefs about what behaviors or characteristics were located in different areas of the brain, it therefore was believed possible to feel an individual's head and know what areas of his or her brain were more developed, and consequently, what his or her behavior was likely to be. Phrenology and physiognomy were rather short-lived scientific endeavors. They largely passed from influence and acceptance because they could not be verified.

LOMBROSO AND ATAVISM

While physiognomy and phrenology had limited influence on public policy and theory, they did set the stage for a more fully developed and influential set of ideas that came about in the latter half of the nineteenth century. Probably the best known of the early biological theorists was **Cesare Lombroso** and his ideas of **atavism**. Lombroso became widely known following the publication of his book *The Criminal Man* (1876), in which he argued that criminals are essentially less evolved forms of humankind. As he explained it, criminals tended to be "throwbacks" to a lower form of human, or more similar to our apelike ancestors than noncriminals. Building on the growing influence of evolutionary science, Lombroso referred to such individuals as atavistic, and argued that as less-evolved examples of humans, criminals were likely to display a number of physical characteristics that were common and pronounced among apes but not among "evolved" people. And, most important for our discussion here, Lombroso initially argued that atavistic people were criminals because of their less-evolved nature. Many people attribute the idea of a "born criminal" to Lombroso; however, this reference was not used until coined by Lombroso's son-in-law and student Enrico Ferri. The visible features of atavistic people were referred to as "stigmata," suggesting that they were clear signs of something being "wrong" or less developed in the person. Among some of the more common of the atavistic characteristics that Lombroso said suggested one's lower status—and greater likelihood of criminality—were the following:

- Misshapen or overly large head
- Uneven facial features, in which one side differs from the other
- Large or protruding lips
- Large jaw and/or cheekbones
- Low or very narrow forehead
- Large eyes
- A large number of wrinkles (especially very noticeable ones) on the face
- Especially long arms, fingers, or toes
- Bulbous or pouchlike cheeks
- Large ears, or ears that stand out from the head
- Misshapen nose

This is only a partial list of Lombroso's characteristics. Lombroso and his followers identified several dozen characteristics, many of which they associated not only with "criminals" in general, but with particular types of criminals.

The science used to validate these characteristics initially suggested that there was some truth to these claims; numerous researchers were able to document at least some of the stigmata. However, this should not be surprising. Consider the individuals that we all encounter in our daily lives. How many of the people we know could we identify as having one or a few of the short list of characteristics listed here?

The fact that many of these characteristics are fairly common among people, and the fact that it was fairly easy to identify noncriminals possessing some of these characteristics, led Lombroso to eventually modify his position and add to his theory social and environmental influences. In this line of modified thinking—combining biology with social/environmental forces—Lombroso argued that criminals need to be examined not as a universal group or class, but more productively on a case-by-case basis. In this way, he suggested that criminals existed in three basic forms: born criminals, insane criminals, and criminaloids. The first type of criminal, the born criminal, is his original idea of an atavistic individual, less developed physically, mentally, and socially than "normal" people. The insane criminal commits crime(s) because of a mental deficiency or due to alcohol and/or drugs. The third group, the criminaloids, are a general class of people who do not have special physical characteristics or mental disorders, but who under certain social conditions (such as an emotional event or a "need" for some item) may engage in some type of crime.

Enrico Ferri, one of Lombroso's most notable protégés, built on Lombroso's work and added in a sizable component of social, economic, and political factors as contributors to crime. Ferri also proposed a categorization of types of criminals, arguing that offenders could be identified as either born, insane, occasional, or criminal by passion. The born and insane criminals are essentially Lombroso's ideas. Occasional criminals and criminals by passion were categories that refined Lombroso's criminaloid category. Ferri, however, believed that to understand the causes of crime it was necessary to look at physical characteristics of both people and environments, anthropological issues (including an individual's age, sex, and physical conditions) and social aspects (culture, religion, economic and political structures, and so on) of the environments where criminals lived. Ferri's ideas fit well with the socialist thinking of the time in Italy, and he was a political activist who was asked to chair a committee charged with rewriting the criminal laws for Italy following the end of World War I. However, with the rise to power of the Fascist political party his efforts were put aside, and his ideas did not become codified into law.

A third influential early positivist to come from Italy was Raffaele Garofalo. He also believed, like Lombroso and Ferri, that scientific approaches were necessary to understand the cause of crime and he focused his efforts on developing a "universal" definition of crime. Garofalo referred to this as "natural crime." The idea of natural crime is infused with many psychological influences, showing a break in thinking from that originally put forth by Lombroso and modified by Ferri. In fact, Garofalo rejected any association with Lombroso or Ferri and at times was quite critical of their theorizing.

The thinking of Lombroso (and subsequent others) gave rise to an often unrecognized development in the study of crime: the field of criminal anthropology (see Rafter, 1992). This line of thinking began in Europe and developed in the United States in the 1890s. In 1893 Arthur MacDonald introduced the term *criminology* in the United States. This was the first use of the term in the United States, and MacDonald was the first American to be identified as a *criminologist* (a specialist in the study of crime and its causes). The focus of this work and of the criminal anthropological work that was published in the United States through 1911 was on the underdeveloped nature (or "degeneracy") of criminal offenders. As a specialized field, criminal anthropology never gained a stronghold in American intellectual thinking and the field failed to soundly define itself. As a result, it faded from importance and influence (see Rafter, 1992).

The ideas originally put forth by Lombroso and added to and modified by Ferri and Garofalo were popular in Europe for several decades (and in the United States for a shorter time), and inspired numerous followers, as well as those who sought to test and/or refute Lombroso's ideas. The end of Lombroso's influence was most pointedly brought about by the work of **Charles Goring** in the second decade of the twentieth century. Goring (1913–1972) took Lombroso's ideas and tested them using a comparison between imprisoned recidivist criminals in England and a group of noncriminals—university students. Although some have argued that Goring was too determined to prove Lombroso wrong (rather than seeking to do a truly objective assessment of Lombroso's ideas), the result was a convincing showing that most of Lombroso's identified physical features could not be associated with criminality. However, Goring did show that people who experienced frequent and long imprisonments were physically smaller (in both height and weight) than others. Beyond this, however, Goring argued that physical features were not associated with one group or the other, but there was actually a greater degree of variation within each group than between the groups. In simple terms, Goring largely disproved Lombroso's ideas, and as a result Lombroso's theory lost both support and influence.

GENETIC THEORIES

Another way of thinking about why people commit crimes is to work from the idea that not only are some individuals "bad" people that have something wrong with them, but instead there might be entire "bad" families that are likely to continue to produce criminal offspring. This is the idea of a group of people who, because of their shared genetic lineage, are predisposed to share a trait of criminality. Many people believe that some of us are just born into situations and families that are criminal and either we have no real chance not to be criminal, or the family we are born into just makes it more likely that we will be criminal.

Genetic theories are different, yet still build on the general ideas that were put forth by people like Lombroso. Just as physiognomy and phrenology had faded from importance earlier, Lombroso's views lost their importance, although not completely. In fact, a couple of decades after Goring disproved Lombroso, others stepped forward with somewhat similar arguments, suggesting that biological determinism might still be able to explain many criminals' actions.

Theories that emphasize an individual's **genetic predisposition** say that criminal behavior is inherited and runs in families. The premise in these explanations centers on the belief that there is something genetic in the cause of crime, and criminality is passed along some lines of families just like other inherited traits such as appearance, diseases, or genetic mutations. While these theories do not claim to explain all criminals or all crime, they do argue that a significant amount of crime can be explained by looking to families where crime "runs in the family."

Crime as an inherited trait has been a commonly argued part of several theories, with some suggesting that it is a deterministic inheritance (that is, those who inherit the trait definitely will be criminal) and others suggesting that inheritance simply predisposes one to a greater likelihood of being criminal.

The idea of biology being a deterministic influence was most strongly advocated by the anthropologist **E. A. Hooten** in the 1930s and 1940s. Hooten's (1939) ideas were based on a massive study of 14,000 prisoners and a comparison group of more than 3,000 noncriminals. In comparing individuals in the two groups he concluded that there were numerous physical differences between criminals and noncriminals, and in almost every way he compared the two groups the criminals were "inferior." This included physical measurements and assessments as well as mental/intellectual abilities.

Hooten argued in favor of addressing the crime problem in society by targeting the genetically predisposed for either segregation or elimination from society. As he stated in his book *The American Criminal* (1939), "Criminals are organically inferior. Crime is the resultant of the impact of environment upon low grade human organisms. It follows that the elimination of crime can be effected only by the extirpation of the physically, mentally, and morally unfit; or by their complete segregation" (p. 309). His position is clear; criminals cannot be changed, they do not deserve to live in society, and sterilization of known criminals is an acceptable practice. As we might expect, Hooten's work was controversial and drew a large amount of criticism.

Both Richard Dugdale (1877/1895) and Henry Goddard (1912) offered a less deterministic view, although they still emphasized the idea of criminality being something that we inherit. The work of these two men, both coming earlier than that of Hooten, focused on examining family trees to identify lines of inheritance of criminality and concentrations of crime among family members. This theory suggests that criminality is a trait that is inherited, but the inheritance is only of a propensity for criminality, not a definite behavior. Dugdale began his work when as a staff member of the Prison Association of New York he discovered six members of the Jukes family in prison. Intrigued by this fact, he began researching the Jukes family tree and discovered that among the approximately 1,000 descendants he could trace back to one woman, Ada Jukes, nearly 50 percent were criminals. Similarly, Henry Goddard (1912) tracked the family tree of a Revolutionary soldier, Martin Kallikak. The interesting aspect of the Kallikak family study begins with the immediate branching of the tree from Martin Kallikak into a family line born of a legitimate son and one from an illegitimate son. The tracking of both major branches of the family tree showed that there were many more criminals in the family branches stemming from the illegitimate son than from the legitimate son. Goddard attributed this to the fact that the mother of Martin Kallikak's illegitimate son was obviously "not of high quality" (as evidenced by the fact that she had an illegitimate son). The moral aspect of Goddard's interpretation of these data is clear, as is the different way that "crime" and "high-quality" character have been defined at various times in history.

Although there are clearly problems with both Dugdale's and Goddard's work—such as failing to consider social aspects of the families' situations—this type of theorizing had a major influence on American criminal laws and policies. Because it was assumed that criminality ran in families, this meant that the offspring of criminals (and especially criminals who had other criminal family members) could be expected to be criminals themselves. Therefore, it only made sense to many policymakers to remove the possibility of these likely criminals being born. As a result, a number of states implemented laws allowing forced sterilization of habitual criminals as part of their criminal sentences. When these laws were challenged in the courts, the U.S. Supreme Court upheld them as constitutional in 1927. In perhaps one of the most frequently quoted Supreme Court decisions of all time, *Buck* v. *Bell*, 274 U.S. 200 (1926), Justice Oliver Wendell Holmes, Jr., wrote, "it is better for all the world, if instead of waiting to execute the degenerate offspring for crime, or to let them starve for their imbecility, society can prevent those who are manifestly unfit from continuing their kind. . . . Three generations of imbeciles are enough."

Other theorists and researchers have also looked at the idea of crime as an inherited trait, although not focusing so strongly on the idea that crime runs in families. In looking to see whether some genetic factor can be passed between generations, or whether genetics or environment plays a larger role in whether someone engages in crime, some researchers have studied the behavior of twins and others have examined whether adopted children have more similarity to their biological or adoptive families. The questions asked by these studies very clearly focus on whether something is passed between parents and children that is associated with greater or lesser likelihood of being criminal.

One of the best ways to study whether a behavior, such as criminality, may be related to genetics is to examine the behavior of twins. The basic approach to this type of science is to track the behavior of sets of twins (or other multiple birth, but they are much more rare) and see if and how their behaviors are similar and different. Especially when research can include identical twins (who have identical genetic makeup), this can be a very powerful way to study the causes of behavior. In studies of this variety, researchers look for concordance rates of behavior. A concordance rate is the frequency with which twins have the same behaviors. So, if a study of sets of twins shows a concordance rate of 100 percent when one twin is criminal and the second is also criminal, and 100 percent when when one twin is not a criminal and neither is the other, then we would have very strong evidence suggesting that genetics is related to becoming a criminal. While it is unrealistic to expect concordance rates of 100 percent for any type of behavior, it is interesting to note that numerous researchers have shown a higher concordance rate for identical twins than fraternal twins (who do not have identical genetic makeup).

The study of twins and criminality was especially popular in the United States, as well as Europe and Japan, starting in the 1930s. Most of this line of research tapered off, however, in the 1960s. Some large-scale, longitudinal studies continue to be done today, although most are focused on issues other than criminality (health issues, psychological functioning, and so on). The ideal way to study twins is to compare behaviors for identical twins raised in separate families. One of the problems with this approach, however, is that not very many families that have twins choose to give one away. In the early 1900s this may have happened in families that had more children than they could afford to support, but today it is very difficult to find twins who were separated at birth. Therefore, most modern studies of twins look at comparisons of concordance rates for identical twins and fraternal twins.

One of the largest studies of twins was done with more than 6,000 sets of twins born between 1881 and 1910 in Denmark (Christiansen, 1977). Identical twins showed a concordance rate three times as high (36% versus 12%) as fraternal twins. Similar findings were reported for a 1985 study in Ohio (Rowe, 1985). In this study the findings went a bit further and showed that not only criminality is highly correlated among twins, but so too are emotions and actions such as anger and impulsiveness. And in a review of all of the available studies of twins done over nearly a half-century, Wilson and Herrnstein (1985) reported that across the studies identical twins showed a concordance rate of 69 percent compared to only 33 percent for fraternal twins. These studies, taken as a whole, strongly support the importance of genetics in determining behavior, especially criminal behavior.

Twin studies, though, do have some problems. The usual criticism of these studies is that it may be impossible to separate out the influence of genetics and social environment. When twins are raised in the same household, they are exposed to the same sets of social influences. And, as many people know, identical twins are more likely to be treated "identically" than fraternal twins (especially when the fraternal twins are different sexes). We have all seen twins that are dressed alike, given very similar names, and treated more or less as copies of one another. This approach to child rearing is assumed to be more common with identical twins than fraternal twins. The problem this raises for research on the possible genetic link to crime is that if in fact identical twins are more likely to be treated the same than are fraternal twins, it may not be possible to conclude that similarities in criminality are due to genetics.

One way to try to overcome this problem is to study children who are not raised by their biological parents. Studies of adopted children enable researchers to compare the influence of genetics with that of one's social environment. The basic approach of such studies is to compare an adopted child's criminality with that of the biological parents (who provided his or her genetic structure) and that of the adoptive parents (who provided his or her social environment).

The most important of the adoption studies is based on data collected on more than 4,000 Danish boys (Mednick, Gabrieli, & Hutchings, 1984). This research has shown that genetics does seem to play a role in criminality, although the researchers argue that this is only a predisposition to crime, not a true deterministic influence. This study has shown that adopted boys who had both biological and adoptive parents who were criminal were more likely (24.5 percent) than those boys who had only criminal adoptive parents (14.7 percent) and only criminal biological parents (20 percent) to be criminal themselves. It is important to keep in mind, though, that even at the level of having both sets of parents being criminally involved, only one in four of the boys were identified as criminal. And one in eight (13.5 percent) of boys with neither a biological nor adoptive parent that was a criminal ended up as criminal himself. Similar results have also been found among more than 1,700 adopted children in a Swedish study (Bohman, Cloninger, Sigwardsson, & von Knorring, 1982) and adopted children in Iowa born between 1925 and 1956 to female criminals (Crowe, 1972, 1974).

Clearly, then, while genetics appears to be influential, it is not the only, or even perhaps the most powerful, influence on criminality. The conclusion that our genetics plays a role in our behavior may be frightening to some of us. To think that our behavior is not something we can completely control can be scary and disheartening. For others of us, however, it may come as a bit of a relief to realize that different people in fact do have different chances, opportunities, or challenges with which they are born. However, if our behavior is not really completely under our control, questions are sure to arise about what is best and appropriate for responding to the crimes of people who do not have full control.

One additional way of looking at a pure genetic influence on crime is to try to identify the gene that leads to a predisposition for crime. The real push for this research began in the 1960s following the discovery that a small percentage of men (about one-tenth of 1 percent or fewer, or one in every 1,000 to 2,000) have a genetic anomaly of two Y chromosomes (see Amir & Berman, 1970; Fox, 1971). So whereas women have an XX pair of sex-determining chromosomes and most men have an X and a Y chromosome, this very small portion of men have an extra Y chromosome. Research looking at these men with the **XYY chromosome** pattern found that they tend to be physically larger and taller, have more and stronger masculine traits, and also tend to score lower on intelligence tests. Interestingly one of the most common places where researchers found men with the XYY chromosome pattern was in mental institutions. Because these men were "more masculine," the assumption carried that these men were also more aggressive and prone to violence.

Several researchers (Jacobs, Brunton, & Melville, 1965; Kessler & Moos, 1970; Price, Strong, Whatmore, & McClemont, 1966; also see Amir & Berman, 1970; Fox, 1971) have tested the chromosomal makeup of male criminals, looking to see if those with an XYY chromosome are in fact more likely to be involved in crime. Most of the research in this area supports the argument that these men are more likely (but not always) involved in crime. However, the problem with this theory for explaining crime is that this "abnormality" is very rare. The incidence of an XYY chromosome in men has always been shown to be less than 1 percent (and sometimes less than one-tenth of 1 percent) of all men. Also, the most common finding among these men is that they show a lower level of intelligence. So the extra Y chromosome might just make these men more likely to be caught if they are involved in crime, not necessarily more likely to be violent or criminal in the first place.

If in fact an XYY chromosome pattern truly has something to do with someone becoming a criminal, it is still a long way from explaining most crime. The situation with the XYY chromosome pattern research highlights one of the basic problems with much of the biological theory approaches. While a particular factor or physical trait might be shown to be statistically related to criminal activity, if the trait is rare among the population, we still have not explained most, or even very many, criminals.

BODY TYPE THEORIES

The idea that biology and our physical traits may predispose us to a greater likelihood of being criminal is continued, and actually replaces the idea of biological determinism, in the work of biological theorists in the twentieth century. It is interesting to note that although some new theories and slightly different points of focus are presented, some of Lombroso's basic ideas remain prominent in many of the theories that continued to emerge. Some of the more influential of these ideas and views are summarized next, including those that center on body types.

Looking at the size, shape, and form of the human body and correlating these issues with our likelihood of engaging in crime was reintroduced to criminology by the German psychiatrist **Ernst Kretschmer**, and later the Americans **William Sheldon** and Sheldon and Eleanor Glueck. All of the propositions of these thinkers focus on the idea of somatotypes. This is the argument that our body build is associated with our behavioral tendencies, life expectancy, likelihood of disease, and temperament. The science of **somatotyping** involves categorizing individuals based on assessments of their physical traits, and then looking for correlations between certain types of bodies (the categories) and those individuals' behaviors. Basically, somatotype theorists believe that people of differing body types think and behave differently; for criminologists it was important to identify the types of bodies that are most often involved in crime.

Kretschmer (1921/1925) first proposed these ideas and presented three ideal types of bodies (later adding a fourth) found among people. The three body types are the asthenic, the athletic, and the pyknic. The asthenic body type is thin and tall with narrow shoulders. The athletic type, much as the name suggests, is muscular and well developed. The pyknic type tends to be "softer," also described in a less flattering way as "short and fat." Within each category of body type, this theory says, are found different varieties of thinking patterns and mental disorders, which in turn are related to different types of criminal behavior.

So Kretschmer contended that each body type was related to a greater propensity for engaging in different forms of criminal behavior. The asthenic body type individual is most often associated with small thefts and fraud, and tends to both first engage in crime at an early age and end his or her criminality early in life. The athletic body type person is most likely to be engaged in violent crime, and usually has fairly stable patterns of criminal behavior throughout life. Pyknic body type individuals are somewhat more likely to be involved in theft or fraud, although they may also be found among violent criminals fairly frequently. What distinguishes these individuals, however, is that they tend to start their criminal behavior later in life than the asthenic or athletic body types. Later in his career Kretschmer responded to some of the critics of his work by adding a fourth category of body types to his somatotype typology: the dysplastic (mixed) body type. A dysplastic individual, who possessed a combination of characteristics of the other three body types, also engaged in a variety of types of crimes.

William Sheldon, a physician, brought the basic ideas and general directions of the somatotyping school of thought originated by Kretschmer to American thinking about crime in the 1940s. Sheldon's (1940, 1942, 1949) work reflects many of the core ideas originated by Kretschmer, but he is credited with both refining the ideas and using a much more rigorous scientific approach to validate and support his ideas. Sheldon also proposed three basic body types—endomorphs, ectomorphs, and mesomorphs—each associated with certain types of behavior. However, one of the important ways that Sheldon's work advances that of Kretschmer is that Sheldon acknowledged that all people have some degree of characteristics of each body type. With this in mind he proposed a way of evaluating body types and rating the degree to which any individual possesses the ideal type traits of each category. Based on a seven-point rating scale, every individual can be assigned a three-number score, reflecting his or her degree of each ideal type's characteristics. The ideal type endomorph is a shorter, smaller, but heavier individual with small bones and is generally soft/smooth. The pure form of the ectomorph body is a thinner person who is often relatively tall, lean, and "fragile" and tends to have a small face. The ideal type mesomorph body is a more athletic person with more-developed muscles and an overall larger body frame and limbs.

Each of the ideal forms of body types, Sheldon (1942) argued, can be associated with a type of personality or temperament. The variety of temperaments are therefore associated with different likelihood of criminal engagement. People who score high on the endomorph body type tend to be outgoing, comfortable, and a bit "soft." Those who score high on ectomorph body type are much more introverted, tend to avoid crowds and others, and often have allergies, illnesses, and other "functional problems." The mesomorph is typically an active, assertive, and perhaps aggressive type of person. Each of these types of personalities and behavioral sets can be relatively easily translated into types of crimes that are most expected for each body type. Obviously the more assertive or aggressive mesomorph would be most likely to be involved in violence, and the ectomorph who prefers to avoid others is most likely to be involved in property crimes or crimes of theft, those that do not require interacting with or confronting others.

The most likely body type for involvement in crime is the mesomorph. This idea was the foundation for continued study in this area in the 1950s by the husband-and-wife team of Sheldon and Eleanor Glueck (1950, 1956). Their interests focused on the delinquency of mesomorph boys, and after comparing five-hundred chronically delinquent boys with a group of five-hundred nondelinquents, they concluded that twice as many delinquents were of a mesomorph body type than nondelinquents. However, in keeping with the thinking that biological and physical factors only predispose rather than determine behaviors, the Gluecks also showed that involvement in delinquency was also related to social factors, including weak family ties and involvement. This acknowledgement of the role of nonphysical factors fit well with the historical era; as is discussed in other chapters, the midtwentieth century was a time when criminological theories emphasizing social and cultural factors were most prominent. The Gluecks essentially "softened" the role of physical body types in the explanation of crime, although they did see it as an important factor.

RECENT BIOLOGICAL THEORIES

Some more recent theories for explaining why and how crime happens have also looked at biological factors. And, as most biological theories before have argued, the most recent theories also suggest that biological factors may make a person more likely to be involved in crime, but these factors do not mean that a person definitely will be criminal. The more recent versions of biological theories have moved away from suggesting that something about our physical bodies or our genetics predisposes us to crime. Instead, the biological theories of the late twentieth century and early twenty-first century have focused more directly on either the biological and physiological results of things we put into our bodies (such as food or drugs) or on how malfunctioning parts of our brains may be associated with crime.

One of the more commonsense approaches that has been developed to explain crime is a focus on **hormones** and their effects on behavior. These views have looked both at men and women separately, and suggest that the levels of sex hormones (testosterone and estrogen) in our bodies influence our emotions and our levels of aggression. Research on men has focused on the idea that high levels of testosterone produce high levels of aggression. And some theories about women's criminality have suggested that premenstrual syndrome and varying estrogen levels are behind criminal behavior.

The research on men's testosterone levels begins with the idea that men commit most crime. And when we think about the men who do commit crime, especially violent crimes, we often think of a certain type of man. Very masculine, large, and aggressive men are often associated with crime. These men are often found to have higher levels of testosterone in their bodies, so it seems logical to assume that when a man has more testosterone, he would likely be predisposed to violence (that is, crime). Decades of research have shown that boys in general are more aggressive than girls, even at very young ages. Several researchers (Booth & Osgood, 1993; Olweus, 1987; Rada, Laws, & Kellner, 1976; Rubin, 1987; Rushton, 1995) have shown that boys and men with higher testosterone levels are also more likely to be involved in violence and crime.

This line of thinking is often offered as an explanation for the high levels of crime committed by athletes. Recent years have shown a higher-than-expected amount of crime (especially violent crime) committed by high school, college, and professional male athletes. Athletes typically have high levels of testosterone, which facilitates not only muscular development, but also competitiveness and aggression. Therefore, the link seems somewhat obvious: A man with high testosterone levels is likely to behave in ways that are criminal. These ideas have also received a great deal of attention as a result of a number of highly publicized incidents in recent years whereby men (especially bodybuilders and other athletes) who take anabolic steroids have engaged in criminal and violent behavior (Pope & Katz, 1990). When men take anabolic steroids they boost their production of testosterone and in turn facilitate their muscular development and competitiveness (as they increase their levels of testosterone). One common consequence (some would say "side effect") of taking steroids is that the individual often becomes very aggressive and sometimes violent (" 'roid rage"). Such instances are commonly interpreted as yet further evidence supporting the theory that high levels of testosterone are related to criminal behavior. Interestingly, others (Dabbs & Hargrove, 1997) have also shown that testosterone levels are related to violent behavior among women as well as men.

However, the research on testosterone levels and aggression/violence/crime needs to be viewed with caution. A number of social influences may affect both testosterone levels and behavior. In fact, one recent review of the research in this area suggests that testosterone levels may be the result of hostility, and not the cause of or contributor to aggression (Aromaki, Lindman, & Eriksson, 1999).

In regard to women's hormone levels and criminal behavior, some research has looked at whether premenstrual syndrome (in which women's hormones change in volume and intensity) may be related to criminality. Some researchers have reported either that a majority of women's criminal offenses are committed during their menstrual periods (Cooke, 1945; Dalton, 1961; Morton, Addison, Addison, Hunt, & Sullivan, 1953) or that women with premenstrual syndrome are significantly more likely than other women to engage in verbally or physically aggressive acts (Bond, Critchlow, & Wingrove, 2003).

Critics of the hormone-level theorizing, however, suggest that the cause-and-effect order may actually be misinterpreted. According to some (Horney, 1978; Katz & Chambliss, 1991), the fact that hormone levels vary among violent criminals may actually be the result of aggression/violence/crime, not the cause of or a contributor to it. Whether we believe that hormones are related to crime or not, the important point is that it is in many ways a logical proposition, and both theorists and criminal justice officials do see hormones as a factor in why some people are criminally involved.

Another approach to looking at biological factors and their relation to crime draws a bit more on social influence and suggests that our diet may play a role in determining our behavior. Most often this line of research has focused on the idea that eating foods that produce either high or low amounts of sugar in our bloodstream affects how we act. Low blood sugar levels (hypoglycemia) often produce irritability, nervousness, and depression (much like PMS), and these feelings can lead to aggression and crime. On the other end of the spectrum, when we have a very high level of sugar in our systems we are susceptible to hyperactivity and sometimes learning disabilities. As any of us know who have ever interacted with a child who eats a pile of candy, sugar gives us energy and can make us hyperactive. Think of times like Halloween or Easter when children get lots of candy; most parents try to limit the amount of candy their children eat, so as to try to control the child's behavior. Think about a time when you have been under pressure to cram for an exam or to get a paper done. Many of us stock up on candy, soda, or other high-sugar (or high-caffeine) foods/drinks, so that we can stay alert and awake. If you have done this, try to remember what you felt like when you finished eating a couple of donuts or a candy bar or two and washed it all down with some sugar/caffeine drinks. We often end up not only being wide awake, but also feeling jumpy and irritable when something goes wrong. These same types of reactions are likely to lead us to strike out at someone or something that we feel interrupts our efforts or does something to annoy us. This is a perfect situation for aggression (that is, crime) to happen.

One of the more controversial areas of research linking biological factors and crime/violence centers on the role of nutrition. One of the first studies to examine this came from the Italian researcher Liggio (1969), who studied the diets of both delinquent and nondelinquent adolescents and found a correlation between their diets and their status as delinquents. Specifically, delinquents were found to eat more pasta, bread, and potatoes—foods that are high in starch, which when eaten is transformed into sugar. As a result, adolescents who ate more of these foods had shorter attention spans, reduced learning abilities, and a greater likelihood of being delinquent.

More recently other research (Liu, Raine, Venables, & Mednick, 2004) has shown that malnourished 3-year-olds are significantly more likely to be aggressive, hyperactive, and involved in delinquent behavior as they approach and reach adulthood. It has also been shown that nutritionally deprived pregnant women are 2.5 times as likely as other women to have male children with antipersonality disorders (Neugebauer, Hoek, & Susser, 1999). Also, individuals with vitamin and mineral deficiencies are more likely to display aggressive and violent behavior (Breakey, 1997; Grantham-McGregor & Ani, 2001; Werbach, 1992). Perhaps the core of the nutrition and violence/crime link is the fact that malnutrition has also been shown to be linked to lower levels of intelligence (Grantham-McGregor & Ani, 2001; Lozoff, Jimenez, Hagen, Mollen, & Wolf, 2000). What all of this suggests, then, is that perhaps the old adage that "you are what you eat" does have some truth to it: If you eat lots of sugars and starches and do not eat healthy/nutritious foods, you may well end up an aggressive, distracted, and criminal person.

Another approach to this focus on biology says that individuals whose brains and central nervous system (CNS) functioning are "different" process information differently, see the world and others in their world differently, and are likely to react to their environment differently than those of us who have "normal" brain and CNS functions. The research in this area tends to work backward from known criminals and shows that among (especially violent) criminals, there are higher-than-expected rates of individuals with organic brain diseases and excessive amounts of "abnormal" electrical activity in their CNS.

A number of studies have found varying levels of support for these types of explanations. For instance, Satterfield, Satterfield, and Schell (1987) reported that children who were hyperactive when they reached adolescence were six times as likely to be arrested as children not diagnosed as hyperactive. Others (Moffitt & Silva, 1988) have shown that children with attention deficit disorder (ADD) may also be more likely to be involved in crime.

Other researchers have suggested that "abnormal" brain development, from before birth and through the first several years of life, may predispose a person to violence and crime. For instance, Adrian Raine and colleagues (1994; Raine, Brenna, et al., 1997; Raine, Bushsbaum et al., 1997) reported that birth complications and subsequent rejection of the infant by the mother pre-disposed individuals to violence in adulthood. Other forms of prenatal com-plications and maternal behaviors may also be linked to increased levels of violence and crime. One large-scale longitudinal study from Finland exam-ined whether a pregnant woman's smoking had negative consequences for her child. In fact, women who smoked during pregnancy (even if they stopped during their first trimester) had a significantly greater chance of having a child who would grow up to be a delinquent/criminal than non-smoking mothers (Rantakallio, Laara, Ishohanni, & Moilanen, 1992). The development of criminal behavior in these offspring, according to the re-searchers, is not necessarily a biological consequence, as social influences may also be involved. Diana Fishbein (1994) has suggested that brain disor-ders may be related to violence and drug abuse in similar ways.

Also addressing the idea of brain development and crime, Raine, Buchsbaum, and LaCasse (1997) have also shown that murderers who plead guilty by reason of insanity have "indications of a network of abnormal cor-tical and subcortical brain processes that may predispose to violence" (p. 495). This type of research has been made possible by the development of brain imaging technology, which allows researchers to both see and map out the areas of brain activity associated with different types of activities. This line of research (Fishbein, 1990; Goyer et al., 1994; Raine, et al., 1997; Volkow & Tancredi, 1987) has suggested that both the temporal cortex and frontal brain regions are involved in violence.

However, it is important to remember that although some types of bio-logical/physiological factor may be found to be more common among known delinquents/criminals, it may not be possible to separate out the ef-fects of the biological factors from social influences. After all, hyperactive people and those with ADD may simply call more attention to themselves (and their criminal activities) and be more likely to be caught/identified. Or, as others have argued, the diagnoses of ADD or hyperactivity (as well as many learning disabilities) may simply be a labeling process that is applied to disruptive (that is, criminal or "precriminal") children and adolescents. Just because a certain factor is seen more frequently among known criminals does not necessarily mean that the factor is a cause of crime. Remember, it is very important to distinguish between things that are simply correlated and those that have a cause-and-effect relationship.

CONCLUSION

Biological explanations for crime and criminals have been around in one form or another for several centuries. In fact, theories that focused on biolog-ical or physical traits of criminals gave rise to attempts to scientifically explain and understand behavior. This should be expected, however, since several centuries ago people did not understand social influences on behavior or have very developed ways of thinking about psychology. What was available was the body and people's behaviors. So when we wanted to better understand how and why certain people acted in certain ways, we looked at what was available for inspection: the body.

The earliest biological theories differ from our more recently developed ideas in two important ways. First, the content of these theories was on the size, shape, and distinguishing features of the body. These characteristics were assumed to represent something about what was happening inside the body, and our external characteristics were taken as symbols for our internal workings. Second, our early biological theories differed from almost all more recently developed theories (both those with and without a biological focus) in that these early explanations for crime worked from the premise that certain features in an individual meant that the person definitely would be criminal. This deterministic view arose out of fairly simple logic and thinking, and today we recognize that there are so many different characteristics of people, environments, and other influences that one quality of a person cannot and will not control his or her behavior. Today's theories that include biological components place these factors in a social context and emphasize that physical/biological factors may make it more or less likely that someone will act in particular ways.

Biologically centered theories suggest that deciding the appropriate and best ways to deal with criminals will depend on whether it is possible to correct or cure the biological factors that contribute to the individual's criminal ways. Early deterministic theories rather clearly suggested that it was in the best interest of society to remove criminals, because they could not be changed. This often meant permanently removing criminals by killing them. However, more humane approaches have also been used over the years, in which we may not end a criminal's life but severely curtail his or her social life. Incapacitating criminals by removing them from society and relocating them to secure hospitals or correctional facilities is widely believed to be the best way to accomplish this. If we see criminals' biological composition as unfailingly causing them to be criminal, we cannot hope to change their behavior. All we can do in such a situation is protect others from the criminal.

However, deterministic theories are largely a thing of the past. For the last century or so we have seen biological/physiological factors theorized not as causing crime but rather as predisposing individuals to criminal ways. People with particular traits may be more likely than others, especially in certain types of situations, to be criminal. From this view, it may be possible to provide some type of treatment, corrective action, or restrictions on other influences that can prevent the individual from falling into criminal ways. Treatment programs, both during and separate from incarceration, would be appropriate ways to address crime. Most common would be some type of drug therapy in which the individual criminal is provided with "medicine" to either reduce/eliminate or control the biological aspect that may trigger crime. We might also use drugs to limit the ability of the person to act out and have his or her behaviors harm others. Either way, the belief is that something can be done to control or eliminate crime from the individual's behavioral repertoire.

Explaining criminal behavior through reference to biological traits was once the primary way for understanding why crime occurred. By the early twenty-first century, though, such approaches have moved to the margins of criminological theory, largely being replaced by theories that focus on social or psychological issues. This is not to say that biological theories have lost their influence completely, for some theorists and research continue to find connections between socially influenced biological factors and many types of behavior, including crime (see Fishbein, 1990). However, suggesting that our behaviors, whether criminal or otherwise, are a direct and clear result of our body's shape, size, appearance, chromosomal makeup, inherited traits, or internal chemical composition is difficult to support. There may be some value to seeing biological factors that can be triggered by social influences, in some situations, at some times, for some people. But beyond this, biological theories are among our weaker and less supported theories for explaining crime.

SUMMARY

Biological theories are among the oldest explanations offered for why some people commit crimes and others do not. A number of biological factors have been the focus of explanations of crime throughout history. The earliest explanations suggested that criminals were underdeveloped forms of human beings, and that their lack of proper physical development reflected their also being underdeveloped mentally and socially. Other biological theories have suggested that crime is an inherited trait that can be seen either in the family lineage of criminals or in their genetic construction. Other biological theorists have argued that our actual bodies—the size, shape, and form of them—indicate criminal tendencies, and that different types of bodies suggest different types of criminal behaviors. More recently, biological theories have focused on the idea of crime as the result of some socially influenced biological factors such as hormone levels or diet.

KEY TERMS

atavism the condition of being less developed than "normal" people; a "genetic throwback" to an earlier physical and social form of person

genetic predisposition the idea that some people have genes that make them more likely to have a certain trait or behavior (such as criminality) than others

Charles Goring a researcher who largely disproved Lombroso's ideas, although his research showed some degree of physical differences between criminals and noncriminals

E. A. Hooten an anthropologist whose book *The American Criminal* reported on numerous physical and mental "inferiorities" among criminals

hormones the chemicals in the human body that are most responsible for sex characteristics and, according to some theories, different types of behavior

Ernst Kretschmer a theorist who introduced the idea of different body types being associated with different forms of crime; proposed three basic body types: asthenic, athletic, and pyknic

Cesare Lombroso the father of positivism; he believed that criminals were under-developed forms of humans and exhibited a wide range of atavistic stigmata, indicating their less-developed state

phrenology an idea from the 1790s and early 1800s that as different parts of the brain developed to a different degree, this could be seen through bumps on the head; the belief that bumps on certain parts of the head indicated criminality

positivism the belief that it is possible to identify causes of a phenomena using scientific methods

William Sheldon a theorist who refined and revised the idea of different body types being associated with crime; proposed three body types: endomorphs, ectomorphs, and mesomorphs

somatotyping the theory and practice of measuring and assessing body types and associating different forms of physical bodies with different types of criminal behavior

XYY chromosome a genetic abnormality found among less than 1 percent of men; argued by some to be a cause of a high level of aggression and, hence, criminality

DISCUSSION QUESTIONS

1. How have the factors on which biological theories focus changed over time?

2. What are the strengths and weaknesses of trying to explain crime from a biological perspective?

3. What are the common threads/ideas that run through the biological theories, from those originally proposed in the eighteenth century through those still discussed today?

REFERENCES

Amir, M., & Berman, Y. (1970). Chromosomal deviation and crime. *Federal Probation, 34*(2), 55–63.

Aromaki, A. S., Lindman, R. E., & Eriksson, C. J. P. (1999). Testosterone, aggressiveness and anti-social personality. *Aggressive Behavior, 25*(2), 113–123.

Bohman, M., Cloninger, C. R., Sigwardsson, S., & von Knorring, A. L. (1982). Predisposition to petty criminality in Swedish adoptees: Genetic and environmental heterogeneity. *Archives of General Psychiatry, 39,* 1233–1241.

Booth, A., & Osgood, D. W. (1993). The influence of testosterone on deviance in adulthood: Assessing and explaining the relationship. *Criminology, 31,* 93–117.

Breakey, J. (1997). The role of diet and behaviour in childhood. *Journal of Paediatric and Child Health, 33,* 190–194.

Christiansen, K. O. (1977). A preliminary study of criminality among twins. In S. A. Mednick & K. O. Christiansen (Eds.), *Biological Basis of Criminal Behavior.* New York: Gardner Press.

Cooke, C. R. (1945). Presidential address: The differential psychology of the American woman. *American Journal of Obstetrics and Gynecology, 49,* 457–472.

Crowe, R. R. (1972). The adopted offspring of women criminal offenders. *Archives of General Psychiatry, 27,* 600–603.

Crowe, R. R. (1974). An adoption study of antisocial personality. *Archives of General Psychiatry, 31,* 785–791.

Dabbs, J. M., Jr., & Hargrove, M. F. (1997). Age, testosterone, and behavior among female prison inmates. *Psychosomatic Medicine, 59*(5), 477–480.

Dugdale, R. L. (1895). *The Jukes: A study in crime, pauperism, disease and heredity* (3rd ed.). New York: Putnam. (Original work published 1877)

Fishbein, D. H. (1990). Biological perspectives in criminology. *Criminology, 28*(1), 27–72.

Fishbein, D. H. (1994). Neuropsychological function, drug abuse, and violence: A conceptual framework. *Criminal Justice and Behavior, 27*(2), 139–159.

Fox, R. G. (1971). The XYY offender: A modern myth? *Journal of Criminal Law, Criminology and Police Science, 62*(1), 59–73.

Glueck, S., & Glueck, E. (1950). *Unraveling juvenile delinquency.* Cambridge, MA: Harvard University Press.

Glueck, S., & Glueck, E. (1956). *Physique and delinquency.* New York: Harper & Brothers.

Goddard, H. H. (1912). *The Kallikak family: A study in the heredity of feeblemindedness.* London: Macmillan.

Goring, C. (1972). *The English convict: A statistical study, 1913.* Montclair, NJ: Patterson-Smith. (Original work published 1913)

Goyer, P. F., Andreason, P. J., Semple, W. E., Clayton, A. H., King, A. C., Compton-Toth, B. A., et al. (1994). Positron-emission tomography and personality disorders. *Neuropsychopharmacology, 10,* 21–28.

Grantham-McGregor, S., & Ani, C. (2001). A review of studies on the effect of iron deficiency on cognitive development in children. *Journal of Nutrition, 131*(Suppl. 2), 649S–666S.

Hooten, E. A. (1939). *The American criminal: An anthropological study.* Cambridge, MA: Harvard University Press.

Horney, J. 1978. Menstrual cycles and criminal responsibility. *Law and Human Nature, 2,* 25–36.

Jacobs, P. A., Brunton, M., & Melville, M. M. (1965). Aggressive behavior, mental subnormality and XYY male. *Nature, 208,* 1351–1352.

Katz, J., & Chambliss, W. J. (1991). Biology and crime. In J. F. Sheley (Ed.), *Criminology: A contemporary handbook.* Belmont, CA: Wadsworth.

Kessler, S., & Moos, R. H. (1970). The XYY karyotype and criminality: A review. *Journal of Psychiatric Research, 7,* 164.

Knoblich, G. & King, R. (1992). Biological correlates of criminal behavior. In J. McCord (Ed.), *Facts, frameworks, and forecasts: Advances in criminological theory* (Vol. 3). New Brunswick, NJ: Transaction.

Kretschmer, E. (1925). *Physique and character.* New York: Harcourt, Brace. (Original work published 1921)

Liggio, F. (1969). Interference in the performance of mental activities due to the wrong diet which lacks the protein factor of animal origin and nervous disorders which are complementary and reversible. *Acta Neurologica, 24,* 548–556.

Liu, J., Raine, A., Venables, P. H., & Mednick, S. A. (2004). Malnutrition at age 3 years and externalizing behavior problems at ages 8, 11 and 17 years. *American Journal of Psychiatry, 161,* 2005–2013.

Lombroso, C. (1876). *L'uomo delinquente.* Milan: Hoepli.

Lozoff, B., Jimenez, E., Hagen, J., Mollen, W., & Wolf, A. W. (2000). Poorer behavioral and developmental outcome more than 10 years after treatment for iron deficiency in infancy. *Pediatrics, 105,* E51.

Mednick, S. A., Gabrieli, W. F., & Hutchings, B. (1984). Genetic influences in criminal convictions: Evidence from an adoption cohort. *Science, 224,* 891–894.

Moffitt, T., & Silva, P. (1988). Self-reported delinquency, neuropsychological deficit, and history of attention deficit disorder. *Journal of Abnormal Psychology, 16,* 553–569.

Morton, L., Addison, H., Addison, R., Hunt, L., & Sullivan, J. (1953). A clinical study of premenstrual tension. *American Journal of Obstetrics and Gynecology, 65,* 1182–1191.

Neugebauer, R., Hoek, H. W., & Susser, E. (1999). Prenatal exposure to wartime famine and development of antisocial personality disorder in early adulthood. *Journal of the American Medical Association, 4,* 479–481.

Olweus, D. (1987). Testosterone and adrenaline: Aggressive antisocial behavior in normal adolescent males. In S. A. Mednick, T. Moffitt, & S. Stack (Eds.), *The causes of crime: New biological approaches.* Cambridge, UK: Cambridge University Press.

Pope, H. G., & Katz, D. L. (1990). Homicide and near-homicide by anabolic steroid abusers. *Journal of Clinical Psychiatry, 51,* 28–31.

Price, W. H., Strong, J. A., Whatmore, P. B., & McClemont, W. R. (1966). Criminal patients with XYY sex-chromosome complement. *The Lancet, 1,* 565–566.

Rada, R. T., Laws, D. R., & Kellner, R. (1976). Plasma testosterone levels in the rapist. *Psychosomatic Medicine, 38,* 257–268.

Rafter, N. H. (1992). Criminal anthropology in the United States. *Criminology, 30*(4), 525–545.

Raine, A., Brenna, P., & Mednick, S. A. (1997). Interaction between birth complications and early maternal rejection predisposing individuals to adult violence. *American Journal of Psychiatry, 154,* 1265–1271.

Raine, A., Buchsbaum, M., & LaCasse, L. (1997). Brain abnormalities in murderers indicated by positron emission tomography. *Biological Psychiatry, 42,* 495–508.

Raine, A., Buchsbaum, M. S., Stanley, J., Lottenberg, S., Abel, L., & Stoddard, S. (1994). Selection reductions in prefrontal glucose metabolism in murderers. *Biological Psychiatry, 36,* 365–373.

Rantakallio, P., Laara, E., Ishohanni, M., & Moilanen, I. (1992). Maternal smoking during pregnancy and delinquency of the offspring: An association without causation? *International Journal of Epidemiology, 21*(6), 1106–1113.

Rubin, R. T. 1987. The neuroendocrinology and neurochemistry of antisocial behavior. In S. A. Mednick, T. Moffitt, & S. Stack (Eds.), *The causes of crime: New biological approaches.* Cambridge, UK: Cambridge University Press.

Rushton, J. P. 1995. *Race, evolution and behavior: A life history perspective.* New Brunswick, NJ: Transaction.

Satterfield, J. H., Satterfield, B. T., & Schell, A. M. (1987). Therapeutic interventions to prevent delinquency in hyperactive boys. *Journal of the American Academy of Child and Adolescent Psychiatry, 26,* 56–64.

Sheldon, W. 1940. *The varieties of human physique.* New York: Harper.

Sheldon, W. 1942. *The varieties of human temperament.* New York: Harper.

Sheldon, W. 1949. *Varieties of delinquent youth.* New York: Harper.

Volkow, N. D., & Tancredi, L. (1987). Neural substrates of violent behavior: A preliminary study with positron emission tomography. *British Journal of Psychiatry, 151,* 668–673.

Werbach, M. R. (1992). Nutritional influences on aggressive behavior. *Journal of Orthomolecular Medicine, 7,* 45–51.

CHAPTER 4

PSYCHOLOGICAL THEORIES OF CRIME

One way to think about crime is to see it as the result of actions of people who just do not think "right" or who have something wrong with them mentally. This is an easy way to view criminals, especially for those of us who do not consider ourselves criminals. After all, nearly everyone knows that crime is wrong, so if we know that it is something that we should not do, and that it harms others, who would do such things? One way many people would answer this is to suggest that only someone who has a disturbed personality or diminished mental abilities would act in criminal ways. We might also think of this as only someone who is "different" from the rest of us.

A focus on people who are different, especially in the ways they think, is at the core of most psychological theories of crime. Common approaches in the psychological perspective suggest that a criminal's personality is the result of poor or flawed socialization, or that the criminal is not able to (fully) understand the harm that crime does, or that criminals are simply less intelligent than the rest of us (and therefore they cannot understand that crime is wrong). We usually see that psychological theories place the blame for criminals' thinking on their socialization experiences or on some traumatic event in their past that caused them to process information and make decisions differently than the rest of us. A few psychologically based theories, however, are less concerned with the source of our ways of thinking, and more interested in how criminal thinking is supported and maintained.

Psychological explanations for crime are some of our most popular views, and are regularly reinforced through media presentations about crime and criminals. Hundreds if not thousands of movies and television shows every year portray crime and criminals, with many of them showing offenders as deranged, psychotic, mentally ill, thinking in ways that do not fit with "normal" people, or just not as intellectually capable as law-abiding citizens.

The psychological view of crime has been around for more than a hundred years. The idea of a psychological explanation for crime paralleled the development of psychology as a science and as a way of understanding people's behavior in general. Psychological approaches to crime also offer the promise of being able to fix problems in individuals that lead them to crime, just as psychology usually offers to fix or correct problems in individuals' thinking that cause them problems in any aspect of life. Basically, the thinking goes that if we can identify a cause of crime in an individual that does not have a permanent or organic foundation, we should be able to engage experts to work with the individual to overcome problems in thinking or ways of processing and understanding information.

Because psychological theories of crime suppose that it is possible to find and isolate mental problems that lead one to commit crime, these theories are closely tied to the idea of **rehabilitation** of criminals. For criminal justice practice, then, those who adhere to a psychological explanation for crime tend to favor treatment of criminals, not punishment. These efforts, and the days of prominence for psychological theories, were seen most clearly in the mid to late twentieth century when prisons emphasized rehabilitation and treatment, not punishment simply for the sake of punishment. The move from imprisoning criminal offenders as a means of punishing them to the use of correctional institutions as places to work with offenders to correct their problems came largely as a result of the influence of psychological theories on our thinking about criminals as flawed (not just "bad") people who could benefit from treatment and interventions. However, the success of such efforts would be based on the accuracy of theorists in identifying what types of mental problems are associated with crime, and the abilities of experts doing diagnoses and treatments to accurately pinpoint an individual offender's problems and how best to address those problems. The successes of rehabilitation efforts have largely been questioned (Martinson, 1974), although many critics believe that the failures of such efforts have more to do with inaccurate diagnoses than poor theorizing. Regardless of the reason, today we continue to move further and further away from thinking about criminals as individuals with illnesses or deficiencies that can be corrected.

In order to fully understand our current thinking about the role of mental illness and mental deficiencies in crime, it is important to trace the development of this line of thinking. This chapter will present and discuss some of the major and most influential psychological theories regarding crime, including psychoanalytic theory, criminal personalities and personality disorders, mental illness, and mental deficiency (low intelligence) perspectives for explaining crime and criminals.

PSYCHOANALYTIC THEORY

A **psychoanalytic perspective** on crime offers explanations based on the ideas of Freudian psychology and its theory of personality. The essential idea as it relates to why people commit crimes is that the three parts of the personality (id, ego, and superego) conflict with one another as a result of some early life trauma or deprivation. Alternatively, one part of the personality dominates the other two so strongly that various types of deviant behavior (including crime) are likely to occur. It is important to keep in mind, though, that Sigmund Freud actually wrote very little about how his theory could be used to explain crime. Instead, later followers of his ideas, most notably August Aichorn (1935), applied his concepts and perspective to the study of crime (discussed shortly).

One way that psychoanalytic theory stands apart from most other theories is in its assumption that people are basically antisocial from the start. Most theories seek to explain why some people commit crime, which is thought of as the exception and the "different" sort of behavior. However, criminological theory based on Freudian psychology suggests that we should expect people to be involved in crime, because people are not generally caring and concerned about others. Only a few other theories (as you will see in the remaining chapters) take this approach, including the ideas of some early biological theorists that we read about in the previous chapter.

Freudian psychology proposes that the personality is composed of three primary parts. The id is the part of the personality that represents the set of instincts and drives that need (or demand) immediate gratification. The id is the unsocialized part of the personality and is focused on seeking pleasure and fulfilling wants and needs for the individual. The superego represents opposite forces and serves as the social authority or conscience of the person. The superego is the part of the personality that seeks to have the person "fit in" with society and others, and seeks acceptance and positive views of the person by others. The ego is the mediating force between the id and superego. The ego attempts to balance the drives of the id and superego and in a well-adjusted person provides balance and continuity for meeting personal needs and achieving social acceptance. The ego is the conscious part of the mind and the id and superego represent the unconscious mind.

In order for a person to be well adjusted and socially productive and functional, the id needs to be socialized and the superego needs to be kept in check. Crime, in the psychoanalytic perspective, is the result of one of three basic types of situations:

1. Some people are not appropriately socialized and the id controls the personality and the individual's activities. The id drives these people to do as they please and be concerned only with their own desires. As a result, social rules and norms for behavior (including laws) may be ignored, go unnoticed, or simply be disregarded in pursuit of their own wants and needs.

2. Some people are overly socialized, with the superego dominating the personality and establishing behavior patterns. When this happens the id is so tightly held in check that it is all but silenced and repressed. If the id of these individuals leads them into actions and situations early in life for which they later feel guilty, the superego may lead them into situations and behaviors that will draw attention to them and lead them to be caught by authorities. This may be done so that the person is subsequently punished, because it is needed and deserved, which also alleviates the individual's feelings of guilt. This process is the primary cause of crime, according to Freud.

3. Some people who effectively (or overeffectively) repress their guilt over early misdeeds may eventually experience a breaking through of the repressed guilt and id, which will lead to an "explosion" of acting-out behavior. In essence, the id is so extremely held down that the pressure on it eventually gets so great that it pushes through and overtakes the superego (and ego) and runs wild. We can think of this as analogous to a balloon (with the air inside being the id) being pushed down more and more (the force outside being the superego). Eventually the id is under so much pressure that it breaks through both the pressure of the superego and the controlling force of the balloon (the ego) and explodes. The explosion is the socially unacceptable behavior (the crime).

Theorists starting in the 1930s brought forward refinements and applications of Freud's ideas and explanations for crime. These new interpretations and applications of basic Freudian psychology are generally referred to as neo-Freudian theory. The best known of the neo-Freudians for applying the psychoanalytic perspective to the explanation of crime is August Aichorn (1935). Basically, Aichorn argued that three factors must be in place in order for crime to emerge from the individual. First, the individual (via the id) needs to have a strong desire for immediate gratification. Second, the id must be in control and outweigh the influence of the superego and ego, making the primary drive of the individual self-gratification, not a concern with relationships the individual has with others. Third, the individual must have a lack of guilt regarding his or her actions. This third factor is a direct departure from Freud's principal view on crime, in which attempts to draw punishment to oneself to alleviate and satisfy guilt were central to most criminal actions.

Most neo-Freudian theorists have argued that criminals experience damage to their ego early in life and as a result the id becomes overly dominant. When the id is dominant, the individual's behavior is "out of control" and is not kept within the bounds of social norms or laws. In this way the neo-Freudian approach is very similar to the ideas of theorists who identify the cause of crime as a personality disorder. These perspectives will be discussed in the next section.

PERSONALITY THEORIES

One commonly heard view about criminals is that "they just seem to think differently than other people." A view such as this is the foundation of the theories that focus on what some call a criminal personality, as well as theories that say particular types of disorders are the root cause of criminal behavior. When we talk about a criminal's **personality**, we are referring to a conceptually broad term that describes the totality of an individual's behavioral and emotional characteristics. Psychologists have defined personality in a wide range of specific ways, and different aspects of the concept are emphasized in various psychological theories. For our purposes, it is sufficient to recognize that criminological theories emphasize different aspects of personality as the reason for crime. Yet what all of the personality theories have in common is that they all focus on the idea that something about the process and contents of people's thinking patterns leads to crime. Some personality theorists point to a particular disorder or problem in the thought process of criminals as the reason for the individual's criminality. For other theorists the overall way in which the individual processes and uses information is the cause of crime.

Among the more influential personality approaches to explaining crime is the idea of a **criminal personality** (Yochelson & Samenow, 1976). Yochelson and Samenow did psychiatric clinical work during the 1960s and 1970s with offenders in a psychiatric hospital, and through their work they identified common traits and ways of thinking that when taken together they called the criminal personality. While focused on the idea of personality, just as the psychoanalytic theorists did (and, in fact, both Yochelson and Samenow were trained in Freudian psychoanalysis), the work of Yochelson and Samenow directly refuted the neo-Freudians' claims that the causes of crime are deep-seated, inner aspects of the personality/mind. Rather, Yochelson and Samenow's approach largely relies on the assumption that criminal ways of thinking are something with which an individual is born, not something that develops due to social influences. A second core assumption of this approach is that the criminal personality is not a deterministic approach to crime, but instead serves to predispose individuals to criminal behavior. Criminal ways of thinking begin early in life, and such thought patterns lead individuals to make choices about their behavior—often decisions to commit crime.

The criminal personality theory provides a focus on the thought patterns that Yochelson and Samenow claimed were common among offenders. These thought patterns are called errors of criminal thinking; fifty-two different traits or processes are included in the overall view of the criminal personality. Generally speaking, criminal thinking tends to be concrete rather than abstract. As Yochelson and Samenow originally proposed their ideas, they claimed that all fifty-two errors of criminal thinking could be found in all offenders; however, as you might imagine, research proved it very difficult (actually impossible) to apply all fifty-two criminal thinking errors to all criminal offenders. Included among these errors of criminal thinking are impulsivity, self-centeredness, chronic lying, perceiving property of others as available for anyone to take, lacking interest in education/school, being sexually active early in life and having a "great deal of sexual thinking," extreme optimism about the future and the risks of dangerous situations, getting great amounts of enjoyment from reckless and illegal activities, manipulativeness, being very energetic, having intense fear of pain and injury, feeling superior to others, having a very high self-image, and becoming extremely angry very quickly. These last four traits often combine when the individual feels that his or her self-image is being attacked or threatened; when such individuals feel threatened (whether that perception is accurate or not), they are likely to quickly become extremely angry and lash out at what they perceive is threatening them.

A somewhat similar approach is presented in the works of White and Walters, who present what is known as the **lifestyle perspective** (1989; Walters, 2002). However, instead of focusing narrowly on the idea of personality, these theorists emphasize what they term *lifestyle criminality*. Crime, in this theory, arises from how individuals live their lives, including the social environment they are in, the choices they make about their behaviors, and the thinking patterns they use to make choices in their everyday lives. Stated succinctly, "Lifestyle theory holds that crime is a consequences of the *conditions* to which a person is exposed, the *choices* he or she makes in life, and the *cognitions* he or she invokes in support of an evolving criminal pattern" (Walters, 2002, ix, emphasis in original).

In the view of these theorists, lifestyle is centered on thought processes, specifically the beliefs the individual holds and uses to interpret and make sense of his or her environment and situations. These belief systems are generated by a collection of four critical and interrelated factors: irresponsibility, self-indulgence, interpersonal intrusiveness, and patterns of social rule breaking. Irresponsibility is the general unwillingness of individuals to see themselves as accountable for their behavior. Instead, they see their behavior as the result of other factors, especially social factors that are beyond their control or influence. Self-indulgence is the tendency of criminals to put their own desires and wants ahead of any concerns about others or considerations of how their actions may negatively affect others. Interpersonal intrusiveness refers to how criminal individuals pursue their self-indulgent goals, ignoring and acting without regard to the rights of others. Finally, because of their disregard for others, dedication to pursuing their own desires, and being unwilling to see that their behaviors are the result of their own choices, criminal behavior is often the result.

Important in understanding how these cognitive factors influence decisions about behavior is the position that reality—the way the world is known to exist and how we experience it—is a socially constructed phenomenon. Individuals all experience the world somewhat differently, and we strive to maintain our belief systems about how our world is put together. We do this through our considerations of schematic representations, or tools for interpreting and making sense of things: attributions, outcome expectancies, efficiency expectancies, goals, values, and thinking styles.

It is also important to consider that "measurements" of personality, or evaluations to determine an individual's "type" of personality or the characteristics of one's personality, are based on tests developed and used by psychologists. Perhaps the most common of these is the Minnesota Multiphasic Personality Inventory (MMPI). This test, commonly used in clinical settings, court cases, correctional classification decisions, and many other types of settings, was originally developed in the late 1930s and then completely revised in 1989. The test is actually a compilation of a number of scales that measure various personal components using true/false questions. The patterns of responses to items on each scale are used to determine the presence and strength of various components of an individual's personality. Included in the MMPI scales are hypochondriasis (falsely believing that one is experiencing a medical condition), depression, paranoia, masculinity/femininity, schizophrenia, and social introversion. The scoring and interpretation (which requires a specially trained psychologist) of the results of an individual's MMPI is often used for making decisions about the diagnosis and treatment of mental illnesses and personality disorders. While tests such as the MMPI are obviously very useful in these types of situations, not all theories and assumptions about the role of personality in crime rely on such scientific approaches to measurement and assessment. Instead, many personality-based theories of crime draw on assumptions and commonsense understandings of people's thought processes, behavior, beliefs, and approaches to life.

The similarities between the White and Walters approach and that of Yochelson and Samenow (1976) are in the central role that the offender's thought processes and ways of thinking plays in explaining crime. Very similar to what Yochelson and Samenow argued, although discussed using different terms, lifestyle criminality is about faulty thinking. This way of thinking in turn leads to decisions about behavior that may well be criminal.

The lifestyle criminality view suggests that criminal events are initiated by the individual's making choices about behavior based on irresponsibility, self-indulgence, and a desire to have power and control over others. The choice to commit a criminal act is supported and reinforced by the individual's being able to attribute his or her behavior to some external factors, not to making a decision. In explaining how a psychology of disresponsibility encourages and supports the criminal actions of individuals, White and Walters explain that a criminal individual "uses the criminologic excuses and myths we have so conveniently provided for him to justify a lifelong pattern of victimizing others" (1989, pp. 259–260). These excuses and myths are the "various psychological hypotheses, complex nonanswers, and inaccurate 'common sense' explanations" (White & Walters, 1989, p. 260) that they claim dominated criminological theory and thinking in the late twentieth century.

The reliance on excuses and justifying one's behavior with reference to existing (but supposedly erroneous) theories serves as a coping strategy for the criminal offender. This is a conscious process, not an unconscious one. Criminals simply live lifestyles that center on disavowing themselves of responsibility for their actions, and the resources for doing this are provided by society. But in the end, "crime is not caused by heredity, drugs and alcohol, psychological trauma, lack of job skills, or social class/status. Rather, crime is caused by criminals, pure and simple" (White & Walters, 1989, p. 260). Lifestyle criminality theory says that individual criminals decide to commit crime, and because of their ways of thinking about themselves, their environments, and what society has suggested about "causes" of crime, these people can be expected to continue committing crimes.

MENTAL ILLNESS

Thinking of criminals as having a **mental illness** is another commonsense, and for most of us logical, way to understand why some people commit crimes and others do not. Mental illnesses, although sometimes difficult to actually diagnose and treat, are usually thought of as misdirected and error-ridden ways of thinking and perceiving the world. There are many different forms of mental illnesses, ranging from relatively minor and occasional disturbances in our emotions and thought processes to severe forms, known generally as psychoses.

We know that many convicted criminal offenders have some type of mental illness. Estimates range from one in five to three in five prison inmates having some form of mental illness. Interestingly, a much smaller number of prison inmates are reported as receiving mental health care or services (Beck & Maruschak, 2001). Eighty-nine percent of state prisons provide mental health services to inmates, with 13 percent of all inmates receiving some form of counseling/therapy and 10 percent being prescribed psychotropic drugs. The two most common mental illnesses associated with criminality are schizophrenia and antisocial personality.

Schizophrenia

Schizophrenia comes in several different forms, varying in degree of severity. Generally speaking, people with schizophrenia are withdrawn and apathetic in their behavior and affect (emotional display). Common symptoms include being unable to remain focused on ideas or behaviors, having delusions, hallucinating (including the stereotypical portrayal of schizophrenics as "hearing voices"), and being unable to follow through with a logical progression or relation of ideas. Schizophrenia is among the most serious and debilitating form of mental illnesses. Sadly, there is no known cause or cure for schizophrenia (American Psychiatric Association, 1994).

The common way most people think of those with schizophrenia is that they are "out of touch with reality." Because their perception of reality significantly differs from that of "normal" people, those with schizophrenia often have (possibly severe) difficulties functioning in the social world. They do not interpret the environment, other people, or others' actions in the ways that most people do. Consequently, they behave in ways that do not fit with the smooth flow of social settings and their behaviors often are unpredictable and violate social norms and laws.

Schizophrenia has been linked with a variety of types of crimes, including both violent and property offenses. However, only a small portion of convicted violent offenders are diagnosed as schizophrenic, and only a very small percentage of people with schizophrenia are arrested for violent crimes. Researchers (Philips, Wolf, & Coons, 1988) report that no more than 2 percent of all people with schizophrenia are arrested for violent crimes, and at most 2 percent of annual violent crime arrests are of people with schizophrenia.

Antisocial Personality

Antisocial personality disorder, also referred to as either *psychopathy* or *sociopathy*, is a state in which individuals experience a significant lack of development of moral order or ethics. A sociopath/psychopath is an individual often referred to as without a conscience. In simple terms, these individuals are self-centered and do not display feelings of guilt or remorse for any of their actions. While this is not an especially common disorder, estimates consistently suggest that between 1 and 3 percent of the adult population are psychopaths/sociopaths. However, in prison populations the rate is typically estimated to be several times higher. This suggests that individuals with antisocial personalities are very likely to be involved in crime (and also very likely to be caught).

Individuals who do not experience feelings of empathy, guilt, or remorse have few checks on their behavior. The disorder of antisocial personality is defined by the American Psychiatric Association (1994, code 301.7) in the *Diagnostic and Statistical Manual of Mental Disorders* as follows:

> There is a pervasive pattern of disregard for and violation of the rights of others occurring since age 18 years, as indicated by three (or more) of the following:
> Failure to conform to social norms with respect to lawful behaviors as indicated by repeatedly performing acts that are grounds for arrest.
> Deceitfulness, as indicated by repeated lying, use of aliases, or conning others for personal profit or pleasure, impulsivity, or failure to plan ahead.

Irritability and aggressiveness, as indicated by repeated physical fights or assaults reckless disregard for safety of self or others.

Consistent irresponsibility, as indicated by repeated failure to sustain consistent work behavior or honor financial obligations.

Lack of remorse, as indicated by being indifferent to or rationalizing having hurt, mistreated, or stolen from another.

As this definition makes clear, individuals diagnosed as such are likely to do things that "normal" personality individuals would never consider actually doing. To understand how this is likely to occur, also consider the following list of characteristics that have been associated with the antisocial personality (Cleckey, 1964):

1. The psychopath is charming and of good intelligence.
2. He is not delusional or irrational.
3. There is an absence of nervousness or psychoneurotic manifestations.
4. The psychopath is unreliable.
5. He is insecure, and he is a liar who can be trusted no more in his accounts of the past than in his promises of the future.
6. He is lacking in either shame or remorse.
7. His antisocial behavior is inadequately motivated. He will commit all kinds of misdeeds for astonishingly small stakes, and sometimes for no reason at all.
8. His judgment is poor, and he never learns from experience. He will repeat over and over again patterns of self-defeating behavior.
9. He is pathologically egocentric, and has no real capacity for love, although he often simulates affection or parental devotion.
10. His emotions are shallow.
11. The psychopath lacks insight to a degree usually found only in the most serious mental disorders.
12. He does not respond to consideration, kindness, or trust.
13. Drunk or sober, but especially drunk, he is guilty of fantastic and uninviting behavior.
14. Psychopaths often threaten suicide but almost never carry it out.
15. The psychopath's sex life is impersonal, trivial, and poorly integrated.
16. The psychopath shows a consistent inability to make or follow any sort of life plan.

Additionally, and directly linked to the high rate and frequency of criminality of the psychopath, four characteristics are common in this population. First, these individuals tend to have a lower arousal level, meaning they get biologically less aroused than "normal" individuals when they encounter what others would perceive as frightening, threatening, or alert-raising stimuli. Second, psychopaths have less ability to learn and benefit from conditioning. Psychopaths are also highly impulsive and tend to display low levels of anxiety. Each of these factors is associated with involvement in crime because these conditions suggest that an individual is not likely to be deterred by threats of punishment or sanction, is not anxious about the possibility of being detected/caught, tends to act on impulse, and is not alarmed by situations that would typically be alarming. Psychopaths often perceive a need for physical stimulation or excitement, because many things are not experienced as exciting for them. This, coupled with a lack of remorse or feelings of guilt, impulsivity, and poor judgment, is likely to lead them to situations in which they commit crimes.

Interest in the link between antisocial personality and criminality has experienced a revival in the last couple of decades. Most of this research has been conducted in other countries, most notably in the Scandinavian countries (Hodgins, Mednick, Brennan, Schulsinger, & Engberg, 1996; Modestin & Ammann, 1996; Tiihonen, Isohanni, Rasanen, Koiranen, & Moring, 1997). This line of thinking is being revived due to the findings of these researchers that there is a statistically significant link between schizophrenia/antisocial personality and violence/crime.

It is important to note here, though, that not all people with one or some of these characteristics are necessarily criminals. We can all think of people we know who do not get very excited by most things that excite others (have a low level of arousal), do not seem to learn very well from experience (are not very susceptible to conditioning), or are either very impulsive or have generally low levels of anxiety. Do not assume that just because a friend has one, or even all, of these characteristics, he or she is a sociopath. Many "normal" people have some or all of these characteristics. The point is not that all people with these characteristics are sociopaths, but that most sociopaths have these characteristics.

Sociopaths/psychopaths are unique among the criminals addressed by psychological theories in that they tend not to be affected by treatment (American Psychiatric Association, 1994). This condition is often thought of as a biological condition, and for this reason it is difficult (if not impossible) to change. However, there simply is no confirmed cause of this disorder, and in fact, *DSM-IV* states, "The cause of this disorder is unknown, but biological or genetic factors may play a role." Note that this is not definitive, only speculative.

All of this also means that in some ways a focus on psychopathy/sociopathy is a biologically grounded theory; in fact, some textbooks discuss this perspective in a chapter on biological theories. Other theories are more clearly and unequivocally psychological in focus and content. As we will see in the next section, some psychological theories focus exclusively on what is in one's mind and how the mind operates.

MENTAL DEFICIENCIES

One of the longest-standing and perhaps most popular beliefs about crime is that criminals are simply not as smart as other people. In many ways this is a very commonsense belief, and one that has been popular with theorists, criminal justice authorities, and the general public for many years. Researchers who investigate the idea that **mental deficiency** is the cause of crime tend to show a relationship between measured intelligence levels and being a known criminal offender.

The first significant and influential research suggesting that intelligence and crime are related appeared almost a century ago (Goddard, 1914). Simply looking at the IQ scores of prison inmates led to the conclusion that between one-quarter and one-half of inmates were unable to "manage their affairs" due to lack of mental ability. However, controversies arose almost immediately, with other researchers suggesting that low intelligence is common among many populations, not just prisoners. Although we might be able to interpret intelligence in several ways, examination of IQ scores for enlisted soldiers during World War I showed that they had lower levels of measured intelligence than prisoners. The most popular conclusion reached from this was that there were problems with the measurement instruments and procedures, not that these populations were necessarily seriously lacking in mental abilities.

In the 1960s and 1970s numerous researchers (Hirschi & Hindelang, 1977; Reiss & Rhodes, 1961; Sorensen & Mednick, 1977; West & Farrington, 1977) reported research results showing that juvenile delinquents and adult criminals had lower IQ scores than noncriminals. Researchers and theorists have argued that intelligence is more influential and important in criminality than other factors including social class, parental education levels, and for some researchers, race. However, the strength and size of this relationship depends on how one chooses to do the research. As Hirschi and Hindelang (1977) showed, when IQ scores are related to official crime records, there is a fairly strong relationship. But when low IQ and self-report data on criminality (which tends to show more crime) are linked, the relationship is significantly smaller and weaker. The research done in the years since Hirschi and Hindelang's conclusions, however, has been mixed, with a significant body of research supporting a link between IQ and crime and a significant body of work showing just the opposite. Some believe that low IQ means that a person has a diminished ability to conduct moral reasoning (Wilson & Hernstein, 1985), which in turn establishes the context for criminal activities.

Those who adhere to the idea that crime is a result of low IQ often cite the idea that intelligence has a strong genetic link. Horn (1983) examined IQ levels of adopted children and showed that they had more similarity to the IQ scores of the children's biological rather than adoptive families (other research has, however, suggested that IQ is not "primarily" biological). Based on these findings it can be argued that intelligence is at least to some degree inherited, and if minority groups tend to have lower IQ scores, this would suggest that they might be (as a group) mentally inferior to white people. And since minority groups in the United States have higher rates of delinquency and criminality, this "natural" factor is seen by some as a logical explanation.

The movement to view crime (among other "weaknesses" or deficiencies) as a result of low intelligence was a central component to a philosophical and political movement in the United States that was prominent during the late 1800s and the first two decades of the twentieth century called the **eugenics** movement. The push of the eugenics movement was to stop the hereditary lines of inferior people by forcibly sterilizing individuals determined to be genetically (as indicated by low intelligence levels) inferior. As numerous scholars have historically detailed (see Haller, 1963; Rafter, 1997), this movement claimed to be for the public good, but was largely a political movement to control society's poor and "different" people. Not only did the eugenics movement push for forced sterilization of many criminals, but it also argued for strict quotas on immigration of people from other nations. The idea was that in order to "keep America strong," the government had to limit the number of inferior people. This meant that poor, undereducated, and criminally involved groups of people should be numerically limited. As we might expect, there were strong racial undertones to this movement, as those who made decisions about who and what behavior constituted inferiority were wealthier, more educated white people (primarily men too).

For several decades various state statutes allowed judges to sentence some categories of offenders to be forcibly sterilized. While these practices were largely abandoned by the middle of the twentieth century, in some jurisdictions and for some types of offenses, such practices have periodically re-emerged in the late twentieth and early twenty-first century.

Although the eugenics movement claimed to show statistical evidence that criminality—via low intelligence levels—was passed on through heredity, these thoughts and practices have always had a racist tone. One of the reasons for the decline in influence of the eugenics movement is the fact that there has not been a consistent view on how intelligence may or may not play a role in explaining crime rates across racial groups. Controversies have raged for many decades about how IQ may or may not be related to race. One of the milestones in this debate occurred in 1967 during a speech by the Nobel Prize–winning physicist William Shockley, who suggested to the National Academy of Sciences that differences in IQ between blacks and whites could explain differences in poverty and crime rates. It is true that nonwhite (especially black) people have higher rates of arrest, conviction, and incarceration in our society. We also know that on the tests that are commonly used to measure intelligence, whites tend to score (as a group) about 15 points higher than blacks. However, this pattern needs to be viewed with caution. Some critics believe that intelligence tests are culturally biased (Greenfield, 1997; Mercer, 1972; Sternberg, 1986). This means that the difference in test scores may have more to do with the actual content of these tests, and not reflect true differences in intelligence.

Robert Gordon (1987) tied these issues together and argued (and supported his claims with research data and results) that the higher rates of delinquency and criminality among black boys and men could best be explained by differences in intelligence levels. Even when controlling for issues such as urban/rural location, income, educational level, and occupation, intelligence levels were the most powerful explanations for high rates of crime among black males. And it is not only whites and blacks for whom intelligence is important in explaining crime rates. Gordon went on to argue that the low rates of delinquency/crime for Japanese, Chinese, and Jews could be explained by their IQ scores, which are slightly higher than those of whites. The reason for the controversial reception of such research and thinking is clear: Gordon was seen as suggesting that black males were simply not as intelligent (as a group) as their white counterparts.

The controversy about the idea that minorities are more involved in crime due to a lower level of intelligence was revived and enhanced in the mid-1990s with the publication of **Richard Hernstein and Charles Murray's** book *The Bell Curve* (1994). In this book Hernstein and Murray provide a detailed examination of the research linking intelligence measures and criminality. Their review argues that the IQ-crime link is among the "most powerful" predictors of criminality that research has uncovered. They then link this idea to research showing that minorities (especially African Americans) are more involved in crime (at least according to official statistics) and have lower average IQ scores. The presentation of this information was taken by many as powerful and convincing evidence for explaining high rates of criminality among African Americans. This was also seen as a highly racist and inflammatory interpretation of research by many others. The critics of this perspective argue that Hernstein and Murray overlook many of the other social contributors to both measured IQ and criminality, and their interpretation is seen as justifying very repressive and unfair responses to crime.

There are a number of problems with mental deficiency theories. First is the often-shown fact that intelligence tests are culturally biased. Gordon's (1987) research is a good example of research findings that can probably be explained (at least in part) by the fact that minority individuals are at a disadvantage on intelligence tests due to cultural biases. Another problem with mental deficiency theories is that while it may be true that known criminal offenders show lower IQ scores, this could easily be attributed to a number of factors other than a greater propensity of less-intelligent people to commit crimes. First, we could attribute this "fact" to what we know about intelligence levels being correlated with poor school performance, and in turn low levels of commitment to pursuing education and abiding by the expectations that school puts on behavior. We might also attribute a large number of known offenders' having low intelligence test scores to these offenders' simply being more likely than "smarter" criminals to get caught. Remember, when we have research that shows a particular trait common among known offenders or prison inmates, this is not research that looks at all criminals, but only a rather small subset of offenders.

CONCLUSION

Psychological theories for explaining crime and criminals are popular with many people because they both seem to make a great deal of sense intrinsically and they rather clearly argue that criminals are distinct and different from the rest of us. Criminals not only act differently from "good people," but they also think differently or have an illness or are just not as smart as the rest of us.

There are really two major problems with psychological theories. First, many of the ideas and concepts that are used by these theories are difficult—if not impossible—to validate scientifically. Much of our thinking about "personality" and what is (or is not) present in the minds of people, whether they be criminals or not, is based on beliefs and hypotheses (theories) and we simply cannot know whether these things are in fact present. The second major problem with psychological theories is that they frequently are just not that effective at explaining why crime happens. This does not mean that crime is not caused by psychological processes and patterns, but our current psychological theories do not enable us to very effectively explain crime.

Despite the problems inherent in psychological theories, identifying the cause of crime as a psychological difference makes sense to many of us. We know that crime is wrong, and in order to try to understand the actions of people who engage in such actions we find it reassuring to think of them as having some type of defect or illness that leads them to interpret their environments, other people, themselves, and even reality in different—and "wrong"—ways.

Psychological theories also offer a great deal of promise to criminal justice officials, treatment providers, and the general public for hopes of ending crime. If we can identify what it is in a person's thinking or mental abilities that lead him or her to break the law, we are already on the path to being able to correct the cause of crime. Psychology as a science offers much hope both for helping people effectively and efficiently cope with their problems and for curing, correcting, or rehabilitating people whose behavior is socially unacceptable. Both biological and psychological theories work from the premise that there is an identifiable problem in a criminal's body or mind. Where and why the problem is believed to have originated will vary across different theories and theorists, but the reason for the problem in thinking and behavior is not the primary concern. Instead, the promise offered by these types of theories is that something can be done to remove, control, or cure the problem in thinking and perception, and this in turn will likely lead to law-abiding behavior.

Psychological theories, especially those such as lifestyle criminality that include the idea that criminal offenders make choices about their actions, emphasize that crime can be controlled. The best way to control crime is through some type of treatment program that focuses on addressing the shortcomings of the individual or curing/controlling their criminally oriented thought patterns. These theories, however, do not dismiss the value of punishment and official criminal justice system processing. When individuals make choices about their behavior, they need to be held accountable for those decisions. Accountability should be combined with treatment, though.

Proponents of psychological theories of crime, then, tend to be optimistic about the possibility for addressing society's crime problem. Although we may not currently have highly effective treatments—although some would argue that drugs, counseling, education, and behavior modification in fact are effective treatments—we know what issues need to be addressed. If we at least know what needs to be fixed, removed, or changed, we can experiment with various treatments until we find out what does work. This is among the more optimistic views of crime in our society.

SUMMARY

Psychological theories for explaining crime focus on the content and processes of people's minds and thinking. The thought processes, parts of the personality, presence and form of mental illnesses, and levels of intelligence are the main foci of psychological theories. Psychological theories have been very popular over the years, largely because they appeal to us in a commonsense sort of way and allow us to see criminals both as "different" from us and as people who can be helped through some sort of treatment.

KEY TERMS

antisocial personality   a form of mental illness in which individuals have no sense of empathy, are highly impulsive, seek immediate gratification, and often harm or take from others in criminal ways; sometimes referred to as sociopathy or psychopathy

criminal personality   the idea of Yochelson and Samenow that some people experience errors of thinking that lead them to have an outlook on the social world that accepts and endorses criminal behavior

eugenics   a movement of the early twentieth century that sought to impose sterilization of criminals and quotas on immigration for "inferior" people in an attempt to rid society of weak, less-intelligent, and criminal groups of people

Richard Hernstein and Charles Murray authors of *The Bell Curve*, a mid-1990s book that argued that minorities' greater involvement in crime could be explained by the "natural" differences in measured intelligence

lifestyle perspective an idea proposed by White and Walters that the thought processes and beliefs of individuals are guided by the factors of irresponsibility, self-indulgence, interpersonal intrusiveness, and patterns of social rule breaking, which lead the individual to make choices in social settings that produce criminal behavior

mental deficiency a mental state in which a person is lacking (usually) in intelligence compared to normal or most people; used to explain crime by saying that those with less intelligence are more likely to violate social rules/laws

mental illness a diagnosable disturbance to the emotional or perceptual abilities of an individual that leads the person to experience interactions and social environments differently from healthy people

personality a conceptually broad term that refers to the totality of an individual's behavioral and emotional characteristics

psychoanalytic perspective an idea first proposed by Sigmund Freud; based on the idea that three parts of the personality—id, ego, and superego—compete and conflict and the result is our mental state and behaviors

rehabilitation processes and activities that seek to change a criminal into a non-criminal

schizophrenia a mental illness that leads the person to perceive reality differently, to be socially withdrawn, and to react to social stimuli in inappropriate ways, including violently/criminally

DISCUSSION QUESTIONS

1. Which personality theory seems the most plausible for explaining crime? Why?

2. What is it about mental illness that would lead such people to be involved in crime?

3. How is a link between low levels of intelligence and criminal involvement explained? Why would a less intelligent person be more likely to be a criminal?

4. What are the policy implications of relying on psychological theories for explaining crime?

REFERENCES

Aichorn, A. (1935). *Wayward youth.* New York: Viking Press.

American Psychiatric Association. (1994). *Diagnostic and statistical manual of mental disorders* (4th ed.). Washington, DC: Author.

Beck, A. J., & L. M. Maruschak, (2001). *Mental health treatment in state prisons, 2000.* Washington, DC: Bureau of Justice Statistics.

Cleckey, H. (1964). *The mask of sanity* (4th ed.). St. Louis, MO: Mosby.

Goddard, H. H. (1914). *The Kallikak family: A study in the heredity of feeblemindedness.* New York: Macmillan.

Gordon, R. (1987). SES versus IQ in the race-IQ-delinquency model. *International Journal of Sociology and Social Policy, 7,* 30–96.

Greenfield, P. M. (1997). You can't take it with you: Why ability assessments don't cross cultures. *American Psychologist, 52,* 1115–1124.

Haller, M. (1963). *Eugenics: Hereditarian attitudes in American thought.* New Brunswick, NJ: Rutgers University Press.

Hernstein, R. J., & Murray, C. (1994). *The bell curve.* New York: Free Press.

Hirschi, T. & Hindelang. M. (1977). Intelligence and delinquency: A revisionist review. *American Sociological Review, 42,* 571–586.

Hodgins, S., Mednick, S. A., Brennan, P. A., Schulsinger, F., & Engberg, M. (1996). Mental disorder and crime: Evidence from a Danish birth cohort. *Archives of General Psychiatry, 53,* 489–496.

Horn, J. M. (1983). The Texas Adoption Project: Adopted children and their intellectual resemblance to biological and adoptive parents. *Child Development, 54,* 268–275.

Martinson, R. (1974). What works? Questions and answers about prison reform. *Public Interest, 10,* 22–54.

Mercer, J. (1972, September). IQ: The lethal label. *Psychology Today,* 44–47.

Modestin, J., & Ammann, R. (1996). Mental disorder and criminality: male schizophrenia. *Schizophrenia Bulletin, 22,* 69–82.

Philips, M. R., Wolf, A. S., & Coons, D. J. (1988). Psychiatry and the criminal justice system: Testing the myths. *American Journal of Psychiatry, 145,* 605–610.

Rafter, N. H. (1997). *Creating born criminals.* Urbana: University of Illinois Press.

Reiss, A., & Rhodes, A. L. (1961). The distribution of delinquency in the social class structure. *American Sociological Review, 26,* 720–732.

Sorensen, L. K., & Mednick, S. A. (1977). A prospective study of predictors of criminal: Intelligence. In S. A. Mednick & K. O. Christiansen (Eds.), *Biosocial Basis of Criminal Behavior.* New York: Gardner Press.

Sternberg, R. J. (1986). *Intelligence applied: Understanding and increasing your intellectual skills.* New York: Harcourt Brace Jovanovich.

Tiihonen, J., Isohanni, M., Rasanen, P., Koiranen, M., & Moring, J. (1997). Specific major mental disorders and criminality: Twenty-six year prospective study of the 1966 Northern Finland birth cohort. *American Journal of Psychiatry, 154,* 840–845.

Walters, G. D. (2002). *Criminal belief systems: An integrated-interactive theory of lifestyles.* Westport, CT: Praeger/Greenwood.

West, D. J., & Farrington, D. P. (1977). *The delinquent way of life.* London: Heinemann.

White, T. W., & Walters, G. D. (1989). Lifestyle criminality and the psychology of disresponsibility. *International Journal of Offender Therapy and Comparative Criminality, 33,* 257–263.

Wilson, J. Q., & Hernstein, R. J. (1985). *Crime and human nature.* New York: Simon & Schuster.

Yochelson, S., & Samenow, S. E. (1976). *The criminal personality: Vol. 1. Profile for change.* New York: Jason Aronson.

CHAPTER 5

THE SOCIAL ECOLOGY
OF CRIME

The natural starting place for explaining crime is often to focus on what is "wrong" or "different" about individual people or certain social groups. We might say, for instance, "That person is simply crazy," or "People of that type are biologically unfit," or "The reason why teenagers commit so much crime is that they are enmeshed in a culture of violence." Perhaps not surprisingly, many theories of crime (for instance, biological psychological, differential association, and social control theories) focus on how people or groups of people are "criminal."

Researchers have found interesting patterns, however, suggesting that focusing on the individual person or social group might fail to offer a complete picture on what is responsible for crime. The consideration of *place* as a cause of crime is one example, and the central focus of this chapter. The idea that place might have something to do with crime is not a new discovery. In the 1830s, two Belgians, Andre-Michel Guerry and Adolphe Quetelet, used some of the first national arrest statistics ever collected and discovered that some regions of France had more problems with crime than other areas (Bierne, 1993). Guerry and Quetelet were also the first to relate regional crime rates to a variety of social factors (such as area poverty and education levels). For instance, they found that areas with less poverty had more property crime (committed, disproportionately, by the poor and unemployed living there), suggesting that the greater wealth in these regions offered more inducements to offend. Moreover, these regional variations appeared to be stable over long periods of time: Areas with the highest arrest rates always tended to have the highest arrest rates, and arrested offenders everywhere (in the 1830s as well as today) tended to be young, male, and poor, although the level of involvement in crime by these individuals varied considerably based on area. But why do some *places* have higher rates of crime?

In this chapter, we will look at two leading explanations for how the characteristics of *places* or *situations* might influence levels of criminal activity. While the two theories presented here are different from each other in significant respects, their common thread is the de-emphasis of the individual or group and an emphasis on the setting. Although criminologists have been aware that certain contexts seem to have unusually high levels of criminal activity since Guerry and Quetelet's work, not until the twentieth century did sociologists begin to give much attention to places as possible breeding grounds for crime. This chapter focuses on two major perspectives for looking at places and situations: social disorganization theory and routine activities theory.

SOCIAL DISORGANIZATION THEORY

Social disorganization theory contains several assumptions that distinguish it from many of the other perspectives that we describe in this text. First, this theory is a "macro theory." That is, social disorganization theory attempts to explain why some *communities* have higher *crime rates* than others, rather than why some *individual people* commit crime and others do not. The theories described in the chapters on control theory, biological theories, and psychological theories explain crime among individual people, and are sometimes referred to as "micro theories." Second, the theory assumes that social organization—schools, churches, business, police, informal networks of friends and neighbors, and government—when functioning normally enables a community to deal with problems of crime. In other words, the theory assumes that effective neighborhood crime control is not really a matter of individual choice, in which an individual decides to clean up an area (because individuals are all assumed to want less crime), but instead that a collective effort on the part of the community is necessary. Third, crime in an area is not primarily due to "defective" people with biological or psychological abnormalities, but happens in communities of otherwise normal people who live where larger institutions have failed. Social disorganization theory, then, is a theory that links an area's high crime rates to the inability of the community to organize in order to act collectively. Moreover, the theory attempts to explain why institutions within a community are unsuccessful.

As individuals, we often have a hard time thinking about how things operate at the macro (community or societal) level, so we digress for a moment to explain this important point. Our personal perspective and experience is entirely focused on the individual (micro) level, so it seems much easier and more natural for us to look at individuals and pick out what is wrong or different about them that leads them into criminal activity than it is to argue that the community one lives in may have some responsibility for supporting high levels of crime. To say that a place or situation matters when it comes to crime causation would be to suggest that you or I could become criminals were we in that same context. But what if our environment can in fact structure our lives in significant ways, meaning that we don't have completely unfettered freedom to make choices? Our location at a certain place might cut off choices we could have made, as well as open the door for other opportunities. For instance, try looking for a job in a community where no jobs are available because an economic downturn led companies to scale back their operations and close offices. In this case, no action the individual can take will successfully result in a job. But we tend not to think in this way, however. Most of the time we think that individuals are completely responsible for their circumstances—that our failure to find a job is because we are not trying hard enough or are just uncompetitive (or not skillful enough at interviewing). The broader influences associated with the characteristics of the community in which we live might be equally relevant to crime as to finding a job, whether we're even aware of these influences or not.

The researchers who started the social disorganization school of thought in criminology were concerned about the huge shift in the population from rural to urban areas that was occurring in the early twentieth century, specifically in the city of Chicago. Between the incorporation of Chicago in the 1830s and 1910, the population of the city had grown from 4,000 people to more than two million, and this growth was associated with the influx of people caused by industry and immigration (Palen, 1981). This rapid degree of change was believed to be the cause of growing levels of disorder in Chicago. Clifford Shaw and Henry McKay (1942), two researchers at the Institute for Social Research located in Chicago, took existing ideas on social ecology and developed the theory of social disorganization as the cause of disorder and high crime in portions of their city.

The notion of social ecology, originally developed by Chicago sociologists Robert Park and Earnest Burgess, held that people struggled for survival in a community of mutual dependence. Consider, for instance, whether you could survive for long if you were entirely on your own (that is, in a world where you would have to find your own food, make your own clothing, provide your own shelter, and see to your own defense). The struggle for survival would be difficult indeed. However, we generally can rely on grocers, clothing stores, builders, and the police to help meet many of our needs. And they, to some extent, depend on us. These networks of interdependence are the basis of communities. Communities would be impossible, or unnecessary, if we did not rely on others.

Park and Burgess also explored how human communities can change. Just as plants can invade a clear field and in turn be succeeded by new plants, the same can happen in human neighborhoods. A particular neighborhood might, for a time, be dominated by a particular ethnic group, but eventually be succeeded by another group. This pattern of invasion, dominance, and succession extends out from the center of the city (that is, the immigrants—"invaders"—do not start at the outer edge of the city). The new immigrants to the city begin in the least desirable parts of the central city and, by stages and over time, move outward toward more desirable property. Burgess in fact developed the five-zone model of an urban area, with each zone radiating outward from the city core (and generally becoming more affluent farther out). We will present this model in greater detail in a moment. Burgess believed that crime and other social problems, such as disease, would be highest in the areas where the newest (and poorest) residents in the city lived, which tended to be very close to the city core. Shaw and McKay borrowed these ideas and set out to see whether Burgess was correct about where crime might be found.

The Location of Crime

Shaw and McKay looked at how crime was spread across Chicago during the 1930s and 1940s. They took a map of Chicago and stuck pins wherever crimes occurred as well as at the home addresses of the juvenile delinquents, in order to see if crime and criminals seemed to cluster in the city core and become less dense the closer one got to the city edge. If place did not matter, then the pins would be scattered all over the map with no real pattern to their location. They found instead something interesting: that crime indeed tended to be concentrated in the slum areas, which were located toward the center of the city, and the concentration of the pins representing crimes grew less the farther away from Chicago's center one went. Place mattered.

Moreover, the pattern appeared to be persistent over time. In other words, the central city zones *always* had more crime than city zones farther out. But why? Most people would conclude that the high-crime areas are merely teeming with criminal people. Back in the early twentieth century, it was common for people to view unpopular ethnic groups, such as the Irish, the Sicilians, and the Poles, as criminal. Think of the movie *Gangs of New York,* for instance, which depicted the violence and disorder in lower Manhattan's Five Points between newly-arrived Irish immigrants during the 1860s. But what might you conclude about these groups if you were to learn, as Shaw and McKay did, that crime appeared to be concentrated in certain areas no matter who lived there? When the slums teemed with Irish, there was high crime; however, the Irish eventually moved out and were succeeded by another ethnic group, and the crime seemed to stay put and not follow the Irish out. In other words, the Irish seemed to abandon their reputed criminal tendencies as soon as they left the slums. Shaw and McKay thus provided further evidence that place, and not necessarily "defective" people, seemed to contribute to the crime problem.

The question then turned to why place mattered. Shaw and McKay looked at how the parts of Chicago differed from each other, using the "concentric zone model" of Burgess that we mentioned earlier. This model broke Chicago into five distinct zones radiating outward from the city's center:

Zone I: (inner city): central business district
Zone II: transitional zone (where the high crime is)
Zone III: working-class zone
Zone IV: residential zone
Zone V: (suburbs): commuter zone

We will describe each of the zones, but we will focus primarily on Zone II (the transitional zone) because crime is most likely to occur here. At least during the years in which Shaw and McKay were doing their research, the *central business district* (Zone I) was located in central Chicago and contained numerous railroads, slaughterhouses, large factories, and stockyards for hogs and cattle. Given the noise, smell, and general unpleasant scenery associated with such industry, one might reasonably suppose that few people would voluntarily choose to live in this area, so the central business district is almost exclusively industrial.

While industry is concentrated in the central business district, the expansion of industry meant that the surrounding neighborhood was changing from residential use to business use—houses were demolished to make way for factories. This area is the **transitional zone**. The homes still standing in the transitional zone tended to be older and in poor condition, as landowners intended to sell their properties to businesses and thus saw little advantage to renovating homes (why would you repair a house when the expense of the repairs would exceed the gain realized from selling the property?). Those of you who live in an apartment or rental unit where the landlord never bothers to maintain the place probably have a good idea of the appearance of homes and apartments in the transitional zone. Additionally, people living in the transitional zone have to put up with being close to the unpleasing features of the central business district. As any real estate agent will tell you, the value of property depends significantly on location, and proximity to what these agents euphemistically call "incurable defects" (such as railroad tracks, factories, and airports) ruins market value. No one is going to pay a premium to live twenty feet from busy railroad tracks (for a vivid example, think of Elwood Blues's inner-city Chicago apartment in the movie *The Blues Brothers* and you'll know what we mean—every time the commuter train passed, within feet of his skid-row hotel room window, everything in the room shook with a deafening noise). Those who can afford higher rents and mortgages move away to neighborhoods where the scenery is a bit more pleasant, while those who cannot afford to move must make do with living near industry and slaughterhouses. Such neighborhoods therefore house the poorest residents of the city, as well as newly arrived immigrants. One may also reasonably expect that residents will move out of the area the moment their financial situation allows.

Traveling farther out from the transitional zone, one encounters the **working-class zone**, where second-generation immigrants live as well as members of the working class. Since industry is not yet moving into the area, homeowners—to the best of their ability, given their limited financial means—are more likely to live in the area for a longer length of time and thus are inclined to maintain their property. This trend continues as one travels out from the city's center. One next encounters the **residential zone**, consisting of middle-class families and better residences. Finally, the affluent **commuter zone** exists on the outskirts of the city, where urban blight, noise, and traffic are minimal.

Social Disorganization and Its Causes

The buildings and scenery in Zone II are not pleasant to look at, but signs of disorder in transitional communities suggest deeper problems. Abandoned cars might line the streets. You might also see unsupervised youth idling in vacant lots, which are also overgrown with weeds and filled with trash to boot. The buildings themselves might be beyond merely old and drab, but decayed to the point where they are falling apart or even burnt-out ruins—and yet nobody ever seems to do anything about it. Even with railroad tracks close by and encroachment from industry, it does not necessarily follow that residents in the transitional zone are incapable of keeping their streets clean and of performing basic maintenance. Why is disorder, as well as crime, associated with transitional zones?

Shaw and McKay concluded, just as Burgess and other Chicago sociologists had suspected, that **social disorganization** is endemic within the transitional zone. That is, the community is unable to function as its residents would desire (to use the jargon of disorganization theory, the area is unable to "realize its values"), by having clean streets, no crime, attractive housing, low disease, and so forth. This is an important point in social disorganization theory: No one in the community wants to live where there is lots of disease, filth, stench, and hoodlums, but some communities are unable to do anything to prevent these problems from occurring. The key to keeping a community from succumbing to disorder is social organization, in which members of the community can communicate with each other and are effective at organizing, mobilizing, and working collectively (as a group). This notion about communities being able to maintain order in public spaces, such as parks and sidewalks, is what the Harvard University sociologist Robert Sampson and his colleagues (1997) termed **collective efficacy**. One can see collective efficacy in action when residents complain to community leaders about problems such as abandoned cars, and when residents organize neighborhood watches and form homeowners associations. The key is that residents are proactive in protecting the interests of their community. In order for there to be collective efficacy, a community must have **social capital**. Social capital consists of the many informal networks within a community. Everyone you know, for instance, is part of your personal network; communities consist of networks as well. Functioning neighborhood networks might organize trash cleanup days as well as plant flowers along the roads, using the collective power of residents to make the community more attractive. Neighborhood groups, who might vote as a bloc, can wield influence with politicians in order to attract municipal resources to the community, as well as work together to attract jobs that might make the area more attractive to residents. It thus takes viable institutions and residents working together to maintain a community that is free from disorder. When there is a lot of social capital— that is, a lot of effective networks for mobilizing community support and resources (residents know each other and are willing to work together)—then there will be less crime.

An organized community makes supervision and detection of deviance more effective, making the area less hospitable for crime. While the families might be able to supervise and control their children on their own, the organized nature of the community means that the parents are nevertheless not alone in their task. One of the authors, when he was much younger, was with a friend who had locked himself out of his house. They tried to enter the house through a window, and were quickly confronted by a neighbor who wanted to know what the two kids were doing. Adults in an organized community are willing to do something about suspicious activity. Beyond direct supervision, the community is also better able to work collectively to socialize youth away from crime.

Where such organizations either do not exist or have failed, however, residents can rely only on themselves. How else can one manage if the neighbors do not speak to each other, or if hardly anyone goes to the local church? Consequently, the community lacks social capital and is socially disorganized, and one sees high crime, teenage pregnancy, and disease because the residents cannot work together to tackle these problems as they emerge. Once crime becomes embedded in a disorganized community, Shaw and McKay theorized that persistent neighborhood "criminal traditions" and values would appear to compete with conventional values among the youth living in the area. In short, crime becomes a tolerated, if not normal, part of life in disorganized communities.

But still, why can't a motivated individual with vision and energy turn a community around? This is easier said than done, largely because we are ourselves often dependent on the assistance of others simply to get on successfully with our own lives. Your parents, for instance, might be paying your tuition. You might depend on student health services or campus organized social activities. In order to change communities for the better, the need to have assistance from others is all the more apparent. So why won't people help each other, even when it can be to their advantage? Shaw and McKay have focused on three factors that might lead to social disorganization:

(1) residential instability, (2) racial/ethnic heterogeneity, and (3) poverty. Each of these sources of disorganization undermines the ability of residents to work in concert and prevent crime from occurring.

Residential Instability. Disorganization theory posits that communities that have a lot of population turnover—in which many residents move from their homes during a given time period—tend to have higher crime. Effective formal and informal community organizations require a relatively stable population, but this isn't possible when the population is always looking to move. For instance, think about how moving affects your own relationships. Would you spend a lot of effort getting to know someone who is going to move away? Would you get to know people in the area, or invest time and energy in community projects, if you know you're going to leave?

Racial/Ethnic Heterogeneity. Shaw and McKay found that communities where lots of different cultures and races lived in close proximity tended to have higher crime rates. At first glance, this finding would appear puzzling. We normally think of diversity as a good thing, but the people of different backgrounds must share something in common and have meaningful interaction with each other. What happened instead in disorganized communities was that the different races and cultures tended to isolate themselves and avoid interacting with other groups. Sometimes this was because the language barrier was insurmountable. Other times the groups saw each other as simply too alien to comfortably interact with. Regardless, communication decreases under such conditions, which means that the community as a whole is less effective at being able to organize and control neighborhood crime.

Poverty. Communities with high poverty tend to lack the resources needed for effective community organization. Concentrated poverty in the community, for instance, seriously weakens the local tax base, which supports such community institutions as schools and recreational facilities. Additionally, the difficult circumstances of poverty mean that a significant portion of residents are focused on survival—asking them to spend time and energy organizing to help the community (which they likely want to leave as soon as possible) is a luxury they can ill afford. Thus, poverty is not in itself a cause of crime, but it facilitates disorganization and prevents the community from being able to effectively deal with local problems.

Empirical Support and Policy Implications

Early research on social disorganization theory tended to focus on "structural" or neighborhood-level correlates of disorganization: poverty, racial heterogeneity, and residential instability. While crime appeared to be connected to these structural factors, the disorganization itself—the weakness of community networks—was not measured in these studies (see Pratt, 2001). Not until the 1980s did criminologists begin to give greater attention to disorganization theory, through more empirical testing as well as many refinements and updates to the theory. Recent work by such criminologists as Robert Bursik, Robert Sampson, and their colleagues (see Bursik & Grasmick, 1993; Sampson & Groves, 1989; Sampson & Wilson, 1990; Sampson, Raudenbusch, & Earls, 1997) have identified weakened social bonds (see Hirschi, 1969) as the mechanism by which social disorganization in a community leads to greater crime. Research by these criminologists and others has found that informal networks, community supervision of youth, and participation in formal organizations in fact predict crime in the community.

Since social disorganization theory appears to have some support, even given the limitations of research testing it, it is worthwhile to think about what the theory says ought to be done in order to reduce crime. On one level, disorganization theory suggests straightforward policy. All one has to do is promote effective community organizations as well as informal mechanisms of social control. If we can get people to attend church and homeowners meetings, agree to watch each other's kids, and keep the streets clean, the residents will be better able to exert control and the community will be a less inviting place for crime.

Shaw and McKay developed one of the first large-scale programs to prevent delinquency with their Chicago Area Project. The objective was to use project staff and social workers to facilitate the creation and maintenance of community organizations as well as the ability of residents to exert social control in their area. Local organizations included youth athletic leagues, recreation programs, and summer camps. The fostering of informal relationships between residents would also give teenagers the opportunity to interact with law-abiding residents, who could serve as conventional role models. If the project was successful, then the community would be better situated to deal with the symptoms of social disorganization, including crime. Assessments of the Chicago Area Project revealed mixed results, however, with some neighborhoods showing decreased levels of crime while others reported higher levels of crime. The Chicago Area Project, as well as later programs such as the Mobilization for Youth, consistently revealed that promoting organization in communities at risk for social disorganization required consistent effort and care, as the organizations cultivated by the projects tended not to be self-sustaining. That is, once financial support for these programs was withdrawn or cut back, the organizations that had formed began to disintegrate. Nevertheless, some communities were able to maintain their ability to organize over the long term, with a correspondingly lower level of neighborhood delinquency than similar, but disorganized, neighborhoods (Schlossman, Zellman, Shavelson, Sedlak, & Cobb, 1984).

Why have policies designed to address community problems been so difficult to implement effectively? A big problem leading to disorganization is residential mobility—in which people, including those who have the talent and inclination to be community leaders, are always looking to leave and as a result never integrate into the community. The challenge is to get these people to love their communities enough to stay—so why can't we seem to get them to do this? One way to understand the basic problem is to relate it to your own life. Let's say that an urban planner wants to reduce high population turnover at an apartment full of college students. Now pretend you're a college student: Would you want to rent that apartment for the rest of your life? Would you do it, especially knowing that college student apartments often are noisy, offer few amenities, and have unresponsive landlords. The urban planner's job is to motivate people to stay and start caring for where they live; however, as a college student, you probably don't see your apartment or dorm as somewhere you would want to spend the rest of your life. This is a problem faced in the policy implications of disorganization theory. If you can think of something the city might do to your apartment complex that would get you to stay even if you were offered a job paying $100,000 per year (but without more amenities, since that would increase the rent and force the poorer people to move away), then you have taken a big step toward solving the problem of disorganization.

Disorganization theory is fairly clear about the efficacy of incarceration as a source of crime control. Since social ties are essential for effective communities, incarceration essentially churns the community and promotes residential instability. That is, many residents are incarcerated, released back into the community, reincarcerated, and so on, which prevents them from building significant ties to their neighborhood. As with many of the theories covered in this book, incarceration would fail to have a beneficial impact on crime.

Criticisms of Social Disorganization Theory

Some researchers, operating from a different set of assumptions from disorganization theorists, have criticized disorganization theory for the value judgment that the term "disorganization" implies. That is, to suggest that a community is *dis*organized might be inappropriate if poor and lower-class neighborhoods are simply *differently* organized. One of the other chapters discusses subcultural theories in which, for instance, members of the lower class simply have different values and needs, and therefore organize their lives in a way that best serves their interests. Crime, then, is merely a by-product of the culture, just like the apparent social organization—crime and community characteristics are correlated with each other, but one does not cause or influence the other. Edwin Sutherland (1947) termed this phenomenon *differential social organization* rather than social disorganization. If you're wondering what the consequence of this different perspective might be for policy purposes, it is actually quite significant. If an area is only differently organized (indeed, functioning exactly as it is supposed to be, according to the values of the area), then it is unclear whether anyone has the moral prerogative to change it. Changing it, after all, would be an ethnocentric act—we would simply be changing the organization of a perfectly functioning community to suit our own tastes. Indeed, the residents of the community would be unable to understand our interference, and would likely view it with suspicion or contempt.

ROUTINE ACTIVITIES THEORY

Routine activities theory focuses less explicitly on networks, informal social control, and community organizations, preferring instead to look at crime-inviting situations and how long-term social change can influence the opportunities for crime to occur. The idea that crime requires opportunity did not originate with routine activities theory (see, for instance, Cloward & Ohlin, 1960), but few earlier theories gave much attention to explaining what opportunity really meant. This neglect of opportunity implies that it (whatever *it* is) is universal, or else of little consequence relative to understanding the criminal offender. Routine activities theory, in contrast, treats opportunity as problematic and the offender as given, and usually focuses on how large-scale social change can be either more or less conducive to crime. Lawrence Cohen and Marcus Felson (1979), two sociologists, provided the initial outline of the theory.

The Necessary Requirements for Crime

Cohen and Felson (1979) reasoned that for a direct predatory crime to occur, three minimum conditions had to be present:

- A motivated offender
- A suitable target (a person or object)
- Ineffective guardianship

In order to prevent crime, all one needed to do was eliminate one of the necessary requirements. We discuss these elements next, so that you might see what they refer to as well as their importance.

Motivated Offenders.   When it comes to understanding the offender, routine activities theory is a rational choice model (similar to classical deterrence theory and the control perspective) in which all people are assumed to weigh the costs and benefits of alternative courses of action and then proceed to do what brings the most advantage. Consequently, routine activities theory does not attempt to explain why some people commit more crime than others, since it is assumed that any "normal" person would do it when the advantages are great enough and the costs low enough. But it is still instructive to create what research indicates to be a profile of the "representative" offender. Felson describes the "typical" **motivated offender** as "a young male with a big mouth who gets into many accidents and makes a mess of everything else" (1998, p. 54). Everything else being equal, situations where such people as this are likely to be found would have the highest potential for crime. One must also remember that being in situations where the advantages of crime appear to be great means that the odds are higher that even the most moral person will get into trouble. But if nobody in the area wants to commit a crime, then crime cannot occur.

Suitable Targets.   For a crime to happen it is not enough to simply have a likely offender in the area—there must also be something tempting nearby. People of a vicious temperament can appear to be saints if they are continuously in situations where there are no opportunities for crime that are worth their time. In order to better understand criminal temptation, and what makes a **suitable target**, it is best to look at it from a prospective offender's point of view rather than necessarily our own. Your professors, for instance, might be tempted by statistical software, but we suspect that most students would pass on an opportunity to steal that. Marcus Felson (1998) elaborated on what makes a target suitable, using the acronym **VIVA** (for *value, inertia, visibility,* and *accessibility*). Each of these characteristics can help us understand which targets will tempt nearby criminal offenders.

As suggested a moment ago, a target's *value* varies from person to person and does not solely depend on objective monetary worth. Think, for example about two music CDs priced at about $18—one by Christina Aguilera and the other by Yanni. Now put yourself in the shoes of a middle-school teen. Which CD will be more valuable to you? On average, teenagers would be more likely to consider the Aguilera CD valuable, scorning the Yanni CD (even though both are worth, in absolute monetary terms, about the same). If you're the owner of a music store frequented by teenagers, then it's a good bet that you will lose more Aguilera CDs to theft than Yanni CDs.

Tedeschi and Felson (1994) analyzed value in the context of a fight. What makes someone a worthwhile target for assault (and possible homicide)? After all, people do not usually randomly punch passersby. Instead, a fight is worthwhile when there is a grievance between two people. Tedeschi and Felson (1994) found that fights were more likely to erupt when people wanted to exert control over the behavior of someone else. If one of the authors dares to look at a pretty female, for example, his wife will slug him in the arm. Additionally, grievances can arise from the need to restore justice. In this case, violence is used to settle a score or get even with a former victimizer. Grievances that might make someone a worthwhile target for violence can arise from the need to save face. This might occur if someone challenged your masculinity/femininity or otherwise insulted you. Without these bases for grievances, there would be no point (or value) in fighting someone.

Inertia, which refers to the size and bulk of a target, is another factor that can make a target suitable. Consider two pieces of merchandise: a handheld digital camera and an entertainment center. Let's evaluate these objects from the point of view of someone who considers them equally valuable. (Let's say that both cost about $1,000.) Which one would be more likely to be shoplifted? You'd be right if you guessed the camera, but do you know why? Digital cameras tend to be small and easily concealed, unlike an entertainment center (which would require a forklift and a truck to move, and thus might arouse the suspicion of store staff as well as give the thief a hernia). Not surprisingly, shoplifting tends to be more of a problem at stores selling expensive light electronic goods, and less of a problem at even the priciest furniture stores (Felson, 1998). Everything else being equal, lighter and less bulky goods would be more suitable as a target. In the case of a possible personal crime, inertia might refer to the physical size and apparent strength of the prospective victim relative to the attacker.

The suitability of a target also depends on the offender's awareness that a target is in the area—that is, the target's *visibility.* In order for a target to be worthwhile to a would-be offender, the offender has to know that it's there. High visibility can be both intentional as well as inadvertent. Stores, simply to stay in business, have to prominently display attractive merchandise and risk tempting shoplifters. If you have parties at your house where lots of people show up, many will have the opportunity to get a good look at what you have. If you annoy other motorists on the road when you crank up your stereo, then you advertise to all that you have a nice set of speakers worth taking. This is the irony of having nice, expensive stuff; we want to flaunt it at least a little bit, but in so doing we alert people that we have something worth stealing.

Finally, the target must be *accessible* to be suitable. Offenders have to be able to easily get to the target and easily get away. One key aspect of routine activities theory is that the typical offender tends to stumble across opportunities for crime over the course of daily routines (the effort it takes to find the target and afterward escape is viewed as a "cost" and is thus a potential deterrent; in this light, routine activities theory assumes that people naturally gravitate toward convenient targets). Attractive targets that are very difficult to get to and get away from will tend to be relatively safe since they are not suitable.

Effective Guardianship.   While motivated offenders and suitable targets help contribute to crime, one final requirement needs to be met before a crime can occur. The target must be poorly guarded. **Effective guardianship** refers to the presence of anyone or anything in the area capable of making the crime more risky. Generally, offenders prefer to be alone with their target. By adding other people or security cameras to the setting, either of which might facilitate protection of the target, things very quickly become difficult for the offender. We normally think of the police as the most important guardians against crime. After all, only the most desperate or brazen criminals would elect to commit a crime in front of them. But if on any given day you were to time how long you can actually see a police officer on duty (including when the police officer is not even watching you and has no idea you're in the area), you'll find that you do not have a whole lot of immediate police protection. In routine activities theory, however, effective guardians can include virtually anyone who can serve as a witness to a crime. Think about the opportunity to steal a backpack containing $500 in cash from a classroom. You might be willing to do it if no one was in the vicinity; however, you wouldn't likely do it if the classroom was full of people, and even if they wouldn't lift a finger to prevent you from leaving the room. Do you see? No police officers are involved, but the presence of eyes watching what you are doing nevertheless makes the theft so much riskier and will probably change your mind. So beside yourself, your parents, friends, and relatives can act as guardians of you and your belongings. Guardians do not even have to be armed—all it takes for guardianship to be successful at deterring most crimes is the knowledge that one is being watched. Guardianship is all the more successful when it is inadvertent and part of natural, everyday routine. Felson (1986), for instance, reasoned that everyday social ties between individuals facilitate guardianship. If you love your parents, you will spend more time around them, but this means that you are under more frequent surveillance. That is, you probably would not smoke marijuana or have sex when your parents are right there, but neither would anyone assault you or steal your belongings with your parents watching.

In sum, for a crime to have the potential of occurring there must be the convergence, in time and space, of the three necessary conditions for crime just described: a motivated offender, a suitable target, and ineffective guardianship. The key factors responsible for this convergence are the everyday routines of individuals—where do they work or go to school, where do they go for entertainment, how do they get home? As the term "routine" implies, the behavior of offenders is not often distinguishable from that of nonoffenders. That is, there is often nothing particularly special, illegal, or even suspicious about the normal routines of offenders before a crime happens. Offenders will not travel miles out of their way and spend hours seeking suitable targets. Instead, they stumble across opportunities for crime because their daily routines place them in situations where they are near worthwhile and poorly protected targets.

The Role of Social Changes

Cohen and Felson (1979) focused their classic article on linking crime rates with large-scale historical social changes. Some social changes might have relevance for facilitating or impeding situations in which offenders are near poorly defended and worthwhile targets. To think about the influence of these changes in everyday social routines on levels of crime, let us first start with an example. Years ago, people tended to spend a lot more time around the house. Women were expected to maintain the home and raise the children, which was no easy task given that labor-saving devices such as dishwashers and washing machines were still evolving. The children of that day—as our parents and grandparents proudly tell us—had to spend much of their time helping with time-consuming chores. Washing the clothes, feeding the chickens, milking the cows—all of these activities took time away from other activities away from the home. But times changed as gender roles evolved and time-saving appliances proliferated in our lives. Rather than the all-day affair that clothes washing used to be, all one has to do now is throw them in the washer, wait a bit, and throw them in the dryer. Freed from labor at home, children have much more free time to spend outside the home than ever before. The times changed for women as well, as over the past several decades a large proportion of women entered the full-time workforce. Women, in effect, were no longer shackled to their kitchens and nurseries.

Think about these social changes from the point of view of a would-be burglar. Years ago, because the household was so high-maintenance, a typical burglar would have to hazard breaking into an *occupied* residence in order to steal the contents. You can probably already see the lack of appeal of this scenario for most burglars—guardianship is naturally quite high if a residence has occupants. Indeed, having people in the house heightens risk and seldom offers any benefit. For example, people in the house may resist entry, could serve as witnesses, and might even attempt to kill anyone who invades their home. On the other hand, an empty home is ideal. With no one there, the only challenge is to get in and get out unobserved by neighbors and passersby. So with women entering the workforce and children freed from chores at home, the job of the burglar became easier and less risky. Not surprisingly, half of all burglaries occur during daylight hours (Gottfredson & Hirschi, 1990).

Recall earlier that Guerry and Quetelet found that the more prosperous regions of France reported higher property crime. At first, this seems odd—prosperity leading to crime? Cohen and Felson (1979), observing crime trends between 1947 and 1970, found a similar pattern in the United States between economic prosperity and property crime and reached the same conclusion as the two Belgians. Offenders were not stealing food or life's essentials. Instead, prosperity increased the availability of items to steal. Between the late 1940s and 1970, there was an increase in the availability of durable (and expensive) electronic goods and automobiles, all of which could be moved relatively easily and quickly sold for cash. In other words, prosperity seems to bring greater temptation in the form of wider availability of suitable targets. One might reason from this that changes in crime rates indeed have less to do with the pool of motivated offenders than with the opportunities available to commit crime.

Policy Implications

The policy implications of routine activities theory are, in the abstract, straightforward: Simply prevent the combination of motivated offenders and suitable targets during moments of ineffective guardianship. Regarding what to do about motivated offenders, Ronald Clarke argued that it is pointless to try to change people. Most theories discussed in this book clearly take the opposite approach, but there may be something to recommend against changing people. Consider the following example. If you have a boyfriend or girlfriend (or significant other), it is highly likely that he or she has an annoying or embarrassing habit like chewing fingernails, belching loudly, or picking his or her nose. Many people try to "improve" their romantic partners and get them to stop being so annoying by nagging and scolding them. In the experience of the authors, at any rate, most people fail at this miserably, and in many cases the attempts at "rehabilitation" are irritating enough and lead to a breakup. Perhaps eliminating opportunity might be simpler.

Routine activities theory thus argues in favor of manipulating the situation in order to keep motivated offenders from becoming tempted (such as by limiting the time they spend around suitable targets), by making the crime too inconvenient to execute, or by increasing the deterrence inherent in a situation (such as by augmenting guardianship). Felson (1998), for instance, recommended that schools could reduce disturbances on campus by cutting back the landscaping and otherwise designing the campus and its buildings to facilitate surveillance. Moreover, he reported that bars were able to reduce the amount of injurious and fatal assaults by serving drinks in plastic cups rather than beer bottles (that is, by reducing the accessibility of potential weapons that might cause injury). It is not easy to kill someone by throwing a plastic cup at her head. Some ideas consistent with routine activities theory actually predate the work of Cohen and Felson. Oscar Newman (1972), for instance, explored the idea of "defensible space" in public housing, such as designing the facilities with natural surveillance in mind. Ronald Clarke (1992) championed increasing the effort and risk of crime via physical barriers to crime (such as a tougher door), alarms, and security guards. One can also ensure that the rewards of crime make the effort not worth the attempt. Convenience stores often clearly display a sign reporting that they have only a few dollars in cash available, for example. Assuming offenders are rational and can accurately perceive the risks, rewards, and potential effort, an obviously tough target will likely be passed. Note that none of these strategies involve changing people, but instead entail manipulating the environment so that people are kept away from targets, or by making targets too well guarded, or by making targets too unsuitable.

Empirical Research and Criticisms

Routine activities theory is perhaps the dominant theory of victimization. Researchers have linked individual routine activities to many types of victimization in many different settings (see Fisher, Sloan, Cullen, & Lu, 1998; Mustaine & Tewksbury, 1998). Wayne Osgood and colleagues (1996) found that the time juveniles spent with peers engaged in unstructured leisure activities away from adults was a predictor of delinquency, even after controlling for how delinquent the child normally was. Other research has explored how macro-level social changes, such as modernization and theft rates, relate to victimization. Neuman and Berger (1988), for instance, found that modernization in different countries was related to theft, though not homicide. Pratt (2001) conducted a meta-analysis of research looking at the correspondence between macro-level changes and crime, finding support for the predictions of routine activities theory (particularly the idea of guardianship). While the empirical literature does not always offer consistent support for routine activities theory, the theory is influential and does appear to offer much promise.

Some have indicated that routine activities theory is a "victim-blaming" theory (see, for instance, Karmen, 2003; Meier & Miethe, 1993). The theory, after all, suggests that victims can facilitate or provoke their own victimization through their daily routines, by making themselves into suitable targets, or by weakening their guardianship. In some respects, this criticism is political rather than scientific. The research does indicate that victims are often, through their behaviors and activities, agents in their own victimization (Meier & Miethe, 1993). That being said, readers should be aware that all theories contain inherent ideology. Nevertheless, while it is one thing to object to a theory because it fails to adequately conform to the facts, it is another matter entirely to reject a theory because one does not like the ideology.

SUMMARY

Theories that focus on the social ecology of crime offer something different from many of the theories of crime that we have discussed so far. Rather than looking at how offenders differ from nonoffenders, these theories instead give attention to how situations or places with high levels of crime differ from those with little crime. Social disorganization theory claims that disorganization undermines ties and institutions within a community, thus making it impossible for residents to work collectively to deal with crime problems in the area. Routine activities theory gives its attention to the immediate situation where crime occurs, namely situations where motivated offenders are in proximity to poorly guarded suitable targets. Both theories have received support in the empirical literature, and both at present are the focus of extensive attention from criminologists. Another common theme for these theories is that neither proposes the rehabilitation of people to prevent future crime from occurring, but they instead suggest that best results might be obtained from changing the situation or the context.

KEY TERMS

collective efficacy the ability of a community to maintain order in public spaces

commuter zone in social disorganization theory, Zone V; the outermost edge of the city that has the least crime; the suburbs

effective guardianship refers to any person or object capable of protecting a victim from an offender, who might report the crime to authorities, or who might serve as a witness. Guardians make crime less likely to occur in that they complicate the execution of a crime

motivated offender in routine activities theory, one of the three necessary requirements for crime; motivated offenders, on average, tend to be young males who get into trouble a lot, but this term can include virtually anyone who might be tempted by crime in a given situation

residential zone in social disorganization theory, Zone IV; exists between the working class zone and the commuter zone and consists of relatively desirable residential property

social capital informal social networks within communities that enable community tasks to get done

social disorganization the inability of a community to organize effectively to prevent social problems from occurring, due to poverty, residential mobility, and racial/ethnic heterogeneity

suitable target in routine activities theory, one of the three necessary requirements for crime; suitable targets can be anything that might tempt a nearby offender

transitional zone in social disorganization theory, Zone II; contains the least desirable residential properties; consequently, only the poorest individuals live here, and they tend to move away when they can; crime is highest in this zone

VIVA an acronym referring to value, inertia, visibility, and accessibility; all of these are elements of what might make a target suitable to a motivated offender

working-class zone in social disorganization theory, Zone III; zone contains residential properties that are older and less desirable than those in the residential and commuter zones, but the residents tend to live in this zone for relatively long durations

DISCUSSION QUESTIONS

1. Which kinds of theories do you believe are most important for understanding and solving crime: theories about places or theories about people?

2. Could disorganization theory be extended to rural areas?

3. According to routine activities theory, is it possible for crime to increase even when the number of would-be criminals remains constant? Explain why.

4. Since 1993, the crime rate has generally declined. How might routine activities theory explain this?

REFERENCES

Bierne, P. (1993). *Inventing criminology.* Albany: State University of New York Press.

Bursik, R. J., & Grasmick, H. G. (1993). *Neighborhoods and crime: The dimensions of effective neighborhood control.* New York: Lexington Books.

Clarke, R. (1992). *Situational crime prevention: Successful case studies.* New York: Harrow & Heston.

Cloward, R. A., & Ohlin, L. E. (1960). *Delinquency and opportunity: A theory of delinquent gangs.* Glencoe, IL: Free Press.

Cohen, L. E., & Felson, M. (1979). Social change and crime rate trends: A routine activity approach. *American Sociological Review, 44,* 588–608.

Felson, M. (1986). Linking criminal choices, routine activities, informal control, and criminal outcomes. In D. B. Cornish & R. V. Clarke (Eds.), *The reasoning criminal: Rational choice perspectives on offending.* New York: Springer-Verlag.

Felson, M. (1998). *Crime and everyday life.* Thousand Oaks, CA: Pine Forge Press.

Fisher, B., Sloan, J., Cullen, F., & Lu, H. (1998). Crime in the ivory tower: The level and sources of student victimization. *Criminology, 36,* 671–710.

Gottfredson, M. R., & Hirschi, T. (1990). *A general theory of crime.* Stanford, CA: Stanford University Press.

Hirschi, T. (1969). *Causes of delinquency.* Berkeley: University of California Press.

Meier, R. F., & Miethe, T. D. (1993). Understanding theories of criminal victimization. *Crime and Justice: A Review of Research, 17,* 459–99.

Mustaine, E. E., & Tewksbury, R. (1998). Predicting risks of larceny theft victimization: A routine activity analysis using refined activity measures. *Criminology, 36,* 829–858.

Newman, O. (1972). *Defensible space: Crime prevention through urban design.* New York: Collier.

Osgood, D. W., Wilson, J. K., O'Malley, P. M., Bachman, J. G., & Johnston, L. D. (1996). Routine activities and individual deviant behavior. *American Sociological Review, 61,* 635–655.

Palen, J. (1981). *The urban world.* New York: McGraw-Hill.

Pratt, T. (2001). *Assessing the relative effects of macro-level predictors of crime: A meta-analysis.* Unpublished dissertation, University of Cincinnati.

Sampson, R. J., & Groves, W. B. (1989). Community structure and crime: Testing social disorganization theory. *American Journal of Sociology, 94,* 774–802.

Sampson, R. J., Raudenbusch, S. W., & Earls, F. (1997). Neighborhoods and violent crime: A multilevel study of collective efficacy. *Science, 227,* 918–924.

Sampson, R. J., & Wilson, W. J. (1990). Toward a theory of race, crime, and urban inequality. In (Eds.), *Crime and inequality*. J. Hagan & R. Peterson (Eds.), Stanford, CA: Stanford University Press.

Schlossman, S., Zellman, G., Shavelson, R., Sedlak, M., & Cobb, J. (1984). *Delinquency prevention in South Chicago: A fifty-year assessment of the Chicago Area Project*. Santa Monica, CA: RAND.

Shaw, C. & McKay, H. (1942). *Social factors in juvenile delinquency*. Washington, DC: Government Printing Office.

Sutherland, E. H. (1947). *Principles of criminology* (4th ed.). Philadelphia: Lippincott.

Tedeschi, J., & Felson, R. (1994). *Violence, aggression, and coercive action*. Washington, DC: American Psychological Association Books.

CHAPTER 6

LEARNING AND CULTURAL TRANSMISSION THEORIES OF CRIME

Like social control theory (see Chapter 8), learning and cultural transmission theories generally assume that criminal behavior is like other forms of human behavior in certain basic respects. First, crime is viewed as a result of social interaction. Social interaction provides both a context and process wherein learning occurs and behavior reflects the nature of what is learned through observation of one's environment, ethnocentric perspective, and the socialization process facilitated by an individual's reference groups, generally, and role models, specifically. Within certain situations crime is simply normative behavior and, reasonably, is to be expected.

Criminal and noncriminal behavior are thought to result from a combination of the socialization process (which, in turn, is heavily influenced by a combination of environmental factors), situational circumstances, and group values. Criminality, then, is not considered innate human character, as contended by determinists such as Lombroso, but rather a product of interaction with others. **Learning theories** (differential association theory and social learning theory) emphasize the process in which criminal behavior is observed, learned, and carried out. Cultural transmission theories are similar to learning theories but focus more on group values (which are shaped and perpetuated from one generation to the next by learning) that encourage and condone crime.

LEARNING THEORIES

Learning theories contend that criminal behavior is learned from others and this learning process necessarily involves the internalization of values, norms, and behaviors that vary across areas and groups. Accordingly, neither free will nor individual characteristics (such as biological or psychological) associated with crime are emphasized, but rather the social environment's effect on the maturation and socialization processes. Learning theory has a rich legacy in criminology and remains an important strand within contemporary theoretical criminology.

By viewing crime as any other behavior that must be learned, a fundamental assumption of the perspective is that behavior results from observing the habits of others and then modeling or copying that which is successful for meeting needs and desires. People model or imitate (Bandura, 1962) what appears to work, which may be conventional (such as educational attainment and legal employment) or unconventional (such as crime). Social environment becomes crucial because role models from family, peer groups, and the larger community can encourage or dissuade delinquency and crime.

In social learning theory, negative outcomes are related to life experiences, such as childhood exposure to domestic violence, sex abuse, recurring conflict with the juvenile and criminal justice system, school failure, poverty, and poor role models. The learning perspective suggests that violent crime, for example, is a rather natural response resulting from observation of adult role models' use of aggression to solve problems. Some youth not only become familiar with domestic violence through firsthand observation, but also come to accept it as normal behavior. Similarly, daily observation of adult hustling, scheming, and stealing may lead to a belief that such behaviors are appropriate means to acquire material goods.

Socially learned behavior typically varies by gender, so much so that criminologists observe the *gendered* nature of both offending and victimization trends. Whereas males use physical force and psychological intimidation to exercise will and access desires, females learn that submissiveness and victimization are the social norms often defining the severity of violence as opposed to its mere occurrence. This chapter examines the two foremost learning theories: differential association theory and social learning theory.

SUTHERLAND'S DIFFERENTIAL ASSOCIATION THEORY

Edwin Sutherland (1883–1950) is often considered the founding father of positivistic criminology. Influenced heavily by the Chicago school and its sociological tradition, he focused on social properties and forces that cause and condition crime and rejected the idea that crime was inherited or otherwise predetermined by biological or psychological factors. While criminologists today readily accept that social structural and environmental factors are essential to understanding crime, Sutherland's ideas were presented during an era when perspectives such as Lombroso's criminal body type (Wolfgang et al., 1972) and Freud's personality theories (Andrews & Bonta, 1998) were dominant.

Sutherland emphasized the role of *socialization* in the development of human behavior and interaction. Socialization refers to a process of human interaction on both one-to-one and group levels wherein behavior is (1) learned from others and (2) reflects society's cultural and subcultural values. Sutherland's *theory of **differential association*** (1939/1942) emphasizes two primary influences: agents of socialization and content of socialization. Agents of socialization refer to who does the socializing, that is, the teaching. Teaching may be in a formal context through a social institution, such as school, church, or family, but also informally through daily interaction in the community and with peer groups. Social interaction directly shapes the socialization process through the related concepts of observation, role modeling, expectation development, and imitation.

Differential association theory might suggest that crime results from those whose role models are criminals and thus who associate with people whose behavior is different or abnormal. While the role of groups is relevant, Sutherland meant that association is based in large part on definitions of behavior that are favorable or unfavorable to breaking the law. Criminals differ from noncriminals in that they are members of groups whose values are favorable to violation of the law. While groups and the idea of association is important, the primary importance of social groups centers on the social interaction and socialization they facilitate. Sutherland's theory is fairly straightforward, presented in nine formal propositions:

1. *Criminal behavior is learned.* This means that crime is not spontaneous or natural, which is opposite from the position taken by many biological theories, as well as the classical and control perspectives. People are basically like computers rolling off an assembly line; computers do not program themselves but acquire their "knowledge" from some external source. Criminality comes from the environment.

2. *Criminal behavior is learned in interaction with other people in a process of communication.* This proposition specifically targets the social environment (as opposed to the physical environment, for instance) as the source of crime.

3. *The principal part of the learning of criminal behavior occurs within intimate personal groups.* This means that not everyone in your social environment will exert the same influence. Your professor might tell you about how cool it would be to go rob a convenience store, but you would be unlikely to do it. But it might be a different matter if the source of your learning was someone close to you, like family or close friends.

4. *When criminal behavior is learned, the learning includes techniques of committing the crime, which are sometimes very complicated and sometimes very simple, and the specific direction of motives, drives, rationalizations, and attitudes.* Thus,

everything associated with crime is learned—even the very reasons why we think we need to commit crime, as well as our excuses.

5. *The specific direction of motives and drives is learned from definitions of legal codes as favorable and unfavorable.* This proposition points to the idea of "normative conflict," in which, in an absolute sense, there is no right or wrong and "crime" is only such relative to the dominant legal code. Some cultures that are ethnocentrically characterized as "criminal" view the reigning legal code with disfavor.

6. *A person becomes a delinquent because of an excess of definitions favorable to violation of law over definitions unfavorable to violation of law.* This proposition says that the preponderance of our socialization will determine whether we turn to crime.

7. *Differential association may vary in frequency, duration, priority, and intensity.* Put differently, the most frequent, longest-running, earliest, and closest influences will be most efficacious or determinant of learned behavior.

8. *The process of learning criminal behavior by association with criminal and anticriminal patterns incorporates all the mechanisms that are involved in any other learning.* This means that criminals are not mentally deficient, but rather "differently learned." Because crime has to be learned, it follows that criminals have average intelligence. Learning crime is also no different than learning arithmetic or anything else.

9. *Although criminal behavior is an expression of general needs and values, it is not explained by those general needs and values, because noncriminal behavior is an expression of the same needs and values* (Sutherland, 1947, pp. 6–8). Stated differently, the motives attributed to crime, such as a need for money, can be satisfied criminally or noncriminally (for example, by getting a job). Which path one follows depends on the environment one is raised in, as the need for money does not require that one commit crime.

While each of these propositions was significant to the establishment of a broad criminological knowledge base, propositions 5 and 6 are the cornerstone of Sutherland's differential association theory. Motives and drives can be thought of as ends and means and they are defined ultimately in either support of or opposition to crime. Intimate group interaction or associations, which vary in frequency, importance, period of time, and level of intensity, effect learning through observation of role models.

These association dimensions make crime more likely when compounded. For example, interacting with people several times a week (frequency) at a sustained level (period of time) has greater influence on attitudes about criminal involvement than occasional and superficial social exchanges. Also, it is generally thought that because motives and corresponding courses of action are learned early in life, attitudes shaped by youth are especially consequential (importance) and largely determine learned behavior into adulthood and throughout life. Differential association theory posits that if a person's primary group interactions provide greater exposure to values and observations that favor rather than discourage crime and delinquency, it is more likely that the individual will also be delinquent.

The nine differential association propositions have shaped numerous leading criminological theories, a testament to Sutherland's "founding father" depiction. Albert Cohen, Donald Cressey, Lloyd Ohlin, George Vold, James Short, and numerous other prominent theorists were either students of Sutherland's or otherwise heavily influenced by his work. The scope of their work is a testament to his impact on the field, particularly in instilling a sociological paradigm that continues to lead theoretical and applied criminology today. Social learning has remained a driving influence in criminological thought (discussed at length shortly), as has the social context (such as culture) in which learning transpires. Because Sutherland's theory draws on and integrates a range of dimensions exacting crime (social interaction, value systems, and cultural factors shaping the nature of learning), it is considered the first *general theory* of crime. As a general theory, differential association moved beyond the question of why individuals commit crime to explaining variation in crime rates across places (countries and cities) and social groups. Differential association is so ingrained in both academic and popular cultural understandings of crime that we readily accept that a delinquent peer group and a community characterized by procriminal definitions of values generates criminality.

AKERS'S SOCIAL LEARNING THEORY

One criticism of differential association theory is that it fails to explain exactly how people learn to commit crime. By the 1960s, researchers had made many advances about learning processes and some criminologists saw the need to update differential association theory to reflect new knowledge on learning. Ronald Akers (collaborating with Robert Burgess) developed perhaps the most significant revision of differential association theory. Differential association remains a significant cornerstone of social learning theory, but Akers's theory incorporates reinforcement/punishment and observational learning as well.

As in Sutherland's theory, everyone is differentially exposed to "procriminal" and "proconforming" values. The people with whom we spend most of our time shape our reality (or how we interpret the world around us), reward and punish behavior, and provide the models for behavior. For differential association to have the best likelihood of an effect on one's behavior, a group has to have the opportunity to shape a person's behavior early, have a lengthier time to work on the individual, and have more frequent contact of a more intense quality. Family and close friends are the most likely sources of influence, but other sources may include teachers, neighbors, and even the media.

Definitions simply refer to how you define a situation. Many things have symbolic value that influences our thought processes and behavior. Think, for instance, of a miniskirt. To a Martian, a leather miniskirt is simply a piece of fabric with no symbolic value. If a miniskirt is being worn by a male football player around campus, some people might define the situation as inappropriate or positively weird. Martians, of course, would wonder what the fuss is about because they were not socialized about the meaning of the miniskirt. More specifically to social learning theory, definitions refer to all the attitudes and values we have about what is right and wrong, pleasurable and unpleasurable, and so forth. Definitions even provide us with our own justifications or excuses for committing crime under certain circumstances.

Learning theory maintains that the continuation of a behavior depends on its consequences. Behavior associated with pleasure is more likely to be continued, but behavior that typically brings pain will be very short-lived indeed, a basic logic quite similar to deterrence and control theories. We will discuss four categories of reinforcement/punishment: positive reinforcement, negative reinforcement, positive punishment, and negative punishment. Reinforcement occurs when you try to get a behavior to continue, while punishment refers to anything that discourages a behavior. The notions of *positive* and *negative* are easy to get mixed up, since we normally think of *positive* as something good and *negative* as something bad. Instead, we suggest that you think of *positive* and *negative* in mathematical terms, where *positive* refers to giving, adding, or introducing something. *Negative* would indicate a situation in which you take something away.

If one wants a behavior to persist in someone, learning theory indicates that one way to accomplish this is to reward the behavior whenever it occurs (such as through approval or money). If you do something and the action or the reaction of others is to give you something you like, that is *positive reinforcement*. If you do something that causes others to take away something you didn't like (say, chores), then that would be *negative reinforcement*. But let's say that you want to get someone to stop doing something you don't like. You could inflict pain on that person (by hitting her or yelling), which would be *positive punishment*. Or you might consider punishing the person by taking away something she likes (such as your friendship), which would be *negative punishment*. Someone who has consistently experienced these rewards and punishments in the past is likely to associate them with present and future behavior, thus influencing whether he or she engages in them at all. So if someone associates crime with pleasure and the punishments are few and inconsistent, he or she is more likely to commit crime in the right situation.

Conversely, someone who figures that the rewards of crime aren't worth it in view of the punishments will be less likely to commit crime.

Imitation occurs when one observes behavior in others and mimics it without necessarily understanding the consequences of the behavior. According to Akers, this is how novel behavior begins in the individual. (Remember that in learning theories people do not spontaneously commit crime or deviance; they have to pick it up from somewhere). Whether the behavior continues depends on the consequences. One of the authors, for example, knew a colleague who repeatedly used the "f-word" and was unsuccessful at guarding his language around his toddler. Swearing in a moment of frustration made him feel good, which the child apparently noticed. Consistent with the notion of imitation, the child began using the word, too. As is the case with toddlers, the child chose probably the most embarrassing moment to loudly and repeatedly imitate his father—in this case, in the middle of a church sermon. You can probably guess the consequences of the behavior!

Social learning theory thus offers ideas for explaining why people become violent. People observe violence in their environment and imitate it. They learn that some situations call for violence, and they learn the rules for when violence is acceptable and when it is not. Their violence is reinforced and the punishments are of relatively less consequence than the rewards. While differential association and social learning theories dwell on the processes whereby people become criminal or law-abiding, the remainder of this chapter will focus on the cultures themselves, which are the contexts in which socialization occurs.

CULTURAL TRANSMISSION THEORIES

Cultural studies inform us that *ideas* form the essence of both cultures and subcultures, the primary difference between the two being that their definitive idea sets are dissimilar and often in conflict. The very term *sub* suggests a separate reality—a distinct set of norms, values, mores, and attitudes that contrast with those of a larger and more dominant culture. In fact, values that conflict with mainstream normative standards characterize the *subcultural* or *cultural transmission* approach to crime.

Cultural transmission theories focus, then, on the ideas that form values and beliefs that differ from conventional ideas. Value systems that conflict with conventional standards largely define subcultures. The values, beliefs, and norms of deviant subcultures are thought to predispose people to commit crime while simultaneously providing a rationalization for being criminal. This rationalization is essentially a technique for neutralizing or minimizing the guilt associated with criminal offending (Sykes & Matza, 1957). Guilt associated with committing crime may be minimal or nonexistent, however, for subcultural members whose social learning process conveys the message that crime is normal.

The Rise of the Subcultural Perspective

Subcultural theories emerged as the dominant perspective on crime during the 1950s and, along with the differential association theory discussed earlier in this chapter, are among the earliest of the criminological theories. The 1950s were perhaps the foremost period during which middle-class values defined social norms and dominated social institutions. Freedom of expression and a widespread liberalization of social behavior and attitudes did not unfold on a national level until the 1960s and 1970s and variation from traditional behavior was still viewed negatively, especially in the context of juvenile delinquency.

Social change usually occurs over time, and attitudes and behavior, particularly by teenagers, during the 1950s moved society away from its traditions. For the first time in American history, middle-class youth owned or had access to automobiles and thus freedom. The rise of rock and roll in popular culture fostered rebellion, greater independence, and outright disobedience. The result was unprecedented levels of juvenile delinquency. Criminologists usually reject the notion that the rise in juvenile delinquency during this era resulted from a general societal moral decay, submitting instead that the delinquency rise was a result of the combination of greater freedom from parents (that is, being less "homebound"); money from part-time jobs; and popular cultural endorsement of rebellion through drinking, indifference toward school performance, and sexual promiscuity.

Cultural transmission theories of crime and delinquency are based on the idea that people *internalize* values and beliefs. Learning shapes and perpetuates values that constitute a belief system representing social attitudes, preferences, and a sense of group identification. Belief systems come to characterize social environments, but some environments are distinguished by atypical, criminogenic value and normative systems wherein crime is encouraged or at least condoned. *Cultural variation* is thus a fundamental assumption, as is the power of conformity. Subscription to the unconventional is rewarded through increased social status and self-esteem that is denied to subgroup members elsewhere in the larger society.

Similarly situated people face social rejection because of their family's socioeconomic status or their race, ethnicity, religion, or place of geographic origin. It is common practice and seems only natural, for example, that people from the same state or region choose to identify and bond together. This reality becomes more pronounced when the group is outside its native environment, largely because its culturally specific practices and patterns of speech and behavior stand out as different. Noticeable differences in dialect, manners, and political or religious attitudes seem to simultaneously push nonnatives outside the mainstream and pull them into social groups and settings with which they are more familiar and feel more comfortable.

Associating with similar others happens all the time and doesn't necessarily involve deviance or crime. College students from the northeast region of the country enrolled in southern universities readily identify with one another and form peer groups that replicate practices reflecting their socialization processes and regional attitudes. The same social pattern holds true for southern students at northern schools as people use culture as a means of defining themselves and to engage social interaction. College students, regardless of where they are from, have a lot in common that dissuades them from crime; they are investing in themselves through education and preparing to compete in the economic arena and therefore are likely to realize upward social and economic mobility. Within subcultures, which are typically found in lower-class settings, college or preparation for college is not the norm. Rather, focus on meeting the more immediate necessities of daily life blocks upward-mobility opportunities for various groups situated throughout the lower class.

Cultural Norms and Legal Process

The study of subcultures from a criminological orientation is necessarily integrated with the study of *legal process*. While the production of law has been more aligned with special interests than those of the populace (Lynch & Groves, 1986), the criminal law is generally regarded (ironically, by the populace) as a product of normative consensus, a parallel reinforced by both the myths and realities of democratic ideals (Lynch & Groves, 1986). The law thus denotes the conventional or *dominant culture*. But an important, and paradoxical, feature of the legal process is the disjuncture between the moral normative value system held by lawmakers and the positional norms of various societal groups.

Positional norms, defined by values correlated with combinations of class status, sex, age, race and ethnicity, religious affiliation, and similar variables, are often underrepresented in the formal definition of authority. A simpler way to state this is that what is considered normal, appropriate, popular, or wrong varies considerably across different social groups throughout society. Repudiation of other groups' societal standards and norms, as formally specified in law and the rules governing societal institutions, fosters greater group cohesion, thus amplifying differences between the value systems of the subculture and the larger society. Thus, another defining characteristic of a subculture is **cultural conflict**.

It is important to make the conceptual distinction between subculture and population segment. The subcultural values of a gang, for example, may intensify although membership is reduced through criminal justice system actions. In short, normative conflict is inherent in social structure; subcultures are very much a manifestation of this conflict. Because American society is so multifaceted and groups often disagree about appropriate standards, the criminal law becomes a kind of glue that holds society together in lieu of the absence of informal standards. Next, we examine the leading theories of lower-class crime that are known by a number of names, most commonly subcultural theory, cultural transmission theory, and cultural conflict theory.

Cohen's Middle-Class Measuring Rod

Most criminology and criminal justice text authors begin discussion of subculture theory with the work of Albert K. Cohen (Lilly, Cullen, & Ball, 1989; Martin, Mutchnick, & Austin, 1990; Reid, 1990; Shoemaker, 2004). Others, however, have chosen to either ignore (Bartol, 1980; Vold & Bernard, 1986) or minimize Cohen's contribution. This lack of consensus raises the question of whether Cohen's theory stands alone as a cultural accounting of crime or is more of an extension and synthesis of previously established theories. The answer lies in examination of not just Cohen's writings, but also his academic background.

Perhaps no student of sociology has ever enjoyed exposure to the high quality of instruction as Albert Cohen. He enrolled in courses taught by prominent sociologists, most notably Talcott Parsons and Robert K. Merton, while an undergraduate during the 1930s at Harvard. While pursuing a master's degree at Indiana University, Cohen studied under Edwin Sutherland. After service in the army during World War II, he returned to Harvard as a doctoral student, where he was mentored by the famous sociologist George Homans (Martin, Mutchnick, & Austin, 1990). Of these scholars, Merton and Sutherland substantially molded Cohen's interests with their strain and differential association theories, respectively. It is because of these influences that his works have occasionally been omitted from reviews of subculture literature. Specifically, it has been alleged that Cohen focuses on internal social conditions of subcultures, culminating in a strain theory dependent on social structural forces, *instead* of a more appropriate focus on the essence of a subculture, ideas (Vold, Bernard and Snipes, 2002). This once dissenting view gained momentum throughout the discipline, evident by Thomas O'Connor's paper "Is Albert Cohen a Strain Theorist?", a 1992 American Society of Criminology Gene Carte Paper Competition winner (*The Criminologist*, 1992). Today, criminological theory texts often discuss Cohen in the context of strain rather than subculture. Nonetheless, Cohen remains a founding pioneer of subcultural theory.

Cohen's repute as the founder of a distinct subcultural theory is based on his most famous work, *Delinquent Boys: The Culture of the Gang* (1955). In this revised version of his doctoral dissertation, Cohen developed a general theory of subcultures through a detailed commentary on delinquent gangs that features five major causal factors: *prevalence, origins, process, purpose,* and *problem.* Prevalence refers to the uneven distribution of delinquency across class sectors in society. From a strain theory orientation, Cohen concluded that some groups were more anomic and moved toward deviance due to societal constraints. The delinquent-prone groups were predominantly from working-class backgrounds.

From a symbolic interactionism perspective, Cohen postulated that individuals from the bottom end of the socioeconomic scale shared difficulty in conforming to the dominant society that largely rejected them. The emergence of subcultures, then, is an alternative created by various people to deal with their mutual rejection, a collective response to shared problems. The process by which subcultures form and evolve is one of trial and error, a redefining of accepted norms likened to crowd behavior. Cohen notes that while "collective outbursts" as a way of solving problems are usually temporary and soon wane, they often succeed in establishing subcultures that, once created, assume a life of their own (1955).

The purpose of the subculture is individual benefit via interaction with the subgroup. The benefit may be material, but also psychological in terms of positive reinforcement, a necessary ingredient for continued group existence. Precisely, individuals may profit by increased self-esteem and social status. These micro-level advantages foster greater group cohesion, making the differences in value systems of the subculture and the larger society pronounced. Repudiation of societal standards and norms thus become a defining characteristic of a subculture and necessarily result in cultural conflict, often referred to as *cultural resistance* (Vetter & Silverman, 1978).

In his focus on delinquent gangs, Cohen noticed class-differentiated degrees of drive and ambition that manifested themselves in individual responsibility. Due to social structural constraints largely beyond their control, lower-class youths experience a socialization process that devalues success in the classroom, deferred gratification, long-term planning, and the cultivation of etiquette mandatory for survival in the business and social arenas (Cohen, 1955). Cohen also observed that working-class juveniles generally did not participate in wholesome leisure activity, opting instead for activities typified by physical aggression, consequently stunting the development of intellectual and social skills valued in the mainstream culture.

The overall learning experience of lower-class males leaves them ill prepared, says Cohen (1955, p. 129), to compete in a world gauged by a **middle-class measuring rod**. The deficiencies of lower-class youth are most noticeable in the classroom, where working-class youth are frequently overshadowed and belittled by their middle-class counterparts. Turning to membership in a delinquent gang is a normal adaptation to status frustration resulting from clashing cultures.

Reviews of Cohen's gang theory of delinquency have been comparatively favorable, one early exception being an *American Sociological Review* article (Kitsuse & Dietrick, 1959) that took issue with methodological considerations. It contended that Cohen failed to present adequate support for what was basically an untestable theory. In response to this criticism, others (Martin, Mutchnick, & Austin, 1990) have considered the matter an issue of perspective. The criticism of verification has merit from a positivistic viewpoint, but Cohen's book is a theoretical commentary with an objective of recognizing qualitative distinctions between juvenile and adult crime and the uneven distribution of delinquency throughout society that prompts the creation of gangs (Shoemaker, 2004).

Cloward and Ohlin's Gang Typology

Whereas a correct chronological listing of subculture theories would move from Cohen (1955) to Walter B. Miller (1958), Richard Cloward and Lloyd Ohlin's subcultural theory of delinquency (1960) is naturally paired with Cohen's, for it too is sometimes classified as a strain theory. Like most criminological theories of this era, Cloward and Ohlin focused on the delinquent behavior of gangs (Williams & McShane, 1988). Not dissimilar from Cohen, their major work, *Delinquency and Opportunity: A Theory of Delinquent Gangs* (1960), is rooted in Merton's anomie and Sutherland's differential association.

In several respects, Cloward and Ohlin further Cohen's hypothesis by offering a more detailed accounting of both subculture emergence and the nature of defiant outgroups via a typology of gangs. Often termed an *opportunity theory* (Bartol, 1980; Lilly, Cullen, & Ball, 1989; Shoemaker, 2004), the basic assumptions are that *limited and blocked economic aspirations lead to frustration and negative self-esteem* and that *these frustrations move youth to form gangs that vary in type*. The ratio of conventional and criminal values to which a juvenile is consistently exposed accounts for the differences in the character of the gangs. Cloward and Ohlin's thesis is that lower-class teenagers realize they have little chance for future success by conventional standards and consequently resort to membership in one of three types of gangs whose different activities result from a shared subcultural perspective.

The typology of gangs is a hierarchy, with the *criminal gang* at the top. Individuals reacting to frustration from failure may blame society rather than themselves. Part of this rationalization includes justifying successful illegal activity. Success models for lower-class youth are not the bankers and lawyers that middle-class youth seek to emulate, but rather thieves and drug dealers whom they observe daily. This suggests an ecological influence as described by Shaw and McKay (1942) wherein children grow into crime, which appears to be an attractive option in depressed environments.

Cloward and Ohlin note that not all have the skills and composure to integrate into the criminal gang, which screens potential members for certain abilities and willingness to conform to a code of values necessary to the unit's success. Mandatory skills include self-control, demonstrated solidarity to the group, and desire to cultivate one's criminal ability (Bartol, 1980, pp. 98–99).

The criminal gang revolves around stealing in a social context, the deviant act itself serving to positively reinforce the mutual codependence between the juvenile and the gang.

Because some strained youth are precluded from gangs that primarily steal, they congregate around violent behavior. This type of subgroup is called a *conflict gang* (Cloward & Ohlin, 1960) and is often the result of an absence of adult role models that are involved in utilitarian criminal behavior. Violent behavior, such as fighting, arson, and serious vandalism, are attributable to a sociological factor, lack of social control. A lack of interest by adults in the future success or failure of their sons and other young males in the neighborhood symbolizes rejection, the adaptation to which is "exploration of nonconformist alternatives" (Cloward & Ohlin, 1960, p. 86).

Cloward and Ohlin also observed that some youth were neither violent nor successful in criminal endeavors. Having failed in both conventional and multiple deviant sectors of society, they formed a third variety of gang, the *retreatist gang*, largely characterized by drug use (Cloward & Ohlin, 1960, p. 183). Members of this kind of comparatively unorganized gang turn to drugs as an escape from status frustration that comes from falling short of both middle-class standards and those of others within their own social class.

While all three gang types emerge in lower-socioeconomic neighborhoods, the particular form they assume is related to the degree of organization of both licit and illicit activity in an area. Although Cloward and Ohlin framed a theory that is more descriptive than Cohen's, it has been criticized for its unnaturalistic rigidity (Empey, 1982, p. 250; Lilly, Cullen, & Ball, 1989). Delinquents do not choose between theft, vandalism, or drug use through a conscious affiliation with gang types. Instead, any one of the gang types may engage in all or a combination of these behaviors.

In sum, Cloward and Ohlin followed a strain tradition to view society as a constraining mechanism that prompted lower-class juveniles to respond by forming gangs. The type of gang a frustrated youth joins depends on the opportunity structure of a neighborhood, particularly the mixture of criminal and law-abiding values held by adult role models. The delinquent acts of gang members are considered normal in that they are responses of conformity by young males to their environment.

Miller's Focal Concerns

Unlike the delinquency theories of Cohen and of Cloward and Ohlin, Walter B. Miller envisioned a pure cultural theory explaining gang delinquency. His theory, presented in an article titled "Lower-Class Culture as a Generating Milieu of Gang Delinquency" (1958), argued the existence of a distinct and observable lower-class culture. Whereas the middle class has values, the lower class has defining **focal concerns**: *trouble, toughness, smartness, excitement, fate,* and *autonomy.*

These concerns advocate the formation of street-corner gangs, while undermining the positive reinforcement needed for the development of conventional values. Smartness, for example, is a skill that warrants respect in the lower-class culture. This refers to the ability to "con" someone in real-life situations, rather than formal knowledge that is relatively inapplicable and even resented in poorer areas. The notion of fate discourages the work ethic and minimizes hope for self-improvement. Deviance is normal and to be expected in lower-class cultures because the focal concerns make conformity to criminal behavior as natural as acceptance of conventional mores for the middle class. Miller observes that juveniles accepting a preponderance of these "cultural practices which comprise essential elements of the total life pattern of lower class culture automatically violate legal norms" (1958, pp. 5–19).

Miller's theory is an explanation of delinquency situated in depressed inner cities, wherein the majority of households were headed by females. Evaluation of the theory has centered on two significant criticisms. First, some of the focal concerns contended to be exclusive to the lower class are also observable in the middle class (Shoemaker, 2004). A second and more controversial issue concerns the use of race rather than class in assessing the relationship between delinquency, matriarchal households, and an exaggerated sense of masculinity associated with physical aggression (Berger & Simon, 1974; Moynihan, 1967). Unfortunately, a focus on blacks and atypical family structure moves discussion away from the veracity of a lower-class value system to differences in racial groups.

The impact of the theories of Cohen, Cloward and Ohlin, and Miller was significant in two respects. First, they developed a general subcultural theory around what was perceived to be a timely issue. Second, the early studies as a whole focused on what was then a novel problem, the emergence of gangs. Gangs in the future were to be defined as delinquent and subcultures considered inherently deviant. Moreover, subculture became a major concept in sociology, a convenient comparative device for highlighting normative standards.

Subculture theories dominated criminological thought during the 1950s and 1960s. In stressing that deviant behavior was more or less normal for those within the subculture, several theorists built on the initial efforts of Cohen (1955), Miller (1958), Cloward and Ohlin (1960), and Wolfgang and Ferracuti (1967). New approaches developed systematic descriptions of the generating processes and patterns of delinquency, often in a gang context (Arnold, 1965; Bordua, 1961; Kobrin, Puntil, & Peluso, 1967). Policing gangs was equated with addressing the larger issue of delinquency, and research funding to address gang delinquency was plentiful. Major studies thus focused on the gang and both relied on and built on subculture explanations of delinquency. In short, the rise of the subculture perspective was aided by the circumstances of social transition, a point that also explains, in part, its decline.

The Demise of the Subcultural Perspective

By the 1960s a number of interrelated social movements (including the civil rights crusade, anti-Vietnam protest, and the counterculture) were under way. In varying degrees they expressed the same themes: distrust and defiance of authority. As the criminal justice system came to be perceived as an instrument of exploitation, theorists' attention shifted to opposing the oppressiveness of the criminal justice system (see Chapter Nine).

As bandwagon shifts to the political left transpired, labeling theory soon replaced cultural transmission as the leading approach to explaining crime (Bookin-Weiner & Horowitz, 1983). The main thrust of labeling theory was that crime and delinquency are definitions and labels that are assigned to people and events by operatives of the criminal justice system. Explaining crime and delinquency from this perspective, then, means explaining how the labeling process works and how it singles out certain people for labeling and not others.

In its more extreme formulations, labeling theory was not concerned with explaining the behavior we call crime and delinquency because criminals and delinquents were not assumed to differ very much in their behavior from other people. Rather, the real difference is said to be the degree of vulnerability to the labeling activities of the criminal justice system.

During this period of interest in labeling, theoretically oriented research on the relationship between crime and culture languished but did not disappear. More moderate versions of labeling theory propelled some research (such as research on gang behavior and emphasis on the role of official processing and labeling in the development of that behavior), but the leading cause of crime and delinquency was considered the criminal justice system itself (Armstrong & Wilson, 1973; Werthman, 1967). Specifically, criminal and delinquent behavior was portrayed as a rational and justified response to social inequality and class oppression (Bookin, 1980).

Much of the contemporary literature of the 1970s, not just on gangs but on social problems generally, was not only indifferent to subculture theory but actively opposed to it. This literature included works such as Chambliss's "The Saints and the Roughnecks" (1973), which emphasized a conflict perspective that viewed the subculture perspective as too conservative. Social control was deemed reactionary because crime and delinquency were considered direct, reasonable, and even justifiable adaptations to injustice.

The rise of social control theory (see Hirschi, 1969) did not seriously factor into the subculture perspective either, though seemingly well-suited to do so (Bookin-Weiner & Horowitz, 1983; Vold & Bernard, 1986). The central elements of attachment to others, degrees of commitment to conventionality, daily routine, and belief in a moral order speak to why subcultures exist and have implications for criminal behavior therein (see Chapter Seven). Ensuing research interests moved toward macro-level determinants of crime and further away from culture and group behavior. Consequently, subcultures were largely ignored until the mid-1980s, when they were seriously connected with gang-related drug and violence problems (Curry & Spergel, 1988).

While historical developments set into motion a chain of events that moved criminological theorizing away from the subculture, the theory was further marred by paradigm shifts in social science research methodology. The rise of positivism delivered subculture theory a would-be deathblow. There was suddenly a disjuncture between the strategy of observation-based data gathering used by most subcultural theorists and a newer preferred theoretical-methodological symmetry involving variable assignment, measurement, and analysis congruent with causality as established by levels of statistical correlation. Critics of subculture theory (see Ball-Rokeach, 1973; Kitsuse & Dietrick, 1959; Kornhauser, 1978) focused on the growing belief that acceptable science must subscribe to particular precepts that subculture explanations did not meet.

The cultural transmission theories could not be adequately tested through the dominant variable analysis methodology that largely defines what is and is not considered acceptable social science. Most central to this discussion is the difficulty that social scientists experienced concerning how to adequately measure subculture and its effects. Another fundamental criticism concerned the problem of *tautological reasoning,* that is, an unclear separation of cause and effect. Does subculture (as an independent variable) generate crime (the dependent variable), or vice versa? For many, the inability to answer this question in terms of statistical clarity moved attention away from the causal effects of the cultural transmission of criminogenic values.

Subcultures of Violence and the Rerise of the Cultural Perspective

A main reason that cultural transmission theory survived intellectual extinction is the work of Wolfgang and Ferracuti (1967), who extended the subcultural perspective beyond a gang context. They argued that homicide resulted from acceptance of a value system that endorsed violence, observing that "Groups with the highest rates of homicide have in the most intense degree a subculture of violence" (p. 78). *Subcultures of violence* were identified by Wolfgang and Ferracuti throughout the social strata. Subcultures are identifiable at the small-group or micro level—for example, delinquent and criminal gangs. They are also recognized at larger social levels, often certain communities labeled "bad parts of town" or even an entire region of the country such as the American South.

Wolfgang and Ferracuti's attention to regional variation in high rates of violence and particularly homicide prompted criminologists to focus on the American South, where violence was far more commonplace. Accordingly, *southern subculture of violence theory* emerged and revitalized the cultural transmission approach to explaining crime. Criminologists have debated whether disproportionately high rates of southern violence stem from cultural or structural properties. Those making the structural argument have focused on the high level of poverty in the region that, when coupled with the related factors of crowded households and a hot climate, seemingly explain frustration and aggravated conditions ripe for violent outbursts. While these factors apply to southern settings, they are also applicable to other areas, such as the Southwest, and thus fail to adequately account for the southern crime phenomenon.

Cultural theorists point, instead, to the South's retention of a distinct identity that characterizes a subsociety or general subculture (Gastil, 1971; Hackney, 1969; Huff-Corzine, Corzine, & Moore, 1991). The high value placed on autonomy, reputation, the glorification of military skills, high levels of gun ownership, and, particularly, the South's history foster a regional subculture of violence. The South's history as a frontier region in the 1700s and 1800s necessitated independence and informal social control realized through vigilante justice. The practice of slavery, the custom of dispute resolution through dueling in the upper class and family feuds in the lower class, high levels of gun ownership, and, most significantly, subscription to a culture of honor came to characterize a distinct culture (Reed, 1972). The southern subculture of violence theorists argued that southern culture and the premium placed on honor moved southerners to approve of violence—but not under all circumstances. Violence is only considered a normal response, and thus more likely, in response to challenge of one's honor and in defensive contexts.

Nisbett and Cohen (1996) have recently presented a **culture of honor** theory that addresses southern crime and extends the general knowledge base on the causal effects of subcultural value systems. They observe that the South is heavily populated by the Scots-Irish who primarily occupy the highland areas of the region, also where the majority of homicides occurs. These groups are physically isolated in remote, rural settings, very homogeneous, and experience little migration in or out, and their social attitudes and standards of behavior are less challenged by changing times or outside ideas. It is contended that the same values of their Celtic ancestors—independence, close-knit kinship groups, defense of personal and family honor, and freedom were transmitted from one generation to the next to generate contemporary values. By comparing levels of violence across lowland, rolling hills, and mountainous areas, the culture of honor theory illustrates that violence is most common in places where the high value placed on honor has been least diffused. Researchers further note that in such places the criminal law reflects ideas that endorse violence, such as support for the death penalty.

Criminologists are considering the effects of migration on the southern subculture of violence, generally concluding that greater exposure to outside influence will weaken beliefs and values that support violence. It is uncertain if this is altogether correct, however, due to the fundamental subcultural assumption of cultural conflict. As traditional southern attitudes and practices begin to erode somewhat proportionally to immigration and the aging of older generations, those still subscribing to the traditional ways will likely "solidify the core" as a reaction to outside pressures and challenges to their way of life.

Criminologists have certainly recognized the importance of youth subcultures in a more general manner recently, largely due to the well-known Columbine High School shootings. Whereas previous attention to culture and crime was limited to lower-class criminality, gangs, or the American South, the Columbine incident portrayed the gothic subculture as a facilitating context in the tragedy.

Elijah Anderson's *Code of the Street* (1999) is perhaps the foremost contemporary statement on subculture and crime. This work interestingly focuses on lower-class and inner-city criminality like the 1950s cultural transmission theories, arguing that it is largely a function of a subcultural norming process. Like Miller (1958), Anderson suggests that distinct culturally-based values or elements generate crime and, like Cohen (1955), he suggests that a lack of competitiveness in conventional arenas leads to reaction formations involving and valuing criminal behavior. The street culture or "code" prescribes violent responses to personal attacks and shows of disrespect. The fundamental assumption that defines the code is that no sign of weakness can be displayed, for doing so invites additional attacks. A major element of this logic is status insecurity, which, similar to Miller's focal concerns, is specific to the lower class. Lacking affluence, occupational status, and professional prestige, young males in depressed socioeconomic urban areas believe that physical aggression is vital to their survival while also bolstering their self-esteem and reputation in the neighborhood.

Anderson's subcultural theory is more complex than the 1950s versions in that, while illustrating deviant values and a socialization process favorable to crime, adoption of the code is adaptation to the immediate environment. Accordingly, the "code" largely applies to public life but carries over to private settings only for those most alienated and socially isolated within high-crime communities. The code is problematic beyond its advocacy of violent retaliation, promoting a "generalized contempt" for the wider society on the perception that the society carries a mutual contempt for inner-city youth. Though based on ethnography conducted during the 1990s, Anderson's attention to a street code is defined, partially, in comparison to a "decent" moral code of the inner city, which is a prosocial and conventional reference point akin to Cohen's utilization of the middle-class measuring rod. Whereas Cohen used the measuring-rod metaphor to accentuate differences between social classes, Anderson's contribution should be credited with calling attention to value differences specific to criminality within the lower social class.

SUMMARY

According to learning and cultural transmission theories, crime, like all behavior, results from a socialization process that encourages crime. Learning theories focus on the social processes wherein youth are exposed to behavioral definitions favorable to crime. Role models and peer groups are important facilitators in the learning process, reflecting the significance of differential association. Cultural transmission theories focus less on the learning process and more on the values characterizing the (sub)culture; the subculture both provides a context in which learning occurs and shapes what is learned through establishing normative behavior.

Social learning theories have become increasingly complex, with Akers's version being the most general learning-based explanation of crime with strong empirical support. Subcultural theories emerged as a major force in criminology during the 1950s and 1960s, were largely ignored during the 1970s, and have reemerged since. Cultural theories have primarily focused on lower-class culture, especially in urban and gang contexts. Attention to subcultures of violence are applicable outside urban settings, most notably the southern subculture of violence thesis emphasizing a code of honor prescribing violent retaliation to threats and insults. Most recently, Anderson's *Code of the Streets* reiterates a code of honor–based value system while returning to the applicability of the culture and crime relationship to urban crime.

KEY TERMS

cultural conflict a repudiation of other groups' societal standards and norms fostering greater group cohesion as a reaction formation ideologically rooted in cultural resistence; conflictual processes typically accentuate differences between groups as a justificatory reference point for group validation

cultural transmission theory a theory that contends that group values, historical customs, and the ethnocentric nature of social learning are intergenerationally transferred normative standards; values that accentuate the role of violence are associated with gangs, the lower class, the American South, inner-city minorities, and fringe social groups

culture of honor a value system of requisite retaliatory and defensive violence for protection and defense of social status threats and personal insults; contextually based in family and immediate group interaction; often identified with southern culture and high violent crime rates

differential association a concept developed by Edwin Sutherland that emphasizes the group nature of delinquency as characterized by the interaction of similarly suited individuals, particularly those with severed ties to conventional social institutions and practices

focal concerns Miller's subcultural elements that combine to characterize lower-class culture; considered less conceptually sophisticated than middle-class values; these elements (smartness, toughness, trouble, autonomy, fate, and excitement) condition the behavioral norms that define a value system condoning and encouraging crime

imitation   mimicking observed behavior, often without much understanding of direct consequences

learning theories   a strand of criminological theory emphasizing the socialization processes involving level of definitions favorable to crime versus conventional definitions; reference group, subculture, and environment are important, additionally relevant factors; differential association is a fundamental assumption; Akers is one of the leading contemporary learning theorists

middle-class measuring rod   a metaphor coined by Albert Cohen, a leading pioneer of the subcultural approach, that references middle-class values, norms, and expected standards of academic, social, and civic achievement against which lower-class youth experience status frustration and strain that is reduced through crime and gang affiliation

DISCUSSION QUESTIONS

1. What is meant by the term *differential association,* and how is this concept significant to the learning process?

2. Why doesn't everyone who is socialized in a deviant subcultural setting become criminal?

3. How does Cohen's middle-class measuring rod have current applicability for lower-class criminality as a reaction formation to status frustration?

4. Do you think W. B. Miller's focal concerns are useful for explaining lower-class criminality today?

5. Will migration patterns in the American South lessen or worsen violent crime, according to the logic put forth by the culture of honor thesis?

REFERENCES

Anderson, E. (1999). *Code of the street: Decency, violence and the moral life of the inner city.* New York: Norton.

Andrews, D. A., & Bonta, J. (1998). *Psychology of criminal conduct* (2nd ed.) Cincinnati, OH: Anderson.

Armstrong, G., & Wilson, M. (1973). City politics and deviance amplification. In I. Taylor & L. Taylor (Eds.), *Politics and deviance.* New York: Penguin Books.

Arnold, W. R. (1965). The concept of the gang. *Sociological Quarterly, 7,* 59–75.

Ball-Rokeach, S. J. (1973). Values and violence: A test of the subculture of violence thesis. *American Sociological Review, 38,* 736–749.

Bandura, A. (1962). *Social learning through interaction.* Lincoln: University of Nebraska Press.

Bartol, C. R. (1980). *Criminal behavior: A psychosocial approach.* Upper Saddle River, NJ: Prentice Hall.

Berger, A. S., & Simon, W. (1974). Black families and the Moynihan Report: A research evaluation. *Social Problems, 22,* 145–161.

Bookin, H. (August, 1980). *The gangs that didn't go straight.* Paper presented to the Society for the Study of Social Problems, New York.

Bookin-Weiner, H., & Horowitz, R. (1983). The end of the youth gang: Fad or fact? *Criminology, 21,* 585–602.

Bordua, D. J. (1961). Delinquent subcultures: Sociological interpretations of gang delinquency. *Annals of the American Academy of Social Science, 338,* 119–136.

Chambliss, W. J. (1973). The saints and the roughnecks. *Society, 11,* 1, 24–31.

Cloward, R. A., & Ohlin, L. E. (1960). *Delinquency and opportunity: A theory of delinquent gangs.* Glencoe, IL: The Free Press.

Cohen, A. K. (1955). *Delinquent boys: The culture of the gang.* Glencoe, IL: Free Press.

The criminologist. (1992). *Official Newsletter of the American Society of Criminology, 17,* 6, 13.

Curry, G. D., & Spergel, I. A. (1988). Gang homicide, delinquency and community. *Criminology, 26,* 3, 381–406.

Empey, L. (1982). *American delinquency: Its meaning and construction.* Homewood, IL: Dorsey.

Gastil, R. (1971). Homicide and a regional culture of violence. *American Sociological Review, 36,* 412–427.

Hackney, S. (1969). Southern violence. *American Historical Review, 74,* 906–925.

Hirschi, T. (1969). *Causes of delinquency.* Berkeley: University of California Press.

Huff-Corzine, L., Corzine, J., & Moore, D. (1991). Deadly connections: Culture, poverty, and the direction of lethal violence. *Social Forces, 69*(3), 715–732.

Kitsuse, J., & Dietrick, D. C. (1959). Delinquent boys: A critique. *American Sociological Review, 24,* 208–215.

Kobrin, S., Puntil, J., & Peluso, E. (1967). Criteria of status among street groups. *Journal of Research in Crime and Delinquency, 4,* 1, 98–118.

Kornhauser, R. R. (1978). *Social sources of delinquency:* An appraisal of analytic models. Chicago: University of Chicago Press.

Lilly, J. R., Cullen, F. T., & Ball, R. A. (1989). *Criminological theory: Context and consequences.* Newbury Park, CA: Sage.

Lynch, M. J., & Groves, W. B. (1986). *A primer in radical criminology.* New York: Harrow & Heston.

Martin, R., Mutchnick, R. J., & Austin, W. T. (1990). *Criminological thought: Pioneers past and present.* New York: Macmillan.

Miller, W. B. (1958). Lower-class culture as a generating milieu of gang delinquency. *Journal of Social Issues, 14* (3), 5–19.

Moynihan, D. P. (1967). *The Negro family: The case for national action.* Washington, DC: Government Printing Office.

Nisbett, R. E., & Cohen, D. (1996). *Culture of honor: The psychology of violence in the South.* Boulder, CO: Westview Press.

Reed, J. S. (1972). *The enduring South: Subcultural persistence in mass society.* Lexington, MA: Lexington Books.

Reid, S. T. (1990). *Crime and criminology.* Fort Worth, TX: Holt, Rinehart & Winston.

Shaw, C. R., & McKay, H. D. (1942). *Juvenile delinquency and urban areas.* Chicago: University of Chicago Press.

Shoemaker, D. J. (2004). *Theories of delinquency: An examination of explanations of delinquent behavior* (5th ed.). New York: Oxford University Press.

Vetter, H. J., & Silverman, I. J. (1978). *The nature of crime.* Philadelphia: Saunders.

Vold, G. B., & Bernard, T. J. (1986). *Theoretical criminology.* (3rd ed.). New York: Oxford University Press.

Werthman, C. (1967). The function of social definitions in the development of delinquent careers. In *Becoming delinquent: Young offenders and the correctional process.* P. G. Garabedian & D. C. Gibbons (Eds.), Chicago: Aldine.

Williams, F. P., III, & McShane, M. D. (1988). *Criminological theory.* Upper Saddle River, NJ: Prentice Hall.

Wolfgang, M. E., & Ferracuti, F. (1967). *The subculture of violence: Towards an integrated theory in criminology.* London: Tavistock.

Wolfgang, M. E., Figlio, R. M., & Sellin, T. (1972). *Delinquency in a birth cohort.* Chicago: University of Chicago Press.

CHAPTER 7

STRAIN THEORIES OF CRIME

To think that crime is more likely to occur when someone fails to get something he or she wants, or else when placed under a great deal of stress, would make a great deal of sense. For instance, students in financial difficulties might feel frustrated and turn to stealing food, beer, or clothes from their roommates. The stress of taking exams and having to find a job after graduation makes drinking alcohol—a *lot* of alcohol—appealing, in order to alleviate the stress. Strain theories, the focus of this chapter, generally make the case that if people get frustrated in their desires, or experience stress, they will be more likely to commit crime.

Strain theories are among the older criminological theories in the literature, and it says something that they still hold currency for today. Robert Merton, a sociologist, formulated a theory of "anomie" (later called "strain theory" by others) during the 1930s, and in the subsequent decades his version of strain theory has seen many refinements (see Cloward & Ohlin, 1960; Cohen, 1955). After a long period as the dominant and influential theory of crime, strain theory waned in importance during the 1970s and 1980s before being revived by such criminologists as Robert Agnew (1992) and Steven Messner and Richard Rosenfeld (1994). Over the years, the various versions of strain theory have received considerable testing, and Agnew's version of strain theory is one of the most frequently tested theories in the literature today.

WHAT DO STRAIN THEORIES ASSUME?

You may have noticed that some theories, such as deterrence and control theories, allege that people are naturally inclined to commit crime and that the reason many people don't is because they are under some sort of restraint. That is, they are afraid for some reason to commit crime or else are unable to do so. In this case, we don't need frustration or stress to explain the causation of crime since people are naturally inclined to do it anyway (or put another way, these theories might say that everyone is pretty much continually frustrated, and whether they act on any given frustration depends on whether the advantages outweigh the costs). Some other theories, however, say that crime is not natural to human beings. Rather, something externally imposed on us must push, prod, or compel us to commit crime. Strain theories take the latter approach, saying that we wouldn't normally commit crime but do so because of external circumstances that place us in a situation we don't like. That is, we generally would like to be law-abiding and live in the manner society would expect us to; however, we encounter obstacles that prevent us from fulfilling this wish. For example, I would like to obey the speed limit, but the construction I ran into earlier will make me late for class if I don't hurry to make up for the lost time. The obstacles we encounter, or else our inability to satisfy our desires, are what push us to commit crime.

While all this talk of stress and inability to get desires satisfied may sound psychological, strain theorists do not usually use ideas originating in psychology. Rather, strain theorists explain how the frustration of our wants leads to crime using sociological concepts like *anomie,* coined by the French sociologist Emile Durkheim (1897/1951). *Anomie* comes from the French word *anomique,* meaning roughly "normlessness." Durkheim believed that people naturally thrive in societies where their desires and wants are socially well regulated. For example, everyone may have a desire for sex, but social institutions such as the church can regulate when and where sexual activity is appropriate, and thereby imposes a limit on that particular desire. When a lack of adequate regulation or social guidance exists because of some breakdown or malfunction in society (that is, there is a state of normlessness), people are more likely to deviate. Durkheim only emphasized the link between anomie and suicide, but strain theorists building from his work suggested that a lack of adequate social regulation, such as regulation of economic desires, leads to crime as well. More specifically, early strain theorists such as Robert Merton argued that anomie was caused by poor integration of the goals of a particular culture with the means available for achieving these goals, as well as with the existing social structure. Culture fails to set limits, and the social structure fails to adequately assist people in achieving culturally valued objectives. All this may sound dry and abstract for now, but the theory will make pretty good sense as we look at it. For now, let us look at Merton's theory and discuss each of the pieces that— working together—lead to crime. Namely, we will focus on the American Dream (or, the culture) and the American social class system. Later in this chapter, we will consider some of the revisions to strain theory by later theorists in response to empirical research and further thinking.

MERTON'S STRAIN THEORY AND ITS VARIANTS

The American Dream

The **American Dream** represents a starting point for some strain theorists to explain why America has the highest crime rates of any industrialized country. Merton was the first to look closely at the "American Dream," which he believed placed excessive emphasis on material and monetary success and too little emphasis on the "proper" way of achieving success. Precisely what our *culture* emphasizes is important, because individual people are not naturally capable of working out the value of material objects on their own; people need the help of culture. For instance, we are not born with any desire for money and the material trappings of success. Money, after all, can't be eaten, so it—in and of itself—doesn't satisfy perfectly natural hunger. Neither is it likely that infants will know anything about the vast difference in prestige between a BMW 545i (a very expensive imported sports sedan with a lot of name cachet) and a Daewoo Nubira (a very inexpensive, very basic automobile). So the fact that we take for granted that money is nevertheless important and that there *is* a difference in prestige among automobiles is because of our culture, and the American Dream is a convenient label for American culture. The aspects of American culture that are relevant for crime concern (1) the "goals," or what we are socialized to want, and (2) the "means," or the rules we're expected to follow while striving to achieve the goals.

Let us first look at the goals. In order to understand what Americans are socialized to desire, one place to begin might be to focus on what the media tells us we're supposed to desire. With few notable exceptions, prime-time sitcoms and "reality" programs show people who live in stylishly appointed houses or high-rise apartments, sport designer clothing, and are fashionably groomed in the latest trendy hairstyles. Many television commercials peddle big-ticket items that only a tiny fraction of the population even has a remote chance of affording. Yet ownership of prestigious material things, such as clothes and cars, is a sign that we've "made it," and many Americans will stretch their finances to the breaking point and beyond to imitate the style of the successful, to advertise their success to others, and to make themselves feel good. Other Americans aren't there yet, and do everything they can to make their dream an eventual reality. Regardless of whether one can actually achieve the American Dream, our culture bestows on everyone the desire to imitate the style of the successful. It is interesting to note that the alleged materialism of American society is not a recent phenomenon; Merton, working during the 1930s, made the same characterization of society that critics make about today (that is, Merton wrote during the Great Depression, the period when nearly 25 percent of the population was out of work and when Americans were supposedly happy just to have enough to eat and a roof over their heads).

Besides socializing us about what to want in life, the American Dream also specifies how one should go about achieving success. Americans are expected to work hard, be honest, defer gratification, become educated, and so forth. By going to college and not slacking off, you are following the ideals set forth about how one is supposed to go about achieving the American Dream.

One is also expected to be competitive and to stand out in front of one's peers. If you get angry with yourself when you score a 96 on a test and somebody else gets a 98, then you have a pretty good idea of how the American Dream works. Should one play by these rules, then the eventual ability to enjoy material success should be all but assured.

So far, so good. But the problem, as Merton saw it, was that the goals of American society are emphasized at the expense of encouraging people to follow the rules. Put more simply, our society stresses that the only important thing is that you are successful—if you fail gracefully (read: by trying hard and following the rules) you're still a failure. There are plenty of easy examples of this to which you might be able to relate. Professional football aficionados will recall that the Buffalo Bills had some of the strongest teams during the early 1990s, but they also lost every Super Bowl game they had ever played in. Therefore, the Bills are not remembered for destroying opponents during the regular season, but rather—if anyone thinks of them much at all—for the fact that they couldn't win the "Big One." The New England Patriots, on the other hand, had very similar success during the regular football season, but they are now referred to as a "dynasty" for having won, as of this writing, three of the past four Super Bowls. Clearly, winning is very important, and it is not enough to merely make a good showing if the result is not victory. Given this emphasis on winning and the very little to be gained by following the rules, there is a natural tendency to shift to "winning at all costs." When only the results matter to us, then we follow the rules only as long as it is convenient for us to do so; as soon as they become an impediment on the way to the American Dream, they get jettisoned. In short, while the culture itself does not encourage us to be criminal, the seeds of crime are present and are likely to bear fruit when one is unable to achieve the American Dream. As Merton (1968, p. 200) wrote, things we normally consider "virtue"—such as ambition—can lead to "vice," such as deviant behavior.

The American Social Structure

Merton thus turned to what the impediments to the American Dream might be. The American Dream promises equal opportunity for all. American history is full of examples of people who raised themselves out of the dirt to become millionaires—if real-life successes were not enough, there were also Horatio Alger stories and other similar American-produced fiction to reinforce the belief that *anyone* can achieve the American Dream as long as one has the necessary pluck and ability. The only impediment our society acknowledges is variation in individual ability, and a lack of ability does not excuse the failure to achieve the American Dream. Some of us are smarter, more clever, harder working, but those who lack these skills are viewed with scorn because they failed to take advantage of opportunities.

Unfortunately, reality is crueler to the majority of us. Depending on where you are in the socioeconomic structure, according to Merton, your road to success can be absurdly easy or impossible. Think of the advantages that rich folks have on the way to success, compared to those people with less economic wherewithal. Rich people have the luxury of not having to practice triage with their budgets—for example, they need not ask themselves, "Do I go to college and get the credentials I need for a better job, or do I buy groceries?" Rich people do not have to worry so much about such dilemmas. Politicians are also more likely to listen to rich people, and thus make laws that are to their advantage. Moreover, rich families have useful social connections that allow them to place even their most mediocre children in the finest colleges and universities, as well as in business and in government. Poor families, on the other hand, are unlikely to have wealthy or influential patrons who are eagerly willing to look out for them, since such families are unable to reciprocate in any consequential way. Merton thus believed that the reality of inequality in America was perhaps the biggest impediment to achieving the American Dream. Things might not be so bad, however, if only the poor had lower and more realistic expectations; however, the American Dream (the need to have expensive stuff), according to Merton, resonates across the *entire* economic spectrum of our society. The poor, like the rich, are socialized to desire pricey cars, plasma TVs, nice watches, and fancy clothes—all of the material trappings of the good life. But the already rich are in the best position to achieve success, while the poor labor at a serious disadvantage where their success is not guaranteed even after enormous effort, honesty, and dedication. People with doctorate degrees do work as cashiers at Wal-Mart. In view of this unfortunate reality, Merton hypothesized that a disproportionate amount of strain falls on the lower social classes.

Responses to Strain

When faced with an obstacle to achieving one's desires, anomie (or strain) occurs and one has to respond to it somehow. Merton proposed that there were five ways people can cope with strain.

Conformity.   In **conformity**, the individual continues to strive for the American Dream as well as obey the rules of society. For example, pretend that you sent an application to be CEO of a major company. Obviously, being a CEO would go a long way toward achieving the American Dream; however, you later received a letter informing you that you were not selected for the job because only Harvard Business School graduates will do for them and you're not good enough. You thus followed legitimate channels toward success and failed. If you continue to strive for similar jobs, sending applications and following all of the rules and working hard, then you have responded to the strain through conformity. Merton believed that most Americans experiencing strain continued to conform.

Innovation.   This response strain is somewhat misleadingly titled. We normally think of **innovation** as a good thing, and something to encourage; however, Merton uses this term to describe those who want to achieve the American Dream but who have rejected the "accepted" and legal means for doing so. Put differently, let's say you are part of a team playing soccer and you lose playing fair. Rather than continuing to play fair, you decide to break the rules in order to improve your chances of winning. In other words, in response to the strain, you continue to strive for success, but no longer employ the socially approved means for doing so. One would expect that crime occurring because of innovation would improve the economic standing of the criminal. The best examples of the innovator would be the white-collar criminal, the "robber barons" of the nineteenth century, and con artists.

Ritualism.   After experiencing strain, some individuals lose their ambition and merely hope to hold on to what little they have. Those who employ **ritualism** still exert effort, but merely for dogmatic reasons (it's all they know) or out of habit; they no longer really strive for the American Dream or believe that their effort will lead to any greater rewards. The lifelong bureaucrat, tired of his or her work and life, might be one example. Ritualists do not commit crime.

Retreatism.   Followers of **retreatism** abandon both the American Dream and the effort expected of citizens. After experiencing strain, their purpose is simply to escape, often through alcohol or drug use. If you have a roommate or a significant other who has no job and who sits on the sofa all day watching *MacGyver* reruns and drinking beer, then you have a good sense of what a retreatist is like.

Rebellion.   The rebel rejects the American system and replaces it with a different set of goals and means. In a sense, these are innovators of a different sort, as their purpose is to change the system. Albert Cohen, for instance, talked about how strained lower-class teenage boys reject the American Dream and replace it with the anti-American Dream (which is basically anything that might offend middle-class sensitivities). The **rebellion** response can be seen in revolutionaries and militants. Rebels may commit crime, but the crime is not intended to promote the economic interests of the rebel so much as to advance society toward the ends the rebel sees as legitimate.

Later Work on Merton's Theory

While Merton's theory of social structure and anomie is widely cited in criminology and sociology, it did not receive much further attention for approximately two decades after its publication in 1938. The reason was more political and ideological than scientific. Murray (1984) observed that poverty, to thinkers in the midtwentieth century, was wholly a product of individual abilities and deficiencies. By the 1960s, however, the idea that individuals are not necessarily at fault for their poverty, but that the system creates and maintains inequality, began to gain momentum among scholars. Indeed, the civil rights movement borrowed from these ideas, arguing that the poverty of minorities had less to do with inherent lack of ability than a system designed to guarantee that minorities have virtually no chance to succeed on their own. Strain theory then began to garner considerable attention. Another lesson here is that many good or interesting ideas in criminology go unnoticed, sometimes for years, not because these ideas were found scientifically inadequate, but because the changing political and ideological landscape made them suddenly fashionable.

In 1960, the sociologists Richard Cloward and Lloyd Ohlin proposed one of the major extensions of Merton's theory, what they called "differential opportunity" theory, which considers access to delinquent opportunities as well as legitimate opportunities. This underlying premise of Cloward and Ohlin's work—that delinquency requires opportunities—certainly makes sense if you think about it. One of the authors spent some time in Craighead County in northeast Arkansas. This particular area had a large number of tiny farming hamlets seemingly isolated from the rest of the world. One of these is a little place in the middle of an endless expanse of rice and cotton fields named Egypt, Arkansas, which consists of a single street scattered with tiny houses and mobile homes landscaped primarily with rusty appliances. There was also a rather dirty-looking fire station and a couple of other buildings in varying degrees of neglect. To be sure, this is not the place where it would be possible to achieve the American Dream through legitimate means, as a visual inspection of the town suggested that there was no sign of any economic activity—even the modest economic activity afforded by a gas station or convenience store. At the same time, it is difficult to imagine how one could achieve the American Dream through illegitimate means, either, since the monetary value of everything in the town—if stolen—would not afford one much of a lifestyle. In view of the limited options for success, criminal or otherwise, in many areas of our country, how can one cope with strain arising from the failure to achieve the American Dream?

Cloward and Ohlin attempted to extend Merton's theory by answering this question. They indicated that the community in which one lives determines the kind and degree of crime present. Economically beneficial crimes require skill and training and are more likely to occur in communities that provide suitable learning environments, such as the presence of criminal role models. Cloward and Ohlin clearly drew these insights from Sutherland's (1947) differential association theory and other work (see Sutherland, 1937) and integrated it with Merton's version of strain theory. The two sociologists also sought to answer the problem of why individuals selected one adaptation to strain over another.

Three criminal subcultures can emerge, depending on the environmental circumstances. The **criminal subculture** comes about when there are no opportunities for legitimate gain, but illegitimate opportunities are still open—that is, strained residents can respond with innovation. Youth gangs form in order to perform income-generating crimes, such as selling drugs, hustling stolen merchandise, and so forth. Other forms of organized crime exist, and youth who are blocked off from the American Dream can consult the criminal element and receive training and mentorship that will allow them to live the high life through crime. If you are affluent, then you might have access to the executive positions necessary to execute white-collar crimes. The **violent subculture** emerges in locations like Egypt, Arkansas, where strain exists but there are no means—legitimate or illegitimate—to deal with the strain. Cloward and Ohlin's theory would indicate that it is highly improbable that an individual from this town, or from another area lacking in income-generating criminal opportunities, will become a wealthy drug distributor or a corrupt chief executive officer of a major company. Consequently, the crime occurring among those in the subculture tends to be of a violent sort—when status cannot be earned through money, being tough becomes the way to have a reputation. Borrowing from the work of Shaw and McKay (1942) on social disorganization theory, Cloward and Ohlin reasoned that the violent subculture is most likely to be an adaptation in disorganized communities. Finally, there is the **retreatist subculture**, for the double failures who were ineffective at achieving the American dream through crime or conformity. As Merton indicated, the retreatists self-medicate their strain with alcohol and drugs. In short, the opportunity circumstances surrounding where one lives go a long way toward determining what adaptation one takes in adjusting to strain.

Empirical Support

Merton's theory, and some of the subsequent updates, generally suggests a certain image of the criminal offender. Criminal offenders are essentially ambitious people—made so by the American Dream—who are no different from upper-class people in terms of their natural abilities, but who are denied material success because of their disadvantageous location in the social structure. Because the social structure gets in the way of material success for the lower class, one might thus reasonably expect that crime would be heavily concentrated among the lower class. Additionally, in areas where a criminal subculture could form, crime should be economically rewarding. As noted earlier, this theory made a great deal of sense to criminologists starting in the 1960s, and was influential in both criminology and in policy.

The theory did have its critics. Some questioned whether American culture was as single-minded as strain theorists allege. For instance, many of you might look with disgust, rather than admiration or envy, upon the multimillion-dollar salaries of professional athletes or corporate executives. Others (see Pfohl, 1985) felt that the contradiction in American society between the culture and the class structure was a worthwhile beginning, but that Merton and others never addressed the question of how this contradiction formed and why it continues. In other words, why America, of all places, and why has America been unsuccessful at tackling the problem?

Critics have also cited scientific research as a reason why strain theory might not be an adequate explanation of crime. It may seem strange to us, but strain theory was not subjected to extensive empirical testing until the late 1960s (that is, nearly three decades after Merton first published the theory). The growth of self-report surveys at this time suggested that the causes of crime were very different from those envisioned by strain theorists. First, social class turned out to be a very weak predictor of criminal activity, apparently refuting the notion that the American social structure was a key facilitator of high crime (see Hirschi, 1969). That is, these studies showed that the poor are only marginally more likely to be delinquent than the rich. These studies also found that criminals lack ambition, and their educational achievements tend to substantially trail those of their peers within the same social class. Moreover, research has found that crime in fact does not pay very well, offering more in the way of short-term gratification than long-term financial gain (Gottfredson & Hirschi, 1990). Strain theorists would suggest, for example, that offenders steal beer in order to sell it and make money. Instead, it appears that offenders steal beer in order to drink it, obviously negating any long-term economic advantage they might have obtained. And even crimes like burglary and robbery net the offender very little from fences and pawnshops. Through the 1970s, criminologists began to believe that strain theory was wrong, and they consequently abandoned it for many years.

More recently, however, scholars have begun to argue whether this research has adequately tested strain theory (see Bernard, 1984). For instance, do people who feel that they are underpaid relative to their skill and effort tend to commit more crime? Much research on strain seldom considers whether individuals actually experience strain. More recently, however, researchers have continued the strain tradition by developing other frameworks, some of which we discuss next.

AGNEW'S GENERAL STRAIN THEORY

During the early 1990s, however, Robert Agnew revived the concept of strain as a cause of crime and formulated a theory he termed "general strain theory" that would become one of the currently influential theories of criminal behavior. Earlier versions of strain theory emphasized how people are socialized to want something—typically material success—but are unable to get what they want. Agnew expanded strain theory beyond this. Agnew's theory broadens the range of the causes of strain and departs from Merton's adaptations to strain, developing more general means of coping.

Types of Strain

Agnew's theory expands the sources of strain from one cause to three. The *failure to achieve positively valued goals,* which is a staple of earlier strain theories, is present here. While earlier strain theories emphasized the failure to achieve the American Dream, Agnew's theory focuses less on culture than on the individual. We may experience strain when we fail to win the approval of a person whom we desire. This example has nothing necessarily to do with economic advancement, but is nevertheless a source of pain and frustration that might lead to crime. Indeed, the music industry has long profited from articulating into sometimes disturbing song the emotions resulting from failed romances and consequent deviant responses. Examples of these run the gamut from stalking (The Police, "Every Breath You Take") to murder (The Beatles, "Run for Your Life"). Other examples of this type of strain might include not making the football team or even not getting to work on time. People may break the law to get what they desire, such as by speeding to make up lost time getting to work.

Strain might also occur when *something positively valued is removed from us.* Imagine how you might feel if your teacher told you that the A you received on a test was a mistake, and that your actual grade was a D! You would likely resent the teacher for taking away your A, and would justifiably feel a great deal of stress and frustration. More generally, this type of strain can occur when parents take away the privileges of their children, when one gets fired from work, or when a relationship ends. Responses to having something desirable taken away would be aimed at restoring whatever had been lost. Conventional responses to the preceding scenarios might include starting a new relationship or getting a new job. There are deviant responses as well. Children have been known to sneak out of their houses at night in response to being grounded by their parents, for instance. The movie *Office Space* details how one employee dealt with his termination (and, worse still, the loss of his red Swingline stapler) by burning down his employer's building.

Strain also occurs if people impose on us *stimuli that we find noxious.* Most people resent it if others ask them to do something, such as clean their room, take on an extra assignment, or take a test. Behaviors in response to this strain would tend to emphasize removing the individual from this situation. For instance, a noncriminal response might be to negotiate with a demanding teacher for reduced work or extended deadlines. Crimes also can deal with noxious situations. For instance, one can shut up another person who is being insulting by punching that individual in the mouth.

In short, Agnew reasoned that strain occurs for more reasons that just expecting something and not getting it. Because Agnew's theory does not focus on social structure or make claims about what Americans want, it is applicable to a broader range of crimes than just those committed by the lower classes for their own economic advantage. Crime nevertheless has a purpose to it, being intended to alleviate the strain in some way. We discuss coping with strain in greater detail next, as strain need not necessarily lead to a criminal response.

Types of Coping

Like other strain theories, Agnew's version does not assert that crime is a necessary consequence of stress. Many of us feel bad, angry, and frustrated, and many people are pretty much miserable most of the time. And yet they do not always turn to crime. As Merton's strain theory suggests, coping with strain can lead to legal as well as illegal consequences. Agnew proposed several ways that people cope with strain.

First, people can cognitively reinterpret the situation (**cognitive coping**). Pretend that you get into a wreck, and your automobile is destroyed. Normally, this event would cause a considerable degree of stress and frustration, but what if you really do feel that "I was driving carelessly, so I deserve it," or "At least I got out of it with my life; the car is not so important," or even "I'm glad to not have to drive that old beater anymore." By minimizing your failures, indignities, or inconveniences, or accepting your responsibility for them, you may still feel unhappy but at the same time you no longer have a reason to act out against others.

We can also deal with strain by using **behavioral coping** strategies. These strategies entail taking some sort of action to deal with the source of the strain, which *might* include delinquency. For instance, if you don't have enough money to live in the style that you would prefer, you might get a job that allows you to live your lifestyle, or else you might steal the money. People who fail their thesis defense in graduate school might cope by revising their work and thus attempt to satisfy the criticisms of their thesis committee. Legitimate coping is not always successful, however, as in the case of a Stanford graduate student who dealt with a stubborn thesis advisor in 1978 by putting a ball-peen hammer through his head (thus negating the source of the strain by forestalling future objections to the thesis).

Finally, one can deal with strain through **emotional coping**. In this case, one does not reinterpret the situation or attempt to deal with the strain, but rather attempts to neutralize the unpleasant emotions that follow from the strain. Do you hate how you feel if you do not do well on a test? Some people take out their anger on the racquetball court. Some pray or go to church. Others go get seriously drunk after finding out their test score. While emotional coping can include deviant or delinquent activity, the common characteristic is the tendency to not deal with the source of the strain but rather to counteract its negative emotional consequences.

When Does Strain Lead to Delinquent Coping?

While there are clearly different ways that people can cope with strain, there is still the question of why some people elect to cope using legitimate strategies while others turn to crime. Under what conditions will strain lead someone to commit crime?

First, Agnew reasoned that strain is more likely to lead to crime *if the strain affects areas that you consider important.* This assertion goes beyond Merton's claim that money—or material success—is the only issue people consider important enough to possibly turn them toward crime. In Agnew's theory, money could be very important to some people, but other people might highly value grades, their masculinity or femininity, their success in sports, and so on. If I don't care about grades, then getting a poor grade on a test is not likely to lead me to assault the teacher, cheat on future tests, or drown my sorrows with Mad Dog 20/20. If grades represent a substantial part of my self-worth, on the other hand, then a low grade is going to have an exaggerated effect on my level of stress and frustration, and that deviance might appear a very tempting response.

Second, those possessing *poor coping skills and resources* are more likely to turn to crime. Some people are better prepared to mitigate potential sources of strain. Those who are diplomatic are in a better position to resolve stressful situations than those who lack tact, for instance. Indeed, a lack of social skills can further aggravate a situation and possibly lead to a physical confrontation. The presence of financial resources can likewise alleviate strain. Money gives us access to therapists, who can make us feel better after a setback. The presence of money also enables us to better deal with financial setbacks.

Third, the *absence of conventional social supports* in one's life makes strain more difficult to deal with legitimately. These social supports include friends, family, and others who might listen to your feelings or give advice and assistance. Conversely, those lacking in social support have no one with whom they can safely vent their frustration, and neither can they expect to receive any assistance through their troubles. Consequently, they are more prone to crime.

Fourth, one is more likely to cope with strain through delinquency if the *advantages of crime are high and the risks are low.* Essentially, when faced with criminal temptation while experiencing strain, the person considers both "What's in it for me?" and "Will I get caught?" If you can get even with an irritating roommate by sabotaging his noisy stereo with an axe, and you can do so without his knowledge, then you are more likely to respond to the strain criminally.

Fifth, strain will tend to lead to crime among those *already predisposed to delinquency.* Agnew's general strain theory borrows from other theories of crime at this point, arguing that such traits as low self-control, criminal beliefs, and exposure to criminal role models predispose some people to react to strain in a criminal way.

Empirical Support

To the extent that researcher attention is a gauge of a successful theory, few can question that Agnew's general strain theory is a successful theory. Since 1992, general strain theory has received considerable empirical testing (see Agnew & White, 1992; Brezina, 1996; Hoffman & Miller, 1998; Katz, 2000; Mazerolle & Maahs, 2000). The research literature is extensive enough to suggest several conclusions about the empirical support for strain theory. Clearly, exposure to strain appears to increase the likelihood that an individual will engage in crime. Less clear, however, are whether a criminal response is more likely given the absence of conventional supports or whether the strain was caused by something important.

The support for strain theory has led Agnew and others to elaborate it in new directions. Agnew (2001) attempted to be more specific about what types of strain are most likely to lead to criminal behavior. In particular, Agnew reasoned that there are four types: (1) when the strain is seen as unjust, (2) when the strain is high in magnitude, (3) when the strain is caused by or associated with low social control, and (4) when the strain creates an incentive to commit crime. Agnew (1999) has also developed his general strain theory to account for crime at the community level, as in social disorganization theory. These new developments have yet to be extensively tested.

MESSNER AND ROSENFELD'S THEORY OF INSTITUTIONAL ANOMIE

In 1994, Steven Messner and Richard Rosenfeld published work on strain theory that builds more explicitly from Merton's original theory than was the case with Agnew's general strain theory. Messner and Rosenfeld specifically focused on institutions that are responsible for regulating our behavior and how many of these institutions have been subverted and rendered ineffective (leading to anomie). Anomie arises as the unbounded desire to succeed pushes people apart, which causes the breakdown of communities and benevolent social institutions. The combination of the breakdown of these institutions and a desire for success that can never be sated (at least through legitimate channels) leads to crime.

When talking about Merton's ideas about the American Dream, we focused primarily on the goals (namely, the desire for money and/or material success) and the means (the rules we're supposed to go by to achieve the American Dream). For Messner and Rosenfeld, the American Dream has four distinctive value orientations: achievement, individualism, universalism, and the money fetish. Many of these ideas were touched on earlier in the chapter, but the theory of **institutional anomie** further develops Merton's ideas.

First, America values *achievement*; Americans are expected to set and achieve goals. Actual achievement is clearly important, since the prestige you have depends very much on the successful outcome of your efforts. If you are a failure, you have little value; if you are a success, then you have great value. Second, *individualism* is an essential trait of American culture. Individuals are expected to make it on their own, overcoming others competing for the same rewards. Those who relied on luck or help from others will see their prestige tarnished somewhat even if they enjoy achievement. In this respect, achievement is most culturally satisfying when taking the best an opponent offers and still winning on one's own merits. For instance, pretend your favorite baseball team is playing a rival that is more than a match for your own team. If your team wins by outplaying the opposition, the victory is all the sweeter than if your team won because the other team played the game without its best hitter. Third, the values of America are *universal*. That is, everyone in society is expected to strive for success. Finally, there is the *money fetish*, in which success is specifically the consequence of getting lots of money. Money, as Messner and Rosenfeld argued, has value beyond its ability to buy things. The acquisition of money is a source of status and prestige in and of itself. How else could one explain why boorish professional athletes and pop stars always seem to be fighting off armies of groupies when the rest of us—who lack the impressive salaries—have to pathetically beg for a date? But there is more to the fetish than getting money. There is the fact that our society sets no upper bound on how much money one gets. As long as somebody out there is doing better than us, we will be resentful. In short, Americans, one and all, are socialized to desire money and, moreover, are expected to achieve wealth through the abilities that they have.

The theory of institutional anomie goes beyond Merton's emphasis on the class system of the United States, arguing for a more general examination of the social structure and its institutions. Institutions normally exist to help the society function better, like the organs within our own body. Each organ—the heart, the brain, and so forth—helps us survive, and so it is with society's institutions. More specifically, Messner and Rosenfeld stated that institutions address the need of the society and its people to adapt to the environment, gather and deploy resources for collective purposes, and socialize members of the society. Four important types of institutions are most relevant for understanding crime: economic, political, family, and education. Economic institutions are concerned with providing goods and services. At a minimum, they are responsible for meeting basic human needs: food, shelter, and clothing. Political institutions are responsible for activities that benefit the community as a whole, such as organizing the police so that everyone is safer. Educational and familial institutions share responsibility for socializing children. These institutions are interdependent, like bodily organs, and the actions, relative importance, and failure of one may have consequences for the others.

Messner and Rosenfeld make the case that the economy holds disproportionate power. One reason for this is that the other institutions are "devalued" relative to strictly economic pursuits. Those responsible for educating and socializing our children, for instance, are paid low salaries or not at all (as in the case with stay-at-home parents). Additionally, other institutions are expected to "accommodate" economic institution needs, rather than the other way around. For example, have your bosses ever demanded that you schedule your classes around your work day? If you do this, then you are accommodating your life to your work rather than to your learning. Even universities are under pressure from economic interests to provide the kind of education that will help students get jobs, and many students go to college not so much to learn but rather to obtain the credentials they need to get a better paying job. Thus, even higher education is expected to have a financial payoff and must therefore accommodate economic interests. Finally, the business mentality "penetrates" into other institutions. Economic institutions are characterized by competition and a concern for the bottom line. This may sound like the business world is fundamentally amoral, and it is; however, businesses that fail to compete and also make decisions that aren't profitable simply fail to survive. So while the business world is brutal, it must be. But what if business values seep into such institutions as government, family, and education? Schools would not be interested so much in educating students as in keeping them happy (and keeping their tuition dollars coming). Parents would spend more time at work, because having and raising their children is not "cost-effective." Government would abandon programs that lose money, including programs that are altruistic in nature—for example, social assistance programs to the poor, such as welfare and food stamps.

What does all this have to do with more crime? The economic institutions are less concerned with following rules than getting profits. Again, following the rules is okay as long as there is some advantage to it, but ultimately getting the money is what really matters. Crime would naturally be very tempting. Consequently, it is up to the remaining institutions to teach people to follow the rules. But if economic institutions devalue and penetrate into other institutions, and force others to accommodate, then the emphasis on social control is less likely to occur within these institutions except superficially and ineffectively. Additionally, families with dual wage earners necessarily have less time to spend socializing their children, so the ability of institutions to socialize people about the rules is lacking even if the willingness is there. Put differently, we have to make choices: Do you give your all to that high-paying job and neglect your family, or do you raise your family and lose the job? If economic ideals predominate, then you would elect to let your family slide while you chase the big bucks. Meantime, your children are taught the rules of the business world—get ahead, whatever it takes. Thus, the overwhelming importance of economic institutions, and the accompanying mindset, means that the other institutions are ineffective at countering the socializing of children into the business mentality. Serious crime is the result.

Unlike Agnew's general strain theory, Messner and Rosenfeld's theory of institutional anomie has not received as much empirical testing. For instance, it is difficult to measure precisely how much business values predominate and have penetrated into other institutions. There does appear to be some support for the theory, however (see Messner & Rosenfeld, 1994; Piquero & Piquero, 1998).

SUMMARY

Strain theory has a long and influential tradition in criminology, starting with the work of Merton through the recent developments of Agnew's general strain theory and Messner and Rosenfeld's theory of institutional anomie. The underlying premise of strain theory is that people who fail to get what they want are more likely to turn to crime, and that they would obey the law if they could, but are forced into crime by various dysfunctions in their society or circumstances.

Strain theories have influenced public policy. Merton's theory suggests that to reduce crime, one might help level the playing field between the poor and the rich in terms of opportunities for success, or else somehow get American culture to better regulate our desires and do so in such a way as to be more realistic. President Lyndon Johnson's war on poverty was an attempt to address the lack of opportunities that poor people faced that might lead them to crime. Examples include welfare and food stamp programs. While Merton and the war on poverty have faded in terms of importance, the resurgence of strain theories may redirect attention toward addressing social class and institutional issues that foster higher rates of crime in the United States.

KEY TERMS

American Dream a convenient label for American culture; specifically, the American Dream maintains that all Americans should strive to achieve wealth

behavioral coping in general strain theory, attempting to resolve the strain through actual behaviors—for instance, assaulting someone who is being insulting

cognitive coping in general strain theory, reinterpreting a situation in order to deemphasize the strain in one's own mind or to accept personal responsibility for its happening

conformity a response to strain in Merton's anomie theory, whereby the individual experiencing strain continues to pursue legitimate ends through legitimate means

criminal subculture in Cloward and Ohlin's theory, the subculture that emerges in areas where criminal role models and financially rewarding crimes are available; offenders tend to focus on using criminal means to make money

emotional coping in general strain theory, resolving the emotional consequences of strain, though not necessarily the underlying reasons for the strain—for instance, crying after experiencing disappointment

innovation a response to strain in Merton's anomie theory, whereby the individual experiencing strain continues to pursue legitimate ends while rejecting legitimate means; crime is one example

institutional anomie the imbalance between institutions essential for a functioning nation; in the United States, in particular, institutional anomie results when economic interests receive precedence over other institutions (such as the family and education), even to the point where other institutions view their roles in economic terms

rebellion a response to strain in Merton's anomie theory whereby the individual

experiencing strain rejects both legitimate means and ends, replacing them with something else

retreatism a response to strain whereby the individual experiencing strain no longer strives to achieve legitimate goals, and abandons legitimate means as well; examples are drug use and alcoholism

retreatist subculture in Cloward and Ohlin's theory, the subculture that emerges when individuals fail at both crime and conformity; retreatists, as in Merton's theory, engage in drinking and drugs

ritualism a response to strain in Merton's anomie theory whereby the individual experiencing strain continues to follow legitimate rules, but has abandoned hope of achieving legitimate goals

violent subculture in Cloward and Ohlin's theory, the subculture that emerges when there are no opportunities for financially rewarding crime; consequently, the only means by which individuals can earn status is through toughness

DISCUSSION QUESTIONS

1. What role do you think the family might play in Merton's strain theory? What about Agnew's general strain theory?

2. How do you feel about the way Merton and other strain theorists view the American Dream?

3. What kind of person would be most likely to respond to strain with crime, according to Agnew's general strain theory?

4. Where does the American Dream fit in Agnew's strain theory?

REFERENCES

Agnew, R. (1992). Foundation for a general strain theory of crime and delinquency. *Criminology, 30,* 47–87.

Agnew, R. (1999). A general strain theory of community differences in crime rates. *Journal of Research in Crime and Delinquency, 36,* 123–155.

Agnew, R. (2001). Building on the foundation of general strain theory: Specifying the types of strain most likely to lead to delinquency. *Journal of Research in Crime and Delinquency, 38,* 319–361.

Agnew, R. & White, H. R. (1992). An empirical test of general strain theory. *Criminology, 30,* 475–499.

Bernard, T. (1984). Control criticisms of strain theories: An assessment of theoretical and empirical adequacy. *Journal of Research in Crime and Delinquency, 21,* 353–372.

Brezina, T. (1996). Adapting to strain: An examination of delinquent coping strategies. *Criminology, 34,* 213–239.

Cloward, R. A., & Ohlin, L. E. (1960). *Delinquency and opportunity: A theory of delinquent gangs.* Glencoe, IL: Free Press.

Cohen, A. K. (1955). *Delinquent boys: The culture of the gang.* Glencoe, IL: Free Press.

Durkheim, E. (1951). *Suicide: A study in sociology.* New York: Free Press. (Original work published 1897)

Hirschi, T. (1969). *Causes of delinquency.* Berkeley: University of California Press.

Hoffman, J., & Miller, A. S. (1998). A latent variable analysis of general strain theory. *Journal of Quantitative Criminology, 14,* 83–110.

Katz, R. (2000). Explaining girls' and women's crime and desistance in the context of their victimization experiences. *Violence against Women, 6,* 633–660.

Mazerolle, P., & Maahs, J. (2000). General strain and delinquency: An alternative examination of conditioning influences. *Justice Quarterly, 17,* 753–778.

Merton, R. (1968). *Social theory and social structure.* New York: Free Press.

Merton, R. K. (1938). Social structure and anomie. *American Sociological Review, 3,* 672–682.

Messner, S., & Rosenfeld, R. (1994). *Crime and the American Dream.* Belmont, CA: Wadsworth.

Murray, C. (1984). *Losing ground: American Social Policy, 1950–1980.* New York: Basic Books.

Pfohl, S. J. (1985). *Images of deviance and social control: A sociological history.* New York: McGraw-Hill.

Shaw, C. R., & McKay, H. D. (1942). *Juvenile delinquency and urban areas.* Chicago: University of Chicago Press.

CHAPTER 8

CONTROL THEORIES
OF CRIME

The control perspective is among the oldest and most popular to have explored the causes of criminality. The basic idea behind the control perspective—which is that people are fundamentally selfish pleasure seekers—dates as far back as the work of the English social philosopher Thomas Hobbes during the seventeenth century. The control perspective also draws insight, or at least shares remarkable similarities with, the ideas of such thinkers and social scientists as Jeremy Bentham, Sigmund Freud, and Emile Durkheim. But not until the 1950s did criminologists begin to give control theory much more than cursory scholarly attention (see Nye, 1958; Reckless, 1955; Reiss, 1951; Toby, 1957). At the time, however, strain theory was at the peak of its influence, and so criminologists tended to focus their thinking and research on strain theories rather than control theories. In 1969, however, Travis Hirschi published a book that integrated the ideas of the early control theorists and presented research supporting his theory. Hirschi's version of social control theory became the definitive social control model as well as the most frequently tested theory of crime during the 1970s and 1980s.

While Hirschi's social control theory continues to shape crime research even today, the 1990s witnessed the advent of self-control theory (Gottfredson & Hirschi, 1990). Although there are many modern varieties of control theory (see Sampson & Laub, 1993; Tittle, 1995), this chapter will focus on the two versions that have been the most influential at shaping criminological research.

WHAT DO CONTROL THEORIES ASSUME
ABOUT HUMAN NATURE?

We begin with a discussion about what makes control theories distinct from the others that we cover in this book, particularly strain and differential association theories. Many theories of crime assume that something must cause, compel, or push people to commit crime. If something must cause crime, then it follows that crime cannot be a *natural* thing for people to do. People can commit crime, for example, only if someone or something else teaches them, or they experience the failure to achieve the American Dream, or they have a biological or psychological "problem." In either case, these theories suggest that people do not decide to commit crime on their own. The idea that criminality is not a normal part of human nature makes so much sense that whenever we hear of a brutal crime, like that of Jeffrey Dahmer killing and eating young boys, the first question that often pops into our head is, "What caused that person to do it?" Put another way, we tend to think that it is natural for us to behave ourselves and obey the law and it is unnatural for us to commit crime.

Control theories, in contrast, usually assume that the willingness to commit crime is natural to all human beings and what needs to be explained is why people resist criminal temptation. Control theories begin with the view that crime is simply a consequence of the rational and self-interested nature with which *everyone* is born. Learning the motivation to commit crime from others is not necessary. We can all naturally anticipate the benefits and costs of our actions, and we choose to behave in whichever way yields the most advantage. Our self-interested nature means that we consider costs and benefits as they relate specifically to our own pleasure. Now imagine the kind of person you might be in your "natural" state, which is how you would be if you did anything and everything that gave you pleasure or advantage. Marriage vows would mean nothing, provided that you had an opportunity for sex and you thought that you could escape undetected or unpunished. Nor would you hesitate to use force if doing so would get you what you wanted and the risk to yourself was not too high. You also might be quick to lie to others, manipulate, cheat, or steal your way to what you wanted if you could get away with it. You would be drawn to eat any food, drink any beverage, or inhale, inject, or snort any substances that made you feel good.

Another factor commonly assumed in control theories is the idea that there is general agreement in the world about what constitutes socially unacceptable behavior. That is, crime is not simply an arbitrary product of moral entrepreneurs (as suggested by labeling theory). As one might expect from the preceding examples, it is not unreasonable to think that people who simply act out their gross desires regardless of the rights of others create chaos and instability in any society. For instance, trust would be foolish if we expected our neighbors to steal from us if they thought they would not get caught. Societies therefore create formal and informal methods of enforcing rules, so as to protect order and ensure a smoothly running society. While there may be gray-area behaviors that are sometimes tolerated and sometimes not—smoking and little white lies come to mind—this viewpoint maintains that no society can function very well when its citizens are free to rob, steal, and kill one another. What all this means is that, unlike differential association and labeling theories, control theories first assume that what crime is does not vary in meaningful ways from one culture to another, and second, the criminal law is not merely a tool used by some people so that they can maintain their positions of power and privilege.

Even though it may be in society's interest to control crime and there is general consensus on what we define as crime, some actions are nevertheless tempting to the individual person because they can be a way of getting what he or she wants. It is much easier and faster to obtain beer and nice clothes by stealing money from a roommate or neighbor than by getting a job and earning the money oneself. In a world where only our natural urges governed our actions, we could expect all of us to do whatever it would take to get what we wanted as long as the payoff outweighed any costs. This does not mean that everyone is essentially evil or bad—after all, control theory assumes that we are capable of obeying societal rules (at least when it is to our advantage; virtue, as they say, is its own reward). Instead the assumption is that we are amoral and that both good and bad actions can ultimately be traced to our ability to be rational in our own self-interest. Control theory says that when we get right down to it, none of us (at the core) are really very nice (although we may see some advantage to giving other people the impression that we are).

Given this somewhat gloomy view of human nature, the basic question for the control theorist is *not* "Why do some people commit crime?" but instead "How do people stop themselves from committing crime when it would have been to their own advantage?" After all, not all of us hit, steal, or rob even when doing so might improve our lifestyle.

We noted earlier that society has adopted formal and informal methods of keeping us from freely acting on our desires. Modern control theories focus on trying to identify which kinds of restraints are most effective at preventing people from committing crime. Social control theories often emphasize how connectedness with society deters crime or eliminates opportunities for crime. Self-control theory, in contrast, focuses almost entirely on an acquired fear of long-term consequences for criminal actions.

As a final note, some people may be able to relate to these assumptions about human nature and find them believable, while others might not. You should be aware, however, that assumptions are not the same things as proven facts. Assumptions—by definition—cannot be scientifically proven, which means that you are under no obligation to accept them. But knowing and understanding the underlying assumptions behind theories is essential for being able to distinguish between and understanding individual theories.

EARLY CONTROL THEORIES

To begin the presentation of the major control theories themselves, we present some of the founders of the modern control perspective. The ideas of these founders provide the basis of contemporary thinking. Most of these ideas are not today used by themselves, but instead have been revised and added to for contemporary use. It is important, however, to first review these "older" ideas for a couple of reasons. First, this can show us how some of the major modern theories developed. Theorists do not pull their ideas out of thin air, but work creatively with the ideas available to them at the time. Second, a historical understanding shows where the dead ends are as far as explaining crime. This latter point is particularly important, as all of us have our own beliefs and opinions about what causes crime—and we may not recognize that these ideas and beliefs may have been considered, tested, and found to be inadequate. As the saying goes, if we fail to understand history, we doom ourselves to repeat it.

This is not to say that control theories historically have been failures like Lombroso's theory of atavism or the explanations of the phrenologists. Rather, the history of control theories has been slowly gathering momentum. The perspective began with only a few isolated studies—but these few ideas continue to influence thinking today. Now, more than a half century later, control theories clearly are among the most important modern explanations of crime.

Albert Reiss (1951) was perhaps the first American criminologist to discuss the idea of "controls," distinguishing between "personal" and "social" forms of control. Personal controls refer to our individual ability to resist temptation, whereas social controls compel us to resist temptation out of fear of what others may do to us—for instance, fear of arrest. A few years later, Jackson Toby (1957) built on this with the idea of **stakes in conformity**, a type of control in which people resist criminal temptation because their very conformity up to the present had led to rewards (such as reputation, job prospects, or educational opportunities) that might be jeopardized were they to engage in crime. Those with few stakes in conformity, on the other hand, have fewer reasons for resisting when faced with the opportunity for crime. F. Ivan Nye (1958) added to control theory, proposing two types of external control: direct (for instance, when you elect to not hit your sibling because your parents are watching you) and indirect (when you worry about the embarrassment you might cause others by failing to resist temptation and getting caught). Internal controls, on the other hand, refer to the guilt that we anticipate feeling were we to engage in delinquency. Such a control essentially takes the fun out of whatever pleasure we might have obtained by giving in to temptation. Of these three types of controls, Nye felt that informal controls were the most efficacious at restraining criminal activity.

During the same period (the 1950s and 1960s), Walter Reckless developed a major branch of control theory called *containment theory*. After going through several rounds of revisions and modification, the final version of containment theory (see Reckless, 1967) lays out a fairly complex model of "pushes" and "pulls" that might lead to crime as well as "inner" and "outer" **containments**, the forces that might buffer or insulate the individual from succumbing to criminal pushes and pulls. "Pushes" to crime are generally internal in focus (some have argued these to be psychological or biological), though sometimes the push might ultimately originate from a social event, structure, or experience, such as poverty or discrimination. Pushes include the need for sex, aggression, frustration, rebelliousness, and a need or desire for immediate gratification. "Pulls," on the other hand, refer to social invitations or encouragements to crime originating from other people. Pulls often come from our role models or companions. For example, you might be at a party where someone is passing a marijuana joint around. The encouragements of your friends to take a puff might pull you into smoking the joint and thus engaging in an illegal activity.

You probably realize that pushes and pulls toward crime are all around us, but that not all of us commit crime. Recall that Reckless identified two types of containments that help us resist pressures to commit crime—inner and outer. Inner containment is our **self-concept,** our conscience, which he believed was formed by about age 12 or so. Individuals with a negative self-concept will be more likely to commit crime. Outer containment is most effective when we receive supervision and discipline. The responsibility for outer containment does not rest so much on the individual as on the ability of the community and the family to provide an effective structure and organization that can provide observation and control. This argument is much the same as that in social disorganization theory (Shaw & McKay, 1942). Indeed, many of the same ideas that Reiss and Nye proposed are evident in Reckless's work—inner containment and self-concept resemble internal control, whereas external containment is similar to social control. The basic idea behind these theoretical terms is very similar.

In some ways, Reckless's theory went beyond the common assumptions of control theory as we know it today, and his theory tends to overlap with some of the other theoretical explanations that we cover in this text (namely, learning and strain theories). Strain theory, for instance, is clearly a theory that emphasizes pushes. One version of strain theory, advanced by Robert Merton (1938), argues that the lack of access to economic opportunities that some people must endure causes them to violate the rules in order to get what they want. As we noted earlier in the discussion of the assumptions behind control theories, this perspective assumes that we need no outside push to commit crime. Differential association theory, which would emphasize how we learn to become criminal from the people closest to us, is clearly one example of a "pull" theory. Control theories, in contrast, argue that we do not "learn" crime nor do we necessarily imitate criminal role models.

HIRSCHI'S SOCIAL CONTROL THEORY

As noted earlier, the control theory formulated by Travis Hirschi has assumed the position as the primary and most frequently drawn-on form of social control theory. Hirschi's conceptualization focuses on the idea of individuals' **social bond** as a means for imposing a variety of restraints on our behavior. The social bond is simply our connectedness to society, and crime—according to Hirschi—is more likely to occur among those with weakened connections to others. Social bonds act as barriers to opportunities for crime, as well as restraints. Thus, criminals are not socialized into crime as other theories might say, but are in fact *undersocialized* into conformity. The social bond consists of four elements: attachment, commitment, involvement, and belief. While each of these bonds may vary independently (that is, it is possible to conceive of somebody with strong commitment but few attachments), Hirschi hypothesized that the four elements of the social bond are interconnected.

Attachment

Imagine that you had the opportunity to cheat on a test at school, but you realized that if your professor caught you your actions would humiliate your parents. If the thought of causing your parents embarrassment, combined with expectation of a loss of their affection, would deter you from cheating, then **attachment**—feelings of sensitivity and affection for others—was what compelled you to take your test honestly. People with strong bonds of attachment genuinely care about what other people think, and appreciate the possibility that people they love and admire will think badly of them. Faced with the opportunity for crime, those with strong attachment to others consider the embarrassment or inconvenience their actions would cause those who are close to them.

On the other hand, Hirschi's theory suggests that if you know someone who is sincere when she says, "I don't care what anyone thinks of me," you might want to guard your wallet, because she is not particularly troubled with the thought that her criminal actions might damage her relationships. People who lack attachment are more likely to succumb to criminal opportunity because they risk less when they participate in crime. We should also note that attachments might lead to greater direct control (as we tend to spend more time around the people we like, who then are in a position to regulate our behavior), but that people who possess strong attachment do not require observation in order to be deterred from crime. Attachment, as Hirschi thinks of it, is something like an "internal parent."

Commitment

The bond of **commitment** refers to stakes we have in following the rules, stakes that we could lose if we were to commit crime. Commitment is somewhat different from attachment in that commitment is more selfish. Commitment means that we care about what people think of us, but only insofar as their having a negative opinion of us impairs our enjoyment of something we *do* care about: wealth, status, or a job. We might not worry about disappointing a teacher by cheating on a test, but we do fear failing the class (and ruining future job prospects) if we are caught. A person who has no long-term job, few educational achievements, and no reputation worth acknowledging would be more likely to be a delinquent; this person would have little to lose by engaging in crime.

Try to think of commitment like this. One person has a stable high-paying job, while another has a low-paying temporary job. Since many bosses take a dim view of crime, employees who get arrested and convicted can expect in many cases to lose their jobs. Of the two people just mentioned, who would you guess would be most likely to be deterred from committing crime that may lead to losing the job?

Involvement

The third element of the social bond, **involvement**, looks at how time acts as a restraint. Many of us feel that we are so busy that it would be hard to take on additional activities. Perhaps the same is true of crime. If we are too busy and engrossed in conventional activity, there should be much less time left for criminal activity. Those who spend more time doing homework have less time to commit crime. Even simply watching television should serve to tie up one's time. In contrast, people who do not spend a whole lot of time engaged in conventional activity, such as by idling on the street corner or in a vacant lot, would have lots of time and opportunity to commit crime.

Belief

Do you believe that killing is wrong under all circumstances? If not, when is it permitted? Any time your own life is in danger? Any time someone threatens your child? Any time someone does something to provoke you beyond your limit? Any time someone you don't like is walking down the street? Whenever it might be fun? Clearly, some of these excuses leave more room for killing someone than others.

Hirschi's theory maintains that those who have a strong **belief** that crime is wrong are less likely to take advantage of criminal opportunities. The less we think that rules have moral authority, the more easily we can find excuses and rationalizations for our criminal actions. Weak beliefs thus do not require that we commit crime, but weak beliefs in the moral wrongness of certain acts function as a poor or weak restraint. It may be more accurate to say that those with weak belief in conventional rules have an ambivalent attitude toward the law. On one hand, people with weak beliefs may not consider crime to be necessarily a good thing. But at the same time, there are many situations when illegal acts would not necessarily be seen as wrong, either. A relative of one of the authors frequently tailgates other cars and feels justified doing such a reckless act (saying "Well I'm in a hurry [so the rules don't apply to me right now]!"), and yet speaks disparagingly of others when they tailgate. People we know who practice such "situational ethics" can be seen as weakly bonded to conventional beliefs and are thus more likely to commit crime. In contrast, strong beliefs—in which we believe that there is no excuse or justification for crime—mean we are more likely to overcome our natural tendency to commit crime.

The element of belief is often thought of as the most difficult to understand. Why would our beliefs not both push and restrain people from crime? After all, we sometimes hear that criminals were taught the "wrong" beliefs at some point in their life—such as from running with a "bad crowd"— and these bad beliefs somehow *pushed* people into crime. This understanding of belief, however, makes sense only if people are not naturally predisposed toward crime (as assumed by control theories). In Hirschi's social control theory, the few people who seemingly hold procriminal beliefs were simply never socialized into conventional values. Their amoral human nature, moreover, means that no push toward crime in the form of beliefs or anything else is even needed. In other words, their procriminal belief system only mirrors what one would expect from those who feel justified to commit crime any time it is to their advantage—that is, people who are completely unsocialized.

Empirical Testing

For at least the first twenty-five years after publication, Hirschi's social control theory was subjected to empirical testing more frequently than perhaps any theory of crime (Stitt & Giacopassi, 1992). Hirschi (1969) himself recognized the importance of testing and provided the first test in the book in which he outlined the theory. He drew on self-reported delinquency survey data from a sample of more than 4,000 juveniles living in California. His results supported his argument that criminal offenders tended to have weaker attachments, commitments, and belief in the moral authority of rules than nondelinquents. The effects of these elements of the social bond on offending tended to be stronger than more traditional crime correlates such as race or social class. One weakness in the theory that emerged, however, is that Hirschi did not find that spending time doing conventional activities had any consistent relationship with crime. Indeed, involvement in many activities had no influence one way or the other on crime. Later tests of Hirschi's theory also tended to confirm these findings (see Kempf-Leonard, 1993).

Empirical testing has also uncovered some other possible weaknesses in Hirschi's version of social control theory. First, Hirschi's own initial test found that juveniles who associated with delinquent peers were significantly more likely to be delinquent as well, and that this predictor tended to have a stronger influence than the elements of the social bond. Other researchers have also confirmed this through other tests through the years (see Conger, 1976; Warr, 2002). Criminologists often interpret this finding about the importance of delinquent peers as evidence of support for social learning theory, which argues that children model themselves on others and learn behaviors based on whether that behavior gets reinforced or punished (see Akers & Sellers, 2004).

One question that you might ask regarding social control theory—and it's a good question—is where bonds come from in the first place. Hirschi (1969) stated that bonds are meaningful only when acquired through personal investment and exertion, not when society gives them away to an individual. But not all people are inclined to exert themselves in order to secure something that has long-term advantage. For instance, colleges and universities frequently award scholarships to those in need, to those who have records of academic and/or civic excellence, and for athletic achievement. Most of us would look on a scholarship as something of great advantage. But who do you suppose would value the scholarship more, and thus be more afraid to lose it by stupidly stealing a book from the university bookstore and/or using school as an opportunity to get away from annoying parents in order to party for a few years: someone who worked hard to get the scholarship and sees the value of obtaining a degree, or someone who did little to earn it? Clearly, opportunities to fashion stronger bonds do not always mean the same thing to different people, and we can probably think of many examples of people squandering opportunities to better their lives. Something else appears to be at work.

SELF-CONTROL THEORY

Some twenty years after Hirschi published *Causes of Delinquency* (1969), Gottfredson and Hirschi (1990) published a revision of control theory in a book titled *A General Theory of Crime*. Apart from the question about what creates bonds in the first place, research had uncovered other reasons why social control theory needed an update (see Hirschi & Gottfredson, 2002). Interestingly, their book in fact said little about social bonds, and instead focused attention on a concept they called **self-control**. Self-control refers to the habit of refraining from grabbing at short-term pleasure out of fear of the long-term consequences. The authors noted that much short-term pleasure has negative long-term pain. For example, pretend you like cheese fries with bacon and ranch dressing. Cheese fries taste really good, and many of us can eat a lot of them. But a plate of cheese fries also contains an awesome number of calories. If we grab at the short-term pleasure of eating a lot of something that tastes really good, we must ignore the long-term fact that (1) we will get fat, or perhaps (2) we will have to exercise and diet to make up for our cheese fries binge if we still wish to fit into our clothes. Clearly, an appreciation of the long-term consequences (self-control) would affect many behaviors besides crime, which is why Gottfredson and Hirschi refer to their theory as a "general" theory. More generally, some forms of pleasure can be reckless (that is, can get us hurt or killed), immoral (offend people), or illegal (criminal). Self-control theory assumes that pleasure appeals to all of us; however, for many of us, our fear of the consequences helps keep us from engaging in such activity. But what makes us fear the consequences? That is where self-control comes in—lots of bad things can happen if we do not take long-term negative consequences into account.

For some people it is difficult to put the long-term consequences into perspective because the consequences are not always immediately apparent or even certain. Obeying a stop sign, for example, makes sense because we risk our lives and those of other people if we violently collide with another car. But this possibility of a collision is a *maybe*. We have all probably run stop signs without getting into an accident; the long-term consequences, while obviously potentially negative, sometimes happen very infrequently. Moreover, running a stop sign is immediately advantageous to us. Without a doubt, we can get to where we want to go faster if we do not have to stop anywhere along the way or yield to other cars. So what do you do when you come up to a stop sign? If you have low self-control, you may think about how much of a hurry you are in (and dismiss the risk of accident) and go through the intersection without stopping. If you have more self-control, you are more likely to shudder at what *might* happen if a car hits you, and therefore stop.

What would a person be like who had low self-control? Gottfredson and Hirschi suggested that low self-control leads to distinctive personality characteristics. In particular, those with low self-control tend to be impulsive, self-centered, belligerent, lazy, and unable to defer gratification. One common thread in each characteristic of low self-control is that all of them are potentially self-destructive. Yet the following traits would be how all of us are naturally inclined to behave if we did not appreciate the potentially negative impact of our actions.

- *Impulsivity.* Do you know anyone who goes out and buys things on the spur of the moment, expensive things such as designer clothes, running up huge credit card debt without even thinking about it? Impulsivity, according to self-control theory, comes naturally and without effort. It takes effort to do things deliberately and with forethought about what the consequences might be.

- *Adventure seeking.* We all naturally prefer to do things that are exciting, but many exciting things can get us into trouble (such as promiscuous sex or lying down on the median of a busy highway for laughs). People with low self-control therefore have a passion for doing thrilling things. Having high self-control and exercising due caution, on the other hand, would have the unexciting—but potentially life-saving—benefit of discouraging us from taking extreme risks.

■ *Self-centeredness.* Have you ever known somebody who acts as if he or she is the only person who matters in the world? Self-control theory argues that we all are basically selfish; we are naturally inclined to look out for ourselves first. In other words, our natural inclination is not to care what others think, except insofar as manipulating other people's feelings can help us to get what we want. It takes self-control to be able to put other people first— genuine empathy toward others takes effort.

■ *Minimal tolerance for frustration.* When a boss or friend yells at you, what is your first reaction? Do you say, "I deserved it"? Probably not. Your first reaction is likely to get angry, and maybe imagine how pleasurable it would be to tell your tormentor where to get off or even deliver a punch to that person's mouth. Frequently venting anger toward someone simply feels good, and it takes effort not to lash out at those who frustrate us.

■ *Lack of diligence.* Self-control theory says that people naturally prefer to do things that bring pleasure quickly and easily, even if there are potential long-term costs to taking the easy way. Tasks that are more complicated and that require effort are more likely to discourage us. A willingness to undertake difficult tasks rather than take the easy way requires effort.

■ *Inability to defer gratification.* Not many people have an easy time waiting for something pleasurable to occur. Nevertheless, many of us can be patient and wait, but patience sometimes takes a great deal of effort. Inability to wait is an indicator of low self-control.

While low self-control includes all these different traits, self-control is at the same time unidimensional. That is, these personality traits are *symptoms* of having low self-control, and all traits should appear in people possessing low self-control. So if someone is unusually selfish, you should also expect that on average this person is also impulsive, lazy, risk seeking, belligerent, and unable to defer gratification. What do you suppose the life of someone like this must be like? As fun as having low self-control might seem to be, low self-control is not a ticket for a happy or stable life. Ignoring consequences would lead to, among other things, accidents, disease, employment instability, brief and volatile social relationships, and even victimization. This is in fact where social bonds fit in: people with low self-control have a habit of frittering away opportunities to form bonds. For example, it is fair to say that most people feel tired when the seven A.M. alarm for an early class goes off. Who is more likely to sleep in and risk failing the class—someone who cares about the long-term consequences of not getting ready for class or someone who does not even think about them? If the thought of failing does not trouble you, then sleeping in sounds like a much better idea than hurrying to get to class. As implied in this example, developing social bonds sometimes requires short-term sacrifice and inconvenience, which someone with low self-control is generally not too willing to make. So Gottfredson and Hirschi would say that social bonds are by-products of self-control.

Besides unpleasant life outcomes and weak social bonds, crime clearly would appeal to someone with low self-control. First, people habitually unable to defer gratification are unlikely to have the kind of patience to wait until they can pay for something, therefore they are more likely to simply take it (especially if they think they can get away without paying). Moreover, most crimes take very little training or skill, which is wonderful if one doesn't have much patience. Anyone, even an uneducated and unskilled person, can thrust a knife at somebody or pull the trigger on a loaded handgun. Second, most crimes really do not require much effort to commit. After all, how much effort does it take to push a handgun in someone's face and demand his or her money (as opposed to working eight hours a day at a job)? Third, Gottfredson and Hirschi (1990) reported that a great deal of crime is spontaneous—very little time elapses between recognition of an opportunity and the actual carrying out of the crime (see also Felson, 1998). Contrary to what television and movies seem to show, the average bank robbery, for instance, undergoes very rudimentary planning, if any. Most crimes simply do not involve much, if any, real planning or thought. Fourth, since crime can lead to inconvenience (if not pain) for a victim, commiting crime is less likely to appeal to someone who genuinely cares about the feelings of others. A person who has low self-control will not worry so much about those he or she hurts. Fifth, although not in every instance, but in many, the danger associated with crime makes it exciting. Finally, committing crime can be a very satisfying way of coping with our frustration. While we would not expect people with low self-control to go out of their way to seek out crime—since that would be a little too much like work—neither would we expect them to resist opportunities for crime, either.

So where does self-control come from? Self-control is an acquired characteristic, so we are not born with it. Gottfredson and Hirschi specifically emphasized child rearing in the family as the primary agent for the development of self-control. In contrast, social learning theories give no particularly important role to the family, and classic versions of strain theory and labeling theory hardly acknowledge the family at all. In self-control theory, childhood socialization is the process of educating individuals about the consequences of their actions. Borrowing from the work of Gerald Patterson (1980), Gottfredson and Hirschi reasoned that three factors must be present before self-control becomes a habit. First, parents must be able and willing to supervise their children. The level of supervision children receive thus substantially depends on how intact the family is, as well as the bonds of love between parent and child. Second, parents must also be able and willing to recognize deviant behavior when it occurs. Third, parents must punish the deviant behavior. Once self-control becomes evident in children, approximately around age 8, differences in self-control remain relatively stable—older children who frequently ignore the consequences of their behavior will show similar tendencies to adults and will engage in more antisocial and self-destructive behavior relative to their same-age peers.

Empirical Research and Criticisms of Self-Control Theory

Since 1990, few theories have garnered as much research attention and discussion as self-control theory (Pratt and Cullen, 2000). Dozens of empirical tests of the theory took place in the decade after *A General Theory of Crime* was published (see Baron, 2003; Grasmick, Tittle, Bursik, & Arneklev, 1993; Keane, Maxim, & Teevan 1993; LaGrange & Silverman, 1999; Sellers, 1999). The results of these tests have generally been supportive—those with low self-control tend to engage in more crime. Research has also explored whether self-control links to crime-analogous outcomes as Gottfredson and Hirschi had speculated. Indeed, there is evidence linking low self-control with adverse circumstances such as contact with delinquent friends, spotty work histories, accidents, and even victimization (see Evans et al., 1996; Schreck, 1999). Consistent with Gottfredson and Hirschi's claims, low self-control does appear to have general effects. Nevertheless, researchers have expressed concern about whether the theory is suitable for explaining crime in general. Some research suggests that the "general theory" of crime may not be very effective for explaining such crime as white-collar crime, where offenders typically must have high self-control in order to achieve the positions necessary to make their crimes possible.

Self-control theory has not lacked for critics. Unlike Hirschi's earlier book, *Causes of Delinquency* (1969), where he provided a detailed guide for measuring the four elements of the social bond, *A General Theory of Crime* did not make positive statements about how to best measure self-control (Akers, 1991). In an effort to move ahead with the testing of the theory, Harold Grasmick and colleagues (1993) developed an "index" of survey question items measuring the personality dimensions (such as impulsivity and self-centeredness) of low self-control, and this index—and variations on it—has become the standard way to measure self-control. Hirschi and Gottfredson (2002) themselves questioned the Grasmick index, stating that the personality traits described in their theory were but consequences of low self-control and not a cause of crime (that is, risk-seeking is a by-product of low self-control just as crime is, and is therefore statistically correlated with crime, but is not a cause of crime). A criterion of a good theory is its ability to be scientifically tested, besides empirical support. Without clear measures of self-control, it may well be that self-control theory, even after more than ten years of considerable scrutiny to which researchers have already subjected it, has still not been adequately tested.

POLICY IMPLICATIONS OF CONTROL THEORY

As control theories assume that offenders are undersocialized, much like a dog that has not been housetrained, the most effective policies to make people less criminal will strengthen the ability of society to socialize its members and successfully integrate people into society. Social control theory in particular suggests policies that would strengthen bonds between individuals and society, especially with such institutions as the family and the school. Big Brother/Big Sister programs likewise strive to create a bond between two people—a youth and an adult role model. Among adults, policies should provide adults with stable employment and community involvement.

Self-control theory indicates that the most far-reaching programs for reducing crime with the greatest long-term benefits would be those that successfully promote development of self-control in children, such as early-intervention programs. Programs such as these train parents how to raise children who have impulse control and self-discipline, for instance. These efforts to develop self-control in children should target families that are struggling in terms of their ability to supervise and socialize children (see Hirschi, 1995). To assist families, the general theory advocates society's striving to maximize the number of caregivers available to each child. Moreover, programs should address the sources of weakened or broken families, in particular teenage pregnancy. We described the successful instilling of self-control as "far-reaching" a moment ago. Remember that low self-control is likely to lead to all manner of self-destructive consequences; instilling self-control in youth can therefore be expected to lead to less crime as well as fewer automobile accidents, teenage pregnancies, drug overdoses, and so on. Children in the habit of behaving as if consequences mattered might be less likely to encounter problems such as these.

As with many theories explored in this book, social control theory questions the usefulness of prison. The specific reasoning is that long-term incarceration is very likely to undermine social bonds. Loved ones might drift away, forming new relationships with others outside prison. Additionally, incarceration disrupts education and employment. Hence, if social bonds are important for keeping individuals from committing crime, incarcerating people—where they are likely to have their bonds of attachment, commitment, and involvement weakened—might actually make them *more* likely to be involved in crime. In short, prison could give offenders less to lose.

Self-control theory is also critical of the emphasis of current policy on the courts and corrections systems. First, the theory indicates that the individuals that these policies seek to protect society from are less capable of appreciating the long-term consequences of their decisions and will simply ignore the tougher sanctions. Thus, threats of exceedingly punitive sanctions are of no value if a person is not in the habit of considering them. Second, the theory also does not recommend efforts to rehabilitate offenders. Self-control, as noted earlier, stabilizes in late childhood, which means that efforts to teach self-control would have no effect in later years. Not surprisingly, rehabilitation programs have been notoriously unsuccessful at providing any long-term effective solution to crime. Self-control theory indicates that the formal justice system offers little crime prevention in return for huge tax expenditures.

SUMMARY

Control theories are recent developments building from ideas that originated long ago. At the core of the control theory perspectives are the ideas of Thomas Hobbes, who believed that people are naturally inclined to be deviant because they are rational and pleasure seeking. This idea is central to understanding control theory and how it differs from other theories. Indeed, the purpose of the control theorist is to make sense of why we do not commit crime in circumstances where doing so would be so gratifying. Hirschi's social control theory says that a person's investment in society creates bonds that make crime impossible or not worth committing. Gottfredson and Hirschi's self-control theory says that during childhood we learn that negative long-term consequences follow from reckless, immoral, illegal, or sinful activity, and so those who learn self-control more or less lose their taste for such activities because they fear the consequences. Hirschi's social control theory and Gottfredson and Hirschi's self-control theory represent the two leading control perspectives today.

Social control theories are distinguished from other theories in that they assume that we are all perfectly capable of crime from birth. In contrast, these other theories argue that crime is a characteristic that is not natural to people (or at least not to "normal" people). You may have noticed that the assumptions behind the control perspective share remarkable similarities to that of classical theory, and this insight would be correct. The key difference is that Beccaria and other classical thinkers were attempting to reform eighteenth-century legal systems and, not surprisingly, argued that the fear of legal sanctions for crime—certainty, swiftness, and severity—were key to promoting order in society. The control perspective, on the other hand, tends to place greater importance on other types of sanctions. Hirschi's control theory, for instance, emphasizes social sanctions. In fact, there is a lot to recommend social sanctions as being more important than legal sanctions. In the legal system, you enjoy (at least nominally) due process protections. You have the right to a formal trial, where you can potentially be exonerated for the crime you are charged with, and you might appeal if proper procedure was not followed in the courtroom. When it comes to what other people think of you, however, you are probably aware that there is no formal trial, no due process, no delays or continuances, and no appeal. The opinions of those who matter to us can be certain, swift, and severe indeed! Self-control theory goes further, adding natural sanctions; however, none—no matter how gruesome—are effective at stopping us if we are not in the habit of thinking about them. At least in these respects, the control perspective offers unique insights.

KEY TERMS

attachment   an element of Hirschi's social bond, referring to the degree of sensitivity that an individual has for the feelings of others, particularly those whom he or she respects or admires

belief   an element of Hirschi's social bond, referring to the degree in which an individual believes that a particular rule of society ought to be obeyed

commitment   an element of Hirschi's social bond, referring to the conventional investments an individual risks losing by engaging in crime

containment   a component of Reckless's containment theory; containment can be both "inner" and "outer," with each insulating individuals from pushes and pulls toward crime

involvement   an element of Hirschi's social bond, referring to how engaged an individual is in conventional activity

self-concept   a component of Reckless's containment theory; a form of inner containment that insulates the individual from pushes and pulls toward crime

self-control   the central component of Gottfredson and Hirschi's self-control theory; refers to the habit of individuals to behave as if long-term negative consequences matter

social bond   in Hirschi's theory, a bond that consists of attachment, commitment, involvement, and belief; it collectively acts to restrain individuals faced with criminal temptation

stakes in conformity   a term coined by Jackson Toby; refers to the stakes (benefits) individuals gain by obeying society's rules—stakes that risk being lost by engaging in crime; a central component in Hirschi's concept of attachment

DISCUSSION QUESTIONS

1. What makes control theories different from differential association and strain theories?

2. Why do you suppose that low self-control would influence crime as well as "crime-analogous" acts?

3. Think of some examples of inner and outer containment. Which forms of containment do you believe are most effective at reducing crime?

REFERENCES

Akers, R., & Sellers, C. (2004). *Criminological theories: Introduction, evaluation, and application.* Thousand Oaks, CA: Roxbury.

Conger, R. (1976). Social control and social learning models of delinquency: A synthesis. *Criminology, 14,* 17–40.

Felson, M. (1998). *Crime and everyday life.* Thousand Oaks, CA: Pine Forge Press.

Gottfredson, M. R., & Hirschi, T. (1990). *A general theory of crime.* Stanford, CA: Stanford University Press.

Grasmick, H., Tittle, C., Bursik, R., & Arneklev, B. (1993). Testing the core implications of Gottfredson and Hirschi's general theory of crime. *Journal of Research in Crime and Delinquency, 30,* 5–29.

Hirschi, T. (1969). *Causes of delinquency.* Berkeley: University of California Press.

Hirschi, T. (1995). The family. In J. Q. Wilson & J. Petersilia (eds.), *Crime.* San Francisco: ICS.

Hirschi, T., & Gottfredson, M. R. (2002). Self-control theory. In R. Paternoster & R. Bachman (Eds.), *Explaining criminals and crime: Essays in contemporary criminological theory.* Thousand Oaks, CA: Roxbury.

LaGrange, T., & Silverman, R. (1999). Low self-control and opportunity: Testing the general theory of crime as an explanation of gender differences in delinquency. *Criminology, 37,* 41–72.

Keane, C., Maxim, P., & Teevan, J. (1993). Drinking and driving, self-control, and gender. *Journal of Research in Crime and Delinquency, 30,* 30–46.

Kempf-Leonard, K. (1993). The empirical status of Hirschi's control theory. In F. Adler & W. S. Laufer (Eds.), *New directions in criminological theory: Advances in criminological theory.* New Brunswick, NJ: Transaction.

Nye, F. I. (1958). *Family relationships and delinquent behavior.* New York: Wiley.

Patterson, G. (1980). Children who steal. In T. Hirschi and M. Gottfredson (Eds.), *Understanding crime* (pp. 73–90). Beverly Hills, CA: Sage.

Pratt, T. C., & Cullen, F. T. (2000). The empirical status of Gottfredson and Hirschi's general theory of crime: A meta-analysis. *Criminology, 38,* 931–964.

Reckless, W. (1955). *The crime problem* (2nd ed.). New York: Appleton-Century-Crofts.

Reckless, W. (1967). *The crime problem* (4th ed.). New York: Appleton-Century-Crofts.

Reiss, A. J. (1951). Delinquency as the failure of personal and social controls. *American Sociological Review, 16,* 196–207.

Sampson, R. J., & Laub, J. H. (1993). *Crime in the making: Pathways and turning points through life.* Cambridge, MA: Harvard University Press.

Schreck, C. J. (1999). Criminal victimization and low self-control: An extension and test of a general theory of crime. *Justice Quarterly, 16,* 633–654.

Sellers, C. (1999). Self-control and intimate violence: An examination of the scope and specification of the general theory of crime." *Criminology, 37,* 375–404.

Shaw, C. R., & McKay, H. D. (1942). *Juvenile delinquency and urban areas.* Chicago: University of Chicago Press.

Stitt, B., & Giacopassi, A. (1992). Trends in the connectivity of theory and research in criminology. *The Criminologist, 17,* 1, 3–6.

Tittle, C. R. (1995). *Control balance: Toward a general theory of deviance.* Boulder, CO: Westview Press.

Toby, J. (1957). Social disorganization and stake in conformity: Complementary factors in the predatory behavior of hoodlums. *Journal of Criminal Law, Criminology, and Police Science, 48,* 12–17.

Warr, M. (2002). *Companions in crime: The social aspects of criminal conduct.* Cambridge, UK: Cambridge University Press.

CHAPTER 9

THEORIES OF SOCIAL CONFLICT

Whereas the majority of criminological theories examined so far have focused on individual, group, and environmental factors, an alternative theoretical tradition views *social conflict* as the root source of most social problems, including crime (Vold, 1958). According to this perspective, social order does not reflect a consensus model of what is right and wrong or best for society as a whole. Rather, the criminal justice system's identification and handling of offenders reflects an uneven distribution of power and resources throughout society.

This conflict, or critical perspective, is traceable to the seminal works of Tannenbaum (1938), Lemert (1951; 1967), and Becker (1963), who first proposed that criminal behavior was attributable to the process of **labeling**. Labeling theory contends that the very act of criminalization is itself an arbitrary label given to certain types of behavior. Moreover, when an individual is described or labeled as delinquent or criminal, the accused then internalizes that characterization, tailoring his or her behavior accordingly.

The rise of American critical criminology transpired during the 1970s, a period characterized by great social upheaval. Current events of the day included the civil rights movement, the Vietnam War, and a general liberalization of the popular culture, as evidenced by the sexual revolution, widespread recreational drug use, and the continuation of the hippie subculture from the 1960s. Theoretical criminology very much reflected the spirit of the times as society's disenchantment with its traditions and customs prompted challenges to authority and the continuation of a form of social control that many believed was not working.

Some came to view the discipline of criminology as part of the problem due to its traditional research focus on crimes committed by the lower class. When we concentrate on street-level crime, we largely ignore the white-collar crimes of the upper class. From this perspective, criminology serves the interests of the ruling class by distracting attention away from their offenses. A number of criminologists became increasingly opposed to class and racial forms of prejudice and discrimination by the criminal justice system and adopted a social justice orientation to their work. This approach advocated social activism to minimize biases against the poor, women, and racial and ethnic minorities.

THE CONFLICT PERSPECTIVE AND CRIME

Crime, from the conflict perspective, is considered a by-product of social inequality, both the result of efforts by those in power to control groups positioned lower in the social structure and a collective expression of deprivation, alienation, and frustration by those in the working class. This power imbalance orientation to explaining crime is, according to some theorists, grounded in and most evident in the conflict that exists between social classes (Lynch & Groves, 1986). A constant tension between "haves" and "have-nots" is considered a fundamental characteristic of modern social life, and this strain is thought to both push and pull individuals into crime.

The conflict perspective is particularly applicable in highly stratified, pluralistic, and multicultural societies, such as the United States, because there is great diversity in values across social groups (by gender, age, sexual orientation, religion, affluence, race, and ethnicity). This mixture of attitudes is observed in a power struggle for the authority necessary to define behavioral standards, formally through the criminal law and informally through the practice of moral condemnation. Those who gain power naturally define crime and deviance in ways that serve their interests, and their designations determine how society's institutions (schools, religion, and the criminal justice system) will be structured. By structuring society toward their interests, then, particularly in regard to what are considered acceptable and unacceptable (that is, legal vs. illegal) forms of wealth building and upward social mobility, the "haves" enjoy a created advantage in competition for economic and social resources.

Those in power are clearly interested in maintaining their advantaged position and use the criminal law as a basis of legitimizing social control, formally exercised through law enforcement and the military. In fact, many conflict theorists contend that the primary function of the criminal law is to protect the property interests of the wealthy (Bonger, 1916/1969; Marx, 1932/1978c; Quinney, 1979, 1980). In so doing, the interests of the "have-nots" are necessarily underrepresented, if at all, thus producing a power imbalance that is accentuated by the fact that the vast majority of people constitute the working rather than the ruling class. Accordingly, theorists are critical of the current system, sometimes calling for radical reform that will effect broader distribution of political power and material resources.

A number of leading critical and radical theories are presented in this chapter and, while they do not specify how power and conflict relate to crime in exactly the same way, they are similar in several respects. They all emphasize, for example, the presence of conflict within society, the importance of social class, and the view of modern capitalist society as the primary source of the inequality that causes or is associated with crime. Scrutiny of capitalism is largely fueled by another commonality, a Marxist heritage.

THE MARXIST HERITAGE

The philosophical underpinnings of the conflict approach are clearly traceable to the writings and revisionist perspective of Karl Marx (1818–1883). Because Marx advocated a mode of government that featured shared ownership of wealth, reference to Marxism typically brings to mind a socialist or communist society. The Marxist view of society includes a number of important related concepts that frame the conflict approach to crime. Marx, in his famous polemical works *Das Kapital* (1867/1978b) and *The Manifesto of the Communist Party* with Friedrich Engels (1848/1978), actually had very little to say about crime. Crime, from the Marxist perspective, is primarily a natural result of the inequality inherent to capitalist societies.

According to Marx (1867/1978b), the economic system of capitalism is the source of most social problems, including crime, because it creates conflict through competition for profit. Profit is considered evil and dehumanizing because it can be realized only by some people taking advantage of others and it minimizes the cultural, educational, and emotional dimensions of social life in exchange for greater emphasis on the dimension of work.

Marxist Concepts

The capitalistic desire for greater profit is realized through extraction of *surplus value* from the working class **(proletariat)** by the ruling class **(bourgeoisie)**. An oversimplified explanation of surplus value is that profit can be realized only through either increasing price or reducing production costs. Through competition, the free market limits profit through price increase, so it is obtained through underpaying laborers, an unfair system that essentially takes advantage of workers.

Profit through surplus value, then, can be realized only through *exploitation* of the proletariat. Because the desire for profit by the bourgeoisie, according to Marx, is insatiable, the degree of exploitation and related forms of dehumanization will lead to *alienation*. Alienation is easy to understand in its tangible forms, such as money and material possession, but the alienation of the working class is a more holistic expression of suffering.

Beyond economic disadvantage, social class distinctions also alienate people in terms of cultural, educational, recreational, and even social deprivation. A good example that illustrates both monetary and social alienation is Greek life on college campuses throughout the United States. Some students (who otherwise would) do not join sororities or fraternities because they simply cannot afford to "go Greek." Because of wealth disparity, then, some students are precluded from this social context—a system that ensures that people from roughly the same economic backgrounds will be segregated into social groups.

Marx predicted that as alienation became obvious and widely recognized throughout the working class, *class consciousness* (an awareness of one's class status) would develop and ultimately unite laborers to revolt against the ruling class and end capitalist-determined society. While various revolutions to end capitalism have not been successful, class consciousness remains a defining aspect of the popular psyche in stratified societies. Definitions of success, marrying well, and social network groups typically factor into the ever-present reality of class consciousness, even if only on a subconscious level.

Orthodox Marxism

Orthodox Marxism, sometimes referred to as **instrumental Marxism**, posits a direct relationship between the interests of the ruling class (profit, power, and prestige) and the functioning of social institutions such as the criminal justice system (Balkan, Berger, & Schmidt, 1980; Quinney, 1979, 1980). In fact, these interests are identifiable in the functioning of the criminal justice system throughout American history.

Workers have not always had a legal right to strike—for example, in protest against unfair working conditions or pay grievances. In the English- and Dutch-owned steel mills in Philadelphia during the 1890s, the first attempts by workers (mostly recent Irish immigrants) to strike were quashed by local police who simply arrested them at the request of the factory owners. Mule-drawn wagons with bars carried the Irish strikers, known as "paddies" (the term *paddy* was a racial pejorative referencing the Irish), away to jail—popularizing into American jargon the term *paddy wagon*. Today, reference to a paddy wagon indicates police vans filled with underage drinkers caught in bar raids, a depiction that is perhaps more than just a coincidence with the original wagons in that heavy drinking was a common practice by Irish workers on the strike line.

Structural Marxism

The acquisition of some political power by the working class over time has forced the ruling class to share some resources (for example, the minimum wage, worker compensation, and health insurance) with the working class (Lynch & Groves, 1986). However, only a token amount of resources are relinquished toward the goal of placating workers into accepting existing class relations rather than achieving greater equality. By spreading some power and wealth across social groups, the ruling class can successfully redirect working-class frustration by placing blame on the shortcomings of individuals, as opposed to a flawed social structure characterized by inequality.

The controversial issue of minority representation in graduate and law school programs, for example, is minimized if low admission rates are viewed relative to other accepted minorities rather than the aggregate reality. This redirection of blame diffuses class consciousness as a *technique of placation* and enables continuation of the status quo and the capitalist mode. Another example of a technique of placation is the institution of religion, which typically advocates versions of morality that do not condone criminal behavior. Moreover, religion usually promotes humility and respect for authority. Accordingly, people self-regulate their behavior and, in so doing, require less expenditure for formal control. More important, the authority and property interests of the ruling class are protected as religion discourages the conflict necessary for change. Marx, in fact, referred to religion as "the opium of the people" (1844/1978a), meaning that religion drugged the lower classes into accepting an unfair social system.

Structural Marxism differs from the orthodox approach by acknowledging an indirect relationship between ruling-class interests and the way social institutions operate (Balbus, 1977; Chambliss & Seidman, 1982). Ruling class interests are often furthered subtly, entrenched in the rules and policies that guide the daily operations of our social institutions. Social institutions normally function so that they typically generate disparate outcomes, which ensures the perpetuation of an elitist hierarchy. While we think of our elected officials, for example, of representing everyone through the democratic political process, the rules governing elections are such that only the wealthy have a realistic chance of being elected. Not surprisingly, the vast majority of our elected representatives are affluent though the majority of their constituents are not.

But what about Marxist thought and crime? Although Marx did not have very much to say about crime, the preceding conceptual line of reasoning has generated several subsequent specific theories of crime, described next. Before examining leading critical and radical statements of crime, it is important to acknowledge the significance of the symbolic interactionist perspective on the conflict perspective, most notably the influence of labeling theory.

LABELING THEORY

The labeling perspective (Becker, 1963; Lemert, 1951, 1967) acknowledges that people first participate in norm violation, either crime or a less serious deviant act, by chance or simply as a part of growing up. Most youth, for example, engage in some form of delinquent behavior as an expression of rebellion or experimentation that is considered part of the maturation process for all teenagers. The difference between delinquents and nondelinquents may be, in large part, an outcome of who gets caught. Simply getting caught can result in **stigma**, a generic negative depiction of a person based on certain aspects of their behavior. The most commonly cited description of labeling theory comes from Howard Becker's famous book *Outsiders* (1963). Becker contended that "social groups *create* deviance by making rules whose infraction constitutes deviance, and by applying these rules to particular people and labeling them as outsiders. From this point of view, deviance is not a quality of the act the person commits, but rather a consequence of the application by others of rules and sanctions to the 'offender.' The deviant is one to whom that label has been successfully applied; deviant behavior is behavior that people so label" (p. 9). Becker's analysis of deviance illustrated that crime and deviance were largely a creation by rule enforcers who held the power to label.

Initial acts of deviance, termed **primary deviation**, prompt negative reactions from those in authority who devalue delinquent youth, due to a combination of the actual trouble they have already caused and the perception that they will cause further problems. These perceptions of youth as delinquent generate stereotypes that cause a sort of ripple effect wherein others also come to see the designated youth in a negative light.

Common stereotypes include portrayals of the lower-class criminal, whose criminality stems from little education, blocked opportunities for advancement, and adherence to criminogenic subcultural values. The process of labeling necessarily involves a power dynamic that pronounces the inequality between those who have position to assign labels and those who are labeled. Labeling, through the concept of *master status,* can become a self-fulfilling prophecy. Once a person has engaged in unacceptable behavior and has been identified as a violator, he or she becomes disvalued proportionate to the severity of the offense. Deviant status can come to altogether define a person ("thief," "stoner," "slut"), overshadowing other socially desirable dimensions of his or her behavior.

After individuals have acquired a deviant label, others view and interact with them in such a manner that further misbehavior is expected. Continued participation in delinquency and crime, called **secondary deviation**, reflects both the ironic outcome of the social construction of crime through the labeling process and the importance of self-concept. Symbolic interactionist influence on the labeling approach can be seen in the sociological works of Mead (1934), Cooley (1902), and Becker (1963). Charles Horton Cooley introduced the idea of the *looking-glass self,* suggesting that the self-image reflected in a mirror is a metaphor for perceptions of self determined through the collective eyes of others. A brief example of the looking-glass self might be new clothes for a social event. Do you see an outfit on you as it actually appears or the way you want others to see you? Probably the latter, according to the labeling perspective.

George Herbert Mead (1934), in turn, is credited with a similar concept termed "the generalized other," the idea that our behavior is affected by perceptions and related expectations. By comparing personal behavior and decisions to a perceived appropriate social standard, people create a meaningful reference point. The reference, however, often reflects distinction.

William Chambliss's well-known study "The Saints and the Roughnecks" (1973) depicted the relevance of social class in the labeling process. The Saints were eight delinquent male high school students whose behaviors included heavy drinking, truancy, vandalism, and minor theft. They particularly enjoyed pranks, some of which involved harm, such as changing traffic and warning signs that caused accidents. As the label "Saints" implies, these middle-class youth from traditional families were seen as "good kids" whose behavior was largely excused by authorities as youthful indiscretion. They were rarely arrested and many grew up to become professionals such as doctors and lawyers.

The "Roughnecks," on the other hand, were six male high school students from the same town who also engaged in various forms of delinquency. They did tend to fight more than the Saints but engaged in far less vandalism resulting in monetary damage. They were all from lower-class families and had frequent interaction with the police who, along with most of the town, viewed them as troublemakers. This perception was reinforced by their frequent arrests, which officially labeled them and arguably affected their futures. In fact, they ended up either working as wage laborers in low-paying jobs or in prison.

Another study that demonstrated the importance of labeling, more so than actual harm specific to behavior, centered on a shoplifting experiment (Steffensmeier & Terry, 1973). With the permission of a department store's management, students dressed explicitly to depict either a "hippie" or "preppie" appearance and then shoplifted. The study focused on whether reactions to the shoplifting differed between the groups and found that witnesses were far more likely to report the hippies. Even though the students in each group committed the same offense at the same rate, it appeared that simply projecting a lower-class or antiestablishment image elicited a harsher reaction. These and numerous subsequent studies (see Mann, 1993; Tittle & Curran, 1988; Wilbanks, 1987) have confirmed the importance of *extralegal factors,* such as class and race, on the practices of arrests, due process, and sanctioning. The current controversy over racial profiling is a straightforward example of the continued importance of labeling.

Braithwaite's theory of **reintegrative shaming** (1989) is the foremost recent contribution to the labeling perspective. Building on the observation of the power of shaming to affect behavior, Braithwaite argued the illogic of stereotyping offenders. Whereas reintegrative shaming sought to punish offenders and bring them back into conventional society, *disintegrative shaming* stigmatized them as deviant through such labels as "ex-con." Blocked from rejoining mainstream society, offenders further develop a self-image of being criminal and ultimately become more entrenched in crime.

While the idea of reintegrating offenders back into society is appealing in theory, it is difficult to achieve due to both social realities and current criminal justice policies. Because the United States is a pluralistic society (heterogeneous, multicultural, and socially stratified), people do not always agree on which behaviors are inappropriate and should be sanctioned. Shaming, as an informal sanctioning mechanism, depends on social consensus, which varies across groups and by particular topics. Americans are divided concerning the legalization of marijuana, prohibition of abortion, regulation of gun ownership, and numerous other issues. Differences of opinion minimize the effectiveness of informal sanctioning, leaving crime problems to the criminal justice system.

The criminal justice system invokes policies involving both disintegrative and reintegrative forms of shaming. Convicted drunk drivers made to wear bright orange vests while picking up trash alongside highways and sex offender notification laws are examples of criminal justice practices employing shame for deterrence (at public and individual levels) and punishment purposes. Offender reentry programs, commonly referred to as "aftercare," seek to facilitate offender transition from incarcerated settings to society. These efforts, often executed in the context of "halfway houses," are consistent with the logic of reintegration. Unfortunately, aftercare is not a high rehabilitation priority, moving many criminologists to observe that policies concerning offender reintegration are largely "image over substance."

In sum, labeling theory contends that through stigmatization, the criminal justice system creates crime and deviance as offenders come to identify themselves according to the expectations suggested by labels. The point where labeling theory ends and critical theories begin is blurred, but the act of labeling and the power dynamic inherent in the labeling process is a recurring theme throughout critical and radical theories.

MARXIST CRIMINOLOGY

Marxist or radical criminologists use the Marxist conceptual framework to examine the criminal law, crime itself, and the government's practice of social control (policing, prosecution, and sanctioning). The *social origins of the law* are observed as reflecting special interests that are traceable to class interests, be they profit or protection from potential threats by the lower class. The offense of vagrancy, for example, is especially class focused and seems to be a means for legitimizing the displacement of lower-class people (whose appearance or behavior is deemed "undesirable") from public, often affluent, places—apart from any violence or threat posed to person or property (Chambliss, 1964). Marxist criminology interprets vagrancy laws as dehumanizing in that the pursuit of profit is clearly valued more than the human suffering associated with being a vagrant. Marx himself contended that "There must be something rotten in the very core of a social system which increases in wealth without diminishing its misery, and increases in crime even more than its numbers" (Marx, 1867/1978).

Marxists contend that the criminal law both serves to control the lower classes and provides immunity for crimes of the ruling class. Why, for example, are drug enforcement efforts focused more on crack cocaine? Relatedly, why are the criminal penalties for using and selling crack more severe than for powder cocaine? Marxists reject the argument that crack-related activities warrant greater policing and harsher sentences because crack is more addictive and incites greater violence. Rather, radical criminologists allege *selective enforcement* against social groups (mostly the poor and minorities) that primarily use and sell crack.

The criminal law from the Marxist perspective, then, is seen as a tool of repression by the ruling class. The criminal behavior of the lower class is largely seen as an expression of resistance to economic and social oppression, with some Marxists going so far as to argue that criminals are political activists or revolutionaries whose behavior represents resistance and is oriented toward social change. Criminals, or at least lower-class offenders, are depicted as victims of social inequality. Not surprisingly, mainstream criminologists respond that such a view excuses personal responsibility for criminal behavior.

WHITE-COLLAR AND STATE CRIME

Marxist criminology redirects attention away from the street crime of the lower class to white-collar and political or state crime. **White-collar crime** was first addressed by Edwin Sutherland, who defined it as "a crime committed by a person of respectability and high social status in the course of his occupation" (1983). Although this definition suggests individual wrongdoing, the scope of white-collar crime also involves activities engaged in by businesses and corporations.

Some theorists submit that crimes such as consumer fraud and false advertising inflict far greater social harm (by affecting more people and involving far greater amounts of money) than do lower-level personal property crimes, such as burglary and theft (Chambliss, 1988, 1999; Quinney, 1980). In some instances, the white-collar crimes of the upper class can also directly inflict personal injury similar to violent crime. The infamous Ford Pinto case during the 1970s serves as a primary example. In this conspiracy, the automobile company discovered that the casing design around the gas tank in the Pinto model was not sufficient and could lead to fire and explosion in the event of accidents under certain conditions. After calculating the costs of issuing a recall to install appropriate parts to ensure consumer safety versus the amount to settle a projected number of lawsuits (including the loss of lives), the company chose to settle the suits. More recently, executives at Ford Motor Company and Firestone Tires made a similar decision when evidence emerged suggesting that tires used on the popular Ford Explorer sport-utility vehicle would deteriorate when driven at high speeds.

Political crime, or **state crime**, differs from white-collar or corporate crime in terms of its primary objectives—political as opposed to economic. Political objectives are rooted in the state's need to exercise or establish power and authority. State crime is typically dichotomized as crimes of negligence and crimes of omission. The former is defined as the result of a conscious choice on the part of the state not to do something about a potential or observable social harm. Crimes of omission are the result of implicit state support for structural conditions (such as capitalism and patriarchy), which in turn lead to socially harmful consequences. White-collar crime and state crime are often considered in conjunction, as the government enables exploitation through its trade policies and leniency for upper-class violators.

LEFT REALISM

Left realism evolved in response to critical theorists' neglect of inner-city crime, specifically, and the plight of the urban underclass, generally. The English criminologist Jock Young (1987) is among the most prominent theorists associated with left realism, being one of the first to call attention to the intense and multifaceted nature of victimization within inner cities. Inner-city residents are dually victimized by the capitalistic economic system and also at the hands of their immediate neighbors who engage in criminal activity. Left realists also criticize other Marxist criminologists whose primary concern is opposing the criminal justice system rather than providing support for the victims of lower-class crimes. For example, critical theorists' attention to disproportionate involvement in crime by disenfranchised urban African Americans is in the context of institutionalized racism within American society. The focus on why this group is heavily involved in crime, however, ignores that they also suffer disproportionately from high rates of victimization, particularly homicide (LaFree, Drass, & O'Day, 1992).

Left realists suggest that *relative poverty* is a more accurate determinant of crime than *absolute poverty*. After all, poverty has a qualitative dimension that necessitates comparison between groups—that is, poverty can be assessed only in relation to others' wealth, a condition captured by the concept *economic disparity*. Young and others (Dekeseredy & Schwartz, 1991; Lea, 1992; Lowman, 1992; Matthews, 1992) argue that relative deprivation combined with the competitive individualism of capitalism fosters discontent and instigates behavior labeled criminal.

Left realists are critical of those whom Marx himself described as "armchair sociologists"—criminologists who are content to wait for revolution to create significant changes in the criminal justice system rather than proactively effect change themselves. The prospects for change are thought to be most likely through advocacy of short-term policy revisions that effect economic improvement and increase justice conditions for the lower and working classes. Left realism, then, is one of the most radical conflict theories.

CULTURAL CRIMINOLOGY

Cultural criminology is closely related to the field of cultural studies and is influenced by postmodern insights (Pfohl, 1985; Schwartz & Friedrichs, 1994) that claim that images presented by the mass media are (falsely) seen by many as reality. This perspective, championed most notably by contemporary criminologist Jeff Ferrell (1993; Ferrell & Sanders, 1995), examines *crime control* rather than crime itself and does so by means of *media analysis.* Specifically, cultural criminologists investigate the ways in which the mass media and popular culture influence the general public's understanding of crime in society and, more important, how they influence policy development. The central premise of this perspective is that crime is a definitionally subjective term, as is its control. In other words, both the public and policymakers are greatly influenced by what the media presents as socially problematic, and their responses are constructed accordingly.

Cultural criminology is influenced, as well, by alternative qualitative methods (Ferrell & Hamm, 1998; Miller, 1995; Miller & Tewksbury, 2001). It is argued that through the *immediacy of crime,* that is, firsthand observation of offending and victimization, criminologists can come to fully understand the complexity of crime. Cultural criminology is also closely associated with the perspective of **social constructionism**, which is addressed in the following section.

THE SOCIAL CONSTRUCTION OF CRIME, POSTMODERNISM, AND CONSTITUTIVE CRIMINOLOGY

The theories addressed in the preceding chapters have all considered crime from an objectivist viewpoint; however, crime (as well as other social problems) can also be examined from a *subjectivist* perspective. Subjectivists, also known as *constructionists,* contend that crime is a definitionally subjective reality. Accordingly, no act is inherently deviant, criminal, or necessarily a threat to society. Rather, crime is constructed by a process called *claimsmaking.* The claimsmaking process originates from groups or organizations that single out a particular phenomenon, cause, or issue, subsequently drawing or demanding attention to it. Such groups are referred to as *claimsmakers* and their endeavors are considered a two-stage process. First, a given issue or problem (for our purposes, crime) is identified by primary claimsmakers, thereby drawing attention to a particular problematic condition and demanding a response to it. Second, the condition is discovered and investigated by the media and then presented to a national audience as a pressing social concern. The specified problem is often contended, through exaggeration, to be of epidemic proportions.

Constructionists suggest that those acts labeled criminal and afforded the most attention by the public, media, and agents of social control are not those that necessarily are the most serious, but rather acts that threaten those in power. Constructionists stress the importance of the *discrepancy* between perceived and actual threats, positing that social harm is presented in a manner that draws attention away from the more serious infractions committed by the upper classes. The construction of crime is a diversionary tool, much like the Marxist concept technique of placation, which allows those in power to cover up their own violations by highlighting the deviance of others.

Essential to the social construction of crime perspective is the identification of *folk devils,* described as unambiguously unfavorable symbols whose real or imagined behavior is a threat to social welfare (Cohen, 1972). Folk devils are necessary because they provide a readily identifiable culprit for the social problem at hand—in our case, crime. An example of using the folk devil construct can be found in the reported church-burning "epidemic" of the mid-1990s (Carter, 1999). In this instance, government officials, special-interest groups, and the media joined forces to perpetuate the claim that a string of church arsons across the southern United States was the result of a nationwide Ku Klux Klan conspiracy to terrorize African Americans. Despite official law enforcement investigations that revealed no evidence of such a conspiracy, all interested parties continued to stand behind their accusations. These claims were easily accepted by the general public as truth in part because the KKK was a likely suspect that had engaged in such behavior previously during the civil rights movement and the South's history of racial strife. If claimsmakers had had no one specific to blame, tales of a racial conspiracy might not have been as easily accepted.

Postmodernism is a movement that began in the humanities and transcended to the realm of social science in the 1980s. Postmodernist thought is not particular to criminology alone; rather it is more of a philosophy of knowledge production and accumulation. Criminology, along with other social and natural sciences, traditionally has stressed the use of the positivistic framework in determining causal mechanisms among phenomena. Postmodernist criminology, however, suggests that much of the knowledge related to crime and criminality has been socially constructed and that no real "truth" is readily available for criminologists.

Despite the shortcomings of the traditional criminological approach, postmodernism contends that deconstruction and then a preferable *reconstruction* of the facts is possible. By examining crime and social control in a social, historical, and cultural context, criminologists can then more adequately understand the scope and nature of both criminal offending and criminalization. Postmodernism essentially demands reconsideration of that which we take for granted—that which is assumed as irrefutable empirical "facts."

Constitutive criminology is a wide-ranging critical theory whose roots are traceable to Marxism and postmodernism. Among the most prominent theorists associated with this tradition are Henry and Milovanovic (1991, 1996), both of whom stress the importance of how humans shape their social worlds. Constitutive criminologists argue that the roots of crime are traceable to unequal power relations that shape society's impressions of and responses to criminal behavior. Constitutive criminology focuses, then, on the processes by which crime is "constructed" rather than caused.

FEMINIST CRIMINOLOGY

There are many varieties of feminist criminology: liberal, radical, and Marxist or socialist. While slightly different, these perspectives have common assumptions. First, although biological differences are acknowledged, gender is seen as a socially constructed reality shaped by cultural, historical, and social factors (Gelsthorpe & Morris, 1990). Feminists reject that behavior is attributable to being male or female; rather it is the result of the prevailing cultural values concerning gender roles and relations. Also, social order and interaction are seen as a function of male dominance. A patriarchal society influences females, according to feminist criminology, in such a way that they have a unique perspective on class, race, and gender interrelationships.

Feminist criminologists have traditionally examined the role of extralegal factors and how they result in more lenient treatment for women than men (Chesney-Lind, 1997; Chesney-Lind & Shelden, 1992; Gelsthorpe & Morris, 1990). It is a matter of some controversy whether the criminal justice system's leniency for women is a matter of less-serious female crime, a lower rate of criminal charges, or other social factors. The two most frequently considered social factors are *chivalry* and *paternalism*. Chivalry refers to traditional gender relations with women placed on a pedestal and needing protection. Paternalism is, in feminist criminological thought, a condescending concept that devalues women by perpetuating a view of them as feeble and even childlike.

Feminist criminology is characterized by intuitive, tentative, and sometimes circular theorizing. Traditional criminological theorizing, in comparison, is more objective and linear—stated in a format suitable for testing by the logic of variable analysis more so than feminist theories. Feminist criminologists have argued that traditional methods of evaluating theory are not applicable, largely because the objectives are not to confirm hypotheses but to effect change through social movement.

Feminist criminologists take issue with criminology's neglect of women offenders and how they are misrepresented through stereotyping. This perspective addresses two general problems: the gender ratio and the issue of generalizability. The *gender ratio* refers to the relative level of criminal involvement by males and females. A fundamental question addresses why women are less likely, and men more likely, to commit crime. The *generalizability* problem refers to whether the traditional criminological theories, largely framed by male criminologists focusing on male offenders, can adequately account for female crime.

A general assumption of feminism is that the production of knowledge (the process of theorizing and research) reflects a male perspective on the natural and social world. Virtually everything—social life, social order, and social institutions—is *gendered.* Feminism is consistent with the conflict perspective in its observation that a gendered society generates inequality. Male superiority and dominance in politics, economics, and social life ensures gender discrimination. The nature and intensity of this inequality varies across versions of feminist theory.

Liberal feminism is a cultural orientation to gender differences, such as separate socialization experiences for boys and girls. Traditional attitudes about gender roles, particularly female participation in the labor market, are blamed for power imbalances. By promoting policies that eliminate, or at least soften, traditional dimensions of power, it is thought that greater social harmony and less gender inequality will result.

Freda Adler (1975) and Rita Simon (1975) were early feminist theorists who sought to explain what they observed as the shrinking gender ratio between male and female crime. The central thrust of their argument, referred to as the *liberation perspective,* is that as women gain more equality in a range of life spheres, including education, occupation, and the family, equality will spill over into criminality. Despite the logic of this argument, empirical support for this theory is scant (Chesney-Lind, 1997; Steffensmeier & Streifel, 1992) and has been generally rejected by many feminist theorists as not being feminist enough, or at all.

Radical feminism is a more aggressive approach to gender relations in that men are viewed in a negative light for taking advantage of women, primarily through sexuality. A key concept of radical feminist thought is **patriarchy**, which is used to describe a social order dominated in all respects by males. This domination extends into both criminality and official responses to it (that is, the criminal justice system). Formal control mechanisms reflect the patriarchal social order in that laws benefit and enable male domination. Women's biological dependence during childbearing years and fundamental physical strength differences subjugate women and situate them in a disfavorable gender-based power dynamic. Also, the male-based social origins of law are thought to be a root source of the objectification of women. In short, radical feminism sees the criminal law and its enforcement as serving the interests of men at the expense of women.

Women who comply with the gendered social system are considered to have been effectively co-opted by male society through material and social rewards that only reinforce the status quo. Additionally, the labeling of various female behaviors, especially sexual deviance, is thought to be a form of dominance that ironically, furthers similar deviant behavior.

John Hagan's *power-control theory* (1989), though not a radical feminist theory per se, attempts to empirically validate claims that the patriarchal social order is related to criminal offending in terms of gender. Specifically, Hagan hypothesizes that females who are raised under more egalitarian familial structures (families where there is more equality between husbands and wives in terms of occupational prestige and income) will engage in higher incidence of criminal behavior than their counterparts hailing from traditional, male-dominated families. Although Hagan's own findings have supported this premise, other research (Jensen & Thompson, 1990; Morash & Chesney-Lind, 1991) has failed to adequately confirm his predictions.

A third feminist perspective, *Marxist* or *socialist feminism,* attributes gender oppression to the inequality inherent in capitalistic economies. Derived from Marxist principles, socialist feminism argues that capitalism, through a gendered labor market structure, allows men to assert economic dominance over women. This economic dominance, in turn, influences all other aspects of social life, including the extent and nature of female criminality. Socialist feminists support the creation of egalitarian societies that would be free from both class and gender divisions.

Feminist criminology has become increasingly influential in recent years. Traditional projections of masculinity (toughness, heterosexuality, and breadwinner status) in subcultural settings have been found instrumental to explaining violence. Beyond attention to female criminality and the treatment of female offenders, attention to the social origins of gender has furthered understanding of crime in general. James W. Messerschmidt has been a prominent voice in calling attention to the gendered nature of behavior. Messerschmidt, in *Masculinities and Crime* (1993), argues that the prevalence of male offending is due primarily to socialization processes that emphasize male success and domination. Both street and white-collar crime are dominated by men, then, in an attempt to assert their strength and supremacy.

PEACEMAKING CRIMINOLOGY AND RESTORATIVE JUSTICE

Peacemaking criminology (Pepinsky & Quinney, 1991), like most conflict perspectives, does not address why people commit crime. Like similar theories, this view acknowledges the importance of the labeling process that splits people into either a criminal or a noncriminal group. The theory's name references the government's "war" language in the context of crime (such as "the War on Drugs"). Peacemaking criminologists are concerned about minimizing social inequality, but also place responsibility for victimization and harm with offenders.

Another perspective very similar to peacemaking criminology is **restorative justice** (Strang & Braithwaite, 2001), in which crime is seen as an outcome of damaged social relationships and the solution is thought to be in bringing people together through community and individual interaction. The foremost assumption is that the criminal justice system's approach of deterrence and punishment is faulty and should be replaced with less-formal approaches emphasizing reconciliation and the restoration of strained relationships. Accordingly, informal solutions to disputes, such as arbitration and juvenile alternatives to court, are advocated as they divert people away from the justice system and prevent formal criminal labeling.

Restorative justice advocates attention to victims' rights, offender accountability, and public safety. Consequently, proponents of this perspective stress the need for interpersonal reconciliation as opposed to traditional state-sponsored responses to crime wherein victims have little or no say in the justice process. Additionally, restorative justice mandates offender accountability such that perpetrators must face their victims and publicly acknowledge responsibility for their actions. Restorative justice, then, is a systems-based approach to an alternative means of achieving social justice. A recent example of restorative justice in practice is the advent of the national youth court movement, which adjudicates juvenile crime through informal, community-based processes that divert youth from entanglement in the juvenile justice system.

SUMMARY

The conflict perspective views the fundamental causes of crime as the economic and social forces operating within society, especially the influence of capitalism. The criminal law and criminal justice system are thought to function on behalf of the ruling social class. The ruling class defines the criminal law with its own interests in mind, and criminal justice policy both controls the poor and perpetuates existing class relations. The working class is economically exploited but also socially alienated, as ruling-class standards of morality are represented in criminal and deviant labels imposed on them.

The criminal justice system's focus on the lower class distracts attention away from crimes of the ruling class, such as white-collar crime and state crime. High levels of property crime and violence in the urban underclass and impoverished rural areas are seen as expressions of deprivation and frustration. Morality crimes, such as sex, drug, and gambling offenses, are considered control mechanisms that punish those whose income is not taxed to the benefit of capitalistic government.

The Marxian heritage has heavily influenced various critical and radical theories. While these theories differ by specifying different aspects of the criminogenic effects of inequality, they all are discontent with the current social system and consider it an underlying basis for many social problems. The terms *critical* and *radical* suggest criticism of the criminal law and its role in contributing to social inequality, and the need for radical action to effect change in the criminal justice system. Critical criminologists believe that they can help effect this change through demystification of equitable social relations as shaped by the forces of capitalism.

KEY TERMS

bourgeoisie the Marxist conception of the ruling or capitalist class, which controls the means of production and exploits the proletariat

labeling a process by which a negative attribute (that is, delinquent or criminal) is assigned to an individual, resulting in internalization of that identity

orthodox/instrumental Marxism a perspective that posits a direct relationship between the interests of the ruling class and the functioning of social institutions

patriarchy a social order dominated in all respects by males

political/state crime crime committed on behalf of governments toward political objectives

postmodernism a philosophy that questions traditional means of inquiry and knowledge production and accumulation

primary deviation the initial incidence of deviant behavior occurring in the natural course of adolescence or young adulthood

proletariat the Marxist conception of the lower or working class that is exploited by the bourgeoisie

reintegrative shaming a process by which a community admonishes and shames individuals with the purpose of bringing them back into conventional society; popularized by the Australian criminologist John Braithwaite

restorative justice a perspective that views crime as a function of damaged social relationships and calls for a reparation of those bonds

secondary deviation continued participation in delinquency or crime due to an internalized self-concept reflective of negative labeling

social constructionism a perspective that addresses the subjectivity of crime and its control

stigma a generic negative depiction of an individual based on certain aspects of his or her behavior

structural Marxism a perspective that acknowledges an indirect relationship between ruling-class interests and social institutions

white-collar crime crimes committed by people of high status in the course of their occupation

DISCUSSION QUESTIONS

1. What are the key differences between orthodox/instrumental Marxism and structural Marxism?

2. How do the main assumptions of the conflict perspective differ from positivistic theories of crime?

3. Do you believe that affirmative action will decrease social inequality, consequently lowering the overall crime rate?

4. What is patriarchy, and what is its impact on the criminal justice system?

5. Do you think restorative justice programs will really make a difference, or is this movement more likely to be viewed by offenders as just a way of "getting off" easy?

REFERENCES

Adler, F. (1975). *Sisters in crime: The rise of the new female criminal.* New York: McGraw-Hill.

Balbus, I. D. (1977). Commodity form and legal form: An essay on the "relative autonomy" of the state. *Law and Society Review, 11,* 571–588.

Balkan, S., Berger, R. J., & Schmidt, J. (1980). *Crime and deviance in America: A critical approach.* Belmont, CA: Wadsworth.

Becker, H. S. (1963). *Outsiders: Studies in the sociology of deviance.* New York: Free Press.

Bonger, W. (1969). *Crime and economic conditions.* Bloomington: Indiana University Press. (Original work published 1916)

Braithwaite, J. (1989). *Crime, shame and reintegration.* Cambridge, UK: Cambridge University Press.

Carter, C. S. (1999). Church burning in African American communities: Implications for empowerment practice. *Social Work, 44,* 62–68.

Chambliss, W. J. (1964). A sociological analysis of the law of vagrancy. *Social Problems, 12,* 67–77.

Chambliss, W. J. (1988). *On the take* (2nd ed.). Indianapolis: Indiana University Press.

Chambliss, W. J. (1999). *Power, politics, and crime.* Boulder, CO: Westview Press.

Chambliss, W. J., & Seidman, R. B. (1982). *Law, order and power* (2nd ed.). Reading, MA: Addison-Wesley.

Chesney-Lind, M. (1997). *The female offender: Girls, women, and crime.* Thousand Oaks, CA: Sage.

Chesney-Lind, M., & Shelden, R. G. (1992). *Girls, delinquency, and juvenile justice.* Pacific Grove, CA: Brooks/Cole.

Cohen, S. (1972). *Folk devils and moral panics: The creation of the Mods and Rockers.* New York: St. Martin's Press.

Cooley, C. H. (1902). *Human nature and the social order.* New York: Scribner.

Dekeseredy, W. S., & Schwartz, M. D. (1991). British and U.S. left realism: A critical comparison. *International Journal of Offender Therapy and Comparative Criminology, 35,* 248–262.

Ferrell, J. (1993). *Crimes of style: Urban graffiti and the politics of criminality.* New York: Garland.

Ferrell, J., & Hamm, M. S. (1998). *Ethnography on the edge.* Boston: Northeastern University Press.

Ferrell, J., & Sanders, C. R. (Eds.). (1995). *Cultural criminology.* Boston: Northeastern University Press.

Gelsthorpe, L., & Morris, A. (Eds.). (1990). *Feminist perspectives in criminology.* Philadelphia: Open University Press.

Henry, S., & Milovanovic, D. (1991). Constitutive criminology: The maturation of critical theory. *Criminology, 29,* 293–315.

Henry, S., & Milovanovic, D. (1996). *Constitutive criminology: Beyond postmodernism.* London: Sage.

Jensen, G., & Thompson, K. (1990). What's class got to do with it? A further examination of power control theory. *American Journal of Sociology, 95,* 1009–1023.

LaFree, G., Drass, K. A., & O'Day, P. (1992). Race and crime in post-war America: Determinants of African-American and white rates, 1957–1988. *Criminology, 30,* 157–188.

Lea, J. (1992). The analysis of crime. In J. Young & R. Matthews (Eds.), *Rethinking criminology: The realist debate* (pp. 69–94). London: Sage.

Lemert, E. M. (1951). *Social pathology.* New York: McGraw-Hill.

Lemert, E. M. (1967). *Human deviance, social problems, and social control.* Upper Saddle River, NJ: Prentice Hall.

Lowman, J. (1992). Rediscovering crime. In J. Young & R. Matthews (Eds.), *Rethinking criminology: The realist debate* (pp. 141–160). London: Sage.

Lynch, M. J., & Groves, W. B. (1986). *A primer in radical criminology.* New York: Harrow & Heston.

Mann, C. R. (1993). *Unequal justice: A question of culture.* Bloomington: Indiana University Press.

Marx, K. (1978a). Contribution to the critique of Hegel's *Philosophy of right:* Introduction. In R. C. Tucker (Ed.), *The Marx-Engels reader* (2nd ed.). New York: Norton. (Original work published 1844)

Marx, K. (1978b). Das Kapital. In R. C. Tucker (Ed.), *The Marx-Engels reader* (2nd ed.). New York: Norton. (Original work published 1867)

Marx, K. (1978c). The German ideology: Part I. In R. C. Tucker (Ed.), *The Marx-Engels reader* (2nd ed.). New York: Norton. (Original work published 1932)

Marx, K., & Engels, F. (1978). Manifesto of the Communist Party. In R. C. Tucker (Ed.), *The Marx-Engels reader* (2nd ed.). New York: Norton. (Original work published 1948)

Matthews, R. (1992). Reflections on realism. In J. Young & R. Matthews (Eds.), *Rethinking criminology: The realist debate,* (pp. 1–24). London: Sage.

Mead, G. H. (1934). *Mind, self, and society.* Chicago: University of Chicago Press.

Messerschmidt, J. W. (1993). *Masculinities and crime.* Lanham, MD: Rowman & Littlefield.

Miller, J. M. (1995). Covert participant observation: Reconsidering the least used method. *Journal of Contemporary Criminal Justice, 11,* 97–105.

Miller, J. M., & Tewksbury, R. A. (Eds.). (2001). *Extreme methods: Innovative approaches to social science research.* Boston: Allyn & Bacon.

Morash, M., & Chesney-Lind, M. (1991). A reformulation and partial test of the power control theory of delinquency. *Justice Quarterly, 8,* 347–378.

Pepinsky, H. E., & Quinney, R. (Eds.). (1991). *Criminology as peacemaking.* Bloomington: Indiana University Press.

Pfohl, S. J. (1985). *Images of deviance and social control: A sociological history.* New York: McGraw-Hill.

Quinney, R. (1979). The production of criminology. *Criminology, 16,* 445–458.

Quinney, R. (1980). *Class, state and crime* (2nd ed.). New York: Longman.

Schwartz, M. D., & Friedrichs, D. O. (1994). Postmodern thought and criminological discontent: New metaphors for understanding violence. *Criminology, 32,* 221–246.

Simon, R. (1975). *Women and crime.* Lexington, MA: Lexington Books.

Steffensmeier, D. J., & Streifel, C. (1992). Trends in female crime: 1960–1990. In C. Culliver (Ed.), *Female criminality: The state of the art.* New York: Garland.

Steffensmeier, D. J., & Terry, R. M. (1973). Deviance and respectability: An observational study of reactions to shoplifting. *Social Forces, 51,* 417–426.

Strang, H., & Braithwaite, J. (Eds.). (2001). *Restorative justice and civil society.* Cambridge, UK: Cambridge University Press.

Tannenbaum, F. (1938). *Crime and the community.* Boston: Ginn.

Tittle, C. R., & Curran, D. (1988). Contingencies for dispositional disparities in juvenile justice. *Social Forces, 67,* 23–58.

Vold, G. B. (1958). *Theoretical criminology.* New York: Oxford University Press.

Wilbanks, W. (1987). *The myth of a racist crim-* *inal justice system.* Monterey, CA: Brooks/Cole.

Young, J. (1987). The tasks facing a realist criminology. *Contemporary Crises, 11,* 337–356.

CHAPTER 10

EVALUATING AND INTEGRATING THEORY

Our understanding of the causes of crime, how its occurrence is unevenly dispersed throughout society in a fairly systematic manner, and how various policy responses might fare is certainly greater than it would be without the benefit of theoretical insight. Theoretical criminology is complex and involves multiple levels of analysis and may vary in degree of abstract thought. Criminology entails both macro and micro levels of analysis of both rational and irrational behavior; it engages both structure and process; it offers diverse conceptions of society through consensus and conflict perspectives; and it debates the relative influences of free will and determinism.

While each of the separate theories presented in the preceding chapters advances our understanding of crime, no single theory adequately explains or can predict *all* of the crime in society. This basic shortcoming has moved criminologists to evaluate theories, both individually and collectively, toward the goal of developing more thorough explanations. The development of new theories and the refinement of existing ones are typically referred to as **theory construction**—a process wherein factors that are known to be correlated with crime are connected to new ideas. The basic idea is that something new can be explained or existing explanations can be improved through the identification of previously unidentified concepts. New concepts come from a more abstract definition of a reality that involves ideas, images, and often a new way of expressing a phenomenon through more precise or descriptive language.

Most theories tend to better address certain types of offenses by featuring explanations that more effectively account for either violent or property crime. Other theories are more specific to juvenile delinquency than adult criminality or otherwise account for the criminal behavior of some social groups more so than others, as specified by, for example, social class or age group. While all of the individual theories emphasize certain causal factors (the various separate empirical realities that are known to be correlated with crime), none of them successfully incorporate all of the many identified causes. This basic shortcoming gives rise to specific questions concerning theoretical criminology, particularly, "Which theories are right?" and, conversely, "Which theories are wrong?" Unfortunately, the answers to these questions aren't obvious and entail consideration of several relevant issues.

EVALUATING THEORY

To begin a discussion of comparing the relative value and "correctness" of individual theories, we must first consider both the *diversity* and *complexity* of the many statements that combine to constitute theoretical criminology. Neither of these characteristics should be surprising. After all, the body of criminological theory has been developed over several decades and we can observe how individual theorists' conceptualizations of social problems reflects the spirit and values of their respective times. The prominence of subcultural theories during the 1950s and early 1960s, for example, reflects the identification of value systems that did not coincide with middle-class standards of the day and, consequently, became a reference point for what was widely believed to be moral decay. As values associated with subcultures became increasingly popularized and the national political pendulum shifted in a general liberal direction, subcultural theories became less popular and were replaced by alternative perspectives.

Similarly, research methodologies have become increasingly sophisticated with the evolution of the social and behavioral sciences. The ability to realize greater precision in determining causal inference due to advances in statistical analytic techniques, for example, have enabled reconsideration of previously accepted relationships and complicated certain assumptions about the causes of crime—particularly in regard to how various crime correlates combine to generate additive and interactive effects. Theories have thus become increasingly complex as today's theorists are more cognizant of the importance of theory-methods symmetry and the need to construct theory that can be empirically assessed.

In order to sort out these concerns, criminologists compare and evaluate theories in three general ways. Theories can be developed and assessed singularly, through theoretical competition, or by theoretical integration. **Singular theory assessment** is the simplest approach to evaluating theory—an approach that simply seeks to identify the level of empirical support that exists for a theory. In short, data is gathered in order to examine whether formally stated propositions that specify causal relationships between theoretical concepts (often in the form of hypotheses) can be accepted—a process known as **theory testing**. If sampling is adequate toward the social science axiom of generalizability, operationalizations of key variables are precise so as to minimize the chance of measurement error, and statistical or qualitative analysis reveals causal relationships, a theory is confirmed. Of course, lack of empirical support for the formally stated propositions that constitute individual theories leads to rejection of hypotheses and the search for alternative explanations.

It is important to understand that theories are not easily confirmed or disconfirmed. Theories are tested by multiple researchers who may, and often do, find contradictory and different levels of support. Theory testing also entails both spatial (place) and temporal (time) variation. That is, a particular theory may be confirmed by a study in one country but not another and, likewise, by past but not present research. Perhaps the value system or social structure is different across countries, or the social demographics of an area change over time due to in and out migration patterns. Last, there is also the basic concern of generalizability—that is, the scope of the applicability of findings. As we have seen in the preceding chapters, some theories work quite well for certain social groups but not others. Accordingly, it is usually not the case that a theory is absolutely confirmed or rejected by any single test. Rather, specific theories are confirmed with noted limitations. Nonetheless, criminologists observe the general relative value of theories according to the amount of empirical support found for each theory and the generality or scope (that is, the extent of the crime problem addressed) that each theory offers.

Moreover, a theory may receive both partial confirmation and partial rejection within and across separate tests. Usually, theory tests prove that at least some of the propositions or major statements of a theory are true. On the other hand, most theory tests fail to prove that all of a theory's propositions are valid and generally applicable to different types of crimes or groups of offenders. A specific theory test might confirm, for example, that the involvement and attachment elements of the social bond (the focal point of social control theory) are correlated with specific types of juvenile delinquency, but that the commitment and belief elements are not.

Most theory tests focus on single theories by subjecting data representative of a theory's primary concepts to empirical scrutiny. These tests enable us to accept and reject various theories according to a systematic scientific standard. Singular theory testing, however, does not permit comparison of multiple theories simultaneously to determine both relative levels of empirical support and the comparative scope of explanation offered. Such comparison is made through a process known as theory competition.

THEORY COMPETITION

Theory competition involves direct and systematic comparison of two or more theories. The "competition" lies in rank-ordering individual theories according to (1) the amount of empirical support (confirming evidence) and (2) the scope of coverage, that is, the breadth of explanation offered. While these two criteria are used to examine individual theories as described previously, assessing several theories at once enables a general appreciation of which theories best explain various aspects of the crime problem. Reference to the level of empirical support demonstrated typically, but not always, means whether variable analysis reveals an acceptable threshold of statistical significance (as discussed in Chapter One). As previously mentioned, statistical evidence confirming causal inference is certainly not the sole standard for accepting, rejecting, and comparing theory. Scholars also regularly engage theoretical comparison in pure conceptual and logical contexts, especially conflict and cultural theorists whose respective explanations are presented in a language that is not particularly well suited for testing through variable analysis.

Theory competition is important in two respects. First, comparing theories in a competitive sense enables us to look for better explanations and disregard (or use cautiously) others that have received only minimal or no support. Inasmuch as theory informs and guides criminal and juvenile justice programs and policies, competitive theory testing has serious implications for real-world program development and continuation. The national youth court movement (sometimes referred to as "teen court"), for example, is directly derived from restorative justice and reintegrative shaming theories. Youth courts and similar other community-based justice programs have been rapidly implemented across the country, but only a few of them have been evaluated. Most youth courts and similar programs are funded by grants that require evaluation, which, in turn, is important for theory construction. As evaluations of initiatives that are based on theoretical propositions occur, research simultaneously informs policymakers about both the effectiveness of specific criminal justice efforts and whether additional programs should be modeled according to similar or alternative theories. The youth court movement is but one of many examples of how theories shape and improve the world of criminal justice.

A second important consequence of competitive theory testing is the generation of knowledge necessary for theory construction and evolution. There is a healthy sense of intellectual competition among theoretical criminologists, whose advocacy of certain perspectives often entails critical attention to the shortcomings and new assertions of rival explanations. Accordingly, theory competition involves close empirical scrutiny of theoretical statements, both in hope of evidencing newly contended relationships (that is, confirming discoveries) and demonstrating lack of empirical evidence toward discontinuation of invalid perspectives. Through this ongoing process of theory competition the field of criminology moves forward and remains current in both the assessment of society's crime problems and informing responses by the criminal justice system.

Theory is generally furthered in one of three ways: (1) the emergence of original theory, (2) theoretical elaboration, and (3) theoretical integration. Original theory is the emergence of a set of propositions explaining a phenomenon (in our case either crime or criminality) which is generally thought to identify a novel cause or source. Many of the theories presented in this text, such as those framed by Sutherland (1947), Cohen (1955), Miller (1958), and Shaw and McKay (1942), are deemed original theory because they identify and emphasize distinct causes of crime—social learning, anomie, subcultures, and social disorganization, respectively. Totally new and unique theories focusing on previously unidentified causes and correlates of crime are very rare, largely due to the breadth and pluralistic nature of the many existing theories. Instead, theory is more often developed through elaboration and integration.

Before moving on to the topics of theoretical elaboration and integration, let's look at the levels of support for some of the different theories we've been examining throughout this text. The theories we've examined view crime as a function of many separate causes—that is, they situate the reasons (and responsibility) for crime across a broad range of personal and social factors. Accordingly, individual theories endorse a range of sometimes competing and ideologically opposed policy responses. At the most basic level, some theories suggest that rehabilitation, prosocial value development, and peer or community-based programs will best alleviate crime rates, while other theories lend credence to a deterrence-based form of justice. So which theories have received the most empirical support when subjected to competitive theory testing?

In reporting the relative empirical support for criminological theories it is important to call attention to one qualifying concern. While theories are compared in terms of strength (empirical evidence) and scope (generalizability), not all of the theories or even all of the leading theories can be examined simultaneously. Attempting to do so would simply be illogical. Comparing all of the theories at once wouldn't be meaningful because the individual theories attempt to explain different dimensions of crime. As we've seen, some explain how the criminal law is formed or constructed according to power struggles (conflict theory) or according to normative consensus (classical criminology), others attempt to account for the criminality of social-demographically identified groups (original strain theory, subcultural and social learning theories), and still others speak to the crime rate through social ecology. This diversity of coverage, then, makes direct comparison of all theories a lot like comparing apples and oranges. Instead, theories are more commonly grouped by type, as they were clustered for presentation in the first nine chapters of this text, and support is discussed in terms of which perspectives seem most fitting for criminological research questions specific to criminality, crime rate, or legal origin.

Perhaps the easiest way to quickly decipher which theories are receiving empirical support is to observe the ones that are currently guiding criminological research and criminal justice practice. Ideally, invalid theories are phased out over time as they cannot withstand empirical scrutiny and the specific juvenile and criminal justice programs modeled after them prove ineffective. Clearly, outdated biological theories of criminality, such as Lombroso's criminal body-typing approach, have been invalidated and are rarely taken seriously anymore. Newer and more elaborate biological theories, however, aren't necessarily seen as taboo anymore and have received a modicum of empirical support that has somewhat revived the biological perspective (Wright & Miller, 1998). Psychological theories that emphasize impulsivity, personality tendencies, and emotional factors, for example, have not received widespread support and seem able to explain the criminality of a fairly narrow group of offenders.

In general, sociological explanations tend to receive more support than either biological or psychological theories, but this claim is partly a matter of classification. Traditional strain theory and similar theories that emphasize the importance of anomie are often considered sociological theories but certainly contain psychological elements. Regardless of whether traditional strain theory is seen as sociological or social-psychological, there is limited empirical support—certainly far less than exists for revised versions such as reverse strain theory. Other sociological or structural theories, such as social disorganization theory, while infrequently tested, are comparatively strong and suggest a consequential correlation between neighborhood cohesiveness and stability and level of crime. Although a dominant perspective for much of the last three decades, social control theory receives only moderate support today.

Newer conflict theories fare better than older Marxist and critical perspectives, but again the statement must be qualified and put into context. Most critical perspectives, be they Marxist, labeling, or conflict theories, address the inconsistencies within and inadequacies of the criminal justice system but with only minimal empirical support. Critical theories focusing on law formation, however, have received greater empirical support.

Subcultural theories are often considered obsolete and, accordingly, almost never tested. Theories emphasizing values and subcultural influence were largely dismissed as tautological during the 1970s but, in all fairness, have received almost no testing—largely due to criminologists' inability to effectively operationalize the key variable of subculture. Recent cultural explanations of crime, such as Nisbett and Cohen's culture of honor hypothesis, contend that value systems have causal effect but are confirmed through mixed methods that do not rise to commonly accepted standards of theory validation. Nonetheless, subculture remains an important, though relegated, concept in criminology whose import is too readily and simplistically explained away as an exogenous variable. The mere fact that criminologists continue to look to subcultures, more so now as a context for than cause of crime, suggests lingering importance and perhaps a neglect that is the fate of most theories that are not neatly tested through variable analysis.

Interest in theory testing most often centers on the well-known deterrence-versus-rehabilitation debate, particularly in response to high-profile crimes involving celebrities or particularly ruthless acts for which the death penalty might be imposed. Rehabilitation advocates essentially believe that society has the ability, through social programs, individual counseling, and education and skills enhancement, to rework the attitudes and belief systems of offenders. Bolstering an offender's level of social bondedness, for example, would presumably vest that person in conventional behavior, yet there is only limited support for social control theory. Supporters of rehabilitation approaches to crime find greater support in tests of social learning and, most frequently, restorative justice theories that seek to rework offenders' psyches and de-escalate conflict with the criminal justice system, respectively.

On the other hand, there is frequent public outcry when a hardened criminal released on parole commits additional crime, particularly when extreme violence is involved. The public often questions why such people are released in the first place and whether society needs harsher punishments to deter repeat offenses. Sociological criminologists have typically found little support for deterrence theory, but again, the matter must be put into context. As we saw in Chapter Two, deterrence is both perceptual and literal and is intended for both individuals and the general public. There is little evidence in support of deterrence, especially for the most serious crimes that society would ideally wish to deter the most. Serious violent crime, however, is often emotive in nature (people become so angry at times that they are not rational), thus negating a meaningful criminal calculus. Accordingly, there is little reason to believe that increasing the severity of punishment will automatically force or motivate people to choose noncriminal courses of action. Nonetheless, it is altogether certain that individual-level deterrence is absolutely effective in regard to capital punishment. On a less-extreme level, emerging evidence shows that deterrence can be effective in situationally specific contexts, such as drug testing for offenders. Despite the presence of limited evidence supporting deterrence theory, the deterrence model remains the single most consequential theoretical perspective in terms of criminal justice practice and policy. In fact, the vast majority of what transpires within and across the three prongs of the criminal justice system is rooted in deterrence principles. The notion of crime prevention (especially efforts at general and perceptual deterrence) and the U.S. Sentencing Guidelines (emphasizing proportionality of punishment), for example, are reflections of a determining deterrence logic.

THEORETICAL ELABORATION

Theory testing and theory competition both effect theory construction as a sort of metaphorical compass pointing the direction for new theory building. As mentioned previously, completely original theory is fairly uncommon—most of the major causes and a great many secondary causes of crime have already been discovered and examined. Theory nonetheless continues to advance in other ways, one of which is **theoretical elaboration.** Theoretical elaboration requires neither the introduction of totally new ideas nor the resolution of differences across theories. Rather, this approach entails building on existing theory by considering what new variables might be added to realize more complete explanations.

A good example of theoretical elaboration is Haynie's (2001) attention to delinquent peer groups. Drawing on concepts from social control and differential association theory, properties of social networks are identified that link these theoretical perspectives and enable elaboration. The delinquent peer explanation recognizes that differential association conditions peer groups and that, at the individual level, the nature of social bonding is predictive of delinquency. By fleshing out the structural properties of peer groups, however, the nature of group delinquency can be better understood. Specifically, the delinquent peer effect specifies that delinquency is a function of the influence exerted by friendship groups whose effect can be observed through the network characteristics of centrality (where someone is located, such as at home or a part-time job, which provides or limits interaction with others), density (how many people are in the group and how frequently they interact), and popularity (the level of acceptance, involvement, and desirability a person realizes within the group). The delinquent peer elaboration on the major differential association and social control theories reaffirms these perspectives but also furthers knowledge about how groups affect behavior. Through this elaboration, new specific research questions can be identified and studied. Popularity, for example, presents interesting queries. On the topic of popularity and teenage sexual victimization, for example, we can hypothesize two opposite trajectories. On one hand, it is plausible that popularity protects people (in this example typically teenage girls) because most people within a youth culture are familiar with who is, in fact, popular. The assumption to be tested here is whether popularity translates into protection from harm as more people desire to look out for those who are well liked. On the other hand, popularity might work the other way—that is, it might actually increase the risk of sexual victimization. Popular youth logically are invited to a greater number of social events, go on more dates, and are thus exposed to a greater number of potential risks. So whether popularity offsets these risks or contributes to victimization is a specific research question stemming from theoretical elaboration.

An argument might be made that virtually all of the theories we've examined are a result of theoretical elaboration, but this is true only in the broadest sense. Cohen's attention to subculture certainly incorporates and builds on Merton's anomie perspective, and Aker's social learning theory clearly extends Sutherland's conceptualization of differential association. Similarly, Braithwaite's reintegrative shaming theory builds on earlier consensus and labeling perspectives. These theories are largely considered original, however, because they introduce and emphasize causal and contributing factors previously ignored or neglected. Theoretical elaboration, then, is better understood as a process of extending existing perspectives to address crime in ways that further our overall knowledge base.

THEORETICAL INTEGRATION

An alternative approach to the shortcomings of single theories and elaboration is **theoretical integration**. Theoretical integration basically enables two main objectives: (1) the construction of models that offer greater accountability for unexplained crime—that is, fuller explanations can be realized by combining complementary and distinct components of separate theories into a single explanation—and (2) the creation of general theory. General theories are grand perspectives that purport to account for all types of crime and deviance, often across time and space, consistent with the label of being "general."

There are two main ways that theoretical integration occurs. The first, **sequential integration**, is fairly easy to understand and is more common. This type of integration, also known as *propositional integration,* involves identifying and combining complementary but conceptually distinct concepts from separate theories toward realizing greater predictability for some crime phenomenon. The term *sequential* is important because the propositions from one theory are simply linked to the propositions of another to form a more elaborate explanation. Consider, for example, how variation in one element of the social bond (attachment) can affect the nature of social learning. According to social control theory, youth form attachments to realize a sense of place and belonging with their primary group, most often parents and immediate family members. Presumably, youth who are poorly bonded with their family—that is, individuals who are not strongly attached—will likely attach to others in their immediate environment. Primary attachments to other youth and adults in the community (social control theory) help us understand how youth develop attitudes and a general outlook that likely approximates the worldview and behavior of the people with whom they interact and whom they emulate (social learning theory). Such a process may result in either a socially desirable or undesirable outcome, depending on the balance of conventional and deviant practices of either parents or neighborhood role models.

Numerous sequential or propositional theoretical integrations during the last two decades have demonstrated the value of combining different schools of thought. Prominent examples include Tittle's control balance theory (1995), Thornberry and colleagues' interactional theory (1991), Krohn's network analysis (1986), and Elliot's integrated delinquency theory (1985). Elliot's theory provides a straightforward example of linking propositions from separate theories to realize greater predictability and explanation. This particular delinquency explanation incorporates dimensions of strain, social control, and social learning theories into a single linear statement. In short, the theory contends that anomic strain (the inability to realize achievements stemming from a means-end discrepancy, for example) negatively conditions social bonds (that is, strain detracts from prosocial bonds), which, in turn, leads to greater exposure to and involvement with similarly situated delinquent others. Through heightened exposure to a delinquent peer group, youth receive social reinforcement (a primary component of social learning theory) for the delinquency and crime to which they are exposed on a regular basis (as confirmed by self-reported delinquency studies).

Krohn's (1986) integrated theory of crime is rooted in the key assumptions and propositions of both social learning and social bonding theories. However, unlike the original versions, his theory is situated in a social network context. A social network is simply a set of individuals or groups associated by friendship or some other type of relationship. Krohn contends that a social network is capable of exerting influence over individual behavior (social control), and similar to Elliot's integrated theory, he rejects the idea that social control is necessarily related to positive, prosocial, or law-abiding behavior. Rather, through incorporation of social learning principles, this theory suggests that if the social network within which one is situated is characterized by delinquency or deviance, exposure to such negative behavior and, presumably, attitudes favorable toward that behavior can encourage delinquent or criminal activity.

Krohn proposes that the strength of the social network's effect is attributable to the network's structural characteristics, specifically its *multiplexity* and *density*. Multiplexity refers to the number of relationships that two or more individuals have in common, such as school, neighborhood, or extracurricular activities. According to Krohn, multiplexity denotes "what individuals' associates do (differential association) and the kind of activities in which they are mutually involved (commitment and/or involvement)" (Krohn, 1986). Density is defined as the ratio of actual social relationships to the total number of possible relationships in a network. Network density is negatively related to crime and delinquency—that is, the higher the density, the lower the delinquency within a social network.

Another example of prepositional integration is found in Thornberry and colleagues' Interactional Theory (1991). This theory, derived from social structural, social bonding, and social learning theories, suggests that the underlying causal mechanism of delinquency is the weakening of the social bond. This weakening, however, only serves to make it *more likely* that one will engage in delinquent or criminal behavior. Compatible with social earning theory, Thornberry contends that only through association, reinforcement, and definitions (favorable to delinquent behavior) will delinquency become a behavioral pattern. According to this theory, the social learning process itself is affected by structural variables such as race, social class, and community and neighborhood characteristics.

The second main type of theoretical integration, **conceptual fusion**, is a little more complex. Whereas sequential integration links complementary concepts in a linear logic model, conceptual integration seeks to merge similar ideas that, while stated differently and presented as distinct variables, actually constitute theoretical overlap. Theoretical overlap refers to concepts and variables across individual theories that account for the same variation in the same or similar dependent variables. Additionally, integration can cross levels of analysis, meaning that fused concepts (or the previously described approach of linking propositions) are drawn from theories that are at a micro level or macro level of analysis. When integration links or combines theories from the same level of analysis, regardless of whether it is at a small-group or societal level, it is considered to be "within-level." Some theoretical integrations are more ambitious and attempt to link the processes of group behavior with structural factors (that is, combining both micro and macro levels of analysis into a single statement), an approach that is labeled "cross-level."

There are fewer examples of conceptual integration than there are for sequential integration. Akers's notion of conceptual absorption (another way of saying conceptual fusion) is important to the topic of theoretical integration, generally, and illustrates how similar ideas expressed in distinct theories can be effectively merged to explain specific behaviors. Akers (1985, 1989) contends that social control theory components, as expressed through the elements of the social bond, are subsumed and fused to assume similar but somewhat unique meaning. Whereas commitment usually refers to the degree of investment in conventional or criminal activity as indicated by the extent to which the other is sacrificed, commitment is "absorbed" in Akers's theory by social learning. Akers contends that the social learning theory concept of differential reinforcement both subsumes and is preferable to commitment. Whereas commitment only denotes sacrifices, differential reinforcement refers to the balance of rewards to punishments. Through attention to punishments (sacrifices), then, differential reinforcement "covers" what is offered by social control theory—at least the commitment component—but also includes consideration of positive influences on behavior and is thus a more complete theory. Similarly, the other social bond elements are arguably subsumed, such as belief being covered by learned definitions of crime as favorable or not.

SUMMARY

After defining the types of theoretical integration and discussing some of the major characteristics, it is important to note that integrated theory has not received the level of support that one might think. The idea of theoretical integration is to realize greater levels of explanation and predictability of crime through linking and fusing the most salient features of independent theories. Once identified, these leading concepts are reassembled into a new and ideally more complete statement. While the practice of combining the strengths of separate theories sounds promising as a thought experiment, in practice integrated theories are not often tested, and the ones that have been tested typically receive about the same or only slightly greater empirical support than in single theory tests. Despite a lack of overwhelming success to date, contemporary criminologists seem to remain enthusiastic about theoretical integration and it is likely to continue as a primary means of theory building for years to come.

KEY TERMS

conceptual fusion   a type of theoretical integration involving the merging of similar ideas into a broader conceptual framework

sequential integration   a type of theoretical integration that involves identifying and combining complementary but conceptually distinct ideas from two or more theories

singular theory assessment   an approach to evaluating theory that seeks to identify the level of empirical support that exists for a theory

theoretical elaboration   an approach to theory building that entails extending existing theory by considering what

new variables might be added for a more complete explanation

theoretical integration   an approach to theory building that incorporates key elements of two or more existing theories

theory competition   an approach to evaluating theory involving the direct and systematic comparison of two or more theories

theory construction   a process wherein factors that are known correlates of crime are connected to new ideas

theory testing   a process wherein data is gathered in order to examine the empirical validity of a theory's propositions

DISCUSSION QUESTIONS

1. How is theory testing related to theory building?

2. What are the similarities and differences between singular theory testing and theoretical competition?

3. How does theoretical elaboration differ from theoretical integration?

4. Identify and discuss the two main types of theoretical integration.

5. What theories do you think could be integrated to develop a general theory of crime?

REFERENCES

Akers, R. L. (1985). *Deviant behavior: A social learning approach* (3rd ed.). Belmont, CA: Wadsworth.

Akers, R. L. (1989). A social behaviorist's perspective on integration of theories of crime and deviance. In S. Messner, M. D. Krohn, & A. Liska, (Eds.), *Theoretical integration in the study of crime and deviance: Problems and prospects* (pp. 23–36). Albany: SUNY Press.

Cohen, A. K. (1955). *Delinquent boys: The culture of the gang.* Glencoe, IL: Free Press.

Elliot, D. S. (1985). The assumption that theories can be combined with increased explanatory power: Theoretical integrations. In R. F. Meier (Ed.), *Theoretical methods in criminology.* Beverly Hills, CA: Sage.

Haynie, D. L. (2001). Delinquent peers revisited: Does network structure matter? *American Journal of Sociology, 106,* 1013–1057.

Krohn, D. M. (1986). The web of conformity: a network approach to the explanation of delinquent behavior. *Social Problems, 33,* 19–29.

Miller, W. B. (1958). Lower-class culture as a generating milieu of gang delinquency. *Journal of Social Issues, 14*(3), 5–19.

Shaw, C. R., & McKay, H. D. (1942). *Juvenile delinquency and urban areas.* Chicago: University of Chicago Press.

Sutherland, E. H. (1947). *Principles of criminology* (4th ed.). Philadelphia: Lippincott.

Thornberry, T. P., Lizotte, A. J., Krohn, M. D. Farnsworth, M., & Jang, S. J. (1991). Testing interactional theory: An examination of reciprocal causal relationships among family, school, and delinquency. *Journal of Criminal Law and Criminology, 82,* 3–33.

Tittle, C. R. (1995). *Control balance: Toward a general theory of deviance.* Boulder, CO: Westview Press.

Wright, R. A. & Miller, J. M. (1998). Taboo until today? The coverage of biological arguments in criminology textbooks, 1961 to 1970 and 1987 to 1996. *Journal of Criminal Justice, 26*(1), 1–19.

INDEX

Volumes in the
New Century Exceptional Lives series . . .

A Desert Daughter's Odyssey:
For All Those Whose Lives
Have Been Touched by Cancer—
Personally, Professionally
Or Through a Loved One

Sharon Wanslee

The Man Who Was Dr. Seuss:
The Life and Work of Theodor Geisel

Thomas Fensch

New Century Books

The Man Who Was

Dr. Seuss

The Man Who Was

Dr. Seuss

The Life and Work of
Theodor Geisel

Thomas Fensch

Copyright © 2000 by Thomas Fensch.

New Century Books
P.O. Box 7113
The Woodlands, Tx., 77387-7113.

This book was printed in the United States of America.

Library of Congress Number:
    00191961
ISBN: Hardcover
    0-930751-11-6
ISBN: Paperback
    0-930751-12-4

Contents

For . . .

Alice in truth . . .

"Behold, I make all things new . . . ."
Revelations 21:5

Acknowledgments

Key Dates in the Life of Theodor Geisel

1904 Theodor Seuss Geisel is born in Springfield, Mass., March 2, the son of Theodor Robert and Henrietta Seuss Geisel.

1921 Theodor Geisel attends Dartmouth College, where he begins writing and drawing for the *Jack-O-Lantern*, the campus magazine.

1925 Theodor Geisel graduates from Dartmouth in June.

1926–1927 Geisel attends Oxford University, in England, meets Helen Palmer and tours England and Europe.

1927 Geisel sells a cartoon to *The Saturday Evening Post*. When it is published, it bears the name "Seuss." Geisel marries Helen Palmer.

1928 Geisel begins drawing an advertising campaign under the title, "Quick Henry, The Flit." That phrase becomes nationally popular. The Flit campaign sustains him financially for 17 years.

1931 Geisel illustrates his first book, *Boners*, published by the Viking Press. His second book, *More Boners*, is published the same year.

1937 *And to Think That I Saw it on Mulberry Street* is published by The Vanguard Press, after numerous (27) rejections. It is the first Dr. Seuss book.

1938 *The 500 Hats of Bartholomew Cubbins* is published by The Vanguard Press.

1939 *The Seven Lady Godivas* is published by Random House. It is his only adult book and his only failure. It begins his life-long association with Random House and publisher Bennett Cerf. *The King's Stilts* is also published.

1940 *Horton Hatches the Egg* is published.

1940–1942 Geisel works as an editorial cartoonist for the newspaper *PM*.

1943–1946 Geisel serves in the Army U.S. Signal Corps, Information and Educational Division, under director Frank Capra; Geisel receives the Legion of Merit for his work on informational films and receives the first of three Academy Awards for his film *Hitler Lives*. (Originally written for the Army under the title *Your Job in Germany.*)

1947 *McElligot's Pool* is published. It is named a Caldecott Honor Book in children's literature. Geisel wins second Academy Award for *Design for Death* (written with Helen Geisel).

1948 *Thidwick the Big-Hearted Moose* is published by Random House. Geisel purchases a hill-top home in La Jolla, California where he will live the rest of his life.

1949 *Bartholomew and the Oobleck* is published; it too is named a Caldecott Honor Book.

1950 *If I Ran the Zoo* is published. It too, is named a Caldecott Honor Book.

1951 Geisel wins third Academy Award for the cartoon film *Gerald McBoing-Boing*.

1952 Geisel writes the script and songs and designs the sets for the film, *The 5,000 Fingers of Dr. T.* It is not successful. Geisel abandons Hollywood.

1953 *Scrambled Eggs Super!* is published.

1954 *Horton Hears a Who!* is published.

1955 *On Beyond Zebra!* is published.

1956 *If I Ran the Circus* is published. Geisel receives an honorary doctoral degree from Dartmouth College, his alma mater.

1957 *How the Grinch Stole Christmas!* is published and becomes one of his most popular books. *The Cat in the Hat* is published, the first of the Random House Beginner Books, for young readers.

1958 *The Cat in the Hat Comes Back* and *Yertle the Turtle and Other Stories* are published; Geisel becomes president of Beginner Books, a division of Random House.

1959 *Happy Birthday to You!* is published.

1960 *Green Eggs and Ham* is published, which has become—in terms of sales—Geisel's most popular book. *One Fish Two Fish Red Fish Blue Fish* is also published.

1961 *The Sneeches and Other Stories* is published. Geisel also publishes *Ten Apples Up On Top!* under the pseudonym Theo. LeSieg (Geisel spelled backwards).

1962 *Dr. Seuss's Sleep Book* is published.

1963 *Hop on Pop* and *Dr. Seuss's ABC* are published.

1965 *Fox in Sox, I Had Trouble Getting to Solla Sollew* and *I Wish I Had Duck Feet* (Theo. LeSieg, pseudonym) are all published.

1966 *Come Over to My House* (Theo LeSieg, pseudonym) is published.

1967 *The Cat in the Hat Song Book* is published.
Helen Palmer Geisel dies by her own hand October 23.

1968 *The Foot Book* is published, the first of the Bright and Early Books for readers pre: Beginner books. *The Eye Book* (Theo. LeSieg, pseudonym) is also published in the same series. Geisel receives an honorary doctoral degree from American International College. *Dr. Seuss's Lost World Revisited: A Forward Backward Glance* is published, despite a legal fight. Geisel marries Audrey Stone Diamond August 5.

1969 *I can Lick 50 Tigers Today! and Other Stories* and *My Book about Me—By Me, Myself, I Wrote It! I Drew It!* are published.

1970 *I Can Draw It Myself* and *Mr. Brown Can Moo! Can You?* are published.

1971 *I Can Write—by Me, Myself* (Theo. LeSieg, pseudonym) and *The Lorax*, about the loss of the environment are published. *The Lorax* becomes the most controversial Dr. Seuss book. He receives a Peabody Award for his television specials *How the Grinch Stole Christmas!* and *Horton Hears a Who!*

1972 *In a People House* (Theo. LeSieg, pseudonym) and *Marvin K. Mooney, Will You Please Go Now!* are published.

1973 *The Many Mice of Mr. Brice* (Theo. LeSieg, pseudonym), *Did I Ever Tell You How Lucky You Are?* and *The Shape of Me and Other Stuff* are all published.

1975 *Because a Little Bug Went Ka-Choo!* (Rosetta Stone, pseudonym), *Oh, The Thinks You Can Think!* and *Would You Rather be a Bullfrog?* (Theo. LeSieg) are published.

1976 *Hooper Humperdink. . . ? Not Him!* (Theo. LeSieg) and *The Cat's Quizzer* are published.

1977 *Try to Remember the First of Octember* (Theo. LeSieg) is published. Geisel receives an honorary doctoral degree from Lake Forest College and receives an Emmy Award for *Halloween is Grinch Night*.

1978 *I Can Read with My Eyes Shut!* is published.

1979 *Oh Say Can You Say?* is published.

1980 *Maybe You Should Fly a Jet! Maybe You Should Be a Vet!* (Theo. LeSieg) is published. Geisel receives an honorary doctoral degree from Whittier College and receives the Laura Ingalls Wilder Award from the American Library Association.

1981 *The Tooth Book* (Theo. LeSieg) is published.

1982 *Hunches in Bunches* is published. Geisel wins an Emmy for the television special *The Grinch Grinches the Cat in the Hat*.

1983 Geisel receives an honorary doctoral degree from John F. Kennedy University.

1984 *The Butter Battle Book*, about warfare, is published. It becomes as controversial as *The Lorax*. Geisel wins a Pulitzer Prize for his contribution to children's literature.

1985 Geisel receives an honorary doctoral degree from Princeton University. The entire graduating class stands and recites *Green Eggs and Ham*, in tribute to Seuss.

1986 *You're Only Young Once!* is published. He receives an honorary doctoral degree from the University of Hartford.

1987 *I Am Not Going to Get Up Today!* is published. He receives an honorary doctoral degree from Brown University, his eighth honorary degree.

1990 *Oh, The Places You'll Go!* is published, and quickly becomes a widely popular high school and college graduation gift.

1991 *Six by Seuss: A Treasury of Dr. Seuss Classics* is published. It includes: *And To Think That I Saw It on Mulberry Street; The 500 Hats of Bartholomew Cubbins; Horton Hatches the Egg; Yertle the Turtle; How the Grinch Stole Christmas* and *The Lorax*.

Theodor Seuss Geisel dies in La Jolla, California, September 24, at 87.

1995 *Daisy-Head Mayzie* is published. It is the only Dr. Seuss book featuring a little girl. *The Secret Art of Dr. Seuss*, pictures that he completed separate from the artwork for his books, is published. Audrey Geisel donates $20 million to the Main Library of the University of California at San Diego. The Library is renamed the Geisel Library.

1996 *My Many Colored Days* is published by Alfred Knopf, Inc. with text by Dr. Seuss and illustrations by Steve Johnson and Lou Fancher. Audrey Geisel donates one million to the library in Theodor Geisel's hometown, Springfield, Mass. A sculpture garden of Dr. Seuss characters is planned for the Library.

Random House publishes *A Hatful of Seuss*, which contains: *If I Ran the Zoo; Sneetches and Other Stories; Horton Hears a Who!; Dr. Seuss' Sleep Book* and *Bartholomew and the Oobleck*.

1997: *Seuss-isms: Wise and Witty Prescriptions for Living from the Good Doctor* is published.

1998: *Horray for Differdoofer Day* is published, based on notes by Seuss left in his study. It is written by Jack Prelutsky and illustrated by Lane Smith.

1999: The Free Press publishes *Dr. Seuss Goes to War: The World War II Editorial Cartoons of Theodor Seuss Geisel.*

Prologue

... one of his earliest memories was playing with lion cubs ...

One of his earliest memories was playing with lion cubs[1] ... and from his bedroom at night, he often heard the sounds of wild animals howling in the night from their cages in the Springfield Zoo, near his home.

Theodor "Ted" Geisel was born March 2, 1904 in Springfield, Mass., the son of Theodor and Henrietta Geisel. Springfield, 90 miles west of Boston, was then a small, idyllic New England town, with a Mulberry Street and family names like Wickersham, Terwilliger and McElligot. There were parades, industry like the Springfield Armory which made Springfield rifles and companies like the G. and C. Merriam company, the dictionary people.

And there was a large German community. His grandfather, also Theodor Geisel, was a co-owner of the local brewery Kalmbach and Geisel, which locals invariably called "Come back and guzzle."[2]

When he was 13, the United States entered the "Great War," against the Kaiser's Germany and the Geisels, of German extraction, faced a hostile Springfield community and, at the same time, cries grew for liquor regulation. Kalmbach and Geisel had become one of the largest breweries in New England—with production over 300,000 barrels a year—but its entire production would be threatened if beer and liquor were regulated.

It was hard to see which was worse on the Geisels; sauerkraut became "victory cabbage," frankfurters became hot dogs and those of German ancestry and German names were suspect. Antiliquor crowds in the statehouse in Boston threatened the Geisel brewery. Loyalty to the United States was never an issue in the Geisel house, but they recognized that German name was suspect and a brewery was a risky business.[3]

Theodor's father worked for 35 years to climb the management ladder in the brewery and, in 1920, when he finally became president of the company, by then called Springfield Breweries, the Volstead Act became law and the Geisel brewery became illegal.

Ted's father was at loose ends, with a succession of jobs until 1931, when he became park superintendent, a job which he held for 30 years.[4] The Zoo grew under Geisel's direction and, as the son of the superintendent, Ted remembered later, he played with lion cubs and listened to the howls of the animals at night from his bedroom.

His first book, *And to Think that I Saw it on Mulberry Street* was published in 1937, remembering the Mulberry Street in Springfield and, in 1950, Geisel published *If I Ran the Zoo*.

One

Theodor Geisel, 1904–1927

*" . . . when he walked into a
room it was like a magician's
act. Birds flew out of his
hands, and endless bright
scarves and fireworks . . ."*

For Theodor Geisel, Springfield, Massachusetts, was always large enough to be a city, but small enough to contain all his dreams and memories.

The Springfield, where he was born March 2, 1904, was a growing manufacturing city: The now legendary Indian motorcycle was made there, beginning in 1901. The Indian company also eventually made airplane engines, bicycles, outboard motors and other equipment. It lasted until 1953.

The Smith and Wesson factory was there; as were the Milton Bradley games company; Duryea and Knox automobiles were made there, and watches, machine parts, bicycles, motorcycles, toys, ice skates, roller skates, railroad and trolley cars.[1]

Springfield was served by three railroads: the New York, New Haven & Hartford and the Boston and Albany and as many as two hundred trains pulled into and left Springfield daily.[2]

And there were breweries. His grandfather, also known as

Theodor Geisel (pronounced *GUY*-sell) was born in the German town of Mulhausen in 1840. At 14, he became a jeweler's apprentice and following his apprenticeship, served in the German calvary in Germany's war with Austria and later in battles between the south German states and Prussia. Mustered out in 1867, he left Germany as so many others did and sailed for America.

He settled in Springfield and again took up his craft of jewelry design and manufacturing; four years later he married Christine Schmaelzlea, also a German immigrant and a year after that he became an American citizen.

In 1876, Geisel and Christian Kalmbach who had apprenticed in the German brewing arts, bought a small brewery. They named it Kalmbach and Geisel. Soon everyone who knew it called it "Come Back and Guzzle."[3]

Theodor Geisel, the son of Theodor and Christine Schmaelzlea Geisel, was born in 1979, beside the brewery. By 1891, it was one of the largest breweries in New England. There were twenty-five matched horses to pull the black and gold brewery wagons through the streets of Springfield. Theodor the son eventually joined his Father's brewery.

Henrietta Seuss (pronounced in the German style as *Zoice*. Years later, the name would be corrupted to rhyme with *juice*) was born the daughter of a baker. When Henrietta, the baker's daughter, married Geisel, the brewer's son in 1901, the sally went: "Seuss the baker puts the staff of life in people's mouths; Geisel the brewer takes it out and pours beer there instead, causing the children of drinkers to suffer the pangs of hunger."[4] But it really wasn't true. The Springfield German community, totaling about a thousand, was prosperous and visible—but a minority nonetheless. Its minority status would be much more obvious and at much more at risk later.

Theodor "Ted" Seuss Geisel (who was the third Theodor Geisel, but not saddled with *3rd*, because he was the first Theodor Seuss Geisel) was born in a home at 22 Howard Street, but early in his life the family moved to 74 Fairfield Street, where he would live until he left for college. Geisel remembered the house, its rooms, furniture, smells and sounds for the rest of his life.

His mother, whom the family called Nettie, had sold pies in her Father's bakery before she was married and every night, as Ted and his younger sister Marnie fell asleep, they didn't listen to Nettie telling fairy stories, but rather to her reciting a poem from the bakery:

> Apple, mince, lemon . . .
> Peach, apricot, pineapple . . .
> Blueberry, coconut, custard . . . and *SQUASH!*[5]

Years later, Geisel couldn't keep the drone of a steamship's engine out of his mind; from his childhood he remembered Nettie's pie poem (with the emphasis at the end . . . *and SQUASH!*). More than anyone, Nettie was responsible "for the rhythms in which I write and the urgency with which I do it," he said.[6]

He learned other lessons from Papa Theodor:

> It was Ted's father, Theodor, who imposed discipline, although he rarely raised his voice or his hand. When he grew angry, he turned away and ignored the offender, sometimes for the rest of his life; this was the fate of a cousin he saw almost daily on the Springfield trolley as he went to his office at the brewery. "You will never be sorry," he counseled his son, "for anything you never said." A tall, straight-backed man with black hair and a mustache, he dressed impeccably and looked especially dashing when he donned riding clothes and boots and took his horse for a canter. He drank beer and rye whiskey and smoked cigars, made in Springfield from tobacco grown in the Connecticut Valley. He was an expert marksman who, in 1902, held a world title at two hundred yards. Each morning, as calisthenic discipline, he held his favorite rifle above his head for ten or twelve

minutes. "My Father had an all-consuming hobby," Ted recalled, "that I always thought was silly and unproductive. It was shooting holes in paper targets. But he was an inspiration. Whatever you do," he told me, "do it to perfection."

Judith and Neil Morgan wrote, in their biography, *Dr. Seuss and Mr. Geisel.*[7]

From Ted's window, at the right rear corner of the second floor of the house, he could see into the country, to a deserted house (neighborhood children thought it was haunted) and, beyond the haunted house (inspiration for the Once-lers house, perhaps?), Ted could hear the sounds and songs of animals in the Springfield Zoo.

When Ted was three, a second sister named after their mother, died of pneumonia, at eighteen months. Ted and his sister Marnie couldn't escape hearing the "terrible sounds of her cough" throughout the house. Her little coffin was displayed in the house and later the family owned a "Pooley cabinet," a narrow New England-made chest in which their Father kept Caruso records. Ted was always haunted by the sheer similarity of the Pooley cabinet to the small narrow coffin which held his sister.

The cabinet, Ted recalled, was about the size, if you laid it on its side, of my sister's casket. No matter how thrilled I was later by my Father's voice and my mother's accompaniment, I always saw Henrietta in her casket in the place where the Pooley cabinet was.[8]

Ted fell asleep night after night listening to Nettie's pie poem; she discovered that he had a peculiar affinity for rhymes. He knew all the words to "Holy, Holy, Holy, Lord God Almighty!" and memorized this rhyme:

> The great Jehovan speaks to us
> In Genesis and Exodus;
> Leviticus and Numbers, three,
> Followed by Deuteronomy.

Much later Ted admitted he added *three* to make it rhyme; it was surely, his biographers Judith and Neil Morgan wrote, a portent of nonsense to come."[9]

His father was appointed to the Springfield park board in 1909 and Ted entered a whole new world, a world which he never left. His new domain, Forest Park, was

> flanked by enormous Victorian homes painted in combination of egg-yolk yellow, fire-truck red and peak-soup green. Here Springfield families fished, picnicked and swam in the summer, and went sledding and ice-skating in the winter. Its maze of dead-end paths delighted Ted, as did the bicycle paths. He remembered the first time he saw pink trees and heard their strange name: dogwood.[10]

Decades later, Geisel would be able to remember the colors, the sounds, the animals.

He took a pencil and pad to the Zoo and began to draw the animals that he saw. But his animals were awkward, mis-shapen and, well, tended toward the bizarre. Any normal parents inspecting the drawings of a precocious child might reasonably expect that the drawings would become more accurate and realistic over time and the experiences and age of the child. Ted Geisel's animals remained awkward, mis-shapen and bizarre. Over the years, he *sharpened his skill at making them awkward, mis-shapen and bizarre.*

Consider two other elements of Ted Geisel's world: every night his father came home with the local newspapers and Ted eagerly grabbed the comics. Ted was influenced by George Herriman's

"Crazy Kat" and the other comics in the papers . . . and he was influenced or perhaps hypnotized by his father's inventions, which took on a Rube Goldberg world of their own. His father "invented" a biceps straightening machine; a spring clip to keep flies off the spigots of beer cases and a device which Ted later called a "Silk-Stocking-Back-Seam-Wrong-Detecting Mirror."[11]

But World War One was brewing far over the horizon from idyllic Springfield. The *Lusitania* was torpedoed in 1915 and anti-German sentiment grew. Many senior citizens today remembered when German-style frankfurters suddenly became hot dogs and sauerkraut was patriotically re-named "victory cabbage."

History collided with the Geisels quickly. In 1917, America went to war with Germany and many German-Americans faced increasingly difficult times maintaining a normal life. The Geisel household, along with the 1,200 other German-Americans in Springfield now faced a hostile world: the enemy wasn't a vague shadow from across the Atlantic—for many others in Springfield, and indeed, across the United States, normal American families whose lineage happened to be Germanic who migrated to the United States a generation or two back, were embodiments of the Kaiser. The Hun. The dreaded enemy. The Geisel family did indeed, speak German at home, prayed in German, ate bratwurst, sauerkraut and drank beer. And Ted didn't quite understand why suddenly he had become the neighborhood boy to be picked on.

Prohibition was coming to Springfield, too, and for the Geisels it was even more threatening than the anti-German sentiment.

Theodor Geisel entered Springfield's Central High in the Fall of 1917. One of the courses he chose to take was art. He later explained what happened:

> Our model that day was a milk bottle containing a
> few scraggly late autumn daisies. I was having a real
> bad time trying to capture the beauty of this set-up
> and immortalize it with a hunk of charcoal and a sheet

of paper. To add to my frustration, my teacher kept fluttering about and giving me hell for turning my drawing board around and working on my picture upside down. "No, Theodor," she said, "Not upside down! There are rules that every artist must abide by. You will never succeed if you break them."

At the end of the class period, Ted Geisel transferred out of that art class and became manager of the high school soccer team. "We lost every game," he later said, "but I was forever free from art-by-the rule book, so I considered it a successful season."[12] We can almost hear it as a Dr. Seuss rhyme:

> *No Theodor, No Theodor.*
> *Not upside down, not upside down,*
> *Not even once, not ever more . . .*
> *This I implore, not ever more. . . .*

Geisel was doing as other youngsters always do—he was creating a world with no rules. Why shouldn't you, *why shouldn't you, draw upside down?* He was also drawing from the right side of his brain, and making perfect sense while doing so. And when he acknowledged to himself that he would take no more art-by-the-books classes, he permanently freed himself for any further *not upside down* rules.

(It's a wonder that the high school let him transfer out of his art class to become manager of the soccer team . . .)

When his Boy Scout Troop, number 13, sponsored by his Methodist Church, began a war bond drive, Ted went from house to house (perhaps along Mulberry Street) selling war bonds. It helped his family escape the stigma of being *those people.* When Grandfather Theodor, the first brewer, head of young Ted's bond selling, he bought one thousand dollars of bonds, enough to make Ted one of the top ten boy scouts in Springfield in bond sales.

In early May, 1918, Ted and nine other scouts stood on the

stage of the Municipal Auditorium to receive special awards from former President Theodore Roosevelt himself. Roosevelt presented an award personally one-by-one to the nine other boy scouts on the platform, parents beaming in the audience.

When Roosevelt got to Ted, he was inadvertently out of awards. Instead of saving the situation by wit or charm, Roosevelt made the mistake infinitely worse.

"What's this boy doing here?" he loudly asked of adult scout officials. Ted was hustled off the stage, humiliated and mortified and no award was presented.[13]

Years and years later—decades later, as Theodor Geisel or as Dr. Seuss, he remembered the burning, searing embarrassment of his childhood. It became a phobia with him—he would forever be uneasy in crowds and seldom at ease speaking in public. Perhaps it's significant that when he moved and settled in La Jolla, California, he chose a mountaintop where he could be alone, no neighbors crowding in, no one to look at his home and ask "what's he doing here?"

(Eventually, it would be easy to say "I can't be at this event—or that event—because I haven't done such things in years." His phobia at facing crowds became a self-fulfilling personality trait.)

Can we listen closely?

(How might Dr. Seuss explain what Ted Geisel could not articulate. . . ?)

> *I blame it all, I blame it all,*
> *for you see, can't you see,*
> *There was no medal,*
> *no medal at all*
> *that day for me.*

In high school he made "B" averages without really trying. He found Latin impossible to comprehend and occasionally cut Latin classes to go to the movies. For the school newspaper,

The Recorder, he wrote one-line quips, known in Springfield as "grinds:"

> It'll just be our luck to be in Latin class
> when they turn back the clocks.

And he drew cartoons, published poetry and satire. Because he contributed so much, he was forced to use a pseudonym: T. S. LeSieg: Geisel spelled backwards. He was to use it again, much later, but it wasn't the first time that pseudonym was used.

When his father played the numbers games, he had to sign the slips so he used T. S. LeSieg. Nettie Geisel didn't particularly mind that her husband played the numbers, but she demanded he use a pseudonym to protect the family's good name.[14]

Prohibition was in. The Eighteenth Amendment—our grand exercise in national self-control—became legal in January, 1919. But grandfather Geisel, the first *brewmeister*, didn't live to see it; he died just before Prohibition was enacted.

Kalmbach and Geisel ("Come Back and Guzzle") had grown and merged and became Liberty Breweries and eventually it became Springfield Breweries, one of the largest in New England. Ted's father's career had grown with the brewery and he had become president. Just before Prohibition. Then he was out of a job.

Geisel starred in a minstrel show which he wrote; he appeared in "Twelfth Night" and was the "grind and joke editor" for his senior high school yearbook, *Pnalka*. With the advice and encouragement of his English teacher, who had graduated from Dartmouth two years previously, Geisel applied to Dartmouth and was accepted.

He chose Dartmouth because a teacher he liked at Central High, Edwin A. "Red" Smith had graduated from Dartmouth two years earlier. As Geisel remembered it, years later:

> The reason why so many kids went to Dartmouth at that
> particular time from the Springfield high school was prob-
> ably Red Smith, a young English teacher who, rather

than being just another English teacher was one of the gang—a real stimulating guy who probably was responsible for my starting to write.

I think many kids were excited by this fellow. . . . And I think when time came to go to college, we all said, "Let's go where Red Smith went."[15]

His classmates voted him Class Artist and Class Wit, but in group pictures he stood in the back row, tall and unsmiling.[16]

And, while waiting to attend Dartmouth, Geisel discovered the writer Hilaire Belloc (1870–1953). In an introduction to a reprint edition of *Cautionary Tales*, Sally Holmes Holtze writes:

Readers of the Introduction might understandably assume that Belloc was a children's book writer, but in fact his humorous writing was only a minute part of what he published in his 83 years. Belloc was born in France in 1870 and became a British subject in 1902. After graduating from Balliol College, Oxford, where he was a Brackenbury History Scholar, he began writing short pieces for publication in magazines. He was astonishing prolific as an essayist, novelist, historian, poet, translator, and editor and wrote well over 100 books; yet he was always troubled by debt and poverty. He was also a fascinating character, a devout Roman Catholic who doggedly applied his religion to every aspect of his life, including his political views, and this devotion was a handicap to his career. Belloc wrote, "I am used to Insult, as I combine in one person . . . A)Poverty. B) Papistry. C)Pugnacity. Any one of three can just swim, but when all three come together the victim sinks" (from *Yesterday's Authors of Books for Children*, 1977). Indeed, he was a difficult man to deal with; he was so unpredictable in temperament that a friend describes him as "ruder and more courteous, kinder and yet more pugnacious than any man I have ever met" (*Selected Cautionary Verses*, Penguin Puffin edition, 1964). Despite any problems he felt other people had with his Catholicism—he complained that his historical perspective wasn't what either Catholics *or* Protestants wanted to teach, and he was told that his religious fervor would prevent him from being elected to a professorship at Glasgow University in 1899—he received many honors in his lifetime. He served in Parliament from 1906 to 1910; he was honored by the Pope; he had honorary degrees from Glasgow University and from Dublin University. Belloc was a passionate man of great knowledge, who worked unceasingly. And he was a man who understood and liked children.

He knew children's tastes for the kind of incredible disasters that occur in *Cautionary Tales*, and he produced these calamities in just the right exaggerated style, so that children could never take the punishments seriously. Because of his skill, his humor, and his art, readers of *Cautionary Tales* continue to find the book memorable and enjoyable.[17]

Geisel was enchanted by *The Bad Child's Book of Beasts: Verses*, first published in England in 1896. The first printing sold out in four days. Belloc published *More Beasts (for Worse Children)* in 1897 and *Cautionary Tales for Children: Designed for the Admonition of Children Between the Ages of Eight and Fourteen Years*, was published in 1907. Geisel memorized chunks of Belloc poems like:

Matilda,
Who Told Lies, and was Burned to Death.

They galloped, roaring through the Town,
"Matilda's House is Burning Down!"

> Inspired by British Cheers and Loud
> Proceeding from the Frenzied Crowd,
> They ran their ladders through a score
> Of windows on the Ball Room Floor;
> And took Peculiar Pains to Souse
> The Pictures up and down the House,[18]

It was Belloc, Ted said, years later, who introduced him to the hypnotic joys of rhyme.[19] And, we can assume, to Belloc rhyme schemes like:

> And took Peculiar Pains to Souse
> The Pictures up and down the House.

Geisel surely realized that Belloc's poems were satires of pure and oh-so-dreary moralistic rhymes of the day, just as Lewis Carroll's poem "You are Old, Father William," from *Alice In Wonderland* is a parody. The original (with the same title) was written by Robert Southey (1774–1843):

> You are old, father William, the
>   young man cried,
> the few locks which are left you
>   are grey;
> You are hale, father William, a
>   hearty old man;
> Now tell me the reason I pray. . . .

Lewis Carroll's version:

> You are old, father William, the
>   young man said,
> And your hair has become very white;
> And yet you increasingly stand on your head—
>   Do you think, at your age, it is right?"[20]

Sally Holmes Holtze writes:

> How could children go back to the plodding verses
> that condescended to them in such tiresome moralizing,
> after they had met the girl in "Rebecca, Who slammed
> Doors for Fun and Perished Miserably"? The very lan-
> guage of Belloc's tales seemed to inform children that
> the stilted phraseology of their previous books had been
> a sham.[21]

Readers need not know the original to understand how Belloc
was using parody, she says, just as readers did not need to know
the Robert Southey original to enjoy how Lewis Carroll mocked
the lessons of age in "You are Old, Father William."

Children clearly understood the rollicking rhymes and
phrases—the freedom—of Belloc's style. And he understood
children's tastes for "incredible disasters."

They were lessons not lost on Ted Geisel.

He began classes at Dartmouth College, four hours north of
Springfield, in the fall of 1921. Although Geisel's father was now
unemployed when the brewery sat idle during the Depression,
there was enough money from Grandfather Geisel to allow Ted to
pay Dartmouth's tuition, then $250. annually.

Fraternity pledge week came and went and although Geisel
made no real efforts toward fraternity life, he was surprised and
perhaps chagrined when no offer at all came from any fraternity.
Months later, Geisel discovered that his dark hair and sharp nose
made Dartmouth fraternity members believe that he was Jewish
and thus effectively blackballed from fraternity life.

But shortly after Pledge Week, Geisel discovered the *Jack-
o-Lantern*, the Dartmouth humor magazine and he turned to
the *Jacko* (as the staff called it) with relief and enthusiasm.
And he quickly found a friend, Norman Maclean, son of a Pres-
byterian minister from Montana. Maclean would eventually

become a professor of English at the University of Chicago and, later in his professional career, publish *A River Runs Through It*, now considered a classic.

Geisel began cartooning for the *Jacko*; one of his first cartoons showed a co-ed with a short skirt and an unnaturally large leg. The cartoon bore the title: "The Fatted Calf."[22]

His habits echo those of thousands, or perhaps hundreds of thousands of young men in college, then or now. A college friend, Frederick "Pete" Blodgett said, of him:

> He never had any money but he never spent much. He was always raising hell and laughing a lot and didn't study worth a damn.[23]

His best grade at Dartmouth during his freshman year was an "A" in first semester German (an automatic since he spoke German at home), but even that slipped to a "B" during the spring semester.

His sophomore grades weren't much better. In Botany, he only survived when his professor Arthur H. Chivers, promised him and Blodgett a raise of one letter grade if they memorized four tree species in Latin. (Geisel had spent hours in class sketching, rather than taking notes. Blodgett's notes weren't much helpful.) They made a game of the memorization and both got a "C," up from their previous "D" work in Botany.[24]

During his second year at Dartmouth, fraternities which had ignored him, now rushed him. Geisel joined Sigma Phi Episilon but was an indifferent frat member during his years at Dartmouth, although he remembered the Sig Ep rituals throughout his life.

Geisel found another importance influence in the Dartmouth English Department:

> . . . my big inspiration for writing there was Ben Pressey (W. Benfield Pressey . . .). He was (as) important to me in college as Red Smith was in high school.

> He seemed to like the stuff I wrote. He was very informal, and he had little seminars at his house (plus a very beautiful wife who served us cocoa). In between sips of cocoa, we students read our trash out loud.
>
> He's the only person I took any creative writing courses from ever, anywhere, and he was very kind and encouraging.
>
> I remember being in a big argument at one of Ben's seminars. I maintained that subject matter wasn't as important as method. . . .
>
> To prove my point, I did a book review of the Boston and Maine Railroad timetable. As I remember, nobody in the class thought it was funny—except Ben and me.[25]

Geisel also had a memory for cartoons, situations, phrases. "When I went to college," he remembered, "it was a campy thing to say, 'Oh, the places you'll go! The people you'll meet!'"[26]

Dr. Seuss published *Oh! The Places You'll Go!*, a *paean* to high school and college graduates everywhere, over six decades later, in 1990.

At Dartmouth, in his junior year, he finally made the mental leap of joining pictures and text:

> This was the year I discovered the excitement of "marrying" words to pictures.
>
> I began to get it through my skull that words and pictures were Yin and Yan. [sic] I began thinking that words and pictures, married, might possibly produce a progeny more interesting than either parent.
>
> It took me almost a quarter of a century to find the proper way to get my words and pictures married. At Dartmouth I couldn't even get them engaged.[27]

Norman Maclean and Geisel developed a fanciful technique for collaboration:

> Norman and I had a rather peculiar method of creating literary gems, Geisel recalled.[28] Hunched behind his typewriter, he would bang out a line of words.
>
> Sometimes he'd tell me what he'd written, sometimes not. But, then, he'd always say, "The next line's yours." And, always, I'd supply it.
>
> That may have made for rough reading. But it was great sport writing.

As others discovered, writing and editing a college newspaper or magazine was a better education than mere college classes.

> My big desire . . . was to run that magazine. If Mac (Norman Maclean) hadn't picked me as his successor my whole life at college would have been a failure.[29]

He was elected editor in mid-May, 1924. In the summer prior to his senior year, the Geisel family financial crisis eased, as his father sold a piece of Springfield property he had owned for six months—for a thirty thousand dollar profit. But Geisel senior still had no real job; he had been elected to the Springfield Park Board, but that was almost an honorary title. Only later, in 1931, when he was appointed Park Superintendent, did he earn a real paycheck.[30]

In his senior year, Geisel was one of twenty elected to Casque and Gauntlet, the Dartmouth senior honorary. One member, Kenneth Montgomery remembered Geisel:

> He was not gregarious in the sense of hail-fellow-well-met; there was no sense of self-importance about him. But when he walked into a room it was like a magician's act. Birds flew out of his hands, and endless bright scarves and fireworks. Everything became brighter, happier, funnier. And he didn't try. Everything Ted did seemed to be a surprise, even to him.[31]

But, at the same time, Casque and Gauntlet members voted him "least likely to succeed."

But one Saturday night in April, 1925, Geisel got caught after sharing some bootleg liquor with friends; the Dartmouth Dean demanded that he write to his parents explaining that he was on probation. And although his name remained in the magazine, he was forbidden to contribute to the *Jack-O-Lantern*. But Geisel was not banned from the magazine's offices, so he continued to contribute, using a variety of pseudonyms, including L. Burbank (a bow to Arthur H. Chivers, his Botany professor) and Thomas Mott Osborn, who was then warden of Sing Sing, the infamous prison in New York.[32]

Geisel also used the pen-name Seuss.

He approached graduation with no career in sight, no job on the horizon, no plans, and—and no real ambition to do anything. But when his Father asked what he was to do, Geisel grandly said that he was going to win a scholarship—a Campbell Fellowship from Dartmouth—to attend Oxford University, in England.

Geisel's father took the news to the editor of *The Springfield Union*, who lived across the street from the Geisel's. The news was promptly printed. Geisel remembered that it was on the front page:[33]

GEISEL WINS FELLOWSHIP TO GO TO OXFORD

Then Ted was forced to tell his father that he had *applied* to receive the Campbell Scholarship, but didn't get it.

Ted didn't receive any punishment from his father, nor even a lecture—his father's disapproving silence was enough. Geisel the elder then admitted that since Ted had announced he would be attending Oxford, then he must attend. Readers of *The Springfield Union* and friends of the family would forget about the scholarship.

Looking back on his career at Dartmouth, Ted said:

> English and writing was my major, but I think that's
> a mistake for anybody. That's teaching you the mechan-
> ics of getting water out of a well that may not exist.[34]

True advice, ignored by thousands of English majors everywhere.

Geisel spent the summer after his graduation working for
The Springfield Union, doing miscellaneous work. When the
Lowell, Mass. *Courier-Citizen* celebrated happy birthday with a
rhymed couplet to the Governor, Ted topped that in the *Union*:

> We'll go you just one better
> (*The Springfield Union* says)
> And wish a happy birthday
> to Calvin Coolidge, Pres.[35]

Theodor Geisel reached Lincoln College, Oxford University
in October, 1925; British academia was worlds away from Geisel's
safe haven of Dartmouth. He arrived just in time for the election
of a student as Guardian of the College Cat.[36]

Again, Geisel was the outsider; he was a Yank in a British
University and he was of German extraction in a land which had
just fought Germany bitterly and had not yet forgotten World War
One. So he read and studied by himself. Eventually he found
other outsiders, including a young lady named Mirabel who had
spent her earlier years in "the India of the Raj, where Papa wore
a pith helmet and shoulder straps." When Geisel and Mirabel
staged a dramatic love affair for a fellow student with a movie
camera—with the Dean of the College, J.A.R. Munro looking on
from a distance—Munro never spoke to Geisel again.[37]

Geisel found much of Oxford life trivial, tedious or bizarre.
He was treated as an underling in the dining halls even though
he was older than many of the British students. He did not

participate in rugby, didn't like the British food, didn't care much for the beer drinking contests in the dining halls, didn't like the hours and the classes. Perhaps most of all he didn't like the classes.

Oxford was very, very pompous and deliberately so. Oxford had centuries of pomposity to live up to and in the 1920s, was doing nothing to change. Ted Geisel was leery of, or alternatively, bemused by pomposity.

But instead of keeping a diary of his thoughts, emotions and reactions, Geisel kept a sketchbook.

His future life lay literally in the margins.

He had to attend lectures:

> on Geoffrey Chaucer (whom he called Jeff), Shakespeare and Milton. Among its sixty-eight pages are a few with words only, but most are thronged with pen-and-ink Seussian cartoons. Sometimes a sketch erupted from the subject of the lecture, but any Oxford don confronted with the result would have felt ready to suggest to the young American (as one eventually did) that his future lay elsewhere. Beside his notes in Anglo-Saxon for Beginners stands a drooling milk cow burdened with a sagging udder, rams' horns and angels wings. A pair of baroque daggers decorates the margin, along with a coat of arms from which a trapped bird struggles to free itself. On the same page as desultory notes on Keats' odes, three dogs move in terror across high wires, a small chicken wears a windmill for a tail, and a despondent devil contemplates his failures. As Ted noted dutifully that the translation of the holy Bible was the greatest literary achievement in the reign of King James he was also deep at work creating a Chaplinesque clown, slumping beneath the weight of military epaulettes and a crown from which grew a soaring cross. In a lecture by Emile Legouis, an authority on William Wordsworth and Jonathan Swift,

Ted sketched himself, sinking into deep water, with the caption "Mr. Legouis attempts once more to attract my attention in a lecture entitled. . . ?" Among his notes on Dryden, a black-faced Cupid appears with a quiver of arrows. So does the profile of a chic young woman wearing a snug cloche. "You hoo," cries a male profile as he peers up the loose-leaf binder at the cloche.[38]

And his future wife literally read his life through the margins of his sketchbook.

Helen Marion Palmer, a graduate of Wellesley, was almost six years older than Geisel. She had come to Oxford a year earlier, after teaching English in Brooklyn for three years.

She watched Geisel illustrate Milton's *Paradise Lost* in his own way.

Geisel remembered Uriel:

> While I was at Oxford I illustrated a great hunk of *Paradise Lost*.
>
> With the imagery of *Paradise Lost*, Milton's sense of humor failed him in a couple of places. I remember one line, "Thither came the angel Uriel, sliding down a sunbeam."
>
> I illustrated that: Uriel had a long locomotive oil can and was greasing the sunbeam as he descended, to lessen the friction on his coccyx.[39]

> "You're crazy to be a professor," (Helen) said, after a class.
>
> "What you really want to do is draw." And, looking at his sketchbook, said, "that's a very fine flying cow."[40]

Any young woman who could appreciate Uriel and his oil can and the flying cow and the drooling cow with a sagging udder, rams' horns and wings, a Chaplinesque clown, dogs walking along high wires, the chicken with a windmill for a tail, the black-faced Cupid, the young woman wearing the snug cloche and the leering male in the margins, was for him.

Theodor Geisel fell in love with Helen Palmer and just as quickly she fell in love with him.

The two became inseparable; Geisel knew that first year students were not allowed to own cars or other motor vehicles, but Helen wasn't a first year student. So after Christmas break, they pooled their money and bought a motorcycle, with a sidecar. Ted appropriated some Oxford ducks and maintained the fantasy that he was a deliveryman, with live ducks in tow.

By the end of the first year, Geisel knew as well as Helen that Oxford wasn't for him. And he wasn't for Oxford.

> My tutor was A.J. Carlyle, the nephew of the great frightening Thomas Carlyle. I was surprised to see him alive. He was surprised to see me in any form.
>
> He was the oldest man I've ever seen riding a bicycle. I was the only man he'd ever seen who never should have come to Oxford.
>
> This brilliant scholar had taken a "First" in every school in Oxford, excepting medicine, without studying. Every year, up to his eighties, he went up for a different "First," just for the hell of it.
>
> Patiently, he had me write essays and listened to me read them, in the usual manner of the Oxford tutorial system. But he realized I was getting stultified in English schools.
>
> I was bogged down with old High German and Gothic and stuff of that sort, in which I have no interest whatsoever—and I don't think anybody really should.
>
> Well, he was a great historian and he quickly discovered that I didn't know *any* history. Somehow or other I got through high school and Dartmouth without taking one history course.

He very correctly told me I was ignorant, and he was
the man who suggested that I do what I finally did: just
travel around Europe with a bundle of high school history books and visit the places I was reading about—go
to the museums and look at pictures and read as I went.
That's what I finally did.[41]

Years later, Geisel clearly remembered the final academic
straw. . . . He had a don (Sir Oliver Onions) who had produced a
variorum edition of Shakespeare and who was chiefly interested
in punctuational differences in Shakespearean texts:

That was the man who really drove me out of Oxford.
I'll never forget his two hour lecture on the punctuation
of *King Lear*.

He had dug up all of the old folios, as far back as he
could go. Some had more semi-colons than commas. Some
had more commas than periods. Some had no punctuation at all.

For the first hour and a half he talked about the first
two pages in *King Lear*, lamenting the fact that modern
people would never comprehend the true essence of
Shakespeare, because it's punctuated badly these days.

It got unbelievable. I got up, went back to my room
and started packing.[42]

Ted and Helen spent some months in Europe, beginning in
the summer of 1926 (Helen chose to remain in Oxford to complete her degree); he met his parents and his sister Marnie. They
toured Switzerland, Munich, Nuremberg, Dresden and Berlin.
They stopped in Mulhausen, to honor the memory of the Geisels
who emigrated to Springfield. In the hamlet of
Kleinschwarzenbach, they hosted a dinner for the Seusses and
sixty-seven people attended.[43] His family finally returned to the
United States and Geisel stayed in Paris.

Geisel recognized that he wasn't exactly in the wave of American expatriate literature of the 1920s; one night in Paris, he caught a glimpse of Ernest Hemingway:

> . . . a worldly man of twenty-seven, smoking a pipe and writing from time to time on a thick pad. "What he was writing, I never knew," Ted admitted. "I was scared . . . to walk over and ask him, lest he ask me what I was writing. I was a twenty-two-year-old kid writing knock-kneed limericks about goats and cheese and other stuff that I couldn't sell. He was probably writing *A Farewell to Arms*."[44]

Geisel met Helen for a short tour of Vienna, then returned to Paris where he gave academics one more try. At Oxford, he had met Emile Legouis, an expert on Wordsworth and Swift. And Geisel had admired *Gulliver's Travels*.

> At Oxford I went to a lecture (I was very interested in Jonathan Swift) by the great Emile Legouis. Although he was a Frenchman, he was the greatest Swift authority in the world at that time.
>
> He talked to me at the end of the lecture and began selling me on going to study with him at the Sorbonne. And, after I left Oxford, I did so.
>
> I registered at the Sorbonne, and I went over to his house to find out exactly what he wanted me to do.
>
> He said, "I have a most interesting assignment which should only take you about two years to complete." He said that nobody had ever discovered anything that Jonathan Swift wrote from the ages of 16 and a half to 17.
>
> He said that I should devote two years to finding out whether he *had* written anything. If he had, I could analyze what he wrote as my D.Phil. thesis. Unfortunately, if he hadn't written anything, I wouldn't get my doctorate.

I remember leaving his charming home and walking straight to the American Express Company and booking myself a passage on a cattle boat to Corsica.

There I proceeded to paint donkeys for a month. Then, I proceeded with Carlyle's idea and began living all around the Continent, reading history books, going to museums and drawing pictures.

I remember a long time period in which I drew nothing but gargoyles. They were easier than Mona Lisas.[45]

Which was not exactly true. He journeyed to Italy and met Helen, who was touring with her Mother. He visited Florence, witnessed the growth of the Mussolini movement and, with Helen, saw Michelangelo's David. Helen's Mother appeared shocked. She would have been happier "if all art, including Raphael's pre-puberty cheribs, wore jockstraps," Geisel said.[46]

He produced some drawings based on what he saw, which he called his "Roman and Florentine Period":

These fractured bits of Roman history include a Seussian version of Romulus and Remus, a group of vestal virgins on the forum, and a dragon, drawn directly from the central monster in *Perseus Frees Andromeda* by Piero di Cosimo in the Uffizi Gallery, Florence. This was the last time that art history was to intrude on Geisel's work.[47]

He also tried to write a novel:

While floating around Europe trying to figure out what I wanted to do with my life, I decided at one point that I would be the Great American Novelist. And so I sat down and wrote the Great American Novel.

It turned out to be not so great, so I boiled it down into the Great American Short Story. It wasn't very great in that form either.

> Two years later I boiled it down once more and sold
> it as a two-line joke to *Judge* (magazine).[48]

Finally, Geisel sailed home, presumably full of Europe, and especially full of academia. He arrived in New York in February, 1927, with no graduate degree, no job, no prospects for a job, no *talent* for a job. He returned to Springfield and drew at his Father's desk. The animals he drew were the animals he had always drawn—odd, mis-shapen, bizarre—but animals which were somehow comical and entertaining. They weren't frightening, just odd. Helen told her relatives and others that his animals were "the sort you'd like to take home to meet the family."[49]

He journeyed to New York and knocked on doors all over Manhattan. In a letter to Dartmouth friend Whitney Campbell he said:

> I have tramped all over this bloody town and been
> tossed out of Boni and Liveright, Harcourt Brace, Para-
> mount Pictures, Metro-Goldwyn, three advertising agen-
> cies, *Life*, *Judge*, and three public conveniences . . . [58]

He returned to Springfield, dismayed. Again he aimed for *Life*[51] magazine and *The New Yorker*.

Finally, one day, the mailman left an envelope from *The Saturday Evening Post*. Geisel had sent them a drawing of two American tourists riding camels and comparing their journey to Lawrence of Arabia. It was his first professional sale. *The Post* had sent a check for twenty-five dollars. When it ran, the by-line said: Seuss.[52]

Two

1927–1939

The drone of the Kungsholm's engine became the driving force of Dr. Seuss's career.

With that thin blade of success of his one cartoon in *The Saturday Evening Post*, and one thousand dollars, his profits from working on the *Jack-o-Lantern* at Dartmouth, Geisel moved to New York. He shared a dingy apartment over a nightclub with a friend, John C. Rose, and this time, Geisel had better luck in New York.

He knew that his best chances as a cartoonist lay with *Judge* magazine (Harold Ross had left *Judge* in 1925 to start *The New Yorker*). Geisel made an appointment with the editor, and promptly got a job as writer and artist (read cartoonist). His salary was seventy-five dollars a week and on that salary he and Helen Palmer could get married. (Some relatives thought that Geisel and Palmer had already been married in Europe. Years later, when he was asked about any such European wedding, Geisel only smiled.[1])

They delayed their wedding because Ted's sister Marnie was due to have her first baby and they didn't want Ted's parents to miss one happy event because of the other. On November 29, 1927, four weeks after her daughter Peggy was born, Theodor

Geisel and Helen Palmer were married in the living room of her home. He was twenty-three; she twenty-nine.

Back at *Judge*, after an Atlantic City honeymoon, Geisel contributed his first cartoon as a staff member. It showed two unicyclists, on very tall unicycles, one speaking to the other. "And to think that today I could have been the wife of a six-day bicycle racer, if I hadn't listened to your rot about Higher Art."[2]

Only weeks later, Geisel added "Dr." to his by-line Seuss, explaining it made up for the doctoral degree he never got in Oxford. Much later, he also explained that he "saved" his own name to use as the by-line on the novel he intended to write. He never used his own name again and he never really attempted to write the Great American Novel.

Quickly after using "Seuss," he used "Dr. Theophrastus Seuss" for an on-going *Judge* feature, "Boids and Beasties, A Department for Indefatigable Naturalists." Some of the creatures for this series were taken almost line-for-line out of the margins of his Oxford notebook.

He used a tipsy elephant to illustrate a feature, "Quaffing with the Pachyderms: Why I Prefer the West Side Speakeasies" (it easily could have been the precursor of Horton the elephant, hero of *Horton Hatches the Egg* and *Horton Hears a Who*[3]) and he began a series, "being ye inside dope on King Arthur's Court translated from Merlin's memoirs." His experiences in the cloistered halls of Oxford gave him more than enough images for that series.

> Among Ted's first fan letters at *Judge* was a curt note from a condemned murderer on death row in Huntsville, Texas, written on the eve of his electrocution. "If your stuff is the kind of thing they're publishing nowadays," the prisoner took the time to write, "I don't so much mind leaving." Ted was enraptured with the letter and kept it at his desk throughout his long life, always feigning fear of running into the felon, whose sentence had been commuted at the last minute.[4]

Critic George Jean Nathan was on the staff of *Judge*, and S. J. Perelman was in the magazine as was Pare Lorentz, who wrote film reviews, but the new *New Yorker* judged *Judge* its main competition and advertisers began deserting *Judge* for *The New Yorker*. Geisel had to take a pay cut to fifty dollars a week.

He clearly remembered those days at *Judge*:

> And the *next* week they instituted another fiscal policy (I was getting a little bit worried by this time) in which they dispensed with money entirely and paid contributors with due bills. "Due bills . . ?"
>
> *Judge* had practically no advertising. And the advertisers it attracted seldom paid for the ads with money; they paid the magazine with due bills. And that's what we, the artists and writers, ended up with in lieu of salary.
>
> For instance: a hundred dollars, the only way for me to get the hundred dollars was to go down to the Hotel Traymore in Atlantic City and move into a hundred-dollar suite.
>
> So, Helen and I spent many weeks of our first married year in sumptuous suites in Atlantic City—where we didn't want to be at all.
>
> Under the due-bill system I got paid once, believe it or not, in a hundred cartons of Barbasol Shaving Cream. Another time I got paid in 13 gross of Little Gem nail clippers.
>
> Looking back on it, it wasn't really so bad, because I didn't have to balance any checkbooks—or file any income tax.
>
> How can you file an income tax when you're being paid in cases of White Rock soda?[5]

He also said . . .

. . . I sort of loved trading my stuff for their stuff. I was happier in one way under the barter system than I've ever been since. When you get paid in money, it leads to accountants and lawyers.[6]

Geisel always claimed that serendipity played a large part in his career. And when *Judge* was faltering, a financial godsend was near.

In the late 1920s, well before air conditioning, families had to keep the windows or screens open, and use flyswatters, flypaper or bug sprays to keep the inside insect population down.

I'd been working for *Judge* about four months when I drew this accidental cartoon which changed my whole life. It was an insect gag.

It was a picture of a knight who had gone to bed. He had stacked his armor beside the bed. Here was this covered canopy over the bed, and a tremendous dragon was sort of nuzzling him.

He looked up and said, "Darn it all, Another Dragon. And just after I'd sprayed the whole castle with . . ."

With *what?* I wondered.

There were two well-known insecticides. One was Flit and one was Fly-Tox. So, I tossed a coin. It came up heads, for Flit.

So, the caption read, " . . . another dragon. And just after I'd sprayed the whole castle with Flit."

Here's where luck comes in.

Very few people ever bought *Judge.* It was continually in bankruptcy—and everybody else was bankrupt, too.

But one day the wife of Lincoln L. Cleaves, who was the account executive at the McCann-Erickson advertising agency, failed to get an appointment at her favorite hairdresser's, and went to a second-rate hairdresser's, where they had second-rate magazines around.

She opened *Judge* while waiting to get her hair dressed, and she found this picture. She ripped it out of the magazine, put it in her reticule, took it home, bearded her husband with it, and said, "Lincoln, you've got to hire this young man; it's the best Flit ad I've ever seen.

He said, "Go away." He said, "you're my wife and you're to have nothing to do with my business."

So she finally pestered him for about two weeks and finally he said, "All right, I'll have him in and buy one picture."

He had me in. I drew one picture, which I captioned "Quick Henry, The Flit!"—and it was published.

Then, they hired me to do two more—and 17 years later I was still doing them.

The only good thing Adolph Hitler did in starting World War II was that he enabled me to join the Army and finally stop drawing "Quick Henry the Flit!"

I had drawn them by the millions—newspaper ads, magazine ads, booklets, window displays, 24-sheet posters, even "Quick Henry, the flit!" animated cartoons. Flit was pouring out of my ears and beginning to itch me.[7]

The Flit campaign, all seventeen years, entered America's vernacular, just as other phrases would, throughout the years. Geisel drew situation after situation involving Flit. In one cartoon, a prisoner is surrounded by insects during a prison break; in another, a genie is also surrounded by bugs during a seance. A song was written about the phrase; Flit sales grew wildly. The only other comparable campaign was the Burma Shave four-line highway signs.[8] Flit insured Geisel's financial security, year after year.

And it allowed Geisel very considerable freedom of time:

My contract with the Standard Oil Company was an exclusive one and forbade me from doing an awful lot of stuff.

Flit being seasonal, its ad campaign was only run during the summer months. I'd get my work done in about three months, and I had all this spare time and nothing to do.

They let me work for magazines, because I'd already established that. But it crimped future expansion into other things.[9]

The Geisels were so comfortable, from the Flit income, they were able to tour Greece during the spring of 1928. They moved into a better apartment and, one morning while shaving, Geisel thought of a party they attended the night before. He completed this poem.

> Mrs. Van Bleck
> Of the Newport Van Blecks
> Is so goddam rich
> She has gold-plated sex
> Whereas Miggles and Mitzi
> And Blitzie and Sue
> Have the commonplace thing
> And it just has to do.[10]

Geisel began selling cartoons to *Liberty* and *Life* (the old *Life*, not the Luce *Life*). The first *Life* was the one that was *intentionally* funny, one New York wag said.[11]

To celebrate their first anniversary, the Geisels took a train to southern California, at the suggestion of John Rose, Geisel's former New York City roommate. There, they were impressed by La Jolla, a small village between the ocean and San Diego. Everything in La Jolla was a marked contrast to their previous lives in New York: they had the seascapes, fresh air; even in the winter there were swimmers in the surf. They saw plants in wild profusion they had never seen before. It had a Mediterranean look and feel. Much of the architecture was Mediterranean/ Spanish. They were enchanted by it all. And they quickly resolved, somehow, to move to La Jolla.

Geisel became fascinated by words; how they were spelled, how they were pronounced; how they *behaved*. Readers of *Judge* shared his fascination with *ough* words, in his feature, titled "Ough! Ough! Or Why I Believe in Simplified Spelling":

"The Tough Coughs As He Ploughs the Dough":

It was forty-five years ago, when I first came to America as a young Roumanian student of divinity, that I first met the evils of the "ough" words. Strolling one day in the country with my fellow students, I saw a tough, coughing as he ploughed a field which (being quite near-sighted) I mistook for pie dough.

Assuming that all "ough" words were pronounced the same, I casually remarked, "The tuff cuffs as he pluffs the duff!"

"Sacriledge," shrieked my devout companions, "He is cursing in Roumanian! . . ."

"Mr. Hough, Your Bough is in the Trough"

The ministry being closed to me, I then got a job as a chore boy on the farm of an eccentric Mr. Hough, who happened to spend most of his time in the bough of a tree overhanging a trough. I was watering a colt one morning when I noticed that Mr. Hough's weight had forced the bough down into the water. "Mr. Hoo!" I shouted, "Your Boo is in the Troo!" Thinking I was speaking lightly of his wife, Mr. Hough fired me on the spot.

"Enough, Enough! I'm Through!"

So I drifted into the prize ring. But here again the curse of the *oughs* undid me. One night in the Garden, I was receiving an unmerciful trouncing from a mauler twice my size. Near the end of the sixth round I could stand it no longer. I raised my feeble hand in surrender. "Eno! Eno!" I gulped. "I'm thuff." "Insults like that I take from no man!" bellowed my opponent, and he slugged me into a coma! Something snapped! . . . a maddening flash . . . and all became black. Fifteen years later I awoke to find myself the father of three homely daughters named Xough, Yough and Zough. I had become a through-going Augho-maniac.[12]

A collection of schoolroom gaffes was published in England under the title *Schoolboy Howlers*. The Viking Press bought the U.S. publication rights and changed the title to *Boners*. Geisel was paid a set rate (but no royalties) to illustrate the book, published in 1931. It was a surprise best seller; and teachers sent in their own best examples of school room *faux pas*. The sequel, *More Boners*, was also published before the end of 1931. Geisel began to think:

> That was a big depression year. And although by Depression standards I was adequately paid a flat fee for illustrating these best-sellers, I was money-worried. The two books were booming and I was not.
>
> This is the point when I first began to realize that if I hoped to succeed in the book world, I'd have to write as well as draw.[13]

He was also encouraged by a review in *American News*:

> offhand . . . we should have said this would be a flop. But the inimitable illustrations of the renowned Dr.

Seuss, of *Judge, Life* and Flit fame, are not unlikely to put this over. They are simply swell.

He subsequently received a second endorsement from the same publication:

> Seuss puts more naive satisfaction into the face of a cat, more passion into the face of a Cleopatra, more anticipation into the face of a Mark Anthony, than many other cartoonists could do if brought together in the same speakeasy.

So he wrote and illustrated a children's ABC book, full of Seussian animals, with seventeen different colors of blue and three colors of red. He took it to publishers Bobbs Merrill, Viking Press, Simon and Schuster and others . . . where it was promptly rejected. He abandoned it.[15]

But Flit begat Esso.

And pictures begat poems.

For Flit he wrote (about the knight and the dragon):

> If Flit can knock
> *this* monster stiff
> Mere bugs and such
> won't last one *whiff!*

And they even generated three rare Seussian books of advertising cartoons: *Flit Cartoons As They Have Appeared in Magazines Throughout the Country* (Vol. 1, 1929 and Vol. 2, 1930) and *Another Big Flit! Year* (1931).

The cartoons were all the same; neither Flit nor Esso, nor later, Shaeffer Bock Beer, nor Ford, nor Atlas Products, nor New Departure Bearings, nor NBC Radio, or Holly Sugar ever asked Geisel to change the Seuss drawings. They didn't carry a Seuss-by-line; they didn't have to. Seuss creatures and Seuss rhymes were becoming nationally recognized. For Esso, a series of panels with monkeys, dragons and such:

>   Foil the Moto-raspus!

>   Foil the Zero-doccus!

>   Foil the Karbo-nockus![16]

Geisel was doing quite, quite well during the days of the Great Depression.

One day in the early 1930s, Geisel got a package at his apartment door: his father sent him a heavy slab of stone . . . imbedded in it: a dinosaur footprint eleven inches wide and sixteen inches long. The Geisels couldn't find a good place for it—they tripped over it and stubbed their toes on it. For a while Geisel thought he'd hang it on the wall for visitors to kiss, like an ancient Blarney Stone, but his wife didn't go for that.[17] It was a perfect Seussian gift: it reminded him of the minuteness of man in the vast time of the universe and he kept it with him, move after move; it took his mind back to prehistoric days, where he could visualize dinosaurs thumping and thundering about and then it would be a very slight jump—or no jump at all—to think of far different Seussian creatures.

It also taught—and retaught—him a valuable lesson:

> It keeps me from getting conceited. Whenever I think I'm pretty good, I just go out and look at it. Half the people I show it to think I've made it myself.[18]

In 1935, Standard Oil, which produced Flit, asked Geisel to work on another campaign, leading to his long "Naval Career." As he remembered it:

They had a product called Esso marine, a lubricating oil for boats, and they didn't have a lot of money to spend on advertising.

They decided to see what we could do with public relations. So, Harry Bruno, a great PR man, Ted Cook and Verne Carrier of Esso and I cooked up the Seuss Navy.

Starting small at one of the New York motorboat shows, we printed up a few diplomas, and we took about 15 prominent people into membership—Vincent Astor and sailors like that, who had tremendous yachts—so we could photograph them at the boat show receiving their certificates.

We waited to see what would happen. Well, Astor and Guy Lombardo and a few other celebrities hung those things in their yachts. And very soon everyone who had a putt-putt wanted to join the Seuss Navy.

The next year we started giving annual banquets at the Biltmore. It was cheaper to give a party for a few thousand people, furnishing all the booze, then it was to advertise.

And it was successful because we never mentioned the product at all. Reporters would cover the party and *they* would write our commercials for us. So, we would end up with national coverage about "The Seuss Navy met . . . ," and then they would have to explain it by talking about Esso Marine.

At the time war was declared, in 1941, we had the biggest navy in the world. We commissioned the whole Standard Oil fleet, and we also had, for example, the *Queen Mary* and most of the ships of the U.S. lines.

Then, an interesting thing happened. I left to join the Army. And somebody said, "Thank God Geisel's gone, he was wasting a great opportunity. He wasn't *selling* the product. We have Seuss Navy hats and we have Seuss

Navy glasses and Seuss navy flags." He said, "These
things should carry advertising on them."

They put advertising on them, and the Navy
promptly died. The fun had gone out of it and the Seuss
Navy sank.[19]

For the Seuss Navy, Geisel had even designed a Naval flag.
It showed the skeleton of a red herring in profile, wearing an
admiral's hat, with a vague Mona Lisa smile on its face.[20]

In May, 1934, he was interviewed for the first time, by a
reporter from Dartmouth College.

> You want an interview, a sort of life story, as
> it were, he asked the reporter.
> The student nodded.
> Truth or fiction?

Geisel proceed to explain:

> I just came back from Peru. . . . (where I) looked into
> the llama situation. . . . They can spit at you and aim
> every shot they make. . . . The biggest disappointment
> I ever had . . . was when I went to Dalmatia to study the
> Dalmatian dog situation. . . . I got there and found all
> the Dalmatian dogs were in England . . . I go all over
> looking for peculiar animals (and) I've discovered that
> God has turned out even more ridiculous creatures
> than I have.[21]

The interview proved three universal truths about Seuss:

* He always embellished (with a twinkle in his eye) the story
of his life and books. He became particularly wary of questions
that began "how you develop your (book) ideas?" That invariably launched him into a widely fanciful Seussian tale of strange
lands with unpronounceable names, where he visited to get ideas;

* He and his wife Helen *were* world travelers (they visited Peru twice in two years—and after nine years of marriage, they had visited thirty countries[22]) and he did, indeed, get story ideas in wild locales: *The Lorax* (1971) was developed and written completely during a visit to Kenya (with his second wife Audrey);

* God did, indeed, create even more fanciful creatures than Seuss did.

Much later, science writer Chet Raymo compared the World of Seuss to the World of Nature, in an article "Dr. Seuss and Dr. Einstein: Children's Books and Scientific Imagination":

> A few years ago, when an insect called the thrips—singular and plural—was in the news for defoliating sugar maples in New England, I noted in my Boston *Globe* science column that thrips are very strange beasts. Some species of thrips give birth to live young, some lay eggs and at least one species of switch-hitting thrips has it both ways. Not even the wildest product of Dr. Seuss's imagination, I said—the Moth-Watching Sneth, for example, a bird that's so big it scares people to death, or the Grickily Gractus,[23] a bird that lays eggs on a cactus—is stranger than creatures, such as thrips, that actually exist.
>
> What about the Moth-Watching Sneth? Well, the extinct elephant bird of Madagascar stood eight feet tall and weighed a thousand pounds. In its heyday—only a century or so ago—the elephant bird, or Aepyornis, probably scared many a Madagascan half to death.
>
> Pick any Seussian invention and nature will equal it. Dr. Seuss's *McElligot's Pool* (Random) there's a fish with a kangaroo pouch. Could there be such a fish in the real world? Not a fish, maybe, but in South America there is an animal called the Yapok—a wonderfully Seussian name—that takes its young for a swim, in a waterproof pouch.[24]

Before Geisel got completely complacent, serendipity again played a large part in his life.

In the summer of 1936, the Geisels sailed for Europe aboard the M. S. Kungsholm. They visited the Alps; Geisel saw intrepid Alp animals clinging to sheer Alp mountain outcroppings. They traveled to Germany and saw the chill of the oncoming Nazi tide. Geisel was then thirty-two years old and the storm clouds of European politics left him saddened.

They returned on the same ship—the Kungsholm. And Geisel found himself caught in the drone of the engine.

Da-da-*Da*, Da-Da-*DUM*, Dum-De-*Da*, De-De-*Da*—there was some variation, but the rhythm stayed in his head. A lesser man would have turned to the nearest ship's bar and taken a drink, or two, or three to take the noise out of his head.

Seuss listened.

He couldn't shake the engine's rhythm. He found himself forming rhymes to the drone of the engine. He was on the Kungsholm for eight days on his return passage. Eight days of listening to the SAME engine rhythm. Eight days of rhyme schemes in his head.

The drone of the Kungsholm's engine became the driving energy of Dr. Seuss's career. It was as simple as that.

Da-da-*Da*, Da-Da-*DUM*, Dum-De-*Da*, De-De-*Da*.

Geisel may not have known what he was hearing, but the rhythm was forceful, hypnotic. Once captured by it, he was hooked. The rhythm didn't leave his head.

He didn't know what he was hearing, but there was a name to it. He may have heard the name at Dartmouth, or at Oxford. If he did, he probably forgot it.

He was hearing the rhythm of:

"'Twas the night before Christmas . . ." or . . .

"He flys through the air with the greatest of ease . . ."

He was hearing *anapestic tetrameter* (or something very much like it), which dates as far back as the ancient Greeks, who used it as a marching beat.

Geisel began hearing. . . . *And to Think That I Saw It on Mulberry Street*, surely the Mulberry street of his hometown of Springfield.

And he remembered:

> I was on a long, stormy crossing of the Atlantic, and it was too rough to go out on deck. Everybody in the ship just sat in the bar for a week, listening to the engines turn over: da-da-ta-ta, da-da-ta-ta, da-dat-ta-ta . . .
>
> To keep from going nuts, I began reciting silly words to the rhythm of the engines. Out of nowhere, I found myself saying, "And that is a story no one can beat; and to think that I saw it on Mulberry Street."
>
> When I finally got off the ship, this refrain kept going through my head. I couldn't shake it. To therapeutize myself I added more words in the same rhythm.[25]

The story began with a horse and wagon. Geisel made a list:

> A stupid horse and wagon
> Horse and chariot
> Chariot pulled by flying cat
> Flying cat pulling Viking ship
> Viking ship sailing up volcano
> Volcano blowing hearts, diamonds and clubs
>
> I saw a giant eight miles tall
> Who took the cards, 52 in all
> And played a game of solitaire. . . . [26]

It did not come easy—Geisel had to marry words with the rhythm (and he probably still didn't know what it was). What he perhaps knew instinctively, but did not, or could not, verbalize was: *the rhythm dictated the story; and the rhythm galloped.*

Without knowing why it worked, he may have sensed it was a perfect rhythm for a children's story.

*　　*　　*

There must be something about oceanliners. Compare Theodor Geisel's experience to an earlier experience of John Philip Sousa, returning from Europe: "In November, 1896, Sousa and his wife were conducting a vacation in Europe when he received a cable telling him that his band manager had died in New York City. Suddenly the many responsibilities of arranging his next tour fell on Sousa's shoulders. He booked passage for home immediately.

"As the ship began its voyage across the Atlantic, Sousa paced restlessly on the deck, absorbed in the many details and decisions awaiting him once he reached the United States. Suddenly, as he described it, 'I began to sense the rhythmic beat of a band playing within my brain.'

"The music didn't stop but continued for the entire voyage, playing the same themes and distinct melody over and over again. Although he didn't write down a note of the music while on board the ship, the moment Sousa reached shore he wrote it just as he heard it in his mind during the voyage. Not one note of the composition has been changed since that day," Elizabeth Van Steenwyk wrote in "It's a Sousapalooza," in the *A & E Monthly* magazine for July 1996 (Now *Biography* magazine). The composition Sousa heard in his head? "The Stars and Stripes Forever," named by President Reagan in 1987 as the official march of the United States. Van Steenwyk writes that a fragment of the musical store of "The Stars and Stripes Forever" is engraved on Sousa's tombstone.

*　　*　　*

He added picture after picture. And, fortunately kept the rhythm scheme. It took him six months before he was happy with the final manuscript. The working title was *A Story That No One Can Beat.*

And here the Geisel story turns into legend.

He took it into New York and showed it to children's book publishers. One, two, three turned it down, four, five—more. And more. And more turned it down. Much later, newspaper and magazine articles set the number from "the twenties" to as many as "into the forties"—the number of publishers who said no. And they said no simply because there had never been a story like his. The rhythm, the Seussian pictures as a children's book.

(We wonder how many book publishers recognized the rhyme scheme as anapestic tetrameter . . .)

And this is a story no one can beat, and to think that I saw it on Mulberry Street. . . .

Rejection after rejection, time after time.

It was too different; it wasn't wholesome enough; it didn't teach the right moral lesson; it wasn't right for children.

Geisel was in Manhattan one day, with the manuscript under his arm. It had been rejected twenty-seven times. *Twenty-seven times!*

And on the sidewalk he met Marshall McClintock, who had been at Dartmouth, one year behind Geisel.

"How are you Ted? And what do you have under your arm?"

Twenty-seven rejections . . .

"It's a book manuscript. A book for children. And I can't do anything with it. . . ."

Serendipity was with Geisel that day. They were standing outside McClintock's office building and he had just been named a children's book editor with The Vanguard Press.

McClintock, Geisel and the manuscript went into McClintock's office. . . . and met James Henle, president of The Vanguard Press and Evelyn Shrifte, staff editor.

And this is a story no one can beat . . .

. . . became literally true. Vanguard Press took the book that day, and only asked for a better title, which became . . .

And to Think That I Saw It on Mulberry Street.
And the little boy who was the hero of the story was renamed after McClintock's son, Marco. And the book dedicated to McClintock's wife, Helene.[27]

If . . . the wife of the McCann-Eriksson executive had been in her usual hairdresser's, she might not have seen *Judge* magazine with Geisel's Flit cartoon and would have never talked her husband into hiring Geisel to draw Flit cartoons . . .

If . . . Geisel had taken a different steamship to and from Europe, he may never have heard such the hypnotic drone that stayed in his mind hour after hour, day after day, until he began to answer it in rhyme. . . .

If . . . Geisel had been five minutes earlier or five minutes later, or even on the opposite side of the street, he might not have met Marshall McClintock and might have abandoned *A Story No One Can Beat* forever. The rhythmic drone of the Kungsholm's engine might just have faded from his inner ear.

Serendipity had again perched on Geisel's shoulder. Can we guess what it looked like? Perhaps it looked something like a Who from Whoville . . .

Marco first sees, on Mulberry Street the "stupid horse and wagon" Geisel jotted down during the Kungsholm voyage.

But the horse turns into a Zebra (on one page); the wagon turns into a chariot (on the next page); the zebra turns into a huge reindeer; the wagon turns into an Eskimo sled; the Reindeer turns into a Blue elephant topped by a Rajah on a covered throne; the sled become a four-wheeled circus wagon, complete with circus band (page after page of changes); a small sled on wheels is pulled behind the wagon and two giraffes help the elephant pull.

The whole parade comes to the corner of Mulberry Street and Bliss Street and needs an escort of motorcycle police. They pass the Mayor and Aldermen on a reviewing stand; a passing airplane drops confetti . . . The parade includes . . .

A Chinese man with chopsticks . . .
A magician doing tricks . . . and . . .
A man with a ten-foot white beard . . .

I swung 'round the corner
and dashed through the gate,
I ran up the steps
And I felt simply GREAT!

FOR I HAD A STORY THAT NO ONE COULD BEAT!
AND TO THINK THAT I SAW IT ON MULBERRY STREET!

Dr. Seuss married text, rhyme and art perfectly.

Here Seuss begins techniques which he uses in almost—almost—all Dr. Seuss books. You could think of it as *escalating sequences* or *escalating action*. The rhyme gallops—the pictures move from left to right, toward the next page and the action builds. Every page—text and pictures—contributes to a bigger—and better—next page. It is no wonder that one of the best critical reviews of a Dr. Seuss book was by a child who simply said:

"Whew!"

Children can read the lines; they can sing the lines; they can *SHOUT!* the lines; they can dance to the lines. And with the emphasis at the end of each page (and on the right side of each page), they are drawn to the next page.

And finally the action climaxes. The child says "Whew!" And often, the reader is back at the beginning.

As children's literature expert Selma G. Lanes wrote much later:

> Seuss cannily manages to magnify and multiply the sense of suspense in his stories, not so much by the ingenuity of his plots as by a clever and relentless piling on of gratuitous anxiety until the child is fairly ready to cry "uncle" and settle for any resolution, however mundane, that will

end his at once marvelous, exquisite and finally, unbear-
able tension. The process is not unlike the blowing up of
a balloon: bigger, bigger, bigger and finally, when the
bursting point is reached, Seuss simply releases his grip
and all tension, like trapped air, is freed.[28]

Mulberry Street appears so remarkably easy: he had the rhyme
from the engine drone; he had some characters from his ship-
board notes. It only took six months to write. Only six months. It
was clearly not that easy. He later said:

> It's hard. I'm a bleeder and I sweat at it. As I've said
> before: The "creative process" consists for me of two
> things—time and sweat. And I've also said that too many
> writers have only contempt and condescension for chil-
> dren, which is why they give them degrading corn about
> bunnies. The difficult thing about writing in verse for
> kids is that you can write yourself into a box: If you can't
> get a proper rhyme for a quatrain, you not only have to
> throw that quatrain out but you also have to unravel the
> sock way back, probably ten pages or so . . . You find
> that you're not driving the car, your characters are driv-
> ing it. And you also have to remember that in a children's
> book a paragraph is like a chapter in an adult book, and
> a sentence is like a paragraph.[29]

The Vanguard Press advertised the book with a line which
would become remarkably accurate over the years:

> Booksellers, hitch on! This is the start of a parade that
> will take you places![30]

Authors often suffer post partum depression when a book is
out and reviews are either nonexistent or fewer than they may
have anticipated.

Mulberry Street generated a few reviews, but they were very favorable. And they managed to match the book. The best was the shortest: writing in *The New Yorker*, Nov. 6, 1937, Clifton Fadiman said:

> They say it's for children, but better get a copy for yourself and marvel at the good Dr. Seuss' improbable pictures and the moral tale of the little boy who exaggerated not wisely but too well.[31]

The New York Times wrote:

> Highly original and entertaining, Dr. Seuss' picture book partakes of the better qualities of those peculiarly American institutions, the funny papers and the tall tale. It is a masterly interpretation of the mind of a child in the act of creating one of those stories with which children often amuse themselves and bolster up their self-respect.[32]

Anne Carroll Moore, children's book expert for the New York Public Library reviewed *Mulberry Street* in *The Atlantic Monthly*. She wrote:

> So completely spontaneous that the American child can take it in his heart on sight . . . As original in conception, as spontaneous in the rendering as it is true to the imagination of a small boy.[33]

(Moore wanted him to speak at the New York Public Library, but at the right time, he could get no further than outside the front doors, he was so consumed with stage fright.)[34]

How as it that Geisel, as Dr. Seuss, could remain "true to the imagination of a small boy?"

Helen Palmer Geisel, from the perspective of a loving spouse, later said, "his mind has never grown up."[35]

By the late 1930s, Geisel had developed a whole vast universe of Seussian animals, made of clay, pipe cleaners, odds and ends . . . a vast Noah's Ark of curious creatures great and small, all generated from his imagination, including: "red turtles, purple elephants, and green camels with bizarre beaks and horns."[36] He made one particularly enchanting bearded creature's face by simply using an old-fashioned men's shaving brush.

They were, of course, his creative *workshop*, his *dream works*, to use the name of Steven Spielberg's production company. Did they speak to him and he to them? Figuratively, they spoke louder than words; they spoke in volumes to him. And he gave them voices and personalities in book after book. . . .

And there were his hats. He had a collection of hats from all over the world, including "a fireman's hat from Equator and a hat from a Czech functionary."[37] Hats and hats and hats.

And once, when Geisel was on a commuter train, from New York into New England, he saw a staid businessman sitting ahead of him, wearing a hat on the train.

And the Seuss in him asked: *What would happen if I knocked that hat off his head?* And the answer clearly was: *another would appear. And another. And another. And another.*

And his second book became *The 500 Hats of Bartholomew Cubbins* (1938). Instead of rhyme, Seuss wrote it in prose, but he didn't forget the rhyme scheme from *Mulberry Street*, he just put it aside for a while.

Young Bartholomew Cubbins, who wore a very small and drab red hat, and who lived in the Kingdom of Didd, happened to be on his way into town when the King passed by with his royal entourage. All citizens of Didd were required to remove their hats when the King passed by.

But when Bartholomew took off his hat, another appeared. And when he took that hat off, another appeared. And another, and another. Taken to the royal castle, the king's advisors, the wise men first then the oldest and *very* wisest men, couldn't figure out why hats kept appearing on Bartholomew Cubbins' head.

They kept track, one by one, then more and more; the Grand Duke Wilfred, as young as Bartholomew, couldn't shoot one off with his bow and arrows, without another appearing instantly. The King's best archer, the "Yeoman of the Bowmen" also failed.

Seven royal magicians, each with a lean black cat, attempted to cast a spell, but the king wouldn't wait.

More hats appeared, a hundred and more . . . two hundred and more!

Bartholomew was ordered to the Royal Executioner to have his head cut off . . . but the Executioner wouldn't cut off anyone's head wearing a heat, so Bartholomew was spared.

And so Grand Duke Wilfred offered to pitch young Bartholomew off the highest turret in the castle. And up the winding stairs they went. But on the way, the hats began to change; they grew grander and grander . . . at the top of the tallest turret in the castle, Bartholomew stood, with the 500th hat, a grand, great hat on his head, a turban with jewels and feathers.

The King gave the Grand Duke Wilfrid a royal spanking for talking back to a King; and Bartholomew received 500 pieces of gold for his 500th hat.

> But neither Bartholomew Cubbins, nor King Derwin himself, not anyone else in the Kingdom of Didd could ever explain how the strange thing had happened. They could only say it just "happened to happen" and was not very likely to happen again.

Instead of the rhyme of the Kungsholm, *500 Hats . . .* was in prose; and instead of being completely in color, like *Mulberry Street . . .* it was in black and white; only Bartholomew's hats were in color, a bright, bright red. And unlike *Mulberry Street . . .* which was a contemporary children's story, *500 Hats . . .* was clearly a classic fable.

It also received favorable reviews, including *The New York*

Times and *Book List* and about the same number as *Mulberry Street.* . . .

A fellow member of the Dartmouth *Jack-o-Lantern* with Seuss, Alexander Laing was the most perceptive:

> That he is a rare and loopy genius has been common
> knowledge from an early epoch of his undergrad troubles.
> It now becomes plain that his is the self-consistent,
> happy madness beloved by children. I do not see what is
> to prevent him from becoming the Grimm of our times.[38]

Another serendipitous event approached; Geisel got a call from Bennett Cerf.

Cerf, a native of New York, had attended Columbia University's School of Journalism (when it was an undergraduate school—it later became solely a graduate program). Cerf had inherited $125,000 from a grandmother and decided after Columbia, to be a stockbroker. It wasn't right for him nor he for it.

So, in 1923, Cerf joined Horace Liveright in his firm Boni & Liveright. And for a contribution of $25,000 from Cerf, Liveright immediately made him a Vice President. Boni & Liveright was a quick education for Cerf; Liveright had a number of name authors, including Theodor Dreiser. But Liveright was a born gambler; profits he made by accident through Boni & Liveright were eaten up financing Broadway plays.

Eventually Cerf had to invest another $25,000 to help keep Boni & Liveright afloat.

In 1925, two years after he joined Boni & Liveright, Cerf offered to buy The Modern Library. In a financial bind (Liveright operated in no other way), he sold The Modern Library to Cerf for $200,000 (plus an "adviser fee" which Liveright tacked onto the deal at the last moment). Cerf brought in, as partner, Donald Klopfer, to join him, for $100,000. Klopfer, who came from a wealthy family, had no trouble finding $100,000 to join Cerf. The Modern Library had been sitting idle, making Horace

Liveright virtually nothing; two years after Cerf and Klopfer bought it, they had recouped their entire investment, including the additional $15,000 adviser's fee which they had to play Liveright.[39]

By 1926, Cerf and Klopfer decided to publish other books which they couldn't fit in The Modern Library series. In his autobiography, Cerf writes:

> Rockwell Kent had become a great friend of ours after he did the end papers for The Modern Library. I would say he was at that time the leading commercial artist in America. One day Rockwell dropped in at our office. He was sitting at my desk facing Donald, and we were talking about doing a few books on the side, when suddenly I got an inspiration and said, "I've got the name of our publishing house. We just said we were going to publish a few books on the side at random. Let's call it Random House."
>
> Donald liked it, and Rockwell Kent said, "That's a great name. I'll draw your trademark." So sitting at my desk, he took out a piece of paper and in a few minutes drew Random House, which has been our colophon ever since."[40]

The Random House house, in all its variations over the years, has become one of the most recognizable colophons in the country, matched by few others—the Viking Press Viking ship; the Henry Holt owl; the Alfred Knopf borzoi; the Bantam Books rooster and the Pocket Books kangaroo.

Random House made its reputation in the publishing world in 1934, when Cerf and Klopfer successfully published James Joyce's *Ulysses* in the United States when no other publisher would carry the obvious obscenity case through the U.S. Courts. When Judge John M. Woolsey ruled that *Ulysses* was "a sincere and serious attempt to devise a new literary method for the observation and description of mankind":

> We published *Ulysses* in January, 1934, with Woolsey's landmark decision in it—and it is still included in our edition. The book has had an enormous sale; it is one of the leading Modern Library and Vintage Giants and sells thousands of copies every year.

Cerf wrote.[41]

Random House expanded rapidly. Cerf brought in Eugene O'Neill and Robinson Jeffers, published the first American edition of Marcel Proust's *Remembrance of Things Past*, Gertrude Stein's *The Geographical History of America or The Relation of Human Nature to the Human Mind* (with dust jacket copy written by Cerf saying he didn't understand a thing she had written, but was publishing it anyhow.[42]). Cerf's coterie of known authors brought in more known authors: he added W. H. Auden and Stephen Spender, Havelock Ellis, George Bernard Shaw, William Saroyan, Budd Schulberg . . . Irwin Shaw, and others.

In 1936, Cerf offered to buy a fledging firm, Smith and Hass, which was having a hard time becoming established and staying financially solvent, bringing along founder Robert Hass as partner.

Hass accepted Cerf's offer and immediately Random House included William Faulkner, Andre Malraux, Robert Graves, Edgar Snow . . . and others.

Busy with adult titles and the growth of the firm, Cerf failed to notice that children's books could and should be emphasized in Random. His wife nudged him in the right direction:

> It was Phyllis who was . . . responsible for my thinking seriously about the books we published for children. She felt we were not doing the kinds of books that could

help our own children expand the knowledge they were gaining in school.

The first juvenile book I personally signed for Random House was by the now famous Dr. Seuss—Theodor Geisel. He had written two juveniles for Vanguard Press, but the one he did for us in 1939 was *The Seven Lady Godivas.*[43]

Cerf brought Geisel into Random House not knowing exactly what Geisel wanted to do next.

The Seven Lady Godivas was intended to be an adult retelling of the Lady Godiva saga, with typical Seussian twists. It begins:

Forward. History has treated no one so shabbily as it has the name of Godiva. Today Lady Godiva brings to mind a shameful picture—a big blonde nude trotting around town on a horse. In the background of this picture, there is always Peeping Tom, an illicit snooper with questionable intentions. The author feels that the time has come to speak: *There was not one; there were Seven Lady Godivas, and their nakedness actually was not a thing of shame.*

The stories of each of the seven Godiva sisters (Teenie, Dorcas, Arabella, Mitzi, Lulu, Gussie and Hedwig) illustrates a variation of Horse Truths. And, for Seuss enthusiasts who have never seen a copy of *Godivas* . . .

Father Lord Godiva decides to go to the Battle of Hastings in 1066 on horseback. There are so much good-byes and cheering by the seven Godiva sisters that his horse Nathan reared, throwing him . . . and Lord Godiva was killed.

Each sister swears an oath to bring forth a new Horse Truth: because *"So long as your page remains empty of Horse Truth, so shall your life remain empty of love . . .*

* Teenie inspects a horse in the castle's stables, which had been presented to her late father, Lord Godiva. Imprudently, she opened its mouth to check its teeth . . . and the horse bit off her nose.

Horse truth: *never look a gift horse in the mouth.*

Teenie married Peeping Tom.

* Dorcas invented a Wagon Superior, with the cart above the horse, but it didn't work; she then invented a Wagon Inferior, with a sled below the horse. It too, was failure—the horse had to walk bowlegged. She then invented a Wagon Anterior, with the cart in front of the horse. The cart crashed into a tree.

Horse truth: *never put a cart before a horse.*

Dorcas married Peeping Dick.

* Arabella worked her poor horse Brutus 'way, 'way too hard and the horse turned to a vat of fermented alcohol and got drunk. She tried to pull the horse away from the vat to water, but it refused.

Horse truth: *You can lead a horse to water, but you can't make it drink.*

She left a note for the other sisters: "By the time you Old Maids read this, I'll be Mrs. Peeping Harry."

* Mitzi built a boat (The Peeping Jack I) propelled by a horse on a treadmill but it wasn't powerful enough. She then built a second boat (the Peeping Jack II) with room enough for two horses, who could change places when one was tried. But one ran into the other and the boat capsized.

Moral: *never change horses in the middle of a stream.*

Mitzi married Peeping Jack at sea.

* Lulu got kicked in the hayloft by a horse and when she fell into a haystack, she found Peeping Drexel's diamond stick-pin.

Moral: *horseshoes are lucky.*

She married Peeping Drexel.

* Gussie thought and thought and could discover no Horse Truth of her own. Finally she went to the stable with a large package and when she emerged—she was riding a blue-green horse—proving, awkwardly, but a Horse Truth nonetheless . . .

It was a horse of a different color.
She married Peeping Sylvester.
* Hedwig's horse Parsifal came down with the grippe. She was afraid she would lose him, so she stayed in the barn and nursed him through. She finally collapsed and fell asleep—when she awoke, Parsifal was gone. Parsifal had been stolen. She left, disconsolate . . . but remembered to snap the lock closed as she left.
Moral: *don't lock the barn door after the horse is gone . . .*
She married Peeping Frelinghauysen.

The Seven Lady Godivas is a charming, charming book . . . written in prose, not in Seuss's rollicking rhyme scheme.

But it was an abject failure. "We charged two dollars for *The Seven Lady Godivas*. It was the Depression. Nobody had two dollars," Geisel later said.[44]

But that was only partly true. Since librarians had filed the previous two Seuss books in the juvenile section of local libraries, they assumed that *Godivas* . . . was also a children's book, but they wanted no part of the Godiva fable in any children's literature section, specially with illustrations—any kind of illustrations. There were nudes in the book—the Godiva sisters, but they were the typical lumpy, mis-shapen Seuss drawings; he couldn't draw breasts or knees. It wasn't erotic. The book wasn't prurient enough for adult readers.

It was every author's nightmare: a royalty statement for a six month period ending Dec. 31, 1940 showed:

9 copies sold with a ten percent royalty:	$1.57
14 copies sold at a discount price of 9.80	.98
Total royalty	$2.55

A previous accounting showed a debit balance of $103.43. Thus the debit balance in Seuss's account was $100.88. When he received this royalty, Seuss drew a naked Lady Godiva on the bottom right margin, riding on a discouraged, bedraggled donkey, holding a banner reading "Excelsior!" and returned it to Cerf.[15]

The Seven Lady Godivas was the lowest point in Dr. Seuss's publishing career, but neither he nor Cerf were particularly crushed. Cerf regarded the loss as the price of luring Geisel to Random House. (Geisel cajoled Cerf into re-issuing *Godivas* in a Commemorative Edition years later, but it too, was a failure.)

The "Excelsior!" flag was as much for Geisel as it was for Cerf. Prior to the publication of *Godivas* . . . Geisel had quit working for Standard Oil. He remembered the starving men in the streets during the Depression, with this ode:

> A flock of Obsks
> From down in Nobsks
>
> Hiked up to Bobsks
> To look for Jobsks.
>
> Then back to Nobsks
> With signs and Sobsks . . .
>
> There were, in Bobsks,
> No jobs for Obsks.[46]

Dr. Seuss didn't forget The Obsks. They eventually reappeared in *If I Ran the Zoo* . . .

As children's book critic Selma G. Lanes said later:

> It's hard to resist watching for what will spring next from the mind of a man who would feed an "obsk" a vegetarian diet of "corn on the cobsk."[47]

Bennett Cerf must have known that his gamble on Dr. Seuss would eventually pay off, quite literally for decades.[48]

Three

1939–1948

"I meant what I said and I said what I meant . . . An elephant's faithful— one hundred percent!"

Undaunted by the failure of *The Seven Lady Godivas*, Geisel plunged into *The King's Stilts*, a fairy tale written in prose. His notes show the development of the villain, Lord Droon:

> Even as a baby, (he) was a scowler . . . Had no use for a rattle . . . preferred to rub two pieces of slate together . . . He liked rasping noise . . . When they gave him blocks with the alphabet on them, he would only use three. He was always spelling BAH![1]

King Birtram ruled in the kingdom of Binn, which was surrounded on three sides by the sea. Mighty Dike Trees kept the sea from pouring in but a kind of a blackbird called Nizzards kept attempting to eat the Dike Trees. The only thing to keep the Nizzards from the Dike trees were the largest and smartest cats in the kingdom. They were the Patrol Cats, who wore badges labeled P.C.

The King worked and worked and his only pleasure was his

pair of bright red stilts. No one begrudged him his stilts except for one old man:

> But there was one man in Blinn who didn't like fun. He didn't like games. He didn't like laughing. This man was a scowler. This man was Lord Droon. "Laughing spoils the shape of the face," he declared. "The lines at the corners of the mouth should go *down*."[2]

So Lord Droon stole the King's stilts and gave them to the king's pageboy named Eric, and demanded Eric hide them. The King went into a funk; the Patrol Cats no longer patrolled to keep the Nizzards away from the Dike Trees and all became hopeless.

But eventually, pageboy Eric couldn't stand keeping the secret of the hidden stilts and he ran to tell the King where he had buried them.

But Lord Droon tricked Eric by making him believe he had the measles and quarantined him in an old house. Eric escaped from quarantine and only just in time discovered sea water which had begun to trickle through the Kingdom. He ran and got the stilts which he had buried and gave them to his King.

On his red stilts, the King commanded the Patrol Cats to attack the Nizzards. It was a terrible battle and beautiful to behold. The Patrol Cats chased away the Nizzards, the Dike Trees again saved the kingdom and . . . The king and Eric both played together on their matching sets of red stilts.

But *The King's Stilts* sold little better than *The Seven Lady Godivas*. In his autobiography, Bennett Cerf was the very soul of courtesy about his new author: "In that same year (1939) we published his *The King's Stilts*, a juvenile which didn't sell many copies either."[4] The first year of publication, *Stilts* sold 4,648 copies and the next year's sales were down to 394 additional copies sold.[5]

Serendipity waited and bided its time, to appear the next year in the shape of a slight breeze from outside his studio window. . . .

Geisel was in the habit of working, then taking a break, and returning to work. He sometimes left a window open in front of his desk. When he returned during the day of January 2, 1940, he discovered that one drawing, of an elephant, had been blown across a drawing of a tree. The elephant appeared to be sitting in the tree. *What would an elephant be doing in a tree?* Geisel asked. *Hatching an egg,* Dr. Seuss replied.

And so he was.

And that led to feverish work—covering months.

In October, 1939, he wrote to Louise Bonino, juvenile book editor at Random House:

> The new book is coming along with a rapidity that leaves me breathless. It is a beautiful thing. The funniest juvenile ever written. I mean, being written. Never before have I stood before myself and pointed so proudly, saying "Genius, you are." I feel certain it will sell over a million . . . (Lew) Miller will hang himself with joy to every lamp post in town . . . (Robert) Haas and Klopfer will buy Tahiti and Bali respectively. (Saxe) Commins will buy Russia. Cerf will buy Hollywood. Louise Bonino will buy a negligee covered with sequins and umlauts and fine Nizzard Maribou . . . P.S.: I like my new book.[6]

The Seven Lady Godivas and *The King's Stilts* were charming stories, but they were stories. They had conclusions, but no real moral. *And to Think That I Saw It on Mulberry Street* had a moral; the moral it taught children was that their imaginations were as real as Marco's—and occasionally they should (or must) shield their imaginations from adults.

With *Horton Hatches the Egg*, Geisel returned to the galloping, rollicking, anapestic tetrameter rhyme scheme of *And To Think That I Saw It on Mulberry Street*.

Geisel worked at the plot as hard as he worked on any plot. Horton was first named Osmere, then Bosco, then Humphrey.

Finally Geisel chose Horton, after a classmate at Dartmouth, Horton Conrad.

Through a rainstorm, (so the story begins) and through snow and sleet of winter he sat while all the other creatures of the forest laughed and laughed . . . at an elephant sitting on a nest, hatching the eggs of a bird named Mayzie.

Hunters came; they aimed rifles at Horton (and Dr. Seuss shows Horton defiantly sitting, his forelegs—arms—folded across his chest).

So the hunters caged Horton—and the egg and the tree—hauling him ("egg, nest and tree") over craggy mountains, across the ocean in a ship, where they sold him as a circus act.

But one day, when the circus was not so far from Palm Beach, a bird flew over the tent, then inside the tent. Horton turned white—it was Mayzie. And she wanted her egg back. But the egg hatched an elephant bird!

> They cheered and they *cheered* and they CHEERED more and more.
> "They'd never seen anything like it before!
> *"My goodness! My gracious!"* They shouted. "MY WORD!
> IT'S AN ELEPHANT-BIRD!!
>
> And it should be, it *should* be, it SHOULD BE like that!
> Because Horton was faithful! he sat and he sat!
> He meant what he said
> And he said what he meant. . . ."[8]

Bennett Cerf and everyone else at Random were pleased with the manuscript of *Horton* . . . when it arrived. Cerf was so pleased that when Geisel requested an additional advance from royalties of five hundred dollars to buy a place in La Jolla, Cerf immediately sent it. When *Horton* . . . was published, it was an immediate hit. There were several reasons why it was a hit when *The Seven Lady Godivas* and *500 Hats* . . . were not: Dr. Seuss had a hero, Horton, which children could identify with—Horton had made a promise and had trouble keeping it.

Horton . . . was the first Dr. Seuss book with the hero speaking in the first person "I"—which children could also repeat: "*I* meant what *I* said and *I* said what *I* meant . . ."; it had a moral that children could understand: *you must keep a promise* and Geisel had gone back to the galloping rhyme scheme of the anapestic tetrameter, instead of static prose. Children could sing, chant, *shout!* the words. And the marriage of pictures and text was again, perfect.

The *New York Times* reviewer said:

> A moral is a new thing to find in a Dr. Seuss book, but it doesn't interfere much with the hilarity with which he juggles an elephant up a tree. To an adult the tale seems a little less inevitable in its nonsense, but neither young nor old are going to quibble with the fantastic comedy of his pictures.[9]

Then the coming war interrupted Dr. Seuss.

Ted Geisel showed a cartoon he had drawn to a friend, Zinny Vanderlip Schoales, who in turn showed it to Ralph Ingersoll, who had been a Jesus (a managing editor; "Jesus" was a *New Yorker* corruption of "genius") on the staff of *The New Yorker* before establishing the liberal newspaper *PM*. Ingersoll liked what he saw and invited Geisel to become a staff cartoonist.

Liberal Geisel was perfect for liberal *PM*.

The fact that *PM took* no advertising made it a perfect Seussian adventure—that was only one step removed from *Judge*, which *got* no advertising. At least Geisel was paid by *PM*; he didn't have to try and live on due bills for rooms in Atlantic City hotels.

Geisel called Charles Lindberg "one of our nation's most irritating heroes," and in cartoon after cartoon, Dr. Seuss ridiculed Hitler, when others were only taking a wait-and-see attitude.

In June, 1941, Ted and Helen Geisel moved to California,

into a home in La Jolla Shores for the summer. The hillside lot and home cost them—in 1940 dollars—eight thousand dollars.

> All the enlightened members of this community know about my books . . . but nobody in Southern California keeps 'em in stock . . . I gotta go now and fight rattlesnakes, bees and man-eating rabbits in the patio, then go fight Lindberg.

he wrote book editor Evelyn Shriffe.[10]

When war was declared, Dr. Seuss entered the fight with surprisingly acidic cartoons. He showed Hitler and a pig-faced Japanese emperor on Mount Rushmore with the caption:

DON'T LET THEM CARVE THOSE FACES ON OUR MOUNTAINS! BUY UNITED STATES SAVINGS BONDS AND STAMPS![11]

His figures, cartoons and icons were right on target: Australian was shown as a kangaroo, with its tail being eaten by the Japanese; Nazis were shown as dachshunds—at least until American dachshund owners complained.

Four months after war with Japan, Germany and Italy was declared by Franklin Roosevelt, Geisel learned that Senator Gerald Nye of North Dakota had still called for the U.S. to stay out of the war.

"He's a horse's ass," Geisel said.

"You shouldn't use language like that," his wife said.

"He is a horse's ass and I'll draw him that way," Geisel said. And he did—in *PM*.

Helen warned him he could get into real trouble for printing a cartoon showing Nye as a horse's ass.

Ingerosoll printed the cartoon but warned Geisel that he could get into real trouble for printing a cartoon showing Nye as a horse's ass.

Then Nye wrote to Geisel: "Dear Dr. Seuss: Please I would love to acquire that charming picture you made of me for my rumpus room."

But did he really write that? Seuss embroidered the tale slightly. What Nye did write was: "(The) issue of Sunday, April 26th . . . carried a cartoon, the original of which I should like very much to possess. May I request its mailing to me?"

Geisel asked Helen if he should mail it.

"No," she said, "he's a horse's ass."[12]

The Geisels moved from New York to their La Jolla home. But before leaving, Theodor Geisel, at thirty-eight, was inducted into the Army as a Captain and assigned to the Information and Education Division, in Hollywood.

California had become threatened by supposedly imminent invasion by the Japanese; with their property in La Jolla, the Geisels found that the war had indeed, come to them. Helen Geisel wrote to Evelyn Shrifte, across the country:

> There isn't a maid or gardener to be hand. Literally everyone is working for Consolidated (Aircraft) unless he's in uniform. One house is right up in no-man's land. Once a week the marines invade, and usually capture our hillside. We are dive-bombed at 5:30 A.M.—then we look out of the window to see hundreds of little boats, amphibious tanks, etc., rushing to shore. In a few minutes our house is in the midst of it all—tanks, jeeps, trucks, bayonets bared right on the driveway. The din of black cartridges is so terrifying that I can't even conceive of what the real thing must be like![13]

Geisel joined his unit, which was quickly dubbed "Fort Fox," working under director Frank Capra. Working with Geisel were composer Meredith Willson, novelist Irving Wallace and producer Carl Foreman. Supervising civilians were animators Chuck Jones and Friz Freleng.

> "(Geisel) tried so earnestly in field drills that it was touching. He was warm and full of worthy convictions, and patriotic to the limit, but he was hopelessly uncoordinated. He was tall, skinny, his hair parted in the middle and falling like some of the birds he drew, and with that great beak of a nose. . . .

author Paul Horgan told Neil Morgan.[14]

For Geisel, Hollywood during the war was another kind of Dartmouth or Oxford; this time for adults, not youngsters. They bought a home in Hollywood and Geisel absorbed script writing techniques from Frank Capra and grew to have an intense and lasting friendship with animator Chuck Jones, he of Bugs Bunny fame.

Geisel was part of a training film team to teach G.I.s cleanliness, avoidance of VD and other military matters. Geisel and company learned that if they showed average spokesman in the films, the recruits wouldn't listen; if they used Hollywood actors, the G.I.'s jeered at the screen. They *would* pay attention to cartoons, so Geisel and his troop created Private Snafu to explain things. Snafu was, of course Army slang for: Situation *N*ormal *A*ll *F*—ked *U*p. They changed Snafu to: Situation normal ALL FOULED UP. The troops still loved it.

Geisel also worked on a film titled *Your Job in Germany*, which attempted to teach occupying troops never to fraternize with the defeated Nazis. Geisel wrote:

> The Nazi party may be gone, but Nazi thinking, Nazi training and Nazi trickery remains. The German lust for conquest is not dead . . . You will not argue with them. You will not be friendly. . . . There must be no fraternization with any of the German people.[15]

But Geisel couldn't escape his German-American heritage and he wrote the script half-heartedly, at best.

He was able, however, to tour Europe behind the Allied armies, carrying his film to show to troop units. He flew to Ireland, then England, then France and then throughout the Allied theater. Geisel found Generals Omar Bradley and Frank McSherry who approved the film for their troops. Only General George Patton refused. Geisel didn't have the opportunity to show it to Patton; someone else did and the General's sole comment was "Bullshit."

After Patton's resounding veto, Geisel traveled to a quiet sector of the war for some sightseeing, only to narrowly miss being taken prisoner by the Germans as the Battle of the Bulge erupted in the same area only hours later.

Back in Hollywood, Geisel's next assignment was to warn of a potential World War Three. He had read in *The New York Times* that a bomb could be built with huge destructive power, from only a glass of water, if only the energy in the water could be harnessed for a bomb.

The script made its way up the chain of a command—then Geisel got a call. The script contained vital secrets—Geisel was to burn the source of his information.

"Burn *The New York Times?*" he asked.

"Burn it," the anonymous voice said.

So Geisel found a copy of the *Times*—any copy—and burned it in a wastebasket in front of witnesses. Mission accomplished.[16]

The war ended soon enough, and Geisel survived it, but tragedy struck from another quarter; the Japanese surrendered in August, 1945, but in September, Geisel learned that his youngest sister Marnie had died. He had delayed his marriage for the birth of her baby and now she was dead. Her marriage had gone sour; she had moved back to the Geisel family home, but had become an alcoholic. She died at the age of forty-three, of a coronary thrombosis.

True to his stoic German heritage, Theodor Geisel never spoke of her death—ever.

After the war, Geisel stayed in Hollywood. Warner Brothers had heard about *Your Job in Germany* and had doctored it enough to win an Academy Award for their version, titled *Hitler Lives?*

Warner Brothers hired him and assigned him to director Jerry Wald. Wald assigned him to work on the script for the James Dean vehicle, *Rebel Without a Cause*. Geisel found it impossibly frustrating. The only element of a script he produced which was acceptable was the same title. Wald and Warners took everything else out.

He was then assigned to RKO, who wanted him to write a Japanese version, to be titled *Your Job in Japan*. Geisel hired Helen and the two of them began scripting the film. In one sequence, they had pastoral shots of sixteenth-century Japan. They were more than astonished when they ran the sequence and discovered someone had spliced in shots of American Sherman tanks. The tanks were edited back out.

RKO called the documentary *Design for Death*; it went through thirty-two major revisions to eventually become a forty-eight minute film, with forty-five hundred feet of captured Japanese film spliced in.[17]

It won an Academy Award, the second Geisel had been involved with in two years. Neither of the films survive; they were probably withdrawn by the military and eventually lost of destroyed.

Geisel then got a call from a friend, offering them a vacation retreat in Palos Verdes Estates, near Los Angeles. The Geisels accepted immediately and moved in. The house—rather the estate, for it was built like a villa from the Italian Renaissance—had, as they say, a storied past. Myrna Loy had lived there, with Arthur Hornblower; Paulette Goddard and Burgess Meredith had honeymooned there.

After only a few days, Geisel decided that he wanted to live in a climate where he could "walk around outside in my pajamas."[18] So with the villa as a backdrop, and walking around outside in his pajamas when he pleased, Geisel began work on the first Dr. Seuss book in seven years.

He returned mentally and psychologically to his home town of Springfield and *And To Think That I Saw it on Mulberry Street* for his next book. There are striking similarities—and some differences—between *Mulberry Street . . .* and *McElligot's Pool.*

McElligot's Pool contains the same *escalating sequences* or *escalating action* that Geisel used in *Mulberry Street . . .* and the same hero—Marco. He is told that he won't catch anything fishing in McElligot's Pool, because it is full of junk.

But like Marco's parade on Mulberry Street, this time Marco imagines there is more in McElligot's Pool than boots, cans, tires and bottles.

The pool, Marco believes, winds its way under farm pastures and villages . . . and it might wind its way all the way down to the sea.

*　　*　　*

As a personal aside, *McElligot's Pool* was the first Dr. Seuss book that I remember reading, when I was about four, perhaps, going on five. I remember to this day following the pictures of McElligot's Pool winding its way underground to the sea thinking then: *it could happen just like that.*

Shortly thereafter, I was taken by my parents from our home in north central Ohio to The Blue Hole, a private park, which I remembered as being 35–40 miles from Lake Erie. I rechecked an Ohio map recently. In a straight line, The Blue Hole, in Castalia, Ohio, is about 8–10 miles from Lake Erie. I remember it as a brilliant crystal blue aquamarine spring. I couldn't see any fish. While we were there, a guide told us, "We don't know how, but we believe that The Blue Hole is connected underground to Lake Erie."

Just like Dr. Seuss said, I remember thinking.

Augmented by visiting The Blue Hole, my memory of reading *McElligot's Pool* for the first time never faded.

And that's duplicated, I am sure, by the millions of children who read a Dr. Seuss book for their first time and thought: *It could happen just like that! Just like Dr. Seuss said!* And I still have my copy of *McElligot's Pool.*

*   *   *

And Marco's line might find its way down to the sea.

(Dr. Seuss shows Marco's line with a worm wrapped around it in a loose knot, not hooked to it.)

Instead of merely thinking of catfish first, Dr. Seuss imagines a dog fish, chasing catfish.

Marco imagines fish swimming from the Tropics, and from north beyond Hudson's Bay, just to get caught in McElligot's Pool.

> A fish that's so big, if you know what I mean,
> That he makes a whale look like a tiny sardine!

> Oh, the sea is so full of a number of fish,
> If a fellow is patient, he *might* get his wish!

> And that's why I think
> That I'm not such a fool
> When I sit here and fish
> In McElligot's Pool.

And so *McElligot's Pool* ends very much like *And To Think That I Saw It on Mulberry Street . . .*

And where Dr. Seuss has a choice in illustrations—where slanting or movement is called for—the movement is invariably to the reader's right, pulling the young reader's attention toward the next page.

Geisel was so taken with the Italian vila atmosphere of his retreat in Palos Verdes Estates, that he painted all the illustrations in watercolor, a new technique for his books. But when the manuscript and illustrations reached Random House, production people there declared that the budget for the book only allowed half the color work he wanted. Few readers ever noticed that the first text page is in black-and-white, the next two in color, the next two in black-and-white and so on throughout the book.

McElligot's Pool won Dr. Seuss his first Caldecott award for the best children's book of the year and it was a selection of the Junior Literary Guild.

The dedication was to Geisel's Father—and the dedication was a family joke:

> This book is dedicated to
> T. R. Geisel of Springfield, Mass.,
> The World's Greatest Authority
> on Blackfish, Fiddler Crabs and Deegle Trout

Geisel had gone fishing once with his Father; but they had nothing to show for the excursion. So his father bought some trout at the Deegel Fish Hatchery and tried to pass them off as fresh-caught.[19]

Reviews continued to be very strong:

> This time prepare to chuckle under water for you'll
> be meeting the weirdest, wildest funniest creatures of
> the deep which imagination can conjure.
> —M.B. King, *Chicago Sun* Book Week[20]

> A picture book in rhyme, a book as divinely idiotic
> as the author-artist's And to Think That I Saw It On
> Mulberry Street, Grown-ups will have as much fun over

the fish that the small fisherman MIGHT catch in
McElligot's Pool as the children will.
— S.J. Johnson, *Library Journal*[21]

Children will have nothing but admiration for this
boy who heard that there were no fish in McElligot's Pool
and then saw them swimming in from the sea.
— *Saturday Review of Literature*[22]

What morals can we draw from *McElligot's Pool?* First, be patient and things might happen. Secondly, trust your own instincts—don't believe what others tell you. Finally, and most importantly, there is a unity to all of nature. McElligot's Pool connects to the ocean; The Blue Hole connects to Lake Erie. To use the title of Holocaust survivor Elie Wiesel's memoir, *All Rivers Run to the Sea* (New York: Alfred Knopf, 1995).

Thereafter, Dr. Seuss books usually became an annual event. The next year *Thidwick, The Big-Hearted Moose* made his appearance:

And so (the story begins) a Bingle-Bug hitched a ride on Thidwick's antlers—and then a Tree-spider joined, and began to spin a web on Thidwick's antlers, and then a Zinn-a-zu Bird who pulled hairs out of Thidwick's head.

But the next day Thidwick saw that the bird had been married and brought his wife, and uncle (who was a Woodpecker) along. The Woodpecker drilled four holes in Thidwick's horn.

A fox, some mice, some fleas, a big bear, and a swarm of three hundred and sixty-two bees came along. Hunters wanted to shoot him, for his antlers, to hang on the Harvard Club wall. So he ran, hunters in pursuit, up hills and down, with all his guests jouncing along. Onto a knoll, on the edge of the lake.

And finally his OLD horns came off so that NEW ones can grow!

And he called to the pests on his horns as he threw 'em,
"You wanted my horns; now you're quite welcome to 'em!
Keep 'em! They're yours!
As for ME, I shall take
Myself to the far distant
Side of the lake!"

And he swam Winna-Bango and found his old bunch,
And arrived just in time for a wonderful lunch
At the south of the lake, where there's moose-moss
to munch.[23]

The reviewers chimed in:

The author's rollicking verse is perfectly suited to
this comical tale. His pictures in red, blue and black are
expressive and funny, and though they appear slightly
confusing at first glance, they are well adapted to the
spirit of the story. For little children, it is splendid read-
aloud nonsense.
—*The New York Herald Tribune Weekly Book Review*[24]

How Thidwick asserted himself is told in verses
which march in double-quick time. The pictures are
scenes of happy confusion, a little difficult to see at
first, but as madly absurd as anything Dr. Seuss has done.
This is pure entertainment for almost anyone over 5.
—E. L. Buell, *The New York Times*[25]

This popular author-artist has written another imaginative and hilarious tale which will be received with
enthusiasm and delight by both adults and children.
The pictures, which are in black, red and blue, are as
comical as the text.
—*San Francisco Chronicle*[26]

> The verses that tell this sad tale are very funny in-
> deed, and the drawings of Thidwick are a delight, from
> the first page to the last.
> —M. G. Davis, *Saturday Review of Literature*[27]

An essay, "The Significance of Dr. Seuss," which captured
the differences between Seuss and Disney and differences between how adults perceived the story and how children perceived
the story, was written by David Dempsey in *The New York Times*:

> *Thidwick* is a masterpiece of economy, and a shrewd
> satire on the "easy mark" who lets the conventions of soci-
> ety get the better of him. The genius of the story, however,
> lies in its finale. A man of less consistence than Seuss
> would have let Thidwick be rescued by the creatures he is
> befriending (this is the customary Disney riposte in simi-
> lar situations) but Seuss' logic is rooted in principle, rather
> than sentiment, and the sponging animals get what they
> deserve. Incidentally, this is also what the child expects.[28]

For his next book, Theodor Geisel drew on a fragment of conversation he overheard when he was in Europe during World War
Two. On a rainy night in Belgium, trapped while the Battle of the
Bulge raged nearby, Geisel overheard one G.I. say to another, "Rain,
always rain. Why can't we have something different for a change?"[29]

And the voice of Dr. Seuss inside him asked, "*well, why can't
we have something different for a change? Why is it always rain
that falls from the sky?*"

And he again drew on Bartholomew Cubbins and the Kingdom of Didd. *Bartholomew and the Oobleck* was in prose, not in
his rollicking anapestic tetrameter.

The King summoned his royal magicians to cast a spell to
make something else came down from the sky, when he got tired
of sun and rain and fog and snow.

And then Oobleck began to fall. First lightly, like snowflakes, then like rain, then like *very* heavy rain, then great goops of oobleck, *as big as cupcakes*, covering everything and everyone. Green, pea green oobleck, covering the bell in the bell tower so it couldn't chime; covering the royal trumpeter so he couldn't blow a warning; covering the Captain of the Guards, so he couldn't warn the people . . . and still it came down, as big as *greenish footballs*, covering the Royal Cook and the Royal Laundress and the Royal Fiddlers and—even the Royal King. And the oobleck kept falling, kept raining down on the Kingdom of Didd.

Bartholomew finally had to confront the King. To rid the Kingdom of Didd from the Oobleck would not involve magic spells or magic words—but only two simple words, Bartholomew told the King: "Now, the least you can do is say the simple words, 'I'm sorry.'"

But then Bartholomew heard a great, deep sob. The old King was crying! "Come back Bartholomew Cubbins! You're right! It *is* all my fault! And I *am* sorry! Oh, Bartholomew, I'm awfully, *awfully* sorry!"

And the moment the King spoke those words, something happened . . .

Maybe there is something magic in those simple words, "I'm sorry."

The lesson was obvious for even the smaller reader—or listener—if the story was read to them:

Sometimes you have to say "I'm sorry."

Sometimes you have to say, "It's all my fault."

Even if you're a King.

Bartholomew and the Oobleck won Dr. Seuss his second Caldecott Award, for the best children's book of the year.

In the summer of 1949, Geisel was invited to speak at ten-day writers' conference at the University of Utah. Screwing up his courage to travel and speak to strangers, Geisel made the trip. He was in wonderful company: Vladimir Nabokov, who had come to the United States nine years earlier; western novelist Wallace Stegner, poets William Carlos Williams and John Crowe Ransom.

By that time, Geisel had strong, very strong beliefs about children's literature; those who write it and what made it exceptional. Children couldn't handle ancient myths, except those which were largely visual: Thor and his hammer, Hermes and his winged sandals.

Aesop's fables were too cold, the *Illiad* too complicated for the re-telling, but the *Odyssey* and the Robin Hood tales were adventurous. He also said he liked Hans Christian Andersen, Robert Louis Stevenson and Mark Twain.

Geisel suggested (can we see the twinkle in his eye?) where his place was: "in the realm of nonsense, there are Mother Goose, (Edward) Lear, (Lewis) Carroll, P.L. Travers and Dr. Seuss."[30]

And he analyzed the *logic* of the *insanity* of children's books:

> This is the crux . . . a man with two heads is not a story. It is a situation to be built upon logically. He must have two hats and two toothbrushes. Don't go wild with hair made of purple seaweed, or live fireflies for eyeballs . . . Children analyze fantasy. They know you're kidding them. There's got to be logic in the way you kid them. Their fun is pretending . . . making believe they believe it.[31]

Geisel assembled his lecture notes and suggested that Bennett Cerf and Random House publish a book of writing techniques for children's books authors. His proposal went first to the juvenile book editors at Random (probably the wrong place for it to land, for it would be a book for adults who were novice "kiddie lit" writers), then worked its way up the chain to Bennett Cerf . . .

. . . and came right back to Geisel.

Random House was *not* interested in such a proposal, for such a book.

Geisel was crushed. Perhaps even more so than when he collected twenty-seven rejections before Marshall McClintock and the Vanguard Press took *And To Think That I Saw It On Mulberry Street.* . . .

After all, then he was an unpublished writer; now he was an experienced author, with several books to his credit, Caldecott Awards and glowing reviews for his work. But the proposal was rejected nonetheless. Random editors didn't want him interrupting his usual work *to tell others how to do the same.*

Louise Bonino, juvenile editor, wrote the rejection letter Random House sent to Geisel:

> You enjoy the adulation not only of the general public but also of the children's librarians. . . . Some of them would feel an author-artist of picture books could hardly qualify as an expert in the field of juvenile writing. . . . (Saxe Commins's) concern is that it would interrupt you in the steady production of your marvelous children's books (and bring) down on your head all kinds of criticism for doing a semiformal book which tries to explain method when there is so much inspired madness in your own work . . . I am returning your notes under separate cover.[32]

Could hardly qualify as an expert in the field of juvenile writing. . . .

(We can only wonder now what he would have had to say in book length about the art of writing for children. And oh! what a missed opportunity for such a book from such a man . . . but the book publishing industry is full of such stories, of editors who make—or made—wrong decisions, refusing to allow an author such as Geisel work on a project the author wanted to work on. Or refusing to accept a book manuscript and thus losing a writer to another publishing firm. Bennett Cerf's own autobiography mentions other such cases. But in this case, we can suggest that Random House was truly wrong. What could it have cost them to allow Geisel to write the book he wanted to write?)

But Geisel moved on, figuratively and literally. Geisel's wife Helen had a family trust fund that had been accumulating interest over the years; they decided that they wanted to live someplace high. They turned to San Diego architect Tom Shepard who suggested an old observation tower on Mount Soledad that overlooked everything else in La Jolla, which they had first discovered some twenty years previously. They bought the tower and two acres around it immediately and sold their La Jolla Shores home and their Hollywood home.

And Geisel's purchase of the tower and the surrounding land was a joke on all of La Jolla. No one thought it was for sale; indeed, everyone living in La Jolla thought that it was government property, quite unavailable for sale.

In the past, servicemen had taken their dates there for quiet trysts; the view was spectacular and lovers' initials had been carved everywhere.

The Geisels could not only look over the city of La Jolla, but San Diego, sixty miles of shoreline of the Pacific and on clear days, they could see inland as far as Palm Springs and well into Mexico. They had a picnic on their new property in mid-September, 1948 and year or so later, they moved into their pink stucco home. And he brought his dinosaur footprint along.

For the rest of his life, he seldom left it for long. It would not surprise accomplished writers to learn that when he was concentrating, the vast views from "The Tower" escaped his attention; he literally turned his desk and his back to the view.

It was his aerie and Theodor Geisel was at home at the very top of La Jolla and in the vast high tower of his imagination.

Four

1948–1956

... he began to chart vast regions of his own, the terra incognito of his Seussian world ...

Ted and Helen began to enjoy their new La Jolla home, in the spring of 1949, one year after the construction began. Getting accustomed to his new working quarters, his thoughts turned toward his childhood home in Springfield. And his bedroom, and the nights he heard the night sounds, the howls, the cries of the nearby Springfield Zoo. And he thought of his father, who took him to the Zoo; he remembered the trails, the animals, their names, their cages, their histories, the zoo smells, the workers, the visitors.

And he thought of the Kungsholm's engine drone, the anapestic tetrameter, which he had used so successfully in *And To Think That I Saw It on Mulberry Street* ... , *Horton Hatches the Egg* ... *McElligot's Pool* and *Thidwick the Big-Hearted Moose*, but abandoned in favor of prose in *The 500 Hats of Bartholomew Cubbins* ... *The Seven Lady Godivas* ... *The King's Stilts* ... and *Bartholomew and the Oobleck*. He still heard the drone in his inner ear.

But most of all, he remembered a young boy.

And he thought ...

And what? *And what?*

He liked to "approach a book with a solution or conflict and hen write myself into an impossible position so there is no (apparent) way of ending (the book). . . . people who think about the endings first come up with inferior products," he told biographers Judith and Neil Morgan.[1] Even if that meant "unraveling the sock" much further back in the earlier pages, if the rhyme scheme went off track or the plot didn't flow.

And what? He would fool with the characters on his desk, get up and walk, pace back and forth, smoke, toy with his *dream works*, until the situations and animals came. (And they came logically one step removed from reality, then a second-step removed from the first and then a third . . . until there was nothing in the world like Dr. Seuss creatures—except the little-known Seussian creatures in nature).

And not only *and what?* but *and where?* From the vast High Top tower overlooking the lush California fields and gardens, and the Pacific and Mexico that Theodor Geisel saw in the distance, he also saw a vast geography of locales . . . and places he knew intimately, because he had been there: Peru, Turkey, England, Italy, Europe.

And in *If I Ran the Zoo,* he began to chart vast regions of his own, the terra incognito of his Seussian world unknown to everyone else, but clearly and indelibly pictured to him. He began to chart the cartography of his mind. And there was no better place to begin than his La Jolla aerie, where he had a vast panorama in front of him, where his imagination could take him—as Gerald McGrew—over the horizon of the Pacific, as the first step to . . . the African Island of Yerka . . . the Mountains of Tobsk (near the River of Nobsk) . . . the jungles of Hippo-no-Hungus, Dippo-no-Dungus and Nippo-no-Dungus . . . the Island of Gwark . . . *and so forth and upward and onward, gee whiz!*

He remembered the Obsks, from his last days with Standard Oil, during the Depression, when he saw men selling apples on the streets of New York, bankrupt. And he even knew the Obsks' diet:

I'll go to the far-away Mountains of Tobsk
Near the River of Nobsk, and I'll bring back an Obsk,
A sort of a kind of a Thing-a-ma-Bobsk
Who only eats rhubarb and corn-on-the-cobsk.
Then people will flock to my zoo in a mobsk.
"McGrew," they will say, "does a wonderful jobsk!
He hunts with such vim and he hunts with such vigor,
His New Zoo, McGrew Zoo, gets bigger and bigger!"

If I Ran the Zoo is Theodor Geisel's clearest and most obvious acknowledgment of his own childhood. And in it, he began to take his readers to lands much richer and more fantastic than Mulberry Street and the Springfield Zoo. In doing so, his books became mirrors for the imaginations of his children-readers, reflecting their own worlds back to them—and validating in a way children could clearly understand, their own best-kept secrets—the worlds of their own imaginations: their own African islands of Yerka, their own Mountains of Tobsk (near the River of Nobsk), their own jungles of Hippo-no-Hungus, Island of Gwark and thousands of other enchanting and fantastical places and locales you and I have never dreamed of. . . .

Reviewers seemed to understand that Geisel had taken another step:

> (It) has a range and freedom of extravaganza that I found utterly delightful.
> —A.C. Moore, *The Horn Book* Magazine[2]

> As you turn the pages, the imaginings get wilder and funnier, the rhymes more hilarious. There will be no age limits for this book, because families will be forced to share re-reading and quotation, for a long, long time.

Hurrah for you, Dr. Seuss, and thank you for one of the
funniest children's books in a blue moon.

> —L. Bechtel, Books section,
> *The New York Herald Tribune*[3]

Dr. Seuss has never imagined or created a better or
funnier picture book than this one.

> —*The Saturday Review of Literature*[4]

All the Dr. Seuss books are popular with children,
as well as with the adults who read them aloud . . . This
newest one is among the best.

> —Frances Chrystie, *The New York Times*[5]

While he was waiting for the book to appear from Random
House, Geisel was approached by P. D. Eastman, whom he had
known from the war years. Eastman and begun working for a new
production company, United Productions of America, and they
wanted something other than the typical (read Mickey Mouse)
cartoons. Did Geisel have a story idea they could use?

He created a little boy, who didn't speak in words—he spoke
only in sounds. He wrote a script and quickly received a check
for five hundred dollars. UPA brought the story to life and Geisel
watched as his story gained shape and form.

Gerald McBoing-Boing was almost a predecessor to Charles
Schultz' Charlie Brown. Gerald has a round face with a blond
topknot. He spoke only in sound effects, a crash! a bang! . . . He
has no friends; everyone makes fun of him . . . and so he takes to
the streets, an figurative orphan. But a talent scout spots him
and he makes a fortune doing sound effects on the radio. His
parents listen in the radio studio while he proves (for the first
time) his success and at the end of the show, he and they ride off
in a limousine.

It was, indeed, far, far different than the usual (Mickey) mouse-
(Donald)duck-(Bugs)bunny cartoons of the day. *Gerald*

McBoing-Boing won an Academy Award for UPA in 1951. It was the third Academy Award project that Theodor Geisel had been involved with.

Theodor Geisel's next venture in Hollywood was completely the reversal of his earlier work—instead of everything going reasonably well, his next project went considerably awry.

The project was *The 5,000 Fingers of Dr. T*, a fantasy produced by Stanley Kramer. The Dr. T being Dr. Terwilliker, a name from his Springfield, Massachusetts youth. Bart (played by Tommy Rettig, of the television *Lassie* series), the hero of the story was (like Theodor years before, in Springfield) bored with his piano lessons. Falling asleep, he drifts (somewhat like Dorothy in the tornado swirling toward Oz) to the castle of Dr. Terwilliker (Hans Conreid), who rules over a piano keyboard two stories high, with 500 captive boys playing with all 5,000 fingers at the same time. Eventually Bart breaks the spell cast over the 500 reluctant piano players and Dr. T is defeated.

The Geisel left their Tower aerie in La Jolla, (which must have, itself, been a bad sign) and moved to Hollywood. There Geisel became the script writer, set designer, lyricist, unofficial producer and unofficial director and key cheerleader for the film.

The production was postponed, then postponed again. Geisel suffered agony after agony; the script was revised and revised again. The production was postponed—for the third time. Peter Lynd Hayes and Mary Healey were brought in as additional cast members. Geisel had to request Kramer delete some questionable scenes.

Eventually, the film went into production, but when Geisel counted heads, he found that the 500 young piano layers turned out to be 150.

Geisel's visualization of scenes involving 500 boy piano players was curtailed by the missing 350; his visualization of the plot, the set designs, and the logic of the story were crippled by the actual production. Nothing went as Geisel anticipated. He surely didn't anticipate that 350 of the 500 boy pianists would be AWOL; the 5,000 fingers of Dr. T eventually turned out to be the 1,500 fingers of Dr. T.

The project ended mercifully, with a epic Seussian accident: during a lunch break, all 150 boys were fed hot dogs from the studio commissary. One became ill and vomited on his own piano keyboard:

> That started a chain reaction, causing one after another of the boys to go queasy in the greatest mass upchuck in the history of Hollywood . . . when the picture was finally released, the critics reacted in much the same manner,

Geisel said.[6]

It was, for its time, a major investment. But there was no happiness and light on the set; rather, there was confusion, revisions, problems and boy after boy spewing hot dogs onto the set. The film eventually cost $2,750,000 to make; it was the most expensive film Stanley Kramer had made to that point. When it was previewed in Los Angeles, in January, 1953, patrons began walking out 15 minutes after the film began. By the end of the film, only five audience members were left, beside Geisel, Kramer and the crew.[8]

Even more than *The Seven Lady Godivas*, the disaster of *The 5,00 Fingers of Dr. T* caused Geisel permanent and devastating disappointment and embarrassment. After all, it was to be his supreme accomplishment in Hollywood. And he *had* been involved in three productions which had each won an Academy Award. In his mind, *The 5,000 Fingers of Dr. T* erased all his previous Hollywood accomplishments and added layer after layer of betrayal, distrust, anguish and embarrassment.

He retreated to his La Jolla tower, never ever to trust or believe in Hollywood again.

When he wasn't agonizing over the production of *Dr. T*, Geisel was working on another book for Bennett Cerf and Random House.

It came out after the production of *The 5,000 Fingers . . .* was over and it followed essentially the same plot as *If I Ran the Zoo*, and much of the same rhyme scheme. As much as Theodor Geisel had despaired of Hollywood during the production of *The 5,000 Fingers . . .*, Dr. Seuss remained right on track for his next book—*Scrambled Eggs Super!*:

(Dr. Seuss illustrates the first page with Peter T. Hooper talking to girlfriend Liz and the "when mother was out" will become a key element in other, later Dr. Seuss books—and with good reason: Dr. Seuss speaks to the hidden world of children: what happens to them when their parents are absent. He projects their own world on paper, in rhyme and pictures—he doesn't speak down to them from an adult's omnipotent point of view.)

The logic—and action—escalates just like *And To Think That I Saw It on Mulberry Street, McElligot's Pool* and *If I Ran the Zoo*.

In *Scrambled Eggs Super*, Dr. Seuss delivers even more colorful images than before: did Dr. Seuss make up creatures, like the "Grickily Gractus"?

Nature has given us a creature very much like the Grickily Gractus, writer Chet Raymo tells us ("Dr. Seuss and Dr. Einstein: Children's Books and Scientific Imagination," *The Horn Book Magazine*, September, 1992).

And his rhyme schemes get even more and more engaging and more and more convoluted and more and more fanciful (This is a Mobius loop of a poem):

Then I went for some Ziffs. They're exactly like Zuffs,
But the Ziffs live on cliffs and the Zuffs live on bluffs.
And, seeing how bluffs are exactly like cliffs,
It's mighty hard telling the Zuffs from the Ziffs.
But I *know* that the egg that I got from the bluffs,
If it wasn't a Ziff's from the cliffs, was a Zuff's.[9]

Eventually, Dr. Seuss brings all the bird-chasing and egg-hunting back to the kitchen (still without mother) makes a huge meal of eggs, beans, ginger, prunes, figs, parsley (quite sparsely) cinnamon sticks, and clove.

Scrambled Eggs Super received as much critical acclaim as other, previous Dr. Seuss books:

> When the one and only Dr. Seuss unleashes his famous imagination to run riot across the pages of a large-size picture book, hurrahs sound from every quarter. And so they will again at this wildly nonsensical account.
> —Polly Goodwin, *Chicago Sunday Tribune*[10]

> How one man can makeup such marvelous names and also draw pictures that surpass the names in fantastic imagery is a mystery. The "very best fowls" in this book are just as wild and funny as the animals in "If I Ran the Zoo." To an adult, the precise quality in the tall-tale style of young Peter T. Hooper adds to the fun of a hilarious creation.
> —L. Bechtel, Book Review section,
> *The New York Herald Tribune*[11]

> The bizarre names of the birds and the patter of the verse make this a wonderful book for reading aloud in the family. The pictures will amuse everyone.
> —*U.S. Quarterly Book Review*[12]

In March, 1953, Theodor and Helen Geisel sailed to Japan, to get the distaste of *The 5,000 Fingers* . . . out of their systems and to enjoy a long-delayed vacation. They received their first copies of *Scrambled Eggs Super!* as they were packing for the trip. On board the U.S.S. President Cleveland, sharing the voyage with them as far as Honolulu the Geisels were surprised to learn, were two former presidents, Herbert Hoover and Harry Truman. The bombings of Hiroshima and Nagasaki were only eight years previous and Geisel was eager to learn the extent of the changes (or the lack of changes) in Japan.

In Kyoto, Osaka and Kobe, Japanese schoolchildren had been invited to draw what they expected to be when the grew up: over 15,000 drawings had been submitted and Ted Geisel was somewhat shocked to see how "American" the drawings were. Boys wanted to fly or go to Mars, girls drew themselves as hostesses on busses. They returned on the U.S.S. President Wilson ("We only travel on ships named for Democrats," Geisel said) and he prepared an article about the Japanese children for *Life* magazine. The article, "Japan's Young Dreams"[13] was heavily edited by Henry Luce's staffers ("Henry Luce was always anti-Japanese and pro-Chinese and they raped the article," he said.)[14]

Most importantly, Geisel brought back trunkfuls of drawings by Japanese children.

The 5,000 Fingers of Dr. T was released about the time the Geisels returned from Japan. The reviews were as markedly bad as Geisel anticipated. Over the years, however, some lightness broke the darkness of that time. (After all, no one on the set at the time ever thought that *The Wizard of Oz* would be anything more than a quirky grade C+ film.) *The 5,000 Fingers of Dr. T* has become something of a cult classic—when and if it can be found. It is more highly regarded now than when it was made—but remains largely unavailable[15] (Although Columbia/TriStar released it on home video in 1991).

One day, in the spring of 1953, in New York, Geisel asked his literary agent, Phyllis Jackson if "I dropped everything else, do you think I could count on royalties of five thousand dollars a year?"[16] We can imagine his plaintiveness. But the question was serious. Geisel wanted nothing to do with Hollywood—where he knew he could make much, much more money—and he didn't want the distractions of writing for Luce's *Life* (or writing for *Life's* Luce). He did not yet anticipate (nor did anyone else) the enormous baby-boom generation, nor did he anticipate the eventual demand for Dr. Seuss books.

Every year, countless thousands of children "grow into" the readership level of Dr. Seuss books, just like growing into shoes. And then they would get Dr. Seuss books from their school or community library, take them home, color in them, lose them and the school or library would buy more Dr. Seuss books.

As of 1996, Dr. Seuss books have sold over 150,000,000[17] copies and, as much as we can be amused at Ted Geisel's 1953 question "do you think I could count on royalties of five thousand dollars a year?", it is a lesson for all writers. Eventually, you too, may—*may*—sell like Dr. Seuss. As the new century begins, he has set the benchmark for sales of children's literature. And just as certainly, the critical benchmark as well.

By the fall of 1953, Dr. Seuss again tackled a book, and this time strictly adhered to the rhyme scheme he used back as far as *And To Think That I Saw It on Mulberry Street . . .*

He tied together three key items: 1). The anapestic tetrameter he knew so well; 2). Horton, the elephant from *Horton Hatches the Egg* and a third element. . . .

The working title of the book was *Horton Hears 'Em!* but the 'Em (or them) eventually became Whos and the title was changed to *Horton Hears a Who!*:[18]

And when Geisel toured Japan he towered over his Japanese hosts. And he towered like a benevolent crane 'way, 'way over the heads of the Japanese children he met.

So he added a much more powerful moral then in any of the previous Dr. Seuss books. In *Bartholomew and the Oobleck*, the moral was:

Sometimes you have to say:
I'm sorry. It's all my fault.

But in *Horton Hears a Who!*, the moral was universal, multi-national, multi-ethnic. In a word: Equality. And it was especially meaningful for children, the way Dr. Seuss phrased it:

> I'll just have to save him. Because, after all,
> A person's a person, no matter how small.

(The voice of the Whos are set in type half the size of the Horton's, in much the same style as the Mouse's tale in *Alice in Wonderland*. His tale bends and twists down the page, set in increasingly smaller type. It is literally the Mouse's tale and his *tail*.)

But the Wickersham (another name from Ted Geisel's hometown of Springfield, Mass.) monkeys steal Horton's clover (with the Whos and Whoville) and give it to an eagle named Vlad Vlad-i-koff, who flew with it, Horton in pursuit all night.

Children would not know the metaphor Dr. Seuss uses, but if adults knew of his trip to Japan following World War Two, then the atomic bomb reference is clear:

> From down on the speck came the voice of the Mayor:
> "We've really had trouble! Much more than our share.
> When that black-bottomed birdie let go and we dropped,
> We landed so hard that our clocks have all stopped.
> Our tea-pots are broken. Our rocking-chairs smashed.
> And our bicycle tires all blew up when we crashed.

But the Kangaroos and the Wickersham monkeys and the Wickersham brothers and uncles and cousins all conspire to rope Horton and snare him. . . .

Horton told the Whos that they had to prove they were there—that each and every Who had to shout out loud that he or she was there. They shouted, but the Kangaroos and the Wickersham monkeys couldn't hear them. The kangaroos and the monkeys roped Horton and began pulling him into a cage. All the Whos in

Whoville still couldn't make themselves heard. The Whoville Mayor searched and he searched to make sure everyone was shouting, as loud as he could but nothing happened until the smallest Who shouted out the smallest shout.

Dr. Seuss phrased the moral two ways: The smallest voice can make a difference; and, a person's a person's no matter how small.

He also thought of McCarthyism, when U.S. citizens were afraid to speak their minds; when, he said they were "scared of speaking their thoughts aloud."[20]

After completing the manuscript and drawings for *Horton Hears A Who!* Ted and Helen Geisel relaxed in their La Jolla home; he was approaching his fiftieth birthday. There was some talk (and some work) on a Broadway production of *The Seven Lady Godivas*, but the project came to naught. He wrote the script for a half-hour television show, "Modern Art on Horseback," broadcast in the Excursion series, sponsored by the Ford Foundation. And he received word that he would receive an honorary doctorate from his alma mater, Dartmouth (thus making "Dr. Seuss" legitimate).

And, in an article, "Why do Children Bog Down on the First R," in *Life*,[21] John Hersey suggested that someone—perhaps Dr. Seuss—free the nation's children from the oh-so-dreary Dick and Jane readers, which had bored children for years. The idea lay dormant in the back-waters of Dr. Seuss's mind. . . .

But at a party in May of 1954, Helen Geisel was suddenly jolted by pain her feet and ankles. A doctor, Francis M. Smith, offered help, but the Geisels assured him that rest would be all she needed. Two days later, Helen Geisel was checked into the Scripps Metabolic Clinic, as her condition worsened. She had numbness in her arms, hands and face and she could not swallow.[22]

The diagnosis came soon enough: Helen Geisel had Guillian-Barre Syndrome and she was placed in an iron lung. She became unable to speak or sit up without help. She was moved across

San Diego to the San Diego County Hospital, where she was paralyzed from the neck down. She had to have a tracheotomy so she could breathe.

Except for the death of his sister Marnie, Theodor Geisel had always roller-skated through life; he carved out a career with the art that he loved, he lived on a mountain with unlimited physical and equally unlimited professional vistas—tragedy had never really touched him.

Now his wife and helpmate lay near death.

Before the iron lung became available, Guillain-Barre syndrome was fatal; even after iron lungs became available, chances for survival were slight.

Ted Geisel was devastated by the news.

He lived life day by day. He called Dartmouth, saying it would be impossible for him to come to receive his honorary doctorate. And he rigged up a series of mirrors so Helen could see beyond the confines of her iron lung.

He waited.

By the end of June, Helen had rallied. She could again swallow, the paralysis was at least in remission and she improved. She could again attempt speech.

She was moved to the California Rehabilitation Center in Santa Monica for extensive therapy. The Geisel's La Jolla home was, in effect, closed. Theodor Geisel was faced with a multitude of daily tasks Helen had always handled—he really didn't know how to handle a checkbook—or even make coffee. "Helen had always shielded him from the real world," a friend, Elin Vanderlip said.[23]

Slowly, ever so slowly, she learned how to live again.

In August, they received their first copies of *Horton Hears a Who!* and the positive reviews helped buoy their spirits.

Some critics caught Seuss's moral, others didn't.

> The verses are full of the usual lively, informal language and amazing rhymes that have delighted such a

world-wide audience in the good "doctor's" other books.
The story, with its moral, does not match the gayety of
some of the older books. But the pictures are as wildly
original and funny as ever.

> —L. Bechtel, Book Review section
> *The New York Herald Tribune*[24]

> Silly rhymes and limpid pictures, those products of
> a wonderful imagination, make the story tops in excite-
> ment, too.
>
> —*Kirkus*[25]

Jane Cobb, writing in *The New York Times* plaintively says
Dr. Seuss is beyond her ability to describe:

> It is probably the most morale tale since the first
> "Elsie Dinsmore," but since it is written and illustrated
> by Dr. Seuss it is a lot more fun . . . Children, parents,
> relatives and friends need not come whimpering to this
> reviewer to find out what the Whos and their town look
> like. She knows the limits of her powers of description.[26]

By September, Helen was feeling well enough to move back
to their La Jolla home, but she couldn't be left alone. She had a
mandatory regimen of exercises to perform every day; she took
daily rides on a stationary bicycle, enlivened by her imagination: "I'm en route from Gallup, New Mexico to Shriprock, through
the Navajo country, but am running into many detours and
sheep . . ."[27]

Brightness returned to both Geisels; for *Colliers* magazine,
Ted wrote "A Prayer for a Child" with remarkable simplicity of
style:

> From here on earth,
> From my small place

I ask of You
Way out in space:
Please tell all men
In every land
What you and I
Both understand. . . .

Theodor Geisel next turned to the alphabet for *On Beyond Zebra!*, which follows Conrad Cornelius o'Donald o'Dell, who doesn't know that there are letters past Z:

The un-named friend of Conrad Cornelius o'Donald o'Dell (who narrates the book) then invents 20 new letters to follow Z: Yuzz; Wum; Um; Humpf; Fuddle; Glikk; Nuh; Snee; Quan; Thnad; Spazz; Floob; Zatz; Jogg; Flunn; Itch; Yekk; Vroo; Hi! and a final leter which has no name (he asks each reader to name it). Each is shown in fancy calligraphy, with a slightly near-eastern look. The book echoes every child who has ever drawn his or her own alphabet letters on paper (or on the walls at home if mother isn't watching).

Like the stanza about the Ziffs who live on cliffs and the Zuffs who live on bluffs in *Scrambled Eggs Super!*, Dr. Seuss again offers a stanza which is so convoluted that it wraps back upon itself, much like a Mobius strip:

And HUH is the letter I use to spell Nutches
Who live in small caves, known as Nitches, for hutches.
These Nutches have troubles, the biggest of which is
The fact there are many more Nutches than Nitches.
Each Nutch in a Nitch knows that some other Nutch
Would like to move into his Nitch very much.
So each Nutch in a Nitch has to watch that small Nitch
Or Nutches who haven't got Nitches will snitch.[29]

The book ends with Conrad Cornelius o'Donald o'Dell convinced that there is more to the alphabet than A to Z.

He dedicated the book simply: To Helen.

Reviews matched those of other Dr. Seuss books:

> Squirely-que, pluperfect, misty and bewildered pic-
> tures accompany each of the new categories.
>
> —Kirkus[30]

> For the fun of it all is in the ridiculous word play,
> even more inventive this time than in his other recent
> rhymes. As for the beasts, it is incredible, but he has
> dreamed up still more, large and small, male and female,
> each somehow connected with a feeling you yourself
> wish you could have put into a new word.
>
> —L. B., Book Review section,
> *The New York Herald Tribune*[31]

> Without the Seuss letters there would be no way to
> spell the names of creatures who look like brooms, or
> who live in tiny hutches, or who like to sing in grottos.
> What these creatures look like is indescribable, but they
> are delightful and it is difficult to imagine how we ever
> managed without them.
>
> —Jane Cobb, *The New York Times*[32]

A year after the first painful beginning of Helen's Guillain-
Barre syndrome, Ted and Helen traveled to Dartmouth College,
where, on the thirtieth anniversary of his graduation, he received
an honorary doctorate (as did Robert Frost). Geisel was over-
joyed to have Helen with him, healthy enough to fly to New
Hampshire. The celebration, in May, 1955, was a sweet satisfac-
tion for Geisel, who doubtless remembered the statement he made
to his father years earlier, that he was going to Oxford to get a
graduate degree. Now he had the degree, honorary though it
was. He maintained typical Seussian equilibrium; he was not

only Dr. Seuss, he was, as he laughed, "Dr. Dr. Seuss." The gown he wore at the Dartmouth ceremonies he brought with him from the west coast—where he had bought it in a San Diego second-hand store.[33]

Serendipity.

Serendipity drew him then to Boston, where he met William Spaulding, then head of the Education Division of the publishing firm, Houghton Mifflin. Geisel had met Spaulding in Washington during the war; Geisel knew the then-popular book by Rudolf Flesch, *Why Johnny Can't Read*—and he also remembered the article by John Hersey, "Why Do Students Get Bogged Down on First R?" in *Life*, in which Hersey pleaded for better children's books with illustrations by such geniuses as "Tenniel, Howard Pyle, Dr. Seuss, Walt Disney."

Spaulding wanted Geisel to write a book children simply couldn't put down. But Spaulding offered a caveat—he wanted Geisel to use no more than 225 words. Geisel was intrigued with the possibility, but there was a problem. Geisel was bound contractually to Random House. Spaulding would have to somehow work with Bennett Cerf to satisfactorily obtain Dr. Seuss.

Spaulding did so—in a unique way: Spaulding and Bennett Cerf agreed to cut the book fifty-fifty: Houghton Mifflin would publish an educational version of the Dr. Seuss book; Random House would have the "trade rights." In other words, Houghton Mifflin would have the rights to sell the book in schools; Random House would publish the same book and sell it through the "book trade" to bookstores and any other non-educational outlets. It was an ideal method for Spaulding to obtain a Dr. Seuss title; the agreement allowed Bennett Cerf to keep Geisel satisfied and still keep him in the Random House stable.

The book had to wait; Geisel was committed to work on another Random House book: *If I Ran the Circus*.

Patterned after *If I Ran the Zoo*, the book was dedicated:

This Book is for My Dad
Big Ted of Springfield
The Finest Man I'll Ever Know.

It began in typical Seussian fashion, with Morris McGurk dreaming of what a circus he could build behind Sneelock's Store: *Circus* lacks something of the pizzazz of *If I Ran the Zoo*, but then again, most sequels rarely match the original. Some critics, who read both books, saw that.

This Dr. Seuss creation does not start with so bizarre a premise as some of his other extravaganzas. The idea of a small boy dreaming up an ideal circus is not in itself startling. However when the great man gets going, he turns on his own free-wheeling fantasy, which is both peculiar to himself and just plain peculiar. It is also just plain wonderful.
—Jane Cobb, *The New York Times*[35]

Fantastic animals and people drawn in the familiar Seuss manner—this time in yellow, blues and pinks—with tongue-twisting names and rhymes, make this a book adults and children of all ages will enjoy.
—Norma Rathbun, *The Saturday Review of Literature*[36]

This is a superb fantasy from that talented purveyor of nonsense in rhyme with excruciatingly funny pictures that will amuse children and anyone else who opens this book.
—San Francisco Chronicle[37]

A howling Seuss phantasmagoria . . . Four-to-eight-year-old youngsters will agree that "no other circus is half the great circus the Circus McGurkus is."
—K. T. Kinkead, *The New Yorker*[38]

> Small fry may be happy just poring over the pic-
> tures, but we suspect that parents will demand that they
> be permitted to read aloud from Dr. Seuss' delicious verse.
> —M. M. R., *The Chicago Sunday Tribune*[39]

With *If I Ran the Circus* completed, Geisel was able to turn his attention to the challenge of the Spaulding-Cerf, Houghton Mifflin-Random House collaboration, the book that would be better than the best reader any American school child ever saw.

It was nearly an impossible task for Theodor Geisel and nearly an impossible task for Dr. Seuss.

The book took him a full year.

He examined the problem from every angle, gave every word the evil-eye, considered every possible combination of words, pictures, logic, plot. He thought he had a story going with a "Queen Zebra," but discovered neither the words *queen* or *zebra* were in the word list provided.[40] The only job more difficult was, he said, "when I wrote the Baedeker guide Eskimos use when they travel in Siam."[41]

Finally, finally, he saw what he wanted:

> I read (the list) forty times and got more and more
> discouraged. It was like trying to make strudel without
> any strudels. I was desperate, so I decided to read it once
> more. The first two words that rhymed would be the title
> of my book and I'd go from there. I found "cat" and then
> I found "hat." That's genius, you see![42]

Five

1956–1960

" . . . easily the best Christmas-cad since Scrooge . . ."

Simply stated, matching *cat* and *hat* revolutionized children's literature.

While he worked and he wrote, he thought and he thought, he began drawing the cat and eventually the cat was born, wearing a red-and-white striped top hat. And it had a red bow tie—note that the tie has three loops, not two. And (perhaps with a bow to Mickey Mouse, at least Mickey in the early cartoons) the cat wore white gloves.

And, as others working with words and pictures can imagine, the cat began to dominate the story. Born in Dr. Seuss's La Jolla dream works, the cat became real—jaunty, perhaps even outrageous. It had a personality and a mind of its own. And it had a smile not unlike the curious smile on the Mona Lisa.

The cat began to carry the story. The narrative began to flow. The story unfolded. It didn't quite have Dr. Seuss's usual galloping anapestic tetrameter, but the rhyme carried the story. And all the words were simple, those in the list Geisel was commanded to use.

Dr. Seuss shows two children, without Mother (or Father), which is an important key to the story. (All we know is that "Mother is out of the house for the day"—no mention of Father.)

And To Think That I Saw It on Mulberry Street and other Dr. Seuss books begin with a daydream: Marco imagines greater and greater sights on Mulberry Street; Gerald McGrew imagines greater and more fantastic animals for his Zooski McGrewski . . . but the Cat in the Hat simply appears. There is no daydream— suddenly he is there.

> And we saw him!
> The Cat in the Hat!
> And he said to us,
> "Why do you sit there like that?"

> "I know it is wet
> And the sun is not sunny.
> But we can have
> Lots of good fun that is funny!"[1]

Lots of good fun that is funny clearly means, to the children, the kind of fun without parents that quickly gets out of the child's control. Children, like puppies, can run amok if they are unchecked; lots of good fun that is funny, is clearly fun run amok. And it's the Cat who is the culprit.

In *The Cat in the Hat*, Seuss uses a device as old as storytelling and folklore itself—the trickster figure. The Cat is clearly magical (he appears instantly), as magical as ancient and modern creatures, such as Kokopelli, the trickster figure of the American Indian southwest. The trickster does not think logically; rather it thinks illogically, never planning, using rules all its own, depending on magic to turn events its way. The trickster Cat very much appeals to the sense of rebellion in all children, who secretly wish the world would run their way; who secretly wish they could make the world turn their way by magic.

But the trickster Cat's behavior is counter-balanced by the rigidity of the real world (the world of adults)—the children are constantly worried about what would happen if their mother would return and find the house in such chaos. Indeed, it's every child's nightmare that they will demolish their house only to find Mother at the front door at the worst possible moment.

The Cat in the Hat is one of the greatest topsy turvy trickster stories in all of children's literature (a *bouleversement*, in the French).

The Dr. Seuss illustrations clearly show pandemonium ready to erupt. The children's pet goldfish tries to warn the children and slow down the Cat, but to no avail.

But the Cat begins to juggle a fishbowl (with the goldfish in it) on top of his umbrella, then balances on a ball, with umbrella and goldfish bowl balanced on one gloved hand and a book balanced on the other gloved hand. A teacup teeters precariously on the edge of his top hat. (A reference to the mad tea party in *Alice in Wonderland*, perhaps?)

Then he adds another book balanced on top of the first, a birthday cake hanging at an angle from his top hat, still balanced on one leg on the ball, the other furry foot holding a glass and bottle of milk.

The boy and girl watch the Cat from the very bottom left corner of that page. Children see and read differently, so Dr. Seuss knows to add details, small animals or characters—this time the main characters, the two children—at the far edge of the page. Children's literature critic and authority Karla Kuskin offers an analysis why children see what they see and why their eyes look at books differently:

> The rhythm in a picture book—the way words and pictures move from page to page—is often paced theatrically. In the planning stage a picture book, like film, particularly animated film, is done in storyboard form. The rough illustrations are laid out

and matched to the appropriate words. These storyboards resemble comic strips, usually minus the word balloons. A baby crawling from frame to frame or a dog playing hide and seek from page to page contribute to the rhythm a picture book needs to keep readers involved and turning the pages. It is also not surprising that such minor characters are also common in animated film and comic strips; they may not say much but they catch young eyes and move things along. The littlest animal tumbling after all the others is almost a Disney trademark. Pogo had a puppy. And Snoopy, who over time made the jump from bit player to the big leagues, has Woodstock, his own silent observer, who in turn has his own groupies, that bunch of birds.[2]

But everything comes falling down with a crash. Everything is a mess and the children know the house shouldn't be like that when Mother returns. The goldfish scolds the Cat for making a huge mess, but the Cat says he knows an even better game. He goes out the door and returns with a big box.

And as the children look on, out popped Thing One and Thing Two, small creatures in red suits with greenish hair. (They have Thing 1 and Thing 2 on their chests and backs.) Sally and the boy narrator don't know what to do upon encountering them, except to fall back on their manners.

The Cat assures the children that the Things are harmless; but they began to fly kites inside the house, knocking down pictures, tables, vases, a chair and ruining their mother's good dress. But the goldfish sees their mother is coming, so the children make desperate efforts to catch the Things with a net. The Cat takes them away in the red box with the hook, but the house is a shambles. Everything is knocked over, wrecked, destroyed.

But the Cat returns with a cleaning vehicle, equipped with arms and hands to pick up and straighten everything.

The Cat in the Hat ends much like *And to Think That I Saw It on Mulberry Street*—do we (children) tell our parents what went on in our world today? Dr. Seuss lets his young readers decide.

Dr. Seuss illustrated the book solely in red and a greenish-bluish color.

The Cat in the Hat proved to be an instant success. It was a success because it was everything a Dick-and-Jane reader shouldn't be: it was written from the child's point of view; it encouraged or espoused random mayhem; parents were not in control; it taught no real moral lesson.

But children could read it by themselves; they could enjoy reading without supervision.

Boxed into the parameters of the word list supplied him, Dr. Seuss created an enduring and engaging character in the Cat in the Hat and created a whole new genre of children's literature. And just as suddenly the Dick and Jane readers were obsolete.

The Cat in the Hat became a publishing phenomenon:

> As soon as the first cartons of *The Cat in the Hat* reached stores, Random House recognized the omens that publishers live for. At Bullock's in Los Angeles, the first 100-copy order disappeared in a day and a hurried call went out for a 250-copy reorder. The Random House trade edition quickly outran Houghton Mifflin's school edition, averaging sales at the start of about twelve thousand copies a month and rising rapidly. The book escalated into a sensation: spurred by playground word-of-mouth, children nagged their parents to buy it. "Parents," Ted said, "understand better than school people the necessity for this kind of reader." Within three years *Cat* sold nearly a million copies at $1.95 each, with editions in French, Chinese, Swedish and Braille,

Geisel's biographers Judith and Neil Morgan said. (The copy I have indicates the 99th reprinting . . . [3])

Critics fell in love with the book and the mischievous cat as quickly as children did:

> It's fine, furious slapstick, told in rolling rhythms and lots of conversation. Dr. Seuss has used only 223 different words, according to the publisher, and according to my count, less than a dozen of these are two-syllable, all chosen for an eye to the knowledge and ability of the first and second grade reader. And there are Dr. Seuss' own illustrations to help make this one of the most original and funniest of books for early readers.
>
> —E. L. Buell, *The New York Times*[4]

> "The Cat in the Hat" is elegant nonsense. We were afraid that the limitations Dr. Seuss put upon himself might have shackled his marvelous inventiveness. Quite the contrary.
>
> —M. S. Libby, Book Review section, *The New York Herald Tribune*[5]

> All the old delightful rimes and rhythms, the zany illustrations are here. Together they make a book to rejoice 7 and 8 year olds and make them look with distinct disfavor on the drab adventures of standard primer characters.
>
> —P.G., *The Chicago Sunday Tribune*[6]

> Here is the same delicious nonsense, hilarious fun, cumulative build-up, and surprise ending that distinguish one of America's most original picture books, "And To Think That I Saw It on Mulberry Street."
>
> —H. A. M., *The Saturday Review of Literature*[7]

Recommended enthusiastically as a picture book
as well as a reader. Complete departure from the usual
dull and unimaginative books of this type.

—*Bookmark*[8]

And then, the Cat established a publishing house. Alone it
would have been substantial; inside Random House, it fortified
Random's reputation as one of the premiere publishing houses
for children's books.

Phyllis Cerf, Bennett Cerf's wife, took Geisel to lunch the
next time he visited New York and the Random House head-
quarters. She reminded him that years previously, when he was
working on the Flit campaigns, they worked together. She had
worked at the McCann-Eriksson advertising agency and although
Geisel produced all his Flit illustrations at home, when he wanted
space at the agency, the space provided was her desk.

She suggested that, as big as the success of *The Cat in the
Hat* was, it could be ever bigger. She proposed that Dr. Seuss
begin a series of similar books. He could produce Dr. Seuss books
in a bigger format, using a more complex vocabulary; books such
as *The Cat in the Hat* could and should be completed using much
the same basic vocabulary which Geisel/Dr. Seuss wrestled with
before discovering *cat* and *hat*.

Thus was born Beginner books, a publishing house inside a
publishing house (a room within the Random House house, if
you will). Geisel and Phyllis—and Helen—would hold portions
of the stock (later smaller portions were given to Bennett Cerf
and even later, smaller shares in the firm were given to others at
Random House).

Ensconced in his La Jolla Tower, Geisel put aside the idea of
the new series to work on another Dr. Seuss book he had promised Random House.

And as big as *The Cat in the Hat* had become, this would
become even bigger. (. . . *And so forth and upward and onward,
gee whiz!*)

For the first time, the focus in a Dr. Seuss book would be, not a boy, but an adult; and the focus was on not on good but a villain. As many children might say, "a bad guy."

The Grinch.

Dr. Seuss was not averse to borrowing characters from one book to use again in another. That only meant that his young readers were familiar with the character and would more easily accept a new book. So he had Marco from *And to Think That I Saw It on Mulberry Street* reappear in *McElligot's Pool* ; and he had Bartholomew from *The 500 Hats of Bartholomew Cubbins* reappear in *Bartholomew and the Oobleck.*

So he let the Whos from Whoville reappear in this book. And he pictured the Grinch's personality with a remarkably apt description (which even children—maybe especially children—could understand):

> The Grinch *hated* Christmas! The whole Christmas season
> Now, please don't ask why. No one quite knows the reason.
> It *could* be his head wasn't screwed on just right.
> It *could* be, perhaps, that his shoes were too tight.
> But I think that the most likely reason of all
> May have been that his heart was two sizes too small.[9]

And with that beginning, Dr. Seuss created a fable just as charming as *'Twas the Night Before Christmas* and just as enduring as *A Christmas Carol.* The library service *Kirkus* called the Grinch "easily the best Christmas-cad since Scrooge."

The Grinch hated the Whos's presents and toys, feasting, and joy and singing and NOISE! He says he has tolerated Christmas for 53 years.

(Theodor Geisel was 53 years old when he wrote, and Random House published, *How The Grinch Stole Christmas!*)

The Grinch tied antlers to his dog Max, harnessed him to a sleigh, donned a Santa suit and, on Christmas Eve, like a perverse, reverse Santa Clause, went down a *Who* chimney and took all the presents, all the meats, all the treats, all the feasts. And even their Christmas tree. He was caught, by little Cindy-Lou *Who*, "who was no more than two." She asked "Santy Claus, why, *WHY* are you taking our Christmas tree? WHY?"

The Grinch lied: "a bulb is out—I am taking it to my workshop and I'll bring it right back here."

He returned to the top of Mount Crumpet; with his sledload to dump it, expecting to hear the sobs and the cries of the Who children.

But everyone had a joyous Christmas anyway.

It was, perhaps the easiest Dr. Seuss book to write, except for the conclusion. Geisel didn't have a conclusion for the longest time. He explained to Judith and Neil Morgan how the conclusion came to be:

> I got hung up getting the Grinch out of the mess. I got into a situation where I sounded like a second-rate preacher or some biblical truism. . . . Finally in desperation . . . without making any statement whatever, I showed the Grinch and the Whos together at the table, and making a pun of the Grinch carving "the roast beast" . . . I had gone through thousands of religious choices, and then after three months it came out like that.[10]

Dr. Seuss added a name and virtually a dictionary definition to our culture:

> Grinch: any sour, pessimistic person who dismisses love and attempts to deprive others of happiness..

And the hard GR sound of Grinch is just perfect.

(Some newspaper headline writers and critics of Speaker of the House Newt Gingrich have linked his name, and perceived negative House of Representatives acts, to the Grinch: "The Gingrich Who. . . .")

Dr. Seuss made a strong moral in Bartholomew and the Oobleck:

> Sometimes you have to say *I'm Sorry,*
> Sometimes you have to say *It's my fault,*
> Even if you're a king.

And he made a strong moral point in *Horton Hears a Who:*

> A person's a person, no matter how small.

And he taught an even bigger lesson, about the nation's biggest celebration, in *How the Grinch Stole Christmas!:*

> Maybe Christmas doesn't come from a store.
> Maybe Christmas . . . means a little bit more!

It was a Dr. Seuss lesson not lost on children and certainly not lost on their parents.

While *The Cat in the Hat* was still setting sales records, the first printing the *Grinch* was 50,000 copies.[11]

And the critics raved:

> The inimitable Dr. Seuss has brought off a fresh triumph in his new picture book . . . The verse is as lively and the pages are as bright and colorful as anyone could wish. Reading the book aloud will be a fascinating exercise for parents or for older brothers and sisters, who will pretend they are entertaining the children while secretly enjoying the humor and the moral for themselves.
> —A. O'B. M. *The Saturday Review of Literature*[12]

> Wonderful fantasy, in the true Dr. Seuss manner, with pictures in the Christmas colors.
> —Charlotte Jackson, *The San Francisco Chronicle*[13]

Even if you prefer Dr. Seuss in a purely antic mood, you must admit that if there's a moral to be pointed out, no one can do it more gaily. The reader is swept along by the ebullient rhymes and the weirdly zany pictures until he is limp with relief when the Grinch reforms and, like the latter, mellow with good feeling.

—E. L. B., *The New York Times*[14]

His peculiar and original genius in line and word is always the same, yet, so rich are the variations he plays on his themes, always fresh and amusing.

—M.S. Libby, Book Review section,
The New York Herald Tribune[15]

And the *Kirkus* service, which recognized the Grinch as a modern-day Scrooge:

Youngsters will be in transports over the goofy gaiety of Dr. Seuss's first book about a villain—easily the best Christmas-cad since Scrooge. Inimitable Seuss illustrations of the Grinch's dog Max disguised as a reindeer are in black and white with touches of red. Irrepressible and irresistible.

—*Kirkus*[16]

In New York, Phyllis Cerf compiled a list of 379 words, from which a Beginner Books author could choose 200, plus 20 "emergency" words for each book project.[17]

In California, Beginner Books was housed in Helen's office, formerly a garage at the Geisel's La Jolla aerie. Above her desk was a gift from Phyllis Cerf: a needlepoint portrait of The Cat in the Hat, inscribed:

THIS CAT STARTED A PUBLISHING HOUSE. NO OTHER CAT CAN MAKE THIS CLAIM.[18]

Beginner Books borrowed money from Random House to finance the start-up; the new company may have started well, for a while, but Phyllis Cerf and Ted Geisel soon clashed on the projects the firm would publish; she was a fighter, he wasn't; he demanded (politely) rules for the books which Dr. Seuss had learned the hard, *very* hard way over the years and through the past books. All his rules made perfect sense, in terms of children's books, especially preschool books:

* Only one picture per page;

* The text should never mention anything that wasn't illustrated;

* Pages which faced each other should be inter-locked, so the two pages form one unit, i.e., if page one is the first right-hand page, then pages 2 and 3 are facing pages and the pictures and text for those pages should be a single unit.[19]

As mild-mannered as Ted Geisel was, few other authors could meet his style demands. And thus Beginner Books was often in a collective quandary and without suitable book projects to put into production. Book projects by Truman Capote and Nathaniel Benchley were both rejected by the Beginner Books triumverate.[20]

Robert Bernstein was hired by Random House from Simon & Schuster to help satisfy the public demand for Dr. Seuss; Ted Geisel's plaintive question of only several years earlier, "Can I make five thousand dollars a year on my work" was beginning to be answered, YES, YES, YES because of the post-war baby boom. No one could have anticipated the baby boom and the thousands of children who would "grow into" Dr. Seuss books each year. Not to mention Dr. Seuss books which were bought, colored in with crayons, bought by schools and community libraries and lost by small tykes and then replaced by other copies. Bernstein fueled the Dr. Seuss boom by making sure there were a few, but only a few Dr. Seuss toys, just as Disney had learned to do with Mickey Mouse lunchpails, Mickey Mouse watches (which appreciated hugely in value over the years) Disney "snowdomes" and a vast, never-ending cornucopia of Mickey Mouse-Donald Duck, Disneyiana.

As reluctant as he was to travel, Geisel appeared on behalf of his books during a ten-day marketing blitz during the 1958 holiday season included Boston, Rochester, Washington, D.C.; Chicago; Madison, Wisconsin and Cleveland. Dr. Seuss was mobbed at each stop.

Dr. Seuss returned to his La Jolla desk and completed *The Cat in the Hat Comes Back* and, like *If I Ran the Circus*, it was good Dr. Seuss, which meant that it was light years better than anything everybody else was publishing, but it wasn't *inspired* Dr. Seuss. But critics still appreciated it, nearly almost as much as the original (*98 and 3/4th percent guaranteed. . . .*)

> While not as rib-tickling as the first story, this one is still well above the average book for beginning readers both in imaginativeness and humor and in narrative and pictorial interest. First graders should be able to read it by themselves.
> —*Booklist*[21]

> Using only 252 different words, culled from a beginning reader's list, (Dr. Seuss) tells in hilarious verse and outrageously funny pictures the further adventures of a couple of youngsters and a naughty cat.
> —E.C. Mann, *The Chicago Sunday Tribune*[22]

> A top-notch sequel to "The Cat in the Hat," providing delightful fare for beginning readers. . . .
> —B. M. Doh, *Library Journal*[23]

> It may be awkwardly rhymed in spots and limited by only 252 different words, but the nonsense and

spontaneous fun of Dr. Seuss is here for the first and
second graders to read.
—*Wisconsin Library Bulletin*[24]

The chief difficulty with the new series of "Beginner Books". . . . (is) the problem of keeping misguided
parents, teachers and older children (who enjoy them
immensely) from reading them aloud to children who
have not yet begun to read and so spoiling all the fun
and profit for them.
—M. S. Libby, Book Review section,
The New York Herald Tribune[25]

And to Ted Geisel's pleasure, we can be sure, Beginner Books
published *A Fly Went By,* by Marshall "Mike" McClintock, his
Dartmouth friend who met him on a Manhattan Street all those
years ago, took him into the offices of The Vanguard Press and
agreed to publish *And To Think That I Saw It on Mulberry Street.*
(". . . *an elephant's faithful, one hundred percent . . .*")

As of late summer, 1997, *A Fly Went By* is still in print with
Beginner Books, now in its 55th reprinting.

In 1957, Helen Geisel suffered dizziness and confusion and
was taken to the Scripps Clinic; she was diagnosed as having
suffered a small stroke. She was back at home several days later,
with slight problems in her right hand and right side and lacking
her usual self.

While Random House was putting *The Cat in the Hat* and
The Cat in the Hat Comes Back into production, Theodor Geisel
began working on another Dr. Seuss project. It was the first time
he would combine three shorter stories into one book: *Yertle the
Turtle and Other Stories.* The other stories were "Gertrude McFuzz"
and "The Big Brag."

With the story "Yertle the Turtle" Dr. Seuss posed another
major moral; children understood the story, but many children
(*and* adults) missed the moral:

They *were* . . . until Yertle, the king of them all,
decided the kingdom he ruled was too small.
"I'm ruler," said Yertle, "of all I can see.
"But I can't see *enough*. That's the trouble with me
With this stone for a throne, I look down on my pond
But I can not look down on the places beyond.
This throne that I sit on is too, too low down.
It ought to be *higher!*" he said with a frown.
"If I could sit high, how much greater I'd be!
What a king! I'd be ruler of all I could see!"

So turtles and more turtles and more turtles came and they all climbed on the back of a turtle named Mack, until the pile of turtles grew higher and higher. And Yertle, the King Turtle, could see longer and farther and he was King of all he could see.

And Yertle the King Turtle ordered even more turtles to climb onto the stack, to heighten the stack even more on Mack's back. (Yet he was offended that the moon was higher than he.)

But Mack got tired of being on the bottom and he protested with a "burp!" and the stack came tumbling down.

And what was the moral? That all turtles and all creatures should be free. And on what was it based? Ted Geisel explained the story to Cynthia Gorney, of *The Washington Post*, in May, 1979:

> La Jolla, Calif.—One afternoon in 1957, as he bent over the big drawing board in his California studio, Theodor Seuss Geisel found himself drawing a turtle.
>
> He was not sure why.
>
> He drew another turtle and saw that it was underneath the first turtle, holding him up.
>
> He drew another, and another, until he had an enormous pileup of turtles, each standing on the back of the turtle below it and hanging its turtle head, looking pained.

Geisel looked at this turtle pile. He asked himself, not unreasonably, What does this mean? Who is the turtle on top?

Then he understood that the turtle on top was Adolf Hitler.

"I couldn't draw Hitler as a turtle," Geisel says, now hunched over the same drawing board, making pencil scribbles of the original yertle the Turtle drawings as he remembers them. "So, I drew him as King What-ever-his-name-was, King" (Scribble) "of the Pond." (Scribble.) "He wanted to be King as far as he could see. So kept piling them up. He conquered Central Europe and France, and there it was."

(Scribble.)

"Then I had this great pileup, and I said, 'How do you get rid of this impostor?'

"Believe it or not," I said, 'The voice of the people.' I said, 'Well, I'll just simply have the guy on the bottom burp.'"[26]

Yertle the Turtle was Dr. Seuss's answer to depotism: Fascism and Nazism.

It was as important a moral as *a person's a person, no matter how small,* in *Horton Hears a Who!*

And Theodor Geisel had to fight long and hard to get that single *burp!* into a Random House book.

A must for both remedial reading and reading aloud. The sweeping illustrations and the spontaneous verse of these three stories make them a welcome addition to that nonsensical, but wise, world of the always popular Dr. Seuss.
—*Kirkus*[27]

Dr. Seuss' talent in using ordinary, simple words with vividness, humor and unflagging rhythm, coupled

with his ability to draw eloquently funny illustrations, make his stories easily readable for young children and equally enjoyable for many a well-read adult.
—E. D., *The Horn Book Magazine*[28]

Hurray! Three shining examples of Dr. Seuss' unique art, first published in a magazine, are now out in a book, pointing little morals for our delight and profit. . . . A hilarious addition to the Dr. Seuss shelf.
—P. G., *The Chicago Sunday Tribune*[29]

This three-in-one chuckle bargain in hard covers is sure to delight Dr. Seuss fans, even though they will not regard it as the super-colossal accomplishment characteristic of many of Seuss's more recent extravaganzas.
—Della McGregor, *The Saturday Review of Literature*[30]

As much as Dr. Seuss books were bought by libraries for year upon year of children growing into the reading level of the books, Geisel so far had missed an obvious target: even as *a person's a person, not matter how small,* his next book captured a guaranteed market: *everyone has a birthday, no matter how old.*

So he completed *Happy Birthday to You!* with most of the inside right front cover blank so parents can sign, date and give the book to the birthday boy or birthday girl.

Critics of all ages loved it:

Any child lucky enough to be flown to Katroo on Smorgasbord's back will be reduced to a happy state of hypnosis by the skillful rhymes and Seussian pictures.
—Charlotte Jackson, *The Atlantic Monthly*[32]

The better a child's book is, the more completely it must turn topsy turvy all the characteristic style and attitudes of the school reader—the stammering prose,

the didactic realism of the illustrations, the family relationships, the role of the animal, the unquestioning ad-
justment to petty bourgeois morals and manners.
—Elizabeth Kilbourn, *The Canadian Forum*[33]

This multicolored excursion is a gay and festive
one, though perhaps a little too long and involved. The
rhyming text and imaginative illustrations, however, will
delight not only Dr. Seuss fans, but birthday boys and
girls as well.
—N. B. Childs, *Library Journal*[34]

While he, Helen and Phyllis Cerf squabbled over possibili-
ties for the Beginner Books list, and before *Happy Birthday to
You!* was published, Ted and Helen took a quick vacation and
returned to his studio to begin yet another Beginner Book, *One
Fish Two Fish Red Fish Blue Fish.*

It was smaller in volume, like *The Cat in the Hat* and used
the restricted word list, which Dr. Seuss mastered in *The Cat in
the Hat.*

One Fish Two Fish Red Fish Blue Fish begins with fish, then
continues with Seussian animals of every size, shape and variety. Some have their names on their chests (Mike, Clark); others
only identified by Seussian species: a Wump; a Nook; a Zans; a
Ying; a Yop; small yellow fellows called the Zeds; an Ish; a Gak,
a Zeep.

The most famous creature in *Red Fish Blue Fish* . . . may be
the bear-like Gox, shown wearing yellow boxing gloves, boxing
with the narrator, a small boy:

> I like to box
> How I like to box!
> so, every day,
> I box a Gox.

In yellow socks
I box my Gox
I box in yellow
Gox box socks.[35]

Most critics read *One Fish Two Fish . . .* as simply on a par
with other Seuss books:

> The new Dr. Seuss is fun, just plain fun. Not per-
> haps such a verbal tour de force as "The Cat in the Hat,"
> it is useful for beginning readers. The text, as always
> with Dr. Seuss, shows more subtlety and variety than his
> pictures.
>
> > —M. S. Libby, Book Review section,
> > *The New York Herald Tribune*[36]

> Easy-to-read but hard-to-fathom pastiche. Seven-
> and eight-year-olds may be pleased with the frantic hu-
> mor of this book.
>
> > —*The Saturday Review of Literature*[38]

and:

> However much adults may yawn over Dr. Seuss, and
> sigh over their children's delight, he does seem to know
> exactly what children just beginning to read find un-
> bearably funny.
>
> > —*The Christian Science Monitor*[38]

E. L. Buell, writing in *The New York Times Book Review*, clearly
and completely understood what Seuss was doing in *One Fish
Two Fish Red Fish Blue Fish. . . .*

> This is not a story but a collection of daffy verses
> about the daffiest of subjects and situations, done in the

inimitable Seuss manner, complete with hypnotic rhymes, jokes, a picture-menagerie of Seuss-type animals that never were on land or sea. . . . (This) is designed to ease the reader into an inkling of how phonics work, and in most cases the name is lettered on some prominent part of the animal's anatomy, for quick recognition and word association. Also slipped in are some exercises in counting and recognition of shapes and colors. Of course the great thing about the Seuss books is that they never seem educational, just high-voltage fun to read, to look at and to listen to.[39]

Just as he had done earlier with Smith and Haas, and The Vanguard Press, Bennett Cerf quickly found Beginner Books too valuable to ignore; by April, 1960, it had set exceeded a million dollars in sales.[40] He proposed that Random House simply buy the firm.

The Geisels wasn't terribly interested in that idea; Ted knew that huge profits from the sale would be taxable and thus largely lost. But Cerf suggested a deferred sales plan that would avoid huge taxes; Ted and Helen would continue to run the company. Geisel was an innocent in the world of business, so he acquested to the plan, and invested wisely.

In the process of negotiating about Beginner Books, Cerf offered Geisel a challenge: now that Dr. Seuss could successfully publish a book with about 250 words—could Dr. Seuss write a book with only 50 words?

The bet was $50.

The book was *Green Eggs and Ham*:

> That Sam-I-am!
> That Sam-I-am!
> I do not like
> That Sam-I-am!

Do you like
green eggs and ham?

I do not like them,
Sam-I-am.[41]

    Geisel had worked furiously with charts, checklists, notations; his imagination was aided and abetted by pure, unadulterated hard work.

    Chuck Jones, creator of Bugs Bunny, clearly saw how Geisel succeeded with *Green Eggs and Ham*: he took the common phrase, *ham and eggs*, and commanded attention by reversing it. Jones compared Geisel's phrasing to that of the Pennsylvania Dutch (who are not Dutch at all, but of German heritage, Dutch being a variation of *Deutsch*, German for *German*), or Yiddish, which used phrases like "He doesn't like opera, my Father" or "throw Mother from the train, a kiss."

    Geisel's best, such as *Green Eggs and Ham*, Jones said, "has that quality of puzzlement. He uses Sam-I-am, not just Sam, and Sam-I-am not only rhymes with green-eggs and ham, but has the same metric emphasis."[42]

> Sam-I-am drives his victim crazy, pursuing him everywhere while he urges him to eat something disgusting. Literature has seldom afforded children an opportunity to ally themselves with such open antagonism, Ted was building on the breakthrough of *The Cat in the Hat*, whose boisterous rampage in the absence of adults went unpunished, alarming some of the school establishment who felt safer with Dick and Jane and considered the Cat "a trickster hero."

Judith and Neil Morgan wrote.[43]

    Geisel later said it was "the only book I ever wrote that still makes me laugh."[44]

Mary Malone, in the *Library Journal*, wrote:

> Another beginning reader with Dr. Seuss' usual in-
> genuity in rhyme, telling in a limited vocabulary but
> unlimited exuberance of illustration, of Sam-I-am who
> wins a determined campaign to make another Seuss char-
> acter eat a plate of green eggs and ham.[45]

M.S. Libby, in *The New York Herald Tribune* hit the book
dead-on:

> He limits himself to monosyllables, but his pictures
> and the wonderful dead-pan humor are superb.[46]

Emily Maxwell, in *The New Yorker* wrote:

> Dr. S. can play so many tunes on his simplified key-
> board that, reading him, one is hardly aware that there
> *are* more than fifty words . . . [47]

And *The Saturday Review of Literature* said:

> The happy theme of refusal-to-eat changing to rel-
> ish will be doubly enjoyable to the child who finds many
> common edibles as nauseating as the title repast. The
> pacing throughout is magnificent and the opening five
> pages, on which the focal character introduces himself
> with a placard: "I am Sam," are unsurpassed. . . . [48]

And books like *Green Eggs and Ham*, *Mr. Brown
Can Moo! Can You?* and *Marvin K. Mooney, Will You
Please Go Now!* remind us that Dr. Seuss is one of the
great creators of nonsense verse in the English language—verse in which you can almost hear an unmis-
takable musical accompaniment,

children's literature authority Jonathan Cott wrote, in *Pipers at the Gates of Dawn: The Wisdom of Children's Literature.*[49]

Now in its 99th reprinting, *Green Eggs and Ham* has been presented as a rap song (by the Canadian band Moxy Früvous), and in a memorable occasion, was recited by the Rev. Jesse Jackson, on "Saturday Night Live," as a black minister would intone it during a southern Sunday sermon.

After publication, Theodor Geisel was occasionally presented with plates of green eggs and ham. "Vile stuff," he said.

Six

1960–1971

"And I learned there are troubles of more than one kind. *Some come from ahead and some come from behind.*"

"I'm subversive as hell," Theodor Geisel said and he meant it. Not quite subversive in a totally political sense, but a political sense mixed with literature.

I've always had a mistrust of adults. And one reason I dropped out of Oxford and the Sorbonne was that I thought they were taking life too damn seriously, concentrating too much on nonessentials. Hilaire Belloc, whose writing I liked a lot, was a radical. *Gulliver's Travels* was subversive and both Swift and Voltaire influenced me. *The Cat in the Hat* is a revolt against authority, but it's ameliorated by the fact that the Cat cleans up everything in the end. It's revolutionary in that it goes as far as Kerensky and then stops. It doesn't go quite as far as Lenin.

* * *

Children's literature as I write it and as I see it is satire to a great extent—satirizing the mores and the habits of the world. There's *Yertle the Turtle* (about the turtle dictator who becomes "the ruler of all I can see" by sitting on the backs of hundreds of subject turtles, his throne brought down by the simple burp of the lowliest and lowest turtle), which was modeled on the rise of Hitler. . . .[1]

And then he wrote "The Sneetches," which appeared in *The Sneetches and Other Stories*:

> Now, the Star-Belly Sneetches
> Had bellies with stars.
> The Plain Belly Sneetches
> Had none upon thars.
>
> Those stars weren't so big. They were really so small
> You might think such a thing wouldn't matter at all.
>
> But, because they had stars, all the Star-Belly Sneetches
> Would brag, "We're the best kind of Sneetches on the beaches."[2]

Then Sylvester McMonkey McBean, the Fix-it-Up Chappie, arrived with a curious machine: for three dollars each, every Plain Belly Sneetch could enter the machine and come out with a star:
Then McBean said, to the Sneetches with stars, for *ten* dollars, you can enter my machine, which will take off your stars.
And even Theodor Geisel learned a lesson from *The Sneetches and Other Stories*. The last story in the book is "The Empty Pants," in which the narrator, a small child, is scared of an empty pair of pants in the dark:

And then they moved! Those empty pants!
They kind of started jumping.
And then my heart, I must admit,
It kind of started thumping.

So I got out. I got out fast
As fast as I could go, sir.
I wasn't scared. But pants like that
I do not care for. No, sir.[3]

(The empty pants clearly represented an authority figure which didn't have to be feared. . . .)

When Robert Bernstein, publisher at Random House, visited in La Jolla, Ted Geisel has the storyboards for the book on the walls. "I'd decided to abandon the book," he told an astonished Bernstein, "Someone I respect told me it was anti-Semitic."

"The Sneetches" was Geisel's strong statement: he was *against* anti-semitism. Against prejudice. Against bigotry. Against peoples vs. peoples.

During the Holocaust, Jews were forced to wear stars. Dr. Seuss turned that around, and into, the Plain-Belly Sneetches and the Star-Belly Sneetches.

It was as strong a moral as he had in *Yertle the Turtle*, where he avoided drawing Hitler as Yertle the Turtle King, but made the same point about Nazism.

Robert Bernstein talked him out of abandoning *The Sneetches and Other Stories*. And Geisel, himself, discovered that the person—"someone I respect"—who thought the book was anti-semitic was . . . was . . . well, an empty pair of pants in the dark. That Geisel didn't have to be scared of.

"Those spooky pants and I came face to face," he told Bernstein.[4]

One (story) is a hilarious vignette about a mother who named all of her 23 sons Dave. The other three are parables on prejudice, stubbornness, and fear of the unknown, thumpingly told in the famous Dr. Seuss style that starts with the absurd and the preposterous and goes on from there.

—Joan Beck, *The Chicago Sunday Tribune*[5]

The best, "What Was I Scared of" makes an excellent creepy story for Halloween. . . . The title story, while amusing, is rather too obvious in its moral.

—Alice Daigliesh, *The Saturday Review of Literature*[6]

Ted and Helen Geisel began to regret the work load they had to put into Beginner Books. In late 1961, they received a call from Donald Klopfer, at Random House, telling them that he had sold direct mail rights to Grolier, which was beginning a direct mail children's book club. Helen Geisel asked if there were any other books sold to Grolier in addition to Beginner Books. Klopfer said that Harpers had also sold their children's book line to Grolier, for the new book club.

Helen—and Ted—refused. Helen refused first. Grolier would sell Beginner Books solely, or not at all. It was Klopfer's turn to be astonished. Then even more astonished when Grolier accepted the Geisel's polite demand. Forty years later, Grolier had paid more than forty million dollars to Beginner Books, a very, very substantial portion of those royalties were for Dr. Seuss books. And, in the bargain, Grolier has become the biggest and most successful children's book club in the country.[7]

Ted Geisel then resurrected the pseudonym Theo. LeSieg, for some books, in which he would write the text, but others would do the illustrations. *Ten Apples Up on Top*, was the first, in 1961; *I Wish I Had Duck Feet* was published in 1965 and *Come on Over to My House*, in 1966. Others were released after that. They were not quite top-drawer Seuss but they did fit in the Beginner Book series.

The next Dr. Seuss was not a collection of stories, but a book based on every parent's-every evening predicament: how to get the baby or toddler off to sleep.

Dr. Seuss's Sleep Book was published in 1962 and was in the form of a report, who's asleep where. . . .

Ted Geisel works his way into the wonderful convoluted nonsense that matches the very best of the previous Dr. Seuss books:

> But it isn't too good when a moose and a goose
> Start dreaming they're drinking the other one's juice.
> Moose juice, not goose juice, is juice for a moose
> And goose juice, not moose juice, is juice for a goose.
> So, when goose gets a mouthful of juices of moose's
> And moose gets a mouthful of juices of goose's,
> They always fall out of their beds screaming screams.
> SO. . . .[8]

E. L. Buell, writing in *The New York Times Book Review* caught the book perfectly in his first sentence:

> A rarity among books—one deliberately calculated to make its readers yawn. And anyone who has followed Dr. Seuss's twenty-five years career as author-artist knows how persuasive he is. No one could resist those zillions of astonishing sleepyheads . . . which only he could have invented, pictured and described in hypnotic rhythms which bring yawns right on top of the chuckles.[9]

The Christian Science Monitor offered:

> This new Dr. Seuss, hardly a classic, at least has the considerable virtue of being continually silly and unflaggingly inventive . . . Whether the thought of Biffer-Baum Birds and Collapsible Frinks nestling down will promote drowsiness in young humans I do not know. In a test on one seven-year-old, the result was giggling. The drawings are, if anything, more frazzled, more rubbery than ever.
> —E. W. Foell[10]

With Beginner Books, Dr. Seuss continued to be "subversive as hell"; his books taught children numbers, phonics, words, relationships. And they were taught so easily, in the form of Dr. Seuss stories and Dr. Seuss creatures, that children didn't know they were learning.

And for the next few years, after *Dr. Seuss's Sleep Book*, Geisel concentrated on Beginner Books, which were promoted with the line on the covers, "The SIMPLEST SEUSS for YOUNGEST USE." But they were no less difficult to write: in fact, the shorter the book, the more difficult and the fewest words available to for Geisel to use, the harder to make a plot line.

For *Hop on Pop*, released in spring, 1963, the good doctor matches simple words and their usage:

> NO
> PAT
> NO
> Don't sit on that.[11]

(Pat, a yellow bear, or yellow Seuss bear-like creature, stands perplexed beside a cactus.)

Dr. Seuss's ABC, released the fall of the same year, uses these forms:

> BIG A
> little a
> What begins with A?
> Aunt Annie's alligator. . . . A . . a . . A.

Critics continued to rave about Beginner Books and *Hop on Pop*:

> As for Dr. Seuss, that wizard is bent on removing
> reading frustrations before they start and he deserves a

special fanfare for Hop on Pop. . . . The illustrations are as funny as ever; they also provide clues for figuring out the meanings of words. Dr. Seuss thinks of everything.

—E. L. Buell, *The New York Times Book Review*[13]

A hilarious first reader . . . which will captivate even the average six-year-old.

—*Christian Century*[14]

Superb, simple Seuss. Funny, phonetic, fantastic. It groups one syllable rhythmic and rhyming words together, uses them in brief sentences and illustrates the idea hilariously with the Doctor's ever fresh and amusing oddities . . . Try it on your 4-year-old now that it's pedagogically respectable to allows that age to attempt to read! Or forget about teaching them anything and have fun.

—M. S. Libby, Books section,
The New York Herald Tribune[15]

And *Dr. Seuss's ABC* . . .

Dr. Seuss's ABC will be the special joy of all the siblings whose older brethren chuckle happily over the good Doctor's zany creations. Everyone else will benefit from it, too, because it stresses not only the letter, but the sound it makes as it grows into a word.

—Alberta Eiseman, *The New York Times Book Review*[16]

The zany Dr. Seuss may be the despair of many educators ever since his "Cat in the Hat". . . . Whether Dr. Seuss has any purpose or not, or whether a child will learn ABC's by mouthing phrases like "googoo goggles, quacking quacker-oo and Fiffer-feffer-feff" is perhaps beside the point. Children seem to enjoy Seussy sauciness and although his googoo goggles gobbledygook may not fulfill all the needs of education it certainly put any fear of letters completely at the mercy of a chubby Zizzer-zazzer-zuzz.

—Guernsey La Pelley
The Christian Science Monitor[17]

Bennett Cerf and all his colleagues at Random House came to expect a Seuss title annually, automatically. Lulled into a half-false sense of security about the good doctor laboring away in his tower in La Jolla, Seuss jolted them by adding clearly non-Seussian rhymes, which had to be edited out. *Hop on Pop* went to New York with these lines:

> When I read I am smart
> I always cut whole words apart.
> Con Stan Tin O Ple, Tim Buk Too
> Con Tra Cep Tive, Kan Ga Roo.[18]

The final book read:

> My father
> can read
> big words, too.
> Like . . .
>
> Constantinpole
> and
> Timbuktu[19]

Later, in *Fox in Sox*, Geisel tried using:

> Moe blows Joe's nose
> Joe blows Moe's nose.

And Bennett Cerf and Random House wouldn't go for *that*, either.[20]

The front cover of the next Dr. Seuss book, *Fox in Sox*, carries this admonition:

> This is a book you READ ALOUD to find out just how smart your tongue is. The first time you read it, don't go fast! This Fox is a tricky fox. He'll try to get your tongue in trouble.

Indeed.

The book is a dialogue between Fox, who is a red fox, and Knox, who is a yellow bear-like creature.

Try these Seussian lines from *Fox in Sox:*

> Through three cheese trees
> three free fleas flew.
> While these fleas flew,
> freezy breeze blew.[21]

Couldn't say it, could you? Neither can I.

The New York Times reviewers were always on Seuss's side; as was *The Christian Science Monitor:*

> Tongue trippers . . . from the facile mind and humorous pen of Dr. Seuss . . . Let the beginners read and recite with sly Fox (in sox) the simple words which always accumulate into audible pandemonium. It will be a rigorous and riotous trip.
> —G. A. Woods, *The New York Times Book Review*[22]

(A second-grader) wrote: "I like the pictures. I think sometimes you get mixed up. I think it is funny. I like the words and rhymes and words that sound alike." This confirmed a parental impression that a

young reader will persist in something new and different—even tongue-twisters like these—if there are pleasures to pull him along. Dr. Seuss, involved here with
tweetle beetles in a puddle paddle battle, continues
to supply such pleasures.
—Roderick Nordell, *The Christian Science Monitor*[25]

His next book, a larger Dr. Seuss book, rather than a smaller
Beginner Book, also spoke with a loud voice with a clear moral.

I Had Trouble In Getting to Solla Sollew is Dr. Seuss's most
pessimistic book. (It may have been Dr. Seuss somehow speaking to Theodor Geisel.)

> I was real happy and carefree and young
> and I lived in a place called the Valley of Vung
> And nothing, not anything ever went wrong
> Until . . . well, one day I got walking along. . . .

He meets trouble after trouble on the way . . .

He continues through a storm, a flood, and encounters the
army of . . . General Genghis Kahn Schmitz, who is forced to
retreat facing the ominous Army of the Perilous Poozer of
Pompelmoose Pass.[24]

Finally, the narrator gets to Solla Sollew, but the doorkeeper
admitted one small trouble: the door is locked and a Key-Slap-
ping Slippard always knocks the key out of the door. And they
can't get into Solla Sollew.

The key to the book was:

> And I learned there are troubles
> Of more than one kind.
> Some come from ahead
> And some come from behind.[25]

Despite the fact that Geisel thought "I'm General Genghis

Kahn Schmitz" was a great line, the book was too bleak. Geisel biographers Judith and Neil Morgan called it "a Seussian *Pilgrim's Progress*."[26] The moral clearly was: *there are some troubles you can't avoid; there are some troubles you must face.* But the real lesson was: this book was chronically far too old for Dr. Seuss's typical child-readers and the message was something they couldn't really grasp (or didn't want to know) at their reading level.

Many Dr. Seuss books are near their hundredth re-printing: in 1997, *Solla Sollew* is in its twenty-second reprinting.

It was followed by two Theo. LeSieg books, *I Wish I Had Duck Feet* (1965) and *Come Over to My House* (1966).

In May, 1966, Bennett Cerf sold Random House to the RCA Corporation, at a time when many publishing firms were being bought or merged into conglomerates. It was then thought that the synergy would benefit broadcast and print properties; such isn't really the case and some broadcast/print properties were later divorced. (Time Warner is an example. The synergy between the Time Inc. magazines and the Warner film empire has never met original expectations, although there is some cross-promotion of Warner films promoted in the Time Inc. magazines.)

Back in La Jolla, Ted Geisel counted up and discovered that his stock in Beginner Books (and thus stock in Random House) sold to RCA made him a multi-millionaire. Random House is now part of Advance Publications, Inc. (which also owns *The New Yorker* magazine and other properties). Advance Publications is, in turn, owned by the Newhouse family.

Then Chuck Jones entered the picture (again). Friends from World War Two days, Jones believed that Dr. Seuss material could, and should, be made into a cartoon special for television. Typical negotiations followed, via Geisel's agents, potential sponsors, the Geisels and assorted friends and others.

It was early in 1966 and the calendar made the choice: by the end of the year Jones could have *The Grinch* ready for holiday viewing.

Jones moved The Grinch to animation without using any of the slapdash techniques of the time. Typical cartoons then used abbreviated action—backgrounds repeated (the same trees would reappear behind running figures, for instance) and voices didn't quite match actions. Jones used full-action techniques: 25,000 drawings instead of a typical cartoons 2,000 drawings.

The Grinch had to be reinvented. Colors—which colors should be used? What kind of a voice? How would the Whos be animated? and the length?—typically the Grinch story could be read aloud to an audience in less than 15 minutes. It had to be lengthened to almost a half-hour (minus time for commercials). Would the plot have to be changed, or added to?

Geisel wanted the Grinch to be in black-and-white—but Jones suggested that his eyes be a jealous green.

A Grinch song was added:

> You're a mean one, Mister Grinch;
> You really are a heel.
> You're as cuddly as a cactus, you're as charming as an eel.
> Mister Grinch! You're a bad banana
> with a greasy black peel . . . [27]

And, eventually, narrating the story was—the man with the perfect Grincy-y voice—Boris Karloff.

CBS-TV bought Grinch paying MGM $315,000 for two annual showings in 1966 and 1967. Chuck Jones predicted that it would be rerun "for at least the next ten years."[28]

He was wrong—*How the Grinch Stole Christmas!* has become an annual holiday event, along with Dickens' *A Christmas Carol* and another cartoon classic, *Charlie Brown's Christmas*, by Charles Schultz. Some things should just go on forever. *How The Grinch Stole Christmas!* is one—a holiday story with an obvious holiday moral, without being preachy or overly religious. In other words, perfect for everyone.

Chuck Jones then turned to animating *Horton Hears a Who!* with nearly the same results, except for the lack of seasonal fanfare. And Geisel turned to *The Cat in the Hat Songbook*, which he thought would be a natural for Cub Scout packs, Brownie troops, day care centers, communities, family sing-alongs. But the lyrics didn't match the melodies and the songs proved hard to sing. And *The Cat in the Hat Songbook* was the only other Dr. Seuss title beside *The Seven Lady Godivas* to be allowed to go out-of-print.

The Geisel's work continued. Helen Geisel worked with Beginner Books, with other projects of her own, with Ted and his new projects.

But on the morning of October 23, 1967, the housekeeper entered the Geisel's home and discovered that no one was up. Helen and Ted slept in separate bedrooms—and Ted was often late to bed and late to rise. That in itself was not unusual. But Helen was not up. The housekeeper, Alberta Shaw, found her in her bedroom.

Sometime during the night Helen Geisel, in constant pain since her first onset of Guillain-Barre syndrome and weakened by her bout with polio had taken her own life. She had overdosed with sodium pentobarbital tablets.

The woman who met Ted Geisel for the first time at Oxford, all those many years ago, who had picked him up, by looking over his shoulder while he was doodling, with the line, "say, that's a fine flying cow"—had taken her own life.

Although she had looked fine during the immediate past weeks, her mental condition had declined. No one knows how much physical pain she endured. She had left a note to Ted, surely as mixed a suicide note as there ever was.

> I feel myself in a spiral, going down down down, into a black hole from which there is no escape, no brightness. And loud in my ears from every side, I hear, "failure, failure, failure. . . ."

I love you so much. . . . I am too old and enmeshed
in everything you do and are, that I can not conceive
of life without you. . . . My going will leave quite a
rumor but you can say I was overworked and over-
wrought. Your reputation with your friends and fans
will not be harmed. . . . Sometimes, think of the fun we
had all thru the years. . . . ."[29]

Theodor Geisel was always fond of the mystical Seussian creatures which he created with such love and such abandon. And
he was fond of fanciful names and mythical organizations. Helen
Geisel signed her suicide note to Ted with the name of the law
firm he created (and said he employed): Grimalkin,
Drouberhannus, Knalbner and Fepp.

And I learned there are troubles of more than one kind.
Some come from ahead and some come from behind. . . .

Her obituary was run in the La Jolla/San Diego newspapers,
in all the major California newspapers and, indeed, throughout
the country, carried by the national wire services.

As he had done with the death of his sister, Marnie, Theodor
Geisel bore his wife Helen's death in stoic silence; her part of the
Dr. Seuss legacy was apportioned as she wished. The La Jolla
Museum's Art-Reference Library was renamed the Helen Palmer
Geisel Library; her share of some of the Dr. Seuss royalties went
to Dartmouth for the Helen and Ted Geisel Third Century Profes-
sorship and other royalties and income went into the nonprofit
Seuss Foundation. It was considerable.

Theodor Geisel was determined to stay in La Jolla, living as he
had—as they had—on their mountaintop, where he had the views
of the Pacific, La Jolla and San Diego, of much of California and
parts of Mexico. He could look down on the beaches and the ocean
surf, where he knew retired citizens of La Jolla had yachts in the
water; retirement was not for him—certainly not at this moment.

Ted Geisel carried the grief of Helen's passing into his work. And working on additional books was the center of his life. It *was* his life.

He worked on another project—*The Foot Book*: this would not be a Beginner Books, but rather the first of the Bright and Early Books, whose reading level would pre-date Beginner Books. Ted Geisel believed that there was no time too early to read to children. He even believed that children should be read to in the womb, a notion which many pediatricians accepted as legitimate.

The Foot Book looks remarkably simplistic; for Geisel, the work was hard, made manifestly harder still by Helen's death. Catching the right rhyme and illustrating it appropriately was real work, hard work. Theodor Geisel usually put in eight-hour days when he was at work on a book, ignoring the ocean view to concentrate on the words in his head.

> Left foot
> Left foot
>
> Right foot
> Right

And, as usual, the illustrations marched toward the right, so little ones could follow toward the next page;

> Front feet
> Back feet
> Red feet
> Black feet[30]

The Foot Book was published in 1968 and no one reading it then (or today) could have guessed the tragedy involved during the months prior to its publication. Following the relative failure of *Solla Sollew*, *The Foot Book* marches on; as of mid-1997, it is in its 52nd reprinting and Bright and Early Books have proved as successful as Beginner Books.

And, in the same year, Theo. LeSieg published *The Eye Book*, illustrated by Roy McKie. It carried much the same page-by-page work scheme as *The Foot Book*. It was also a Bright and Early Book.

And Theodor Geisel's life changed, for the better, as do many whose spouses die unexpectedly. Into his life came Audrey Dimond, a La Jolla friend, who had known both Ted and Helen Geisel. She had been married to Grey Dimond, a cardiologist. Judith and Neil Morgan, in their biography, *Dr. Seuss and Mr. Geisel*, reprint this remarkable exchange between Grey and Audrey Dimond:

> . . . Audrey had approached her husband, Grey, in the kitchen of their Ludington Lane house to say that she planned to marry Ted. She realized that "something was lacking" in their marriage; she considered Grey self-sufficient, she told him, "but Ted needs me." The cardiologist had stood silently for a moment as though he were thinking all this over.
>
> "Who," he said finally, "is going to do the driving?"
>
> "Why, I guess, I will," Audrey replied, astonished.
>
> "Good," he said, "I don't want any wife of mine marrying a man who drives the way Ted does."[31]

In June, 1968, Ted Geisel and Audrey Dimond moved to Reno, into the Ponderosa Hotel, for the Nevada-required six-week waiting period to get married.

Theodor Geisel and Audrey Dimond were married quietly in Reno August 5, 1968.

At the end of the year, Geisel found himself in a legal battle over decades old Dr. Seuss material. He learned that the Universal Publishing Co., in New York, had contracted to reprint Dr. Seuss material from *Liberty* magazine, from about 1932. He spent

$100,000 in legal fees; the case went to U.S. District Judge William B. Herland in New York in December, but he ruled that Geisel had sold the material to *Liberty* at $300. per page. *Liberty* had the legal right to re-sell the material to Universal Publishing Co. The book, *Dr. Seuss' Lost World Revisited: A Forward-Looking Backward Glance* was published, but few Seuss enthusiasts have ever seen it. It exists now only in some library special collection departments.[32] Geisel needn't have spent his $100,000 on legal fees. It did nothing to damage his reputation.

Geisel was frequently at odds with contributors who could not live up to his exact standards for Beginner Books. He was particularly frustrated with Mike Frith, who worked with him on *My Book About Me*, an ingenious fill-in-the-blank book, in which the little owner was encouraged to past her or his photo on the front cover of the book and write inside, weight, number of teeth, address, an outline of the child's hand, and foot and on and on. On the inside left front cover is a space for the child's name (and a typical Seussian retort):

> My Name is
>
> _____
>
> I don't care
> if you like
> my name or not.
> *That's* my name.
> It's the only
> name I've got.

Frith actually wanted to take a day off to watch Joe Namath and the New York Jets in Super Bowl III. Geisel was outraged that this heresy and carried his rage to Random House, where they all (including Robert Bernstein, who bore the brunt of his anger) were then astonished at *his* outrage.

So Geisel plotted. . . .

Carolyn See tells the story in "Dr. Seuss and the Naked Ladies," published in *Esquire*:

In March of 1968, a scant month after Philip Roth had published *Portnoy's Complaint*, Theodor Seuss Geisel, the celebrated "Dr. Seuss," creator of grinches and hippografs, foxes in socks and cats in hats, wrote a five-page outline for a dirty book. He sent it to Robert Bernstein, successor to Bennett Cerf, and Seuss's own editor at Random House. Bernstein blanched, it is to be supposed, made emergency phone calls and called emergency meetings, all to discuss this more than dangerous aberration to which one of their leading, and certainly most wholesome, writers had succumbed. Dr. Seuss stayed home, meanwhile, didn't answer the phone and laughed himself sick.

"I finally called Bernstein, after a week, and let him off the hook. He'd caught on by that time anyway."[33]

Interested fans often asked where he got his inspiration for the exotic locales and names in the Dr. Seuss books. Ted Geisel had been a world traveler with Helen Geisel. He and Helen had seen Europe and such areas as Peru, Turkey and the Yucatan region of Mexico; now he and Audrey traveled together. In the fall of 1969, they left California for Hawaii, then to Cambodia for visits to Angkor Watt, to India to see the Taj Mahal, to Tehran, to Jerusalem, where he was made an "Honorary Jew," by Teddy Kolleck, mayor of Jerusalem, then to Paris, then to London and then to New York, just in time for the release of *I Can Lick 30 Tigers Today! And Other Stories*.

(It seems logical, in retrospect, that Dr. Seuss obtained considerable inspiration for the strange locales and equally strange names he created, by visiting Peru, Turkey, the Yucatan, Angkor Watt, the Taj Mahal and on and on and on. These visits should almost be income-tax deductible expenses for Geisel, for the ideas, sketches and schemes he derived from seeing those exotic places. Other writers, not bankrolled by the very substantial royalties flowing from the Dr. Seuss sales, aren't quite lucky enough to travel so extensively.)

He next began *I Can Draw It Myself* , which he called "A revolt against coloring books," and *Mr. Brown Can Moo! Can You?*

In the past, Dr. Seuss had championed equality in *Horton Hears a Who!* and against Fascism/Nazism in "Yertle the Turtle" and against anti-semitism in "The Sneetches" (even though his child-readers may not understand the morals in "Yertle the Turtle" and "The Sneetches").

His pristine views from the top of Mount Soledad, he saw, were beginning to be spoiled by urban sprawl, apartments, condominiums, too much and too many, and that jolted him into action on a greater scale than *Mr. Brown Can Moo! Can You?*

But as much as he wanted to contribute something to what he saw as serious environmental damage, he didn't have a plot, characters or setting.

So he and Audrey decamped to Kenya, in September, 1970.

As typical tourists, they visited the common markets in Nairobi, then went to the Mt. Kenya Safari Club.

Years earlier, Dr. Seuss saw inspiration when a drawing of an elephant blew over a drawing of a tree. "What could an elephant be doing in a tree?" he asked and *Horton Hatches the Egg!* was born.

At the Mount Kenya Safari Club, Theodor Geisel was sitting and looking one afternoon, when a herd of elephants passed across the horizon, in front of the mountains.

Dr. Seuss was galvanized into furious work.

> I don't know what happened . . . I had nothing but a
> laundry list with me and I grabbed it . . . I wrote ninety
> percent of the book that afternoon. I got some kind of
> release watching those elephants

he later said.[34]

The book became one of his most controversial: *The Lorax*.

He took home photographs of the trees in the Serenghetti, which later became his silk-tufted Truffula trees.

He worked and worked on The Lorax, who "speaks for the trees." Eventually, The Lorax was short, old, brown and had a yellow bushy beard.

(To me, he looks like an animal cousin of Old Sneelock, in *If I Ran the Circus. . . .*)

> What was the Lorax?
> And why was it there?
> And why was it lifted and taken somewhere
> from the far end of town where the Grickle-grass grows?
> The old Once-ler still lives here.
> Ask him. *He* knows.

> You won't see the Once-ler.
> Don't knock at his door.

The Lorax begins at night, with dark shades of blues, greens, taupes—and the Once-ler is never completely seen—only his eyes, green arms and green hands.

Like the Ancient Mariner, the Once-ler tells *his* ancient story— but only after you pay him: The Once-ler's story is one of greed, pure and simple. The Truffula Trees had all been cut down for garments called Thneeds.

A Thneed was an all-purpose garment which everybody could wear and everybody could need. But a Lorax popped out of the cut stump and warned against spoiling the forests.

The Once-ler built a whole factory and cut down all the Truffula Trees, to make Thneeds, which everyone needs.

The Lorax warned about losing all the forests.

Children who are too young to understand equality, and surely too young to understand the perils of Fascism and Nazism and 'way too young to understand why some Sneetches wear stars and some have no stars . . . these readers could surely see the poor Brown Barba-loots which looked like Seussian brown bears, waving sadly, as they walked away from their ruined forest.

And we can almost hear some little girl or boy, talking to the pictures: *Goodbye, Bar-ba-loots, Goodbye.* . . .

But the Once-ler's factory worked overtime, making Thneeds which everyone needs and the sky became grey and the Swomee-Swans can no longer sing for the smog in their throats.

And there was pollution in the ponds, too.

And then the Once-ler cut down the very last Truffula Tree.

And the Lorax left, uttering one word: *Unless.*[35]

> The master of nonsense turning his deft pen to such serious subjects as ecological disaster? Nonsense. Yet Dr. Seuss' (book) happens to be very good indeed (though not really vintage Seussiana),

said *The Christian Science Monitor.*[36]

And *Library Journal* wrote,

> The big colorful pictures in Dr. Seuss's typically lively, cartoonish style, and the fun images, word plays and rhymes make this an amusing, if unsubtle, exposition of the ecology crisis.[37]

The Lorax would always be considered his most controversial book.[38]

Seven

1971–1991

Oh, the places you'll go . . .

Before *The Lorax* was published, Ted Geisel had met Liz Carpenter, Secretary to Ladybird Johnson, and during a pleasant conversation, he told her about *The Lorax*. She suggested because of the environmental nature of the book, it would surely help Ladybird Johnson's campaign in cleaning up the environment. Would Geisel consider contributing the manuscript to the Lyndon Johnson Presidential Library in Austin, Texas? So Geisel called Lyndon Johnson at the LBJ Ranch in the Hill Country of Texas. Would the President like to have the manuscript and art for *The Lorax*? The President would indeed, so the Geisels journeyed to Austin to present *The Lorax* materials to the LBJ Library personally.

That was a plus.

Just several years later, Dr. Seuss helped bring down a president.

He had completed a Bright and Early book, *Marvin K. Mooney, Will You Please Go Now!*, in 1972, about a rascal of a kid who wouldn't go home. Dr. Seuss wrote:

The
time
has come.

The time has come.
The time is now.
Just go.
Go.
GO![1]

But Marvin K. Mooney won't leave.

Ted Geisel had previously met Art Buchwald and they had become good friends. When Buchwald published *I Never Danced at the White House*, he sent Geisel a copy and dared Geisel to write a political book.

Theodor Geisel did it faster than Buckwald ever expected.

It was then July, 1974, and the Watergate investigation was juggernauting toward its inevitable conclusion. Theodor Geisel took a copy of *Marvin K. Mooney . . .*

And revised throughout the book:

The time has come.
The time has come.
The time is now.

Just go.
Go.
GO! I don't care how.

You can go by foot.
You can go by cow.
Richard M. Nixon,
will you please go now!

. . . and sent the book to Art Buchwald. Geisel told Random House what he had done with one copy of *Marvin K. Mooney . . .* and "they went nuts," in his words. But he gave Buchwald permission to use it.

Buchwald ran the book, with Dr. Seuss's revisions, in his nationwide column.

And nine days later . . .

> The time had come.
> SO . . .
> Nixon WENT.[2]

Buchwald claimed the credit and Dr. Seuss was a willing accomplice.

Also in 1972, *The Lorax* was made into a cartoon, like *How The Grinch Stole Christmas! The Lorax* was narrated by actor Eddie Albert and it too, was a success.

For 13 years following the publication of *The Lorax*, in 1971, Theodor Geisel worked on an annual release of one or more Beginner Books or Bright and Early books. (Those he published under the pseudonym Theo. LeSieg were books which were smaller in format than the Dr. Seuss books—for either of the two series—and the LeSieg books were written by Geisel but illustrated by Seuss and others.) They were:

* *In A People House*, 1972;
* *Marvin K. Mooney, Will You Please Go Now!*, 1972;
* *The Many Mice of Mr. Brice*, 1973;
* *Did I Ever Tell You How Lucky You Are?*, 1973;
* *The Shape of Me and Other Stuff*, 1973;
* *Great Day for Up!*, 1974;
* *There's a Wocket in My Pocket!*, 1974 in which he writes:

> Did you
> ever have the feeling
> there's a
> WASKET
> in your
> BASKET?

... Or a NUREAU
in your BUREAU?[3]

Here was Theodor Geisel again being subversive; teaching children sounds with nonsense stories . . .

* *Wacky Wednesday,* 1974;
* *Because a Little Bug Went Ka-Choo!,* 1974, and for that book he worked closely with Michael Firth. Because they worked so closely together, the book was hardly just a Theo. LeSieg book. Audrey Geisel walked into the studio during a time when they were thinking of a pseudonym; Firth suggest that they name it after her. Geisel said her maiden name was Stone; instantly the pseudonym became Rosetta Stone.
* *Oh, the Thinks You Can Think!,* 1974;
* *Would You Rather Be a Bullfrog?,* 1975;
* *Hooper Humperdink. . . ? Not Him!,* 1975;
* *The Cat's Quizzer,* 1976;
* *Try to Remember the First of Octomber,* 1977;
* *I Can Read With My Eyes Shut!,* 1978;
* *Oh Say Can You Say?,* 1979;
* *Maybe You Should Fly a Jet! Maybe You Should Be a Vet!,* 1980;
* *The Tooth Book,* 1981;
* *Hunches in Bunches,* 1982.

His readers would never know that, in the mid-1970s, Dr. Seuss and Theo. LeSieg were getting older. Ted Geisel discovered one morning in 1975 that he couldn't see. Momentarily panicking, he called Audrey, who in turned called in an eye specialist. She feared cataracts; the specialists diagnosed cataracts *and* glaucoma. For five years, Geisel endured operations for both cataracts and glaucoma. Some days he could see with his left eye perfectly but his right eye was still damaged. He compensated by making his storyboards larger than normal; when they were shipped to Random House, they were reduced to regular page size.

Surely, his eye problems contributed to the 1978 book, *I Can Read With My Eyes Shut!* although again, young readers couldn't have realized that either. It took five years for the eye problems to be resolved and his sight restored.

In June of 1977, Theodor Geisel was awarded an honorary degree at Lake Forest College, near Chicago. His commencement address took less than two minutes to read; and in an age when 98 and 3/4ths percent of all commencement addresses are forgettable as soon as the graduates and happy parents have left the coliseum, no one could forget this bit of wisdom from Dr. Seuss:

My Uncle Terwilliger on the Art of Eating Popovers

My uncle ordered popovers
from the restaurant's bill of fare.
And when they were served,
he regarded them
with a penetrating stare . . .
Then he spoke great Words of Wisdom
as he sat there on that chair:
"To eat these things,"
said my uncle,
"You must exercise great care.
You may swallow down what's solid . . .
BUT . . .
you *must* spit out the air!"

And . . .
as *you* partake of the world's bill of fare,
that's darn good advise to follow.
Do a lot of spitting out the hot air.
And be careful what you swallow.

*   *   *

Age again crept closer to Dr. Seuss and to Ted Geisel. Although his eye problems had been cleared up, in 1981, he suffered from "indigestion" one day then again the next day and then Audrey took him to the hospital where the diagnosis was that he had suffered a heart attack; relatively small, but a heart attack nonetheless.[5] He had been a chain-smoker but reluctantly gave it up—he found a pipe that he hadn't used for years— decades earlier, really—and filled it with radish seeds. Occasionally, when he was thinking Big Thinks, he would water the pipe with an eyedropper. And when he had forgotten what was in his pipe, radish greens grew out of the bowl.

Age continued to creep closer.

During a dental exam, a lesion was discovered at the base of his tongue; cancerous and potentially very dangerous, Geisel submitted to a procedure that placed an implant under his tongue to neutralize the cancer.

Out of the hospital, Geisel marveled at the Reagan administration's vision of a potential nuclear war with Russia. And then he remembered—or seemed to recall from his European days years earlier, the Guelphs and the Ghibellines of the north of Italy, who fought a war because one side favored the Pope and the other side was anti-Pope. Or, rather, Dr. Seuss remembered them because one side cut their apples vertically and the other side cut their apples horizontally. That was Seussian history, as he recalled it.

Thus was born his second-most-controversial book, *The Butter Battle Book*, Dr. Seuss's statement on the futility of war: about the competing tribes, the Zooks and the Yooks.

And, of course, the Zooks watched the Yooks, and one of the Zooks fired a slingshot at a Yook . . . who got together with a council of Yooks, and made a monstrous triple-threat slingshot . . . and the Zooks replied with a triple-threat slingshot catcher . . . and then the Yooks . . ."carefully trained a real smart dog named Daniel to serve as our country's first gun-toting spaniel."[6]

But the other side invented an Eight-Nozzled, Elephant-Toted Boom-Blitz . . . and . . . a Big Boy Boomeroo . . . of a weapon.

Both sides eventually had bands, and cheerleaders and uniforms and flying machines and bombs . . . for war.

And Dr. Seuss leaves the conclusion hanging on edge:

> "Grandpa," I shouted, "Be careful! Oh, gee!
> Who's going to drop it?
> Will *you*. . . ? Or will *he*. . . ?
> "Be patient," said Grandpa, "We'll see.
> We will see . . ."[7]

When he took the book to Random House, he said "I have no idea if this is an adult book for children or a children's book for adults . . ." and said he always wanted to write a "lady and the tiger" ending.[8]

He and Random House people went 'round and 'round, like the Gingham Dog and the Calico Cat, about the title and the cover and the ending and the message . . . were children old enough to understand war for seemingly trivial principles?

Janet Schulman, editor in chief, sent proofs to children's author Maurice Sendak, who returned the definitive blurb about *The Butter Battle Book*:

> Surprisingly, wonderfully, the case for total disarmament has been brilliantly made by our acknowledged master of nonsense, Dr. Seuss . . . Only a genius of the ridiculous could possibly deal with the cosmic and lethal madness of the nuclear arms race . . . He has done the world a service.[9]

The message was not used on the cover, but it was enough. *The Butter Battle Book* went to press with the cover as Dr. Seuss drew it and with the message that Dr. Seuss had intended.

The Big Boy Boomeroo of age inched closer. In December,

1983, Theodor Geisel had an operation and a deep biopsy of the area of his neck where the lesion was first spotted. His neck was disfigured, but the operation was a necessity to stop any further spread of cancer.

But, as Random House people first thought, *The Butter Battle Book* was received critically with strong reservations:

> The language of the story rhymes and amuses in customary Seuss fashion, and the colorful cartoon drawings are zesty and humorous. Seuss is in a category of his own in both originality and popularity, and the demand for this book will undoubtedly be large. One wonders, however, if a book for young children is a suitable vehicle for such an accurate and uncloaked description of the current stalemate in nuclear arms disarmament. . . . This story ends without the slightest glimmer of hope that a solution to the standoff will be found, and as such can only contribute to a child's sense of helplessness. On this issue, perhaps above all others, it is critical to communicate to children the possibility of finding solutions beyond those immediately visible.
>
> —Anne L. Okie, *School Library Journal*[10]

> "(This) is probably the most thinly veiled allegory Geisel has written. It's not a funny book. Clearly, he feels seriously about the arms race. . . . To some persons, "The Butter Battle Book" may not seem like ideal children's fare. The book depends heavily on the implicit urgency of the arms control issue. We all know it is important (so the argument goes) and therefore our children should know about it. But should they? What Geisel rather disparagingly calls "a happy ending" may in fact be the ray of hope that children need when learning about adult troubles. It is not fashionable to be optimistic about the nuclear arms race. But, if the future of the world rests

with children, shouldn't they learn that, in addition to
seeing evil, mankind is capable of averting it as well?
—Gloria Goodale, *The Christian Science Monitor*[11]

The world survived the nuclear arms race, children everywhere survived Dr. Seuss's moralizing and *The Butter Battle Book* is still in print.

When the book was released, Random House officials, including Donald and Samuel Newhouse (Random House was now owned by the Newhouse family, through their Advance Publications Company), took him to luncheon at New York's "21" club. It was fifty years since Bennett Cerf took him to lunch and took him into the Random House family from Vanguard Press. Bennett Cerf had since died, but Dr. Seuss and Random House continued on. . . .

Dr. Seuss was pleased that right after *The Butter Battle Book* was shown on television in the Soviet Union on New Years Day of 1990, the U.S.S.R. began to fall apart. Since he and Art Buchwald caused the downfall of the Nixon administration with "Richard M. Nixon, will you please go now!" it was only right that Dr. Seuss by himself caused the downfall of the giant Potemkin village that was the Soviet Empire.

And then Dr. Seuss won the Pulitzer Prize. Ted Geisel was astonished. The Pulitzer was "usually given to adults. I'm a writer who had to eat with the children before the adults eat," he said.[13]

Clearly now he was at the head of the table; at about that time, Dr. Seuss books were being published in over 20 languages and the baby-boom generation guaranteed sales that multiplied phenomenally, book after book, year after year.

Audrey tricked him into going to Princeton University in the spring of 1985; he discovered that Princeton would be awarding him an honorary doctorate. When he got up to walk to receive his diploma, in a move that can't be imagined for any other writer, the entire graduating class rose, chanted the full book-length text of *Green Eggs and Ham*.[14]

Back in La Jolla, Geisel considered all his recent illness, operations, for his eyes, which resulted in *I Can Read With My Eyes Shut!* and his recent operation for the cancer in his throat. He retold his latest encounters with doctors and hospitals in another book and that, perhaps more than any therapy or treatment was good for him. For the first time since *The Seven Lady Godivas*, he was not writing a book for children. Ted Geisel had always said, "adults are only obsolete children and to hell with 'em." On the front cover is the subtitle:

A Book for Obsolete Children

The book was *You're Only Old Once!*:

> Just why are you here?
> Not feeling your best . . .
>
> You've come in for
> An Eyesight and Solvency Test.

And here Dr. Seuss shows a progressively larger eye chart which reads:

He is battered by every test imaginable, for every specialty known to science.

Ultimately, after all the testing and poking and prodding (and billing), the best doctor of all, Dr. Seuss, offers a positive diagnosis:

> you're in pretty good shape
> for the shape you are in![16]

And indeed, he was in pretty good shape for the shape he was in: the book was written and published when he was 82. Random House publishing panjandrums had worried that the book would not sell—it clearly wasn't a book for the usual audience for Dr. Seuss books: children. And would adults buy it? Adults really didn't read Dr. Seuss books, unless the Seuss books were thrust at them by small hands to be read at bedtime.

Dr. Seuss was righter than right. As usual. The first printing of 200,000 copies sold out and the book had to go back to press. Early Dr. Seuss children had, by now, become adults (and had children of and perhaps grandchildren of their own). So the "obsolete children" bought this book for themselves and savored the pictures they saw in the book—of themselves getting older.

The book sold and sold. It hit the number one spot on *The New York Times* best-seller list; after five months it had sold 600,000 copies and by the end of the first year had sold one million copies and was in its ninth printing.[17]

Dr. Seuss was much more than a best-selling author; he was a cultural icon. A retrospective collection of his work was displayed in the San Diego Museum and drew huge crowds, although the art critic of the *San Diego Union* panned it as not a collection about *art*. That shows toured the country, stopping at various museums: the Carnegie Museum of Art in Pittsburgh; the Baltimore Museum of Art; the New Orleans Museum of Art and the Queens Museum of Art in New York.

He and Helen toured his hometown of Springfield, Massachusetts, some twenty years after the death of Geisel's father.

They walked along Mulberry Street and the Mayor gave him a metal outdoor sign, *Geisel Grove*, found in the park that Geisel's father had so carefully nurtured. Later on Mulberry Street, sightseeing in an antique bus, Geisel was startled to see two hundred school children appear, holding a huge sign:

AND TO THINK THAT I SAW HIM ON MULBERRY STREET!

Geisel was speechless with tears.[18] And although the situations changed from locale to locale, that spirit was how he was received anywhere he made a public appearance.

But the Big Boomeroo of age and health was still closing in. By 1985 he had weakened. The cancer in his throat had been halted, but the by-product of the cancer treatments was an infection in his jaw, impossible to eradicate. And he was increasingly infirm, with bouts of gout and loss of hearing typical of advancing age, and more and more turned down invitations for social events, especially outside La Jolla.

Projects didn't jell; there was no Horton blown onto an elephant as an idea to seize on. He began books, abandoned them—the outside world saw him as an exalted figure; in his studio, nothing seemed to work.

Except . . . the cynical dictum from his Dartmouth years:

Oh, the places you'll go . . .

That worked: the cynical phrase from his callow college days was the key to another Dr. Seuss book. How graduation, from either high school or college is a pretty scary thing. Stepping into the dark, walking who-knows-where . . . taking tentative steps into the dark of a big world:

Congratulations!
Today is your day.

You're off to Great Places
You're off and away!

You have brains in your head.
You have feet in your shoes.
You can steer yourself
any direction you choose . . . [19]

You're on your own, and you know what you know.
And *YOU* are the guy who'll decide where to go.

It was Dr. Seuss's last book; when he was working on it, he seemed to know that, and so did those around him.

He knew his audience, just like he had known the audience for *You're Only Old Once! Oh, The Places You'll Go!* hit the top of *The New York Times* best-seller lists and stayed there for more than two years. During that time, it sold one and one-half million copies![20]

But while waiting for *The Places You'll Go!* to appear, Audrey Geisel felt herself sinking, sinking into some vague illness, something that she thought might be Alzheimer's. She finally got a diagnosis and discovered that a tumor was pushing against her brain. An operation was successful and she was on her way again.

He read an essay in *The New York Review of Books*, by novelist Alison Lurie, which charged him with sexism. All the main characters in his books, were little boys, she claimed. Geisel believed that most of the characters in his books were animals and "if she could identify their sex, I'll remember her in my will," but in *Daisy-Head Mayzie*, published posthumously, for the first time in a Seuss book, the hero is a little girl.

Slowly, bit by bit, Dr. Seuss put his work away; there was no agony, no pain. He began sleeping on a sofa in his studio. Once, when Audrey awakened him, he asked, plaintively, "am I dead yet?"[23]

In the evening of September 24, 1991, Dr. Seuss died peacefully in his sleep, in his mountaintop studio in La Jolla.

Years earlier, Helen Geisel had to undergo a sudden, traumatic (and unexplained) operation. He never had any children of his own. But in fact, the children of the country and the whole world were his.

He loved them and they loved him.

And they love him still.

Epilogue

" . . . to a unique and hallowed place in the nurseries of the world . . ."

All of the Random House Dr. Seuss books, except for *The Seven Lady Godivas* and *The Cat in the Hat Songbook* remain in print and, following his death, there have also been additional Dr. Seuss books published.

Daisy-Head Mayzie was published in 1995 as was *The Secret Art of Dr. Seuss*, abstract paintings with fanciful names, which were art works unrelated to any of his books. *My Many Colored Days*, with illustrations by Steve Johnson and Lou Fancher and an anthology, *A Hatful of Seuss*, containing *If I Ran the Zoo; The Sneetches and Other Stories; Horton Hears a Who!; Dr. Seuss's Sleep Book* and *Bartholomew and the Oobleck* were also published in 1996.

Seuss-isms: Wise and Witty Prescriptions for Living from the Good Doctor, a "stocking-stuffer"-sized book of aphorisms was published in 1997.

Horray for Diffendoofer Day has been published in 1998; it was based on notes Geisel left uncompleted in his study during his lifetime; it was eventually written by Jack Prelutsky and the art was supplied by Lane Smith.

There is now a "second generation" of Seuss material. His widow and literary agents have licensed the Dr. Seuss name to the Jim Henson Studios and they have created *The Wubbulous World of Dr. Seuss*, a television cartoon series for children. And that television series has resulted in spin-off books also published by Random House.

Theodor Geisel by himself, created a revolution in children's books. He single-handedly eliminated the "See Dick, See Jane, See Spot," readers from millions of classrooms and libraries—simplistic books which had bored children for decades.

His books challenged children to use their imaginations; he took them to imaginary locales aboard fantastical animals and taught them lessons about equality, the environment, duty ("I meant what I said and I said what I meant, an elephant's faithful, one hundred percent . . .") and the true value of Christmas . . .

In the words of a young boy, referring to Seuss, "you have an imagination with a long tail . . ."

By the 1970s he had become an icon. In 1999, the Postal Service issued a Cat in the Hat U.S. stamp.

Interviewed by Hilliard Harper in *The Los Angeles Times Magazine* in 1986,[1] Geisel said,

> I think I had something to do with kicking Dick and Jane out of the school system. I think I proved to a number of million kids that reading is not a disagreeable task. And without talking about teaching, I think I have helped kids laugh in schools as well as home. That's about enough, isn't it?

After his death, *Time* magazine headlined his obituary "The Doctor Beloved By All"[2]:

> He was one of the last doctors to make house calls— some 200 million of them in 20 languages. By the time of his death last week at 87, Dr. Seuss had journeyed on beyond Dr. Spock to a unique and hallowed place in the nurseries of the world.

Bibliography

Books by Theodor "Dr. Seuss" Geisel

1937: *And To Think That I Saw It on Mulberry Street.* New York: The Vanguard Press.

1938: *The 500 Hats of Bartholomew Cubbins.* New York: The Vanguard Press.

1939: *The Seven Lady Godivas.* New York: Random House.

1940: *Horton Hatches the Egg.* New York: Random House.

1947: *McElligot's Pool.* New York: Random House.

1948: *Thidwick the Big-Hearted Moose.* New York: Random House.

1949: *Bartholomew and the Oobleck.* New York: Random House.

1950: *If I Ran the Zoo.* New York: Random House.

1953: *Scrambled Eggs Super!* New York: Random House.

1954: *Horton Hears a Who!* New York: Random House.

1955: *On Beyond Zebra!* New York: Random House.

1956: *If I Ran the Circus.* New York: Random House.

1957: *How the Grinch Stole Christmas!* New York: Random House.

1957: *The Cat in the Hat.* New York: Random House.

1958: *The Cat in the Hat Comes Back.* New York: Random House.

1958: *Yertle the Turtle and Other Stories.* New York: Random House.

1959: *Happy Birthday to You!* New York: Random House.

1960: *Green Eggs and Ham.* New York: Random House.
1960: *One Fish Two Fish Red Fish Blue Fish.* New York: Random House.
1961: *The Sneetches and Other Stories.* New York: Random House.
1961: *Ten Apples Up on Top.* (Theo LeSieg, pseudonym). New York: Random House.
1962: *Dr. Seuss's Sleep Book.* New York: Random House.
1963: *Hop on Pop.* New York: Random House.
1963: *Dr. Seuss's ABC.* New York: Random House.
1965: *Fox in Sox.* New York: Random House.
1965: *I Had Trouble Getting to Solla Sollew.* New York: Random House.
1965: *I Wish I Had Duck Feet.* (Theo. LeSieg, pseudonym.) New York: Random House.
1966: *Come Over to My House.* (Theo., LeSieg, pseudonym.) New York: Random House.
1967: *The Cat in the Hat Song Book.* New York: Random House.
1968: *The Foot Book.* New York: Random House.
1968: *The Eye Book.* (Theo, LeSieg, pseudonym.) New York: Random House.
1968: *Dr. Seuss' Lost World Revisited: A Forward-Looking Backward Glance.* New York: Universal Publishing Co.
1969: *I Can Lick 50 Tigers Today! and Other Stories.* New York: Random House.
1969: *My Book About Me—By Me, Myself, I Wrote It! I Drew It!* New York: Random House.
1970: *I Can Draw It Myself.* New York: Random House.
1970: *Mr. Brown Can Moo! Can You?* New York: Random House.
1971: *I Can Write—by Me, Myself* (Theo. Leseig, pseudonym.) New York: Random House.
1971: *The Lorax.* New York: Random House.
1972: *In a People House.* (Theo. LeSieg, pseudonym.) New York: Random House.
1972: *Marvin K. Mooney, Will You Please Go Now!* New York: Random House.

1973: *The Many Mice of Mr. Bice.* (Theo. LeSieg, pseudonym.) New York: Random House.

1973: *Did I Ever Tell You How Lucky You Are?* New York: Random House.

1973: *The Shape of Me and Other Stuff.* New York: Random House.

1974: *Great Day for Up!* New York: Random House.

1974: *There's a Wocket in My Pocket!* New York: Random House.

1974: *Wacky Wednesday.* (Theo. LeSieg, pseudonym.) New York: Random House.

1975: *Because a Little Bug Went Ka-Choo!* (Rosetta Stone, pseudonym.) New York: Random House.

1975: *Oh, The Thinks You Can Think!* New York: Random House.

1975: *Would You Rather be a Bullfrog?* (Theo. LeSieg, pseudonym.) New York: Random House.

1976: *Hooper Humperdink. . . ? Not Him!* (Theo. LeSieg, pseudonym.) New York: Random House.

1976: *The Cat's Quizzer.* New York: Random House.

1977: *Try to Remember the First of Octember.* (Theo. LeSieg, pseudonym.) New York: Random House.

1978: *I Can Read with My Eyes Shut!* New York: Random House.

1979: *Oh Say Can You Say?* New York: Random House.

1980: *Maybe You Should Fly a Jet! Maybe You Should be a Vet!* (Theo. LeSieg, pseudonym.) New York: Random House.

1981: *The Tooth Book.* (Theo. LeSieg, pseudonym.) New York: Random House.

1982: *Hunches in Bunches.* New York: Random House.

1984: *The Butter Battle Book.* New York: Random House.

1986: *You're Only Young Once!* New York: Random House.

1987: *I'm Not Going to Get Up Today!* New York: Random House.

1990: *Oh! The Places You'll Go.* New York: Random House.

1991: *Six by Seuss: A Treasury of Dr. Seuss Classics.* New York: Random House.

1995: *Daisy-Head Mayzie.* New York: Random House.

1995: *The Secret Art of Dr. Seuss.* New York: Random House.

1996: *My Many-Colored Days.* New York: Alfred Knopf.
1996: *A Hatfull of Seuss.* New York: Random House.
1997: *Seuss-isms: Wise and Witty Prescriptions for Living from the Good Doctor.* New York: Random House.
1998: *Hooray for Diffendoofer Day.* New York: Random House.
1999: *Dr. Seuss Goes to War: The World War II Editorial Cartoons of Theodore Seuss Geisel.* New York: The Free Press.

Secondary Sources

Cerf, Bennett. *At Random: The Reminiscences of Bennett Cerf.* New York: Random House, 1977.

Cott, Jonathan. *Pipers at the Gate of Dawn: The Wisdom of Children's Literature.* New York: Random House, 1983.

Dr. Seuss From Then to Now. New York: Random House, 1986.

Fensch, Thomas, ed. *Of Sneetches and Whos and the Good Doctor Seuss: Essays on the Writings and Life of Theodor Geisel.* Jefferson, N.C.: McFarland & Co., 1997.

Hulbert, Dan. "SEUSS-travaganza." *Houston* (Tx.) *Chronicle*, Aug. 3, 2000, pp. D 1, D 4.

Lanes, Selma G. *Down the Rabbit Hole: Adventures and Misadventures in the Realm of Children's Literature.* New York: Atheneum, 1971.

MacDonald, Ruth K. *Dr. Seuss.* New York: Wayne Publishers, 1988.

Marschall, Richard, ed. *The Tough Coughs as He Plows the Dough: Early Writings and Cartoons by Dr. Seuss.* New York: William Morrow, 1987.

Minear, Richard H., ed. *Dr. Seuss Goes to War: The World War II Editorial Cartoons of Theodor Seuss Geisel.* New York: The Free Press, 1999.

Morgan, Judith and Morgan, Neil. *Dr. Seuss and Mr. Geisel.* New York: Random House, 1995.

Notes

Prologue

1) Wilder, Rob. "Catching Up With Dr. Seuss," *Parents* magazine, June, 1978, pp. 63.
2) Morgan, Judith and Morgan, Neil, *Dr. Seuss and Mr. Geisel*, pp. 6.
3) Ibid., pp. 18–19.
4) Ibid., pp. 34.

One

1) Morgan and Morgan, p. 3.
2) Ibid., pp. 5.
3) Ibid., pp. 6.
4) Ibid., pp. 6
5) Ibid., pp. 6–7.
6) Ibid., pp. 7. The pie poem was one of his earliest memories, but as far as is known, he never used it in any of his books.
7) Ibid., pp. 7.
8) Ibid., pp. 9.
9) Ibid., pp. 11–12.
10) Ibid., pp. 12
11) Ibid., pp. 13
12) Quoted in Morgan and Morgan, pp. 21.
13) Ibid., pp. 21–22.

14) Ibid., pp. 23
15) Edward Connery Lathem, "The Beginnings of Dr. Seuss: A Conversation with Theodor Geisel," *Dartmouth Alumni Magazine*, April, 1976.
16) Ibid.
17) *Hillaire Belloc's Cautionary Tales.* (Reprint ed. Gregg Press, div. of G. K. Hall & Co., Boston, 1979). No pagination.
18) Ibid., pp. 17–24.
19) Morgan and Morgan, pp. 25.
20) Martin Gardner. *The Annotated Alice.* (New York: Clarkson N. Potter Co., 1960). pp. 69–70.
21) Introduction, *Hillaire Belloc's Cautionary Tales*, no pagination.
22) Morgan and Morgan, pp. 28.
23) Ibid., pp. 30.
24) Ibid., pp. 28.
25) Lathem.
26) Morgan and Morgan, pp. 32.
27) Lathem.
28) Lathem.
29) Morgan and Morgan, pp. 33.
30) Ibid., pp. 34.
31) Ibid., pp. 35–36.
32) Ibid., pp. 36.
33) Lathem.
34) Morgan and Morgan, pp. 37.
35) Ibid., pp. 38.
36) Ibid., pp. 41.
37) Ibid., pp. 42.
38) Ibid., pp. 44–45.
39) Lathem.
40) Morgan and Morgan, pp. 45.
41) Lathem.
42) Lathem.
43) Morgan and Morgan, pp. 50.

44) Ibid., pp. 52.
45) Lathem.
46) Morgan and Morgan, pp. 54.
47) Mary Stofflet, in *Dr. Seuss from Then to Now*, pp. 21.
48) Lathem.
49) Morgan and Morgan, pp. 58.
50) Ibid., pp. 58. Boni and Liveright was a book publisher; Bennett Cerf would buy The Modern Library from Horace Liveright to establish Random House. *Judge*, the humor magazine would not long survive.
51) *Life* magazine, the humor magazine. Henry Luce would buy *Life*, kill it in its original form and use just the name for a new magazine he was developing—a picture magazine which his wife, Claire Booth Luce had, in part, suggested.
52) But like a man who wears both a belt and suspenders, under Seuss, the *Post* editors ran: "Drawn by Theodor Seuss Geisel." Morgan and Morgan, pp. 59.

Two

1) Morgan and Morgan, pp. 60–61.
2) Reprinted in Richard Marschall, *The Thought Coughs as he Ploughs the Dough: Early Writings and Cartoons by Dr. Seuss*, pp. 10.
3) Mary Stofflet, in *Dr. Seuss from Then to Now*, pp. 23.
4) Morgan and Morgan, pp. 62–63.
5) Lathem.
6) Morgan and Morgan, pp. 63.
7) Lathem.
8) Morgan and Morgan, pp. 65.
9) Lathem.
10) Lathem.
11) In Marschall, pp. 11.
12) Reprinted in Marschall, pp. 57.
13) Lathem.

14) Morgan and Morgan, pp. 71–72.

15) Ibid., pp. 72.

16) Stofflet, in *Dr. Seuss from Then to Now*, pp. 24–25.

17) Morgan and Morgan, pp. 74–75.

18) Jonathan Cott, *Pipers at the Gates of Dawn: The Wisdom of Children's Literature*, pp. 17.

19) Lathem.

20) *Dr. Seuss From Then to Now*, pp. 23.

21) Bob Warren, *The Dartmouth*, May 10, 1935, reprinted in Morgan and Morgan, pp. 76.

22) Morgan and Morgan, pp. 79.

23) The Moth-Watching Sneth and the Grickily Gractus are from *Scrambled Eggs Super!*—TF.

24) *The Horn Book* magazine, Sept. 1992.

25) Lathem.

26) Morgan and Morgan, pp. 80.

27) Ibid., pp. 82.

28) Selma G. Lanes, *Down the Rabbit Hole: Adventures* and *Misadventures in the Realm of Children's Literature*, pp. 79–80.

29) Cott, pp. 28.

30) Morgan and Morgan, pp. 83.

31) *The New Yorker*, pp. XXX.

32) *The New York Times*, Nov. 14, 1937.

33) *The Atlantic Monthly*, Nov., 1937.

34) Morgan and Morgan, pp. 84.

35) Peter Bunzel, "The Wacky World of Dr. Seuss," *Life*, April 5, 1959; also cited in Morgan and Morgan, pp. 85.

36) Morgan and Morgan, pp. 85.

37) Ibid.

38) *Dartmouth Alumni Magazine*, Jan. 1939, reprinted in Morgan and Morgan, pp. 88.

39) Bennett Cerf. *At Random.* (New York: Random House, 1977), pp. 27–57.

40) Ibid., pp. 65.

41) Ibid., pp. 93.

42) Ibid., pp. 105.
43) Ibid., pp. 153.
44) Stofflet, in *Dr. Seuss from Then to Now*, pp. 31.
45) Cerf, pp. 154.
46) In *Dr. Seuss from Then to Now*, pp. 27.
47) Lanes, pp. 88.
48) Like his purchase of the firm Smith and Hass, which enlarged Random House, Bennett Cerf eventually bought The Vanguard Press at least in part, to bring the first two Dr. Seuss books into Random House . . .

Three

1) Reprinted in Morgan and Morgan, pp. 96.
2) *The King's Stilts*, no pagination.
3) Ibid.
4) Cerf. *At Random*, pp. 153.
5) Morgan and Morgan, pp. 96.
6) Geisel, reprinted in Morgan and Morgan, pp. 97. Miller, Haas, Klopfer and Commins were all executives at Random House.
7) Ibid., pp. 97–98.
8) Dr. Seuss, *Horton Hatches the Egg!*, no pagination.
9) *The New York Times*, Oct. 13, 1940, pp. 10.
10) In Morgan and Morgan, pp. 103.
11) Ibid., pp. 104.
12) Ibid., pp. 101–102.
13) Helen Geisel, quoted in Morgan and Morgan, pp. 105.
14) In Morgan and Morgan, pp. 107.
15) Reprinted in Morgan and Morgan, pp. 111.
16) E.J. Kahn, Jr., "Children's Friend," *The New Yorker*, Dec. 17, 1960.
17) Morgan and Morgan, pp. 119–120.
18) Ibid., pp. 121.
19) Morgan and Morgan, pp. 121.
20) Oct. 18, 1947.

21) Oct. 1, 1947.
22) Nov. 15, 1947.
23) *Thidwick, The Big-Hearted Moose*, 1948, no pagination.
24) Nov. 14, 1948.
25) Oct. 10, 1948, pp. 25
26) Nov. 14, 1948, pp. 12.
27) Oct. 16, 1948.
28) Dempsey, *The New York Times*, May 11, 1958.
29) Theodor Geisel, quoted in *The Raleigh* (N.C.) *Times*, Jan. 6, 1951.
30) Geisel's Utah lecture notes, reprinted in Morgan and Morgan, pp. 123–124. Travers was, of course, the author of *Mary Poppins* and other books.
31) Geisel lecture notes, reprinted in Morgan and Morgan, pp. 124.
32) Louise Bonino to Theodor Geisel, Sept. 29, 1949, reprinted in Morgan and Morgan, pp. 124. Saxe Commins was an editor at Random House.

Four

1) Morgan and Morgan, pp. 128–129.
2) Sept. 1950, 26:354.
3) Nov. 12, 1950, pp. 8.
4) Nov. 11, 1950, pp. 33.
5) Nov. 19, 1950, pp. 42.
6) In Morgan and Morgan, pp. 134–135.
7) Donald Spoto. *Stanley Kramer, Film Maker.* (New York: G.P. Putnam's Sons, 1979), pp. 149.
8) Morgan and Morgan, pp. 135.
9) *Scrambled Eggs Super!*, no pagination.
10) March 29, 1953, pp. 14.
11) May 17, 1953, pp. 10.
12) Sept. 1953.
13) *Life*, March 29, 1954.
14) Morgan and Morgan, pp. 137.

15) The *Movies Unlimited* Catalogue, which lists "thousands and thousands" of films now available in VCR format, does not list *The 5,000 Fingers of Dr. T.*

16) E.J. Kahn Jr. interview with Phyllis Jackson, reprinted in Morgan and Morgan, pp. 140–141.

17) "All Time Best Selling Hardcover Children's Books," *Publishers Weekly* magazine, Feb. 5, 1996.

18) Morgan and Morgan, pp. 145.

19) *Horton Hears a Who!*, no pagination.

20) Geisel, quoted in Morgan and Morgan, notes for pp. 144.

21) May 24, 1954.

22) Morgan and Morgan, pp. 148.

23) Ibid., pp. 150.

24) Oct. 24, 1954, pp. 20.

25) Sept. 1, 1954. *Kirkus* is a publication for librarians which recommends books for library purchase.

26) Sept. 12, 1954, pp. 32.

27) In Morgan and Morgan, pp. 151.

28) *Colliers* magazine, Dec. 23, 1954, pp. 86.

29) *On Beyond Zebra!*, no pagination.

30) Oct. 15, 1955.

31) Nov. 13, 1955, pp. 3.

32) Nov. 13, 1955, pp. 45.

33) Morgan and Morgan, pp. 152.

34) *If I Ran the Circus*, no pagination.

35) Nov. 18, 1956, pt. 2, pp. 47.

36) Nov. 17, 1956.

37) Nov. 11, 1956, pp. 2.

38) Nov. 24, 1956.

39) Nov. 11, 1956, pp. 11.

40) John C. Fuller, "Trade Winds" column, *The Saturday Review of Literature*, Dec. 14, 1957.

41) Dr. Seuss, "How Orlo Got His Book," *The New York Times Book Review*. Nov. 15, 1957.

42) Theodor Geisel, quoted in Morgan and Morgan, pp. 154.

Five

1) Dr. Seuss, *The Cat in the Hat*, no pagination.
2) Karla Kuskin, "The Mouse in the Corner, the Fly on the Wall: What Very Young Eyes See in Picture Books," *The New York Times Book Review*, Nov. 14, 1993.
3) How can you determine whether you have a first edition of a book, or a reprint edition? The page behind the main title page should show copyright; and toward the bottom of the page, if there is a line of numbers, the lowest number indicates the reprint edition. In this case, the copy of *The Cat in the Hat* I have shows: 104 103 102 101 100 99. My copy is part of the 99th printing. What that printing is sold out and the book goes back to press—as it invariably will—the 99 is erased and then the 100 will be the reprint edition. This is Random House. Other firms have other methods of showing first editions. At Charles Scribners Sons, in the late 1930s and 1940s, first editions of Hemingway books and others were shown by an A on the copyright page. The A was then erased for a reprinting. The editions and reprintings, however, do not tell the reader anything about how many books constitute a second printing, or in the case of *The Cat in the Hat*, how many books were printed during the 99th reprinting. Nor do the reprint numbers necessarily indicate the rare book value of the copy.
4) March 17, 1957, pp. 40.
5) May 12, 1957, pp. 24.
6) May 12, 1957, pt. 2, pp. 7.
7) May 11, 1957.
8) April, 1957.
9) *How the Grinch Stole Christmas!*, Random House, 1957, no pagination.
10) Morgan and Morgan, pp. 58.
11) Ibid., pp. 160.
12) Nov. 16, 1957.

13) Nov. 10, 1957, pp. 20.

14) Oct. 6, 1957, pp. 40.

15) Nov. 17, 1957, pp. 30.

16) Sept. 15, 1957.

17) Morgan and Morgan, pp. 158.

18) Ibid., pp. 159.

19) Geisel, op. cit, in Morgan and Morgan, pp. 160.

20) Morgan and Morgan, pp. 165–166.

21) Nov. 1, 1958

22) Nov. 2, 1958, pt. 2, pp. 11.

23) Nov. 15, 1958.

24) Nov. 1958.

25) Nov. 2, 1958, pt. 2, pp. 8.

26) Cynthia Gorney, "Dr. Seuss at 75: Grinch, Cat in Hat Wocket and Generations of Kids in His Pocket," *The Washington Post*, May 21, 1979.

27) May 1, 1958.

28) August, 1958.

29) May 11, 1958.

30) Sept. 20, 1958.

31) *Happy Birthday to You!*, no pagination.

32) Dec. 1959. Ms. Jackson seems to have confused the Birthday Bird, which flew with the child and the Smorgasbord which carried the child as it loped along, a Seussian cross between a horse and (perhaps) a llama.

33) Dec. 1960.

34) Jan. 15, 1960.

35) *One Fish, Two Fish, Red Fish, Blue Fish*, pp. 38–39.

36) May 8, 1960, sec. 12, pp. 21.

37) May 7, 1960.

38) May 12, 1960, pp. 4B.

39) March 20, 1960, pp. 42.

40) Morgan and Morgan, pp. 167.

41) *Green Eggs and Ham*, pp. 9–16.

42) Jones, op cit, in Morgan and Morgan, pp. 170–171.

43) Morgan and Morgan, pp. 171.
44) Michael J., Bandler, "Seuss on the Loose," *Parents* magazine, Sept. 1987.
45) Sept. 15, 1960.
46) Book Review section, Nov. 13, 1960, sec. 12, pp. 16.
47) Nov. 19, 1960.
48) Nov. 12, 1960.
49) pp., 34.

Six

1) Cott, "The Good Dr. Seuss," from *Pipers at the Gates of Dawn*, pp. 28–29.
2) *The Sneetches and Other Stories*, no pagination.
3) Ibid.
4) Robert Bernstein, quoted in Morgan and Morgan, pp. 173–174.
5) Nov. 12, 1961, Sec. 2, pp. 12.
6) Oct. 28, 1961.
7) Morgan and Morgan, pp. 176.
8) *Dr. Seuss's Sleep Book*, no pagination.
9) Sept. 9, 1962, pp. 30.
10) Nov. 15, 1962, pp. 2B.
11) *Hop on Pop*, pp. 18–19, 23–24, 26–31.
12) *Dr. Seuss's ABC*, pp. 3–5, 6–8, 56–57, 61–63.
13) April 14, 1963, pp. 56.
14) June 5, 1963.
15) May 12, 1963, sec. 12, pp. 24.
16) Nov. 10, 1963, pt. 2, pp. 52.
17) Nov. 14, 1963, pp. 2B.
18) Morgan and Morgan, pp. 178.
19) *Hop on Pop*, pp. 62–63.
20) Morgan and Morgan, pp. 179.
21) *Fox in Sox*, pp. 47–48.
22) April 18, 1965, pp. 16.

23) May 6, 1965, pp. 2B.

24) We assume that Dr. Seuss knew he was using a variation on the French word for grapefruit: *pamplemousse.*

25) *I Had Trouble in Getting to Solla Sollew*, no pagination.

26) Morgan and Morgan, pp. 187.

27) Ibid., pp. 191.

28) Ibid., pp. 191.

29) The note became part of the Coroner's report on her death and was reprinted in Morgan and Morgan, pp. 195.

30) *The Foot Book*, no pagination.

31) Morgan and Morgan, pp. 200–201.

32) I was able to read a copy on loan from the Library of the University of South Carolina, Columbia. It is a very drab looking book—T.F.

33) *Esquire*, June 1974.

34) Geisel told the same story to his biographers, Morgan and Morgan (pp. 210) and to Chris Dummit of *The Dallas Morning News*, June 16, 1983.

35) *The Lorax.*

36) Nov. 11, 1971, pp. B4.

37) Nov. 15, 1971.

38) It is now in its forty-second printing.

Seven

1) *Marvin K. Mooney, Will You Please Go Now!* no pagination.

2) This episode appeared in "The Private World of Dr. Seuss" by Hillaird Harper, *The Los Angeles Times Magazine*, May 25, 1986.

3) *There's a Wocket in My Pocket!*, no pagination.

4) Morgan and Morgan, pp. 217–218.

5) His heart attack is described in Morgan and Morgan, pp. 245.

6) *The Butter Battle Book*, no pagination.

7) Ibid., no pagination.

8) Morgan and Morgan, pp. 250.

9) Ibid., pp. 252.
10) May, 1984.
11) March 2, 1984, pp. 2.
12) Morgan and Morgan, pp. 255.
13) Ibid., pp. 255.
14) Ibid., pp. 261.
15) *You're Only Young Once!*, no pagination.
16) Ibid., no pagination.
17) Morgan and Morgan, pp. 265.
18) Ibid., pp. 267–269.
19) *Oh! The Places You'll Go*, no pagination.
20) Morgan and Morgan, pp. 283.
21) "The Cabinet of Dr. Seuss."
22) Quoted in Morgan and Morgan, pp. 286.
23) Ibid., pp. 287.

Epilogue

1) Harper, "The Private World of Dr. Seuss," May 25, 1986.
2) *Time*, Oct. 7, 1991.

Index

About the Author

Thomas Fensch has published 18 books of nonfiction, including books about John Steinbeck, James Thurber, Oskar Schindler and Theodor Geisel. His biographies include: *Steinbeck And Covici; Conversations with John Steinbeck; Conversations with James Thurber; Oskar Schindler and His List* and *Of Sneetches and Whos and the Good Doctor Seuss.*

He holds a doctorate from Syracuse University and lives near Houston, Texas.

Printed in the United States
1760

9 780930 751112